Mexico Megacity

Mexico Megacity

James B. Pick
and Edgar W. Butler

WestviewPress

A Division of HarperCollins*Publishers*

To my wife, Patricia M. Butler
E. B.

To my wife, Rosalyn M. Laudati
J. P.

Copyright © 1997 by Westview Press, A Division of HarperCollins Publishers, Inc.

Published in 1997 in the United States of America by Westview Press, 5500 Central Avenue, Boulder, Colorado 80301-2877, and in the United Kingdom by Westview Press, 12 Hid's Copse Road, Cumnor Hill, Oxford OX2 9JJ

A CIP catalog record for this book is available from the Library of Congress.
ISBN 0-8133-8983-6

The paper used in this publication meets the requirements of the American National Standard for Permanence of Paper for Printed Library Materials Z39.48-1984.

10   9   8   7   6   5   4   3   2   1

Contents

Contents

Figures

Maps

Tables

Preface

This book has as its goal describing various regions within Mexico Megacity. Its orientation clearly is from a traditional, classical view of the city. Much of the description and analyses presented focus on spatial dimensions in the conurbation. We fully recognize that there are other just as viable and useful approaches to examining Mexico Megacity. There are ample historical documents and studies covering the development of Mexico City. Other perspectives have explored life in various areas of the city; among those that most immediately come to mind are those by Lewis (1961, 1974) and Velez-Ibanez (1983). There are, of course, many others.

How any city is studied and data interpreted is influenced by the world view of the authors. We clearly made decisions that influenced what was included in this volume. Inclusion by us did not mean, however, that by excluding certain topics they were not important. We have data and information on many other aspects of Mexico Megacity that were not included because of space and cost considerations. As one might imagine, Mexico City has such a multifarious variety of populations, regions, ecological areas, and other dimensions that we have only singled out some for inclusion given our preferences. For now, this volume will have to suffice.

We clearly have been influenced by what has been called the 'Chicago School' of examining cities and their structures. However, we do not necessarily believe that it is necessary to subscribe to a social evolutionary or organic view of the city as emphasized by the Chicago School. Among other perspectives on cities are those that emphasize disorganization, exploitation of the under-classes, the sustenance school, economic influences, environmental aspects, technology, values, and social power. A little of each of these orientations can be discerned in this book. Thus, it is clear that while we do emphasize certain aspects of the Megacity, ultimately the endeavor is highly eclectic.

We emphasize the spatial structure of Mexico Megacity in its many and various manifestations. However, we believe that we have done more than describe the form of the city; we analyze the demographic forces that exist in Mexico Megacity and we examine and analyze many other dimensions as they exist in a variety of areas within the metropolitan complex. Our cluster analyses demonstrate consistencies among some dimensions and show that Mexico Megacity certainly has many aspects to it that are clearly different from U.S. cities.

What we have done in this volume is to present data, analyses, and narrative so the reader can understand the complex spatial patterning and some of its relationships within the metropolitan complex. While most of the time we have remained neutral regarding conditions in the Megacity, it also is apparent that at times we do make value judgments. We do believe that we have enlightened readers about Mexico Megacity and have not obscured its more important elements. We hope that this volume generates an appreciation of Mexico Megacity and produces more research of various genesis on the metropolitan complex from our orientation and from a variety of other perspectives. We are confident that this volume will assist those who are involved in policy making and decision making in Mexico and the Megacity and who are interested in analyzing other megacities.

We have been conscientious and highly deferent in following the available data. However, all information used in this volume was gathered by others and whatever deficiencies the original data have, of course, were carried over into our description and analyses. As the authors, however, we are responsible for subsequent analyses and interpretations.

Acknowledgments

As with our previous books on Mexico, this project could not have been accomplished without the support, cooperation, and collaboration of many individuals and institutions in Mexico and the United States. We accept full responsibility for the contents of this book, but wish to recognize the important contribution of these many other persons and institutions.

The one person most responsible for the production of this book is W. James Hettrick and we acknowledge his great contribution. He carried out most of the geographic information system analysis (GIS), helped develop the graphs and tables, and at all times was a crucial contributor to the effort. Over the years we have been truly blessed with remarkable graduate students at the University of Redlands and University of California, Riverside. James Hettrick has kept that tradition alive by his dedication, tenacity, and superb contribution.

At the University of Redlands, we thank the office staff of the Department of Management and Business. Karen Philabaum, Joyce Smith, Yolie Figueroa and Cheryl Johnson were always extremely helpful and kind in facilitating and improving this project. We also thank undergraduate student workers in the office who helped. We thank the Armacost Library staff and particularly librarian Linda Barkley for their great help and efficiency. We thank former department chair Hub Segur for graduate student support for this project.

At the University of California, Riverside, we would like to thank the Intramural Research Program and Intramural Travel Funds provided to Edgar W. Butler that facilitated in completing this project. Cathy Carlson and Robin Whittington in the Department of Sociology were unusually efficient and kind in facilitating this research effort. The office staff in the Department of Sociology at UCR -- Anna Marie Wire, Terry deAnda, and Renee DeGuirre-- assisted in many ways the completion of this project. Grace Law assisted in early digitizing work and Glenn Tsunokai also contributed his expertise at different stages in the research endeavor. The staff of the Rivera Library, as usual, went far beyond the call of duty in facilitating this work.

In Mexico, we owe our greatest debt to Dr. Carlos Jarque Uribe who continues to be a constant source of inspiration to us. Since our very first meeting a number of years ago he has constantly been a supporter of our research. He has facilitated our efforts over the years and we offer him our sincere appreciation. At INEGI, we want to especially extend our sincere appreciation to Pilar Garcia Velazquez. At INEGI, we also thank J. Arturo Blancas Espejo, Mario Chavarria, Franciso J. Gutierrez, Pablo Alberto Leon Lozada, Jose Luis Olarte Q., Jesus Olvera Ramirez, Tomas Ramirez, Enrique Ordaz, Mario Palma Rojo, Fernando Zepeda Bermudez, Juan Lobo Zertuche, and others.

In Mexico, we also extend our appreciation to Carlos J. Navarrete, who kindly assisted us in visiting, touring, and photographing Mexico Megacity as well as offering his special knowledge of the area. We extend our appreciation to Tomas Mojarro for several photographs. We thank Gerardo Mendiola at Grupo Editorial Expansion for assistance and expert discussions and thank Jesus Tamayo for expertise on understanding the city.

Maps in this volume were produced by programs now available from Environmental Systems Research Institute (ESRI), Redlands, California. Appreciation is expressed for their support and to the predecessor company of Atlas GIS.

At Westview Press we wish to acknowledge the contribution of Dean Birkenkamp, for his encouragement of this book. Lynn Arts and Jill Rothenberg, Annemarie Preonas, Jim Grode, David Jenemann, Lisa Wigutoff, and others as usual at Westview have been cooperative, helpful, and offered insights and expertise that improved the manuscript.

We thank Leslie Hettrick for her proofreading and other assistance.

Finally, we clearly recognize that this book would not have been possible without all of the contributions gratefully acknowledged here. Again, we take full responsibility for any deficiencies that may exist.

1

Overview

Introduction

Urbanization is a manifestation of historical, social, economic, geographic, demographic forces. "Mankind's future will unfold largely in urban settings" (Fuchs, 1994:1). Much of the world's population in the future will be living in megacities -- that is, cities or urban agglomerations with a population of eight million or more (Chen and Heligman, 1994). Of course, dimensions other than size also are important in defining a megacity. Among other factors are its financial control over a hinterland -- both national and international, its commercial/industrial structure, political role, educational facilities, basic service functions, control over the media, and in many nations whether or not it is a primate city. The growth of megacities has been a relatively recent development.[1] A number of issues arise as a result of population size and urbanization for each country that contains a megacity or megacities. Some of these issues are addressed in subsequent chapters in this volume.

Undoubtedly, these very same dimensions are important in examining Mexico City – what we are calling *Mexico Megacity*. This book focuses on the Mexico City metropolitan zone which is rapidly emerging as one of the largest urbanized complexes in the world. By the year 2000 Mexico City may be the largest city in the world (Chen and Heligman, 1994; Fuchs et al., 1994), or at least as one of the top ten cities in the world (U.N. 1995: 5; Ezcurra and Mazari-Hiriart, 1996).

While research has been accomplished examining some giant cities (Brunn et al., 1983; Dogan and Kasarda, 1988; Sassen, 1991, 1994; Knight and Gappert, 1989), our research is distinctive from other giant city studies because there has been few analyses of districts or areas within Latin America megacities. This research is also unusual because minimal analyses have been carried out on districts or smaller areas within the Central Metropolitan Zone of Mexico -- *Mexico Megacity*. Several comparisons have been made of the Mexico City "core" with the "suburbs" (Schteingart, 1988; Negrete, Graizbord and Ruiz, 1993). Small areas were examined for a smaller metropolitan region in 1980 (Garza, 1987). However, given the size of Mexico Megacity, those comparisons were limited in scope and in their value for scientific research, planning, and policy making today.

This research systematically examines similarities and differences *within* the Mexico City metropolitan region on a variety of dimensions theoretically derived from previous research endeavors concerned with differentiation *within* metropolitan areas (see Goldstein and Sly, 1977: vol. 1, pp. 33-34; Butler, 1976; Butler and Barclay, 1977). Our analysis specifically delineates geographic units within the central metropolitan zone of Mexico City and its surrounding environs. Mexico Megacity includes the Federal District and adjacent, selected municipios in the surrounding State of Mexico. Measures for theoretical concepts are available for areas within the region from Mexican censuses and other sources by delegations and municipios.   The major focus of the book is on demographic, social, economic, environmental, labor force, and corporate themes. The book obviously is a case study of what is one of the largest cities in the world, if not the largest. We believe, however, that our approach expands the base of scientific knowledge of urbanization processes and helps provide a solid base for comparative studies and for decision-making and policy development, especially in Latin America.

---

[1] Chapter 13 presents growth data for selected megacities and illustrates percent of total population that lives in these megacities.

Theoretical Perspectives

One of the basic assumptions of urban studies is that demographic, social, economic, and ecological characteristics of areas within metropolitan regions are systematically interrelated to attitudes and behavior. There have been several theoretical perspectives advanced to explain the variety and types of areas found within the metropolitan complex. The traditional perspectives of the Burgess concentric zone theory (1925), Hoyt's sector theory (1943), and the multiple nuclei theory advanced by Harris and Ulman (1945) probably are the most prominent. The social area analysis orientation developed during the 1940s (Shevky and Williams, 1949) and 1950s (Shevky and Bell, 1955) influenced substantial research on the internal differentiation of cities. Other theoretical approaches have been advanced by Hoover and Vernon (1962), human ecologists (Hawley, 1950; Berry and Kasarda, 1977), and economists (Clark, 1940). A theoretical statistical analyses also have resulted in heuristic typologies of areas within metropolitan regions (for examples, see Carey, 1966; Herbert, 1967; Janson, 1968) and factorial ecology has became prominent (see Sweetser, 1965; Berry and Kasarda, 1977). The 'growth machine' and presumed 'new paradigm' also may have some explanatory power for our analyses (Castells, 1979).

While analysis of the internal structure of Latin American megacities is slim, there are enough similarities among various theoretical perspectives and subsequent research endeavors examining them to suggest hypotheses that need to be tested, variables that should be included in the analysis, and methodologies having utility in such research. As examples of differences that may exist between U.S. cities and Latin American cities, including Mexico Megacity, Figure 1.1 illustrates in broad outline the Burgess (1925) concentric zone perspective. Figure 1.2, developed by Griffin and Ford (1983), implies that there are perhaps concentric zones but also sectors (see Hoyt 1943) in Latin American cities. However, there also is a suggestion of reversal of what exists in the some of the zones, e.g., poverty centralized in U.S. cities but on the periphery in Latin American cities, including Mexico Megacity (see Schnore, 1965).

Without exception, previous studies of both U.S. and Latin American cities have shown that metropolitan areas are highly differentiated into a mosaic of areas and neighborhoods that have relatively similar populations and activities taking place within them, i.e., they are relatively homogeneous because of cost, affinity, and voluntary and/or forced segregation. Thus, major differences that exist in cities are among areas rather than within neighborhoods.

Major dimensions on which areas differ are (1) population characteristics, (2) housing dimensions, (3) economic factors, (4) social class/rank, (5) urbanism/familism indicators, and (6) race/ethnicity. Race/ethnicity research endeavors have engendered the development of a whole host of segregation indices. While specific variables used to measure these concepts have varied among various theoretical approaches, virtually all of them address the primary concepts noted above. Population structure indicators have included population size, growth, sex ratio, and migration. Housing dimensions explored have been single family vs. multiple family units, and examination of various housing deficits. Socioeconomic variables generally are extent of labor force participation, unemployment, education, income, and occupation. Social rank/status factors examined generally include educational level, occupational level, income level, and housing tenure (owner/renter). Familism has been measured by fertility, marital status, and extent of females participating in the labor force. Race/ethnic segregation in the United States typically has focused upon the Black population. However, segregation may be examined for a variety of other dimensions, including the elderly, squatters, religious groups, and so on.

Variables derived from theoretical perspectives are systematically analyzed in this volume. They also are incorporated into several different cluster analyses. One cluster analysis utilizing 30 variables, is briefly presented in this chapter. It is augmented by additional cluster analyses in individual chapters, as deemed appropriate. The 30 dimension analysis also is expressed in more detail in Chapter 12. Part of Chapter 13 presents a model of Mexico Megacity that heuristically employs information from all of the cluster analyses and other information presented in this volume.

The cluster analysis presented in this chapter has as its goal laying the groundwork for various analytic discussions in subsequent chapters. Additional cluster analyses reported in subsequent chapters utilize sets of variables specifically related to that particular chapter. One chapter in the volume is devoted to recapping the development of urbanization in Mexico with an emphasis on larger cities and Mexico-United States border cities. Another chapter analyzes historical population growth and differentiation in Mexico Megacity and demonstrates that the city is a primate city, describes the contemporary Mexico Megacity population, and forecasts future population growth in the region.

Several subsequent chapters explore basic demographic dimensions that influenced Mexico Megacity's growth. The analysis stresses marriage, fertility and family planning, migration patterns, and mortality and health. It is only through the complex interplay of these demographic dimensions that Mexico City grew and its smaller areas became differentiated from the rest of Mexico and each other. Population growth's impact upon the environment and quality of life in the city are examined in detail in a following chapter.

Social and economic factors loom large in any exploration of Mexico Megacity. In Mexico there are substantial variations among states in education, literacy, economic level, indigenous language, consumption of goods and services, and religion, among many other factors. Variation along these dimensions also is highly visible in the various delegations and municipios that make up Mexico Megacity.

Clearly the economy of Mexico is impacted by Mexico Megacity, but also the worldwide and national economy influence the city. Mexico Megacity is home to almost half of the major corporations in Mexico and has numerous transnational corporations located and concentrated in several locations in the metropolitan region. Mexico City has a major impact upon communications and finances throughout Mexico. It influences the oil, automobile, maquiladora, and tourism industries. To a substantial degree, Mexico's economic future is decided in Mexico Megacity; thus investment and development for the rest of Mexico are decided in the city.

Mexico Megacity is the location of the central government and governing Mexico and Mexico Megacity is the concern of all Mexicans. However, there are substantial political differences between Mexico Megacity residents and those living throughout the rest of Mexico in respect to the dominant political party and views as to how Mexico should be governed.

In the latter part of this book we utilize various theoretical perspectives and all of the information and analyses reported in earlier chapters to expand the sophisticated multivariate cluster analyses of the spatial structure of the city introduced in this chapter. This effort focuses on determining the *latent* aspects of the region to develop a more parsimonious view of Mexico Megacity. Finally, we turn to the future urbanization of Mexico and Mexico Megacity, forecasting the future in respect to demographic, social, and economic factors. For those who are interested, we also shed some light upon some possible future policy alternatives. For the scientific community, we present a list of future research priorities. Among them is whether or not Mexico Megacity is becoming more like U.S. cities, e.g., is there a convergence taking place?

In the remainder of this chapter, we first describe the Mexico Database Project including its background, discuss the methodology used in the book, present base maps that are used throughout the volume, describe the Mexico Megacity Geographic Information System (GIS), enumerate variables used in analyses and indicate their source, and present a preliminary discussion of the 30 variable cluster analysis.

Figure 1.1 Burgess's Model

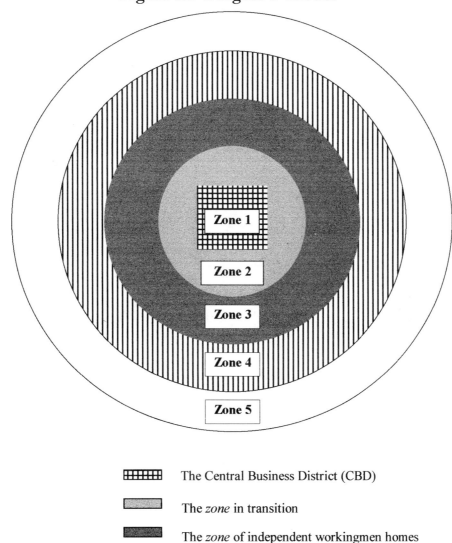

⊞⊞⊞⊞	The Central Business District (CBD)
▓	The *zone* in transition
▓	The *zone* of independent workingmen homes
ⅢⅢⅢ	The *zone* of better residences
☐	The commuter's *zone*

Figure 1.2

Latin American City Structure

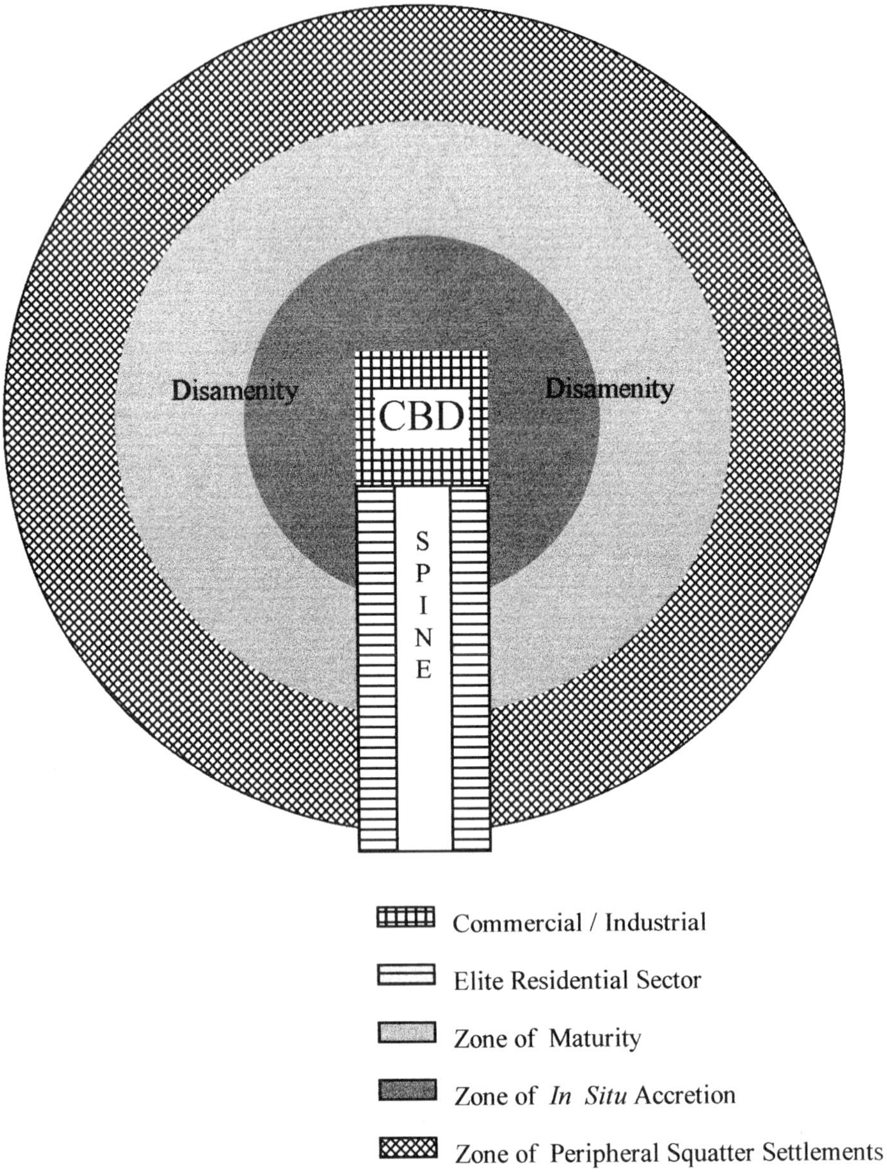

Source: Griffin and Ford in Brunn and Williams (eds.), *Cities of the World: World Regional Urban Development*,1983

Mexico Database Project

This book was developed as part of the continuation of a larger project devoted to developing a database on Mexico. The database project brings together a large array of data on economics, population, housing, and a variety of other information gleaned from a variety of governmental and private sources. All information presented here is from our much larger U.S.-Mexico Database Project (see the Bibliography for citations of project publications).

This volume is both descriptive and analytical and we hope that it will further enhance an understanding of Mexico Megacity, broaden U.S. perspectives on the city, and interest others in using the statistics and maps that we have brought together in one information system (Butler et al., 1987). While emphasis in this volume is on descriptive information, some analyses are in the form of simple correlations and in some instances statistics and maps present more sophisticated multivariate information, as do various cluster analyses.

Virtually all information included in this work is available to the U.S. and Mexican public in the form of census publications, annual statistical volumes (anuarios), electronic media, and in numerous other publications. However, the logistics of gathering data from scattered sources, documents, files, and reports is very time consuming. Some data included in this volume are available only in electronic mode. In every instance we note the source and how to obtain the information for those who may be interested in more detail than presented here. Finally, to our knowledge, no one else has systematized into one database such comprehensive information on Mexico Megacity.[2]

Our view is that this volume will be of use to planners, researchers, businessmen, decision makers, as well as to laypersons who are interested in Mexico and Mexico City. We have found that even the most knowledgeable person about Mexico Megacity can be surprised at some of the data and spatial distributions uncovered in our presentation.

The Mexico Database Project is based upon the assumption that systematized information is necessary for Mexico to take full advantage of its population and natural resources. The Mexico Database Project is a computerized Geographic Information System (GIS) on the states, *municipios*, and *delegaciones* of Mexico. The goal of the Database Project is to make available systematized information of these units of Mexico for administrative, planning, policy decisions, and research.

So far the project has produced several dozen articles and three books. The project's first book was the *Atlas of Mexico* published by the Westview Press in 1989 (Pick, Butler, and Lanzer). That volume reported extensive analyses of the 1980 Mexican census as well as other information. Subsequently, a volume containing extensive analyses was published as *Handbook of Mexico* (Pick and Butler, 1994). That volume focused on the state level but also included some small area analysis for Mexico City and the border region. Also published by the Westview Press in 1991 (Butler and Bustamante, eds.) was a book entitled *Sucesion Presidencial: The 1988 Mexican Presidential Election*. Articles published utilizing the database have focused on fertility, migration, socioeconomic dimensions, election results and projections, the labor force and projections, Mexico City, Oaxaca, and an analysis of continuity and change. Works in progress include a book on urbanization in Mexico, an analysis of the Mexican borderlands and maquiladoras, and extensive analyses of the Mexican '500' and transnational corporations in Mexico. This volume thus represents only a small portion of the work already accomplished using the Mexico Database.

---

[2] Data utilized in this volume are available on diskette from the authors.

Methodology

Data at the Megacity level as well as information on areas or districts within them are necessary to examine systematically internal differentiation. This volume utilizes data from a variety of sources, including the Mexican censuses from 1895-1993 and Garza (1987). In addition, corporate data (*Expansion,* 1995) were used to develop parts of the economic section of this volume. Also *Resumen General* census publications were especially valuable. Further, *Anuarios Estadisticos* (INEGI, various years) were systematically consulted. A variety of other publications were utilized and are referred to at appropriate places in the text and are listed in the Reference section.

Mexico Megacity consists of the 16 delegations (delegaciones) of the Federal District and 53 of the 100 municipios from the surrounding State of Mexico. The data used in this book were obtained the Mexico Database Project.[3] The text emphasizes simple interpretation and comparisons as well as correlation and cluster analyses. Simple descriptive statistics are often utilized including mean, median, range, extreme values, percentiles, and standard deviation. For longitudinal data series, trends and changes over time are pointed out. At times, the text refers to other maps showing similarities and/or contrasts.

To assist in comparisons, a correlation matrix was computed for the entire set of variables included in the book and correlations are often referred to clarify relationships. Generally, correlation coefficients examine the relationship between two variables with a range from -1.0 to +1.0 (Affi and Azen, 1972; Blalock, 1979). Finally, to present some idea of relative homogeneity among variables, on occasions, the coefficient of variation (CV) is reported. The CV is a measure of related variables that takes into account deviation relative to the mean (Affi and Azen 1972; Blalock 1979). The coefficient is defined as 100 times the ratio of the standard deviation to the mean. Thus the CV allows a relative comparison of variation among all variables. In the text, a CV of less than 20 is treated as small or narrow; a CV between 21-99 is considered middle-range, while a CV of 100 and greater is considered as large.

Computer generated maps and graphics, and cluster analysis techniques are used to delineate more or less homogeneous areas within the city. Cluster analytic techniques ascertain the hidden or latent dimensions of a city's internal structure. It involves developing a data matrix containing measurements on m variables for each of n units of observation (Chatfield and Collins, 1980; SAS Institute, 1985). In our CMZ cluster analyses, m refers to the various socioeconomic, population structure, and economic variables whereas n identifies the units of observations, i.e., delegations in the Federal District (Mexico City) and municipios in the State of Mexico. Thus the intent is (1) to reduce dimensions of n units of observation into a smaller number of common units of observation, R, based on homogeneity in sets of variables within the common units. (2) to describe and compare the common units, and (3) interpret the spatial patterns for the CMZ complex.

Once data from various sources were gathered, they were processed for statistical and mapping purposes. Several different software packages were utilized in this process. For most mapping, Atlas from ESRI is utilized (ESRI, 1996). MacDraw and Delta Graph programs were utilized to develop some figures and Excel was used for spreadsheets.

Data were entered and manipulated and maps created by the following steps:

---

[3] The Mexico Database consists of geographic information system on the states, municipios, the cities, and corporations in Mexico.

1. Data were input and tested for accuracy.
2. Many raw values were used to calculate constructed
   variables and/or rates.
3. Data were analyzed to determine the range of data.
4. For most maps, small areas were grouped approximately into quintiles from
   lowest to highest values. However, variables with unusual, extreme
   values, or outliers, were mapped with customized classifications that
   assigned extremes to special thematic categories.
5. Statistical calculations were performed.
6. A systematic set of files was built to include all variables. Computerized
   documentation was maintained to keep track of variable definitions, names,
   data sources, and mapping codes.
7. A computerized codebook was maintained and updated in a file to keep track of
   the organization of all material.

Mexico Megacity Geographic Information System (GIS)

The Mexico Megacity Geographic Information System (GIS) is part of a larger project focusing on all of Mexico. Figure 1.3 presents a conceptual overview of the system which should be helpful in understanding the overall design. Study attributes include demographic, economic, and a variety of other dimensions. They were arranged on master spreadsheets and inputted for electronic analysis. Attributes are keyed to geographic smaller regions of the city, or what is known as *coverages*. Coverages consist of base maps shown earlier which are then linked to attributional information. Outputs from the GIS are available on screen displays or in printed form. The GIS thus contains many attributes and many coverages. Figure 1.4 presents in more detail the process from obtaining data and information to the production of this book. The entire Mexico Megacity GIS is available on diskette with a Codebook detailing variables, their definition and source, and other miscellaneous information. Information on acquiring the diskettes may be obtained from James Pick.

The GIS is suitable for multipurpose uses, such as (1) computerized information to produce maps and statistical analyses for policy makers and businesses; (2) academic studies; (3) data for a variety of demographic, economic, and environmental research; (4) incorporation into an expanded, longitudinal GIS as more data become available; and (5) should be useful for a variety of research and teaching activities in many different disciplines.

Figure 1.3. Conceptual Diagram of Mexican GIS

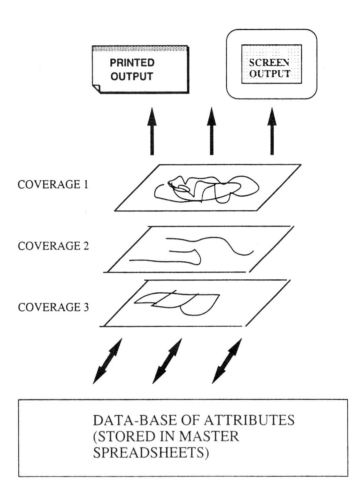

Figure 1.4. System Diagram of Mexican GIS

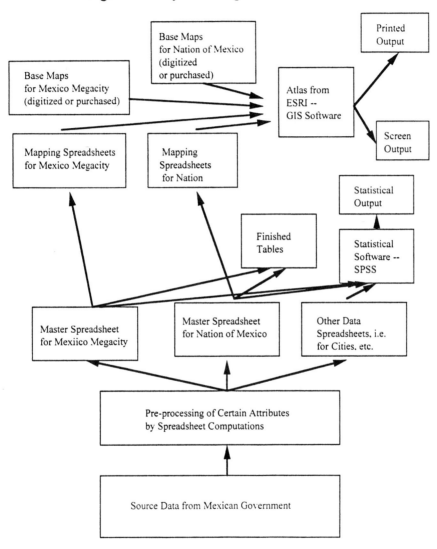

Megacity Variables

Dimensions presented in this volume are only a few of the multitude available from a number of Mexican government publications and reports from private agencies. This work primarily utilizes the 1990 population census, and 1989 and 1993 economic censuses and information gleaned from various *Anuarios* up through the mid 1990s. However, available in these and a variety of other government sources is information covering lengthy time periods of Mexican history, especially beginning in 1895 with the first Mexican census. In addition to variables and time periods presented here, the Mexico Database Project contains a substantially larger computerized database on Mexico and Mexico Megacity. This volume, then, is only illustrative of the range of variables and time periods actually contained in the Mexico Database.

Data sources for this research were primarily various Mexican censuses. However, census data were supplemented by other government and non-governmental information. To our knowledge this effort is the first to examine systematically smaller areas *within* metropolitan Mexico City for a broad range of demographic and socioeconomic attributes. Garza (1987) analyzed small areas in 1980 but for a more limited metropolitan area and smaller range of characteristics. Our examination is partially descriptive, but we also utilize a variety of multivariate techniques, such as cluster analysis, to develop a more systematic view of the city. At all times we attempt to avoid cultural relativism; at times we compare Mexico City with cities in the U.S. and elsewhere throughout the world. Whenever possible we also compare Mexico City with other megacities for which information is available.

The range of dimensions and time periods contained in this volume were constrained by cost considerations rather than by database information. For those who are interested in obtaining the computerized database on diskette, information may be obtained by communicating to James Pick.

Base Maps

This section presents maps essential to understanding subsequent text, statistics, figures, and maps included in this volume. Base maps delineate delegation and municipio boundaries which are referred to throughout the volume. Base Map 1.1 shows the location of the Federal District and State of Mexico within Mexico. Map 1.2 outlines small area boundaries of Mexico Megacity. Map 1.3 illustrates the delegations of the Federal District. These base maps were used for producing most of the other maps found in this volume. Table 1.1 lists the delegations and municipio units in Mexico Megacity with a designated number.

In 1990, Mexico City, as delineated by INEGI (1990), contained 15,440,746 people, which accounted for 19 percent of the total Mexican population. The basic definition of Mexico Megacity used in this volume is that of INEGI (1992). Some analyses focus only on delegations of the Federal District and a few are limited to a more restricted metropolitan region as delimited by Garza (1987).

It is important to picture the setting and proximities of the base map coverage. As seen in Map 1.4, the full extent of Mexico Megacity has maximum dimensions of about 64 miles north and south and 55 miles east and west. For the populous Federal District, the maximum extent is only about 36 miles north and south by about 28 miles east and west. Map 1.4 superimposes on the base map well known features of Mexico City. Many tourists are only familiar with old city center stretching east from Chapultepec Park to the Mexico City Airport and south from the Zocolo to the National Autonomous University. This area is only about eleven miles square and only a small part of the entire conurbation. Tourists do travel to the Aztec Pyramids, which are located in the northeastern arm of the metropolis; that trip gives an idea of the full reach of the conurbation. A few other features of the periphery are shown on Map 1.4 in order to orient the reader more familiar with Mexico City to the extent of our base map.

It is important to mention that Mexico sits in a high altitude basin, surrounded on the south and east by volcanoes, two of which reach heights of nearly 18,000 feet. These huge volcanoes of Popocatepetl and Ixtaccihuatl are at the southeastern outer edge of the conurbation and are marked on Map 1.4. The lowest part of the plain containing Mexico City has a height of 7,350 feet (Ezcurra, 1991). Lake Texcoco is a lake that fills part of the municipio of Texcoco and adjacent municipios. It has been draining and drying for many decades and is surrounded by swampy areas. Lake Texcoco and vicinity are important because they form a barrier to urbanization in certain parts of the eastern metropolis. For detailed information on the physical geography and geology of the city, and the reader is referred to other sources (Garza, 1987; Ezcurra, 1991).

14

Map 1.1
STATES OF MEXICO

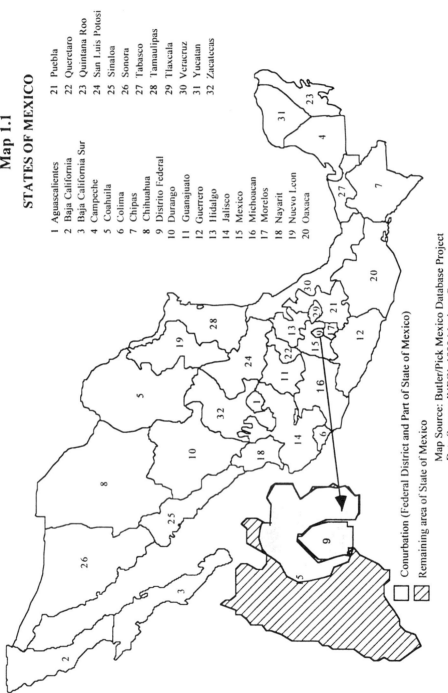

1 Aguascalientes	21 Puebla
2 Baja California	22 Queretaro
3 Baja California Sur	23 Quintana Roo
4 Campeche	24 San Luis Potosi
5 Coahuila	25 Sinaloa
6 Colima	26 Sonora
7 Chipas	27 Tabasco
8 Chihuahua	28 Tamaulipas
9 Distrito Federal	29 Tlaxcala
10 Durango	30 Veracruz
11 Guanajuato	31 Yucatan
12 Guerrero	32 Zacatecas
13 Hidalgo	
14 Jalisco	
15 Mexico	
16 Michoacan	
17 Morelos	
18 Nayarit	
19 Nuevo Leon	
20 Oaxaca	

☐ Conurbation (Federal District and Part of State of Mexico)

▨ Remaining area of State of Mexico

Map Source: Butler/Pick Mexico Database Project
Data Source: INEGI, 1990 Mexican Census

Map 1.2
Mexico Megacity Base Map

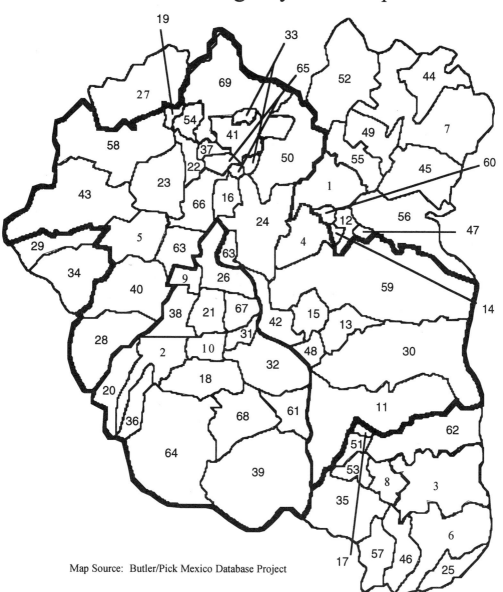

Map Source: Butler/Pick Mexico Database Project

16

Map 1.3
Federal District

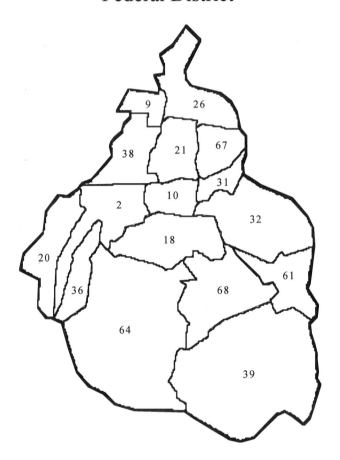

Map Source: Butler/Pick Mexico Database Project

Table 1.1 Delegations and Municipios in Mexico City

No.	State	No.	State
1	Acolman	36	Magdalena Contreras *
2	Alvaro Obregon *	37	Melchor Ocampo
3	Amecameca	38	Miguel Hidalgo *
4	Atenco	39	Milpa Alta *
5	Atizapan de Zaragoza	40	Naucalpan
6	Atlautla	41	Nextlalpan
7	Axapusco	42	Nezahualcoyotl
8	Ayapango	43	Nicolas Romero
9	Azcapotzalco *	44	Nopaltepec
10	Benito Juarez *	45	Otumba
11	Chalco	46	Ozumba
12	Chiautla	47	Papalotla
13	Chicoloapan	48	Paz, La
14	Chiconcuac	49	San Martin de las Piramides
15	Chimalhuacan	50	Tecamac
16	Coacalco	51	Temamatla
17	Cocotitlan	52	Temascalapa
18	Coyoacan *	53	Tenango del Aire
19	Coyotepec	54	Teoloyucan
20	Cuajimalpa *	55	Teotihuacan
21	Cuauhtemoc *	56	Tepetlaoxtoc
22	Cuautitlan	57	Tepetlixpa
23	Cuautitlan Izcalli	58	Tepotzotlan
24	Ecatepec	59	Texcoco
25	Ecatzingo	60	Tezoyuca
26	Gustavo A. Madero *	61	Tlahuac *
27	Huehuetoca	62	Tlalmanalco
28	Huixquilucan	63	Tlalnepantla
29	Isidro Fabela	64	Tlalpan *
30	Ixtapaluca	65	Tultepec
31	Iztacalco *	66	Tultitlan
32	Iztapalapa *	67	Venustiano Carranza *
33	Jaltenco	68	Xochimilco *
34	Jilotzingo	69	Zumpango
35	Juchitepec		

Note: * Federal District (Delegations)

18

Map 1.4
Features of Mexico Megacity

State of Hidalgo

Basilica of
Tepotzotlan

Zocolo

Aztec Pyramids

State of Tlaxcala

Ciudad
Satellite

Lake Bed of Texcoco

Chapultepec Park

Airport

Desierto de
Los Leones Park
(Air Pollution Episode)

Sports Palace

Ixtaccihuatl
Volcano

National Autonomous
University of Mexico
(UNAM)

State of Puebla

Ecological Park
of Xochimilco

Tepozteco
National Park

Popocatepetl
Volcano

State of Morelos

N

Map Scale
0   10 miles

Map Source: Butler Pick Mexico Database Project

Preliminary Cluster Analysis[4]

The 30 variables utilized in the cluster analysis are shown on Table 1.2; they include (1) population, (2) housing, (3) economic, (4) social rank, (5) urbanism/familism, and (6) race/ethnicity. Ten clusters were generated. In order to facilitate comparison with the overall Megacity and to compare each cluster with all other clusters, Table 1.3 presents data for each cluster, variable mean data for each cluster, and mean for the Megacity as a whole. Map 1.5 shows the results of the cluster analysis -- ten clusters. A careful perusal of the data suggest the following as mainly delineating each cluster.

Cluster No. 1:

Cluster 1 has by far the highest mean population size -- 595,176 and influences all other statistics regarding Mexico Megacity. It contains the core delegations of the Federal District (see Map 1.4).

> *Federal District:* Azcapotzalco, Benito Juarez, Coyoacan, Cuauhtemoc,
> Gustavo A. Madero, Iztacalco, Miguel Hidalgo, and
> Venustiano Carranza.

While it has the highest relative population size, the cluster between 1989 and 1990 actually lost population. It has the highest density of all clusters -- almost ten times that of most others -- 10,153/hectare which actually distorts the density measure for all other clusters. It has the lowest gender ratio among all clusters, a very high economically active population, low home ownership, low fertility, but a somewhat average Indian population.

Cluster No. 2:

Cluster 2 contains 20 delegations and municipios, or 29 percent of the 69 units that make up Mexico Megacity. As shown on Map 1.4, these areas are scattered throughout the metropolitan complex. Five Federal District delegations are included in this cluster.

> *Federal District:* Alvaro Obregon, Cuajimalpa, Iztapalapa, Magdalena
> Contreras, and Tlahuac
> *State of Mexico:* Acolman, Chicoloapan, Chiconcuac, Cocotitlan
> Huehuetoca, Jaltenco, Melchor Ocampo, Naucalpan,
> Nextlalpan, Nezahualcoyotl, Temamatla, Texcoco,
> Tlalnepantla, Tultepec, and Zumpango.

Seven of the remaining 15 municipios are located in the far Northcentral and Northwest, four in the mid-Eest, two in the mid-West, and one each in the Northeast and Southeast. These areas have the second highest average population base of 295,678 and density is relatively high compared to all other clusters except No. 1. Generally these are areas that have been long settled. Educational level is equivalent to that of the complex and the percentage of higher income families is about the average level. All in all, as might be anticipated, these areas represent older, more mature areas of the metropolitan complex.

Cluster No. 3:

As shown on Map 1.4, Cluster 3 consists of 19 delegations and municipios, or (27.5 percent of the 69 areas that makeup Mexico Megacity). These areas appear to be intermediate

---

[4] The cluster analysis is explicated in more detail in Chapter 12.

on many dimensions except for their relatively large population size -- 187,164 and a relatively low density of population, compared to clusters 1 and 2.

> *Federal District:* Tlalpan, Xochimilco.
>
> *State of Mexico:* Atenco, Atizapan de Zaragoza, Cuautitlan, Chiautla, Chimalhuacan, Ecatepec, Huixquilucan, Nicolas Romero, Papalotla, La Paz, Tecamac, Teoloyucan, Teotihuacan, Tepotzotlan, Tezoyuca, Tlalmanalco, Tultitlan.

It has an average Indian population. It is primarily a periphery cluster with the two Federal District delegations in this cluster also being located in the far Southcentral. Many units that make up this cluster are relatively small suggesting that they are peripheral areas that have been settled for some time since they appear to have few housing and neighborhood deficits.

Cluster No. 4:

Cluster 4 contains two municipios of the State of Mexico, one located immediately north of the Federal District and the other one more northwest (see Map 1.4).

> *State of Mexico:* Coacalco and Cuautitlan Izcalli

This cluster contains a relatively large population with a relatively high density except when compared with Cluster 1. It has the highest inmigration ratio of all clusters. Residents have a higher level of primary education and double the percentage of high income -- 14 percent vs. 7 percent for the metropolitan region. Perhaps this should be called a transition zone.

Cluster No. 5:

The only area in Cluster 5 is Chalco (See Map 1-4).

> *State of Mexico:* Chalco

Chalco is located in the mid-to south Eastern region of the metropolitan complex; it is a municipio of the State of Mexico. Chalco has a higher than average population size, the next to highest population growth in comparison with the other nine clusters, and has higher than average inmigration. Its density is on the lower end of the scale. Generally, it has substantial neighborhood deficits, especially in housing units lacking running water.

Cluster No. 6:

Cluster 6 contains one delegation of the Federal District and two State of Mexico municipios.

> *Federal District:* Milpa Alta
>
> *State of Mexico:* Ixtapaluca and Juchitepec

As shown on Map 1.4, units making up this cluster are on the periphery and to the mid-east and southeast. This cluster has a lower than average population size of 71,760 and a low density. It has a higher than average lack of running water (22.2%) and more than average number of one room housing units. Otherwise this cluster can be considered as close to the 'average' for Mexico Megacity.

Cluster No. 7:

Cluster 7 has a population mean of 17,142, which is on the lower end of the scale. Areas shown on Map 1.4 that make up this cluster have a low density. All of the units in this cluster are located in the State of Mexico.

> *State of Mexico:* Amecameca, Ayapango, Coyotepec, San Martin de las Piramides, Temascalapa, Tenango del Aire, Tepetlaoxtoc

One municipio -- Coyotepec -- is located in the Northwest periphery. However, all other municipios included in this cluster are located in eastern peripheral areas of the State of Mexico; three of them in the Northeast -- San Martin de las Piramides, Temascalapa, and Tepetlaoxtoc, and three adjacent municipios in the Southeast -- Amecameca, Ayapango, and Tenango del Aire.

Cluster No. 8:

Cluster 8 consists of six municipios in the State of Mexico (see Map 1.4). Three of these municipios are located on the Northeast periphery, two are located on the Southeast periphery, and one, located in the West mid-section of the complex, is similar to these municipios in characteristics but not in geographic location.

> *State of Mexico:* Axapusco, Jilotzingo, Nopaltepec, Otumba, Ozumba, Tepetlixpa

Thus, all municipios that make up this cluster are located on periphery of the Megacity. The mean population size is 13,770, far below the average for the Megacity. It has had some population growth over past few years but mainly by fertility. It has the highest fertility rate of females aged 20-29 for all clusters. Density is on the low end of the scale, while the gender ratio is almost exactly that of the metropolitan complex. This cluster is on the high end of not having a toilet and in the use of coal and/or wood for cooking and heating. It has a relatively low percentage in the labor force and is on the low end of having females in the labor force.

Cluster No. 9:

Cluster 9 contains two municipios in the State of Mexico that are geographically separated from each other; Isidro Fabela is located to the West of the Federal District on the periphery of the metropolitan complex while Atlautla is on the far periphery in the Southeast (see Map 1.4).

> *State of Mexico:* Atlautla and Isidro Fabela

In respect to population size, this cluster averages only slightly over 12,000 and has an extremely low density. The gender ratio is about average for the entire Megacity and there has been little inmigration but has a higher than average fertility for women aged 20-29. Population residing in this cluster has a lower than average working force and of women in the labor force. Over half of the population has no toilet and nearly half of the population uses coal/wood for cooking and heating. While there is very high home ownership, educational level is very low.

Cluster No. 10:

As with Cluster 5, Cluster 10 contains only one municipio -- Ecatzingo (See Map 1-4) and is located at the far bottom of the map and furthest Southeastern part of Mexico Megacity; it is not part of the Federal District but is located in the State of Mexico.

State of Mexico: Ecatzingo

The area has an extremely small population of 5,808, relatively undensely populated, and has had little population growth. It has more males than females. It has some substantial housing deficits with 61 percent of the units not having a toilet and over 80 percent of the population uses coal and/or wood for heating and cooking. It has the lowest level of working population of all clusters, the lowest level of population having more than an elementary school education, the lowest percentage of population that has an upper level income, and has the highest percentage of home owners in the entire Megacity.

Table 1.2 List of Variables for Cluster Analysis

Variable Group	Description
Population	Log of Population
	Relative Population Growth 1970-1990
	Log of Population Density
	Sex Ratio
	Inmigration in Past 5 Years
Housing	Lack of Running Water
	Housing with One Room
	Household Crowding
	Septic Tank or Open Flow for Housing Unit
	No Toilet in Housing Unit
	Firewood or Coal for Heating
Economic	Economic Activity for Population Age 12+
	Unemployment
	Percent Owners/Employers/Salaried Workers
	Percent of Chemical and Petrochemical Revenues, 1993
	Percent of Metal Production and Equipment Manufacturing Revenues, 1993
	Percent of Professional and Technical Services Revenues, 1993
Social Rank	Professional/Technical/Managerial Occupation
	Primary Education
	High Income (more than 5 times minimum wage)
	Home Ownership
Urbanism/Familism	Cumulative Fertility to Women 20-29
	Free Union
	Separated and Divorced
	Ratio of Women Economically Active
Race/Ethnicity	Mixtec Language
	Nahautl Language
	Otomi Language
	Zapotec Language
	Indigenous Language - Remainder

Note: all variables are for 1990 unless otherwise indicated.
Source: 1990 Mexican Census of Population; 1993 Mexican Economic Censuses.

Table 1.3 Overall Cluster Means

Variable	1	2	3	4	5	6	7	8	9	10	Mexico City
Cluster No.											
POPULATION GROUP											
Total Population 1990	4,761,411	5,913,550	3,556,120	478,832	282,940	201,011	120,000	82,621	24,183	5,808	15,440,746
Population 1990	595,176	295,678	187,164	23,916	282,940	71,760	17,143	13,770	12,092	5,808	223,779
Population Growth 1970-1990	-0.08	1.84	2.74	9.88	5.83	1.45	1.04	0.79	0.80	0.60	1.92
Population Density 1990	10153.0	244.8	132.3	123.8	85.6	70.8	58.5	59.1	54.2	43.8	1305.7
Sex Ratio	0.8858	0.9662	0.9714	0.9585	1.0008	0.9784	0.9936	1.0115	0.9885	0.9911	0.9673
Immigration 1985-1990	0.0418	0.0710	0.0647	0.1631	0.1626	0.0123	0.0325	0.0295	0.0221	0.0043	0.0591
HOUSING GROUP											
Lack of Running Water	1.3875	5.0050	12.5105	3.1000	71.4000	22.2000	8.2000	14.3333	18.3000	15.2000	9.9754
Housing with One Room	4.7375	7.6100	9.4684	2.5000	21.0000	12.8667	10.8714	9.4000	8.7500	6.9000	8.5725
Household Crowding	0.2034	0.2897	0.2870	0.2700	0.2172	0.2645	0.3440	0.2942	0.3308	0.2388	0.2826
Septic Tank or Open Flow	0.0343	0.1726	0.1992	0.0443	0.1271	0.1425	0.1237	0.1684	0.1500	0.0836	0.1509
No Toilet	0.0691	0.1563	0.1742	0.0366	0.1718	0.2105	0.3162	0.4388	0.5165	0.6109	0.2077
Firewood or Coal	0.2625	2.0450	3.3684	0.3500	3.3000	8.6667	13.8714	26.9833	46.2000	82.2000	8.2696
ECONOMIC											
Economic Activity 12+	0.4834	0.4330	0.4258	0.3886	0.4338	0.4245	0.4168	0.3329	0.3849	0.3122	0.4222
Unemployment	0.0165	0.0198	0.0187	0.0181	0.0235	0.0171	0.0245	0.0317	0.0219	0.0189	0.0205
Owners/Employers/Salaried	0.7943	0.7230	0.7044	0.9362	0.6685	0.5244	0.8236	0.4500	0.3143	0.1585	0.6531
Wholesale Service Revenues	0.5064	0.2540	0.2376	0.3397	0.2138	0.1340	0.0485	0.1988	0.0937	0.0000	0.2639
Metal Products and Equipment Manuf. Revenues	0.1933	0.2339	0.2275	0.5146	0.3459	0.2009	0.0935	0.1511	0.4149	0.1270	0.1975
Professional/Technical Services Revenues	0.3060	0.0997	0.0553	0.0860	0.0196	0.0095	0.1004	0.0452	0.0000	0.0000	0.1151
SOCIAL RANK											
Prof./Technical/Managerial Occupation	0.1801	0.0846	0.0836	0.1459	0.0319	0.0319	0.0421	0.0325	0.0250	0.0171	0.0826
Primary Education	0.5899	0.4267	0.4173	0.5434	0.2780	0.3544	0.3276	0.2886	0.2583	0.1884	0.4107
High Income (more than 5 x minimum wage)	0.1211	0.0755	0.4173	0.1397	0.0420	0.0335	0.0415	0.0429	0.0321	0.0153	0.0716
Tenure	0.5845	0.7604	0.8017	0.8392	0.8581	0.7931	0.8007	0.8436	0.8662	0.9353	0.7734
URBANISM/FAMILISM											
Cumulative Fertility to Women 20-29	0.8277	1.2894	1.3383	1.1693	1.8336	1.2604	1.5224	1.6243	1.5856	2.1422	1.3262
Free Union	0.1013	0.0886	0.0792	0.0847	0.0668	0.0842	0.0769	0.0792	0.0772	0.0821	0.0844
Separated and Divorced	0.0360	0.0311	0.0188	0.0202	0.0181	0.0183	0.0167	0.0158	0.0169	0.0216	0.0239
Ratio of Women Economically Active	0.3185	0.1814	0.1697	0.1787	0.1468	0.1377	0.1274	0.1252	0.1302	0.1851	0.1798

Table 1.3 Overall Cluster Means (Continued)

Variable	1	2	3	4	5	6	7	8	9	10	Mexico City
Cluster No.											
RACE/ETHNICITY											
Mixtec Language	0.0013	0.0012	0.0016	0.0007	0.0086	0.0018	0.0002	0.0003	0.0001	0.0002	0.0012
Nahautl Language	0.0028	0.0035	0.0025	0.0013	0.0053	0.0114	0.0029	0.0008	0.0004	0.0005	0.0030
Otomi Language	0.0020	0.0020	0.0020	0.0008	0.0024	0.0013	0.0008	0.0007	0.0007	0.0002	0.0016
Zapotec Language	0.0019	0.0010	0.0010	0.0011	0.0000	0.0013	0.0002	0.0001	0.0000	0.0002	0.0009
Indigenous Language-Remainder	0.0050	0.0041	0.0037	0.0027	0.0106	0.0042	0.0025	0.0028	0.0030	0.0016	0.0038

Cluster 1	Cluster 2	Cluster 3	Cluster 4	Cluster 5	Cluster 6	Cluster 7	Cluster 8	Cluster 9	Cluster 10
Azcapotzalco	Acolman	Atenco	Coacalco	Chalco	Ixtapaluca	Amecameca	Axapusco	Atlautla	Ecatzingo
Benito Juarez	Alvaro Obregon	Atizapan de Zaragoza	Cuautitlan Izcalli		Juchitepec	Ayapango	Jilotzingo	Isidro Fabela	
Coyoacan	Chicoloapan	Chiautla			Milpa Alta	Coyotepec	Nopaltepec		
Cuauhtemoc	Chiconcuac	Chimalhuacan				San Martin de las P.	Otumba		
Gustavo A. Madero	Cocotitlan	Cuautitlan				Temascalapa	Ozumba		
Iztacalco	Cuajimalpa	Ecatepec				Tenango del Aire	Tepetlixpa		
Miguel Hidalgo	Huehuetoca	Huixquilucan				Tepetlaoxtoc			
Venustiano Carranza	Iztapalapa	Nicolas Romero							
	Jaltenco	Papalotla							
	Magdalena Contreras	Paz, La							
	Melchor Ocampo	Tecamac							
	Naucalpan	Teoloyucan							
	Nextlalpan	Teotihuacan							
	Nezahualcoyotl	Tepotzotlan							
	Temamatla	Tezoyuca							
	Texcoco	Tlalmanalco							
	Tlahuac	Tlalpan							
	Tlalnepantla	Tultitlan							
	Tultepec	Xochimilco							
	Zumpango								

Map 1.5
Mexico Megacity
Overall Clusters 1 to 10

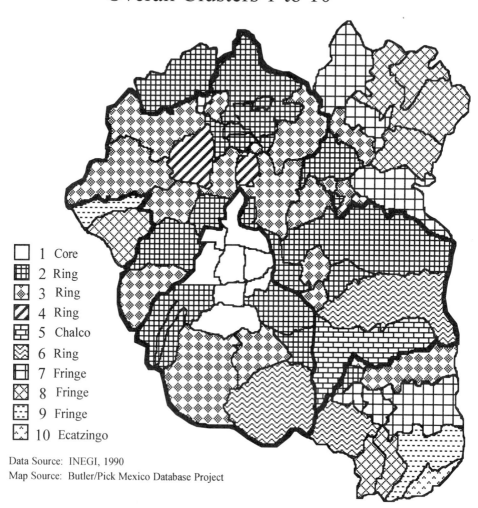

1 Core
2 Ring
3 Ring
4 Ring
5 Chalco
6 Ring
7 Fringe
8 Fringe
9 Fringe
10 Ecatzingo

Data Source: INEGI, 1990
Map Source: Butler/Pick Mexico Database Project

Summary

In summary, overall goals of this book were (1) to delineate systematically areas within Mexico Megacity having similar social characteristics, (2) to compare areas within the city on a variety of dimensions including socioeconomic status, population structure, and segregation, (3) to establish a baseline for analyses of changes taking place in areas within the region which also will allow a comparative analysis across time, (4) to develop a sampling frame of similar and dissimilar areas that can be used by other researchers for a variety of other studies and research endeavors, and (5) to present information in such a manner that the research allows planners and policy makers to utilize scientifically generated information .

Theoretical considerations assisted us in selecting most, but not all, variables examined in this book. Our preliminary conclusions are that the Burgess concentric zone perspective has a lot to offer in way of explaining the spatial distribution of the dimensions we have examined in this book. However, there are substantial differences between Mexico Megacity and cities in the United States; among these differences is the substantial reversal of socioeconomic variables. Primary poverty zones in Mexico City are located on the periphery which would be highly unusual for contemporary U.S. cities. Clearly some dimensions form what loosely might be called sectors, while other variables are formed only in multiple nuclei.

The cluster analysis was found to be useful in demarcating areas that make sense to observers of the metropolitan complex and to consolidate numerous variables into smaller subsets. As a result of this and other preliminary work (Butler and Pick, 1995), we identify the following broad metropolitan areas: (1) an urban core, (2) an inner ring, (3) an expansion zone, and (4) poverty regions -- the fringe. The book will examine this preliminary perception of the metropolitan complex in much more detail. It will seek to arrive at a finalized perception that can be evaluated and compared to well known theories of the metropolis.

A question that certainly will need to be addressed is to what degree our results on Mexico Megacity can be generalized to other times, to other Latin American cities, and to other Megacities. That is, are there similar areas within other large cities including megacities and are there similar kinds and types of clusters in other cities. Subsequent analyses will add variables, carry out more sophisticated quantitative techniques, and evaluate the process whereby the various regions came into being and have their contemporary characteristics.

2

Urbanization in Mexico

Introduction

Unikel (1977: 465) noted that the geographic concentration of population and economic activities is one of the remarkable aspects of twentieth century Mexico. It produced radical changes in the population distribution of Mexico, changed population composition, accelerated transformation of Mexico culture and rural portion of the population, and introduced an 'urban way of life' into society.

Many explanations have been offered to account for the urbanization of a society. In Mexico it undoubtedly was and is a multi-dimensional phenomenon. It involves Mexico's most fundamental societal institutions, including its economic, social, political, demographic, and ecological aspects. The major focus in this chapter is on the demographic and ecological; most other aspects of urbanization of Mexico are explored in subsequent chapters.

The goals of this chapter are (1) to briefly sketch historical population and urban growth in Mexico, (2) analyze urbanization changes between 1950 and 1990, (3) describe the urban population in 1990, (4) present information on the 59 major cities in Mexico in 1990, (5) discuss CONAPO's system of cities model, (6) illustrate cities along the Mexican-U.S. Border, and (7) discuss future urbanization in Mexico. Thus, this chapter places in context urbanization in Mexico and by presenting a brief introduction to Mexico City sets the stage for our more extensive analysis of contemporary *Mexico Megacity.*

Of particular interest in defining the process of urbanization and extent of urbanization is exactly what consists of an urban population. Unikel (1977: 480) proposed the following classification for Mexico:

Rural: Population living in localities less than 5,000 inhabitants.
Mixed-Rural: Population living in localities between 5,000 and 9,999 inhabitants.
Mixed-Urban: Population living in localities between 10,000 and 14,999 inhabitants.
Urban: Population living in localities of 15,000 and more inhabitants.

These definitions differ from the Mexican census, which defined urban to be population living in localities of 2,500 or more. In the chapter and book we generally refer to the census definition, except where we specifically cite other studies.

Historical Urban Growth in Mexico

Population and Urban Growth: 1821 - 1990

Historical population growth in Mexico and several major historical events for 1742 through 1996 are shown on Table 2.1. Figure 2.1 illustrates population growth between 1742 and 1996. Between 1821 and 1860, the Mexican population grew at a relatively slow rate (ca. one percent/year). Reform laws of 1859 dismantled many large civil and religious land holdings, while Mexico City's role as a center of industrialization and transportation attracted migrants from rural areas leading to its being the primary population center of Mexico. During the early part of this period, Mexico was at war with the Texans. Other wars and conflicts with the U.S. eventually ended with population and land transfers (Gadsden Purchase 1853); the net result reduced Mexican territory by almost 50 percent (see Map 2.1). The urban system developed by Spain before Mexican independence changed to a "highly regionalized, weakly articulated urban system in which cities were consumers rather than producers" (Kemper and Royce, 1979: 271).

Mexico's population and urban growth in the twentieth century has been startling. The Mexican population grew from 13.6 million in 1900 to 81.2 million in 1990 and to 94.6

million in 1996. The annual rate of increase was 2.0 percent. However, decennial growth fluctuated with moderate growth before 1940 and after 1980 with the era between 1940 and 1980 being a period of rapid population and urban growth. For Mexico as a whole, its rural population increased from 12.2 to 27 million between 1900 and 1970 (a 2.2 fold increase); however, its urban population increased from 1.4 million to 22 million (a 15.7 increase). National urbanization increased from 28 percent in 1900 to 71 percent in 1990 (see Figure 2.2). The geography of urbanization, however, changed only slightly during the twentieth century. That is, the pattern of urbanization established in 1900 carried over into the 1990s. This pattern of geographic continuity with extensive growth over many decades has been shown for other social characteristics in Mexico during the same time span (Butler and Pick, 1991; Butler, Pick, and Fukurai, in press). Porfirio Diaz ruled Mexico from 1877 to 1911, during which time the first census of Mexico was taken in 1895. He encouraged international investment to assist in industrializing Mexico and he actively promoted development of a national railroad system (Portes and Bach, 1985). There was relatively little internal migration in Mexico prior to 1910. This was primarily because of the dominance of the hacienda system which kept workers "virtually bound to the soil as indentured labor" (Whetten and Burnight, 1956). In addition, there were inferior transportation and communication networks and a poor economy. A few cities grew during this era and Mexico City had an annual growth rate of 3.1 percent, absorbing 36 percent of gross increase in urban population (Unikel, 1977: 490).

The Revolutionary Era, beginning around 1910, engendered a mobile population and many refugees sought shelter in cities and towns. As a result of this shifting about of the population and deaths related to internal strife, the 1910 and 1921 censuses (see Table 2.1) showed that the Mexican population decreased in population from 15.2 million in 1910 to 14.3 million in 1921 (Alba, 1984). While the number of smaller settlements decreased drastically, the urban population increased from 11.7 percent to 14.7 percent. Mexico City absorbed 60 percent of the increase in urban population during this intercensus period. The urban impetus engendered by the revolutionary era continued unabated and urban migrants flooded other towns and cities.

During the late 1930s, the government focused on agrarian reform and urbanization slowed (Tamayo, 1986; Unikel, 1977). However by 1940, 20 percent of the Mexican population lived in places 15,000 or larger (Unikel, 1977), and the Mexico City urban area ad 7.9 million residents (INEGI, 1994).

Initially urban increase proportionately was substantially a result of migration, but natural increase (excess of births over deaths) starting in the 1950s and thereafter was the major component of urban population increase (Unikel, 1977). Table 2.2 illustrates urbanization for the states of Mexico 1930, 1950, 1980, and 1990. Between 1940 and 1970, the Mexican population grew from 20 to 49 million and urbanization continued apace. In 1930, the least urbanized states were Chiapas, Guerrero, Hidalgo, Oaxaca, Queretaro, and Tabasco. During the 1930 - 1950 time period, all states except Baja Sur and Nayarit increased in urbanization. The least urban states in 1950 were the same states that were the least urbanized in 1930. At the same time in Mexico, life expectancy increased from 42.5 to 60.3 years. The decline in mortality rates, accompanied by continuing high fertility rates and increased life expectancy, accounted for the great population increase. Mexico's fertility rate has declined somewhat in more recent years so that it is now about average for Central America but remains above world-wide averages (see Chapter 4).

Unikel's (1977) major analysis of Mexican urbanization from 1900 and 1970 illustrated this dramatic growth (see Table 2.3 and Figure 2.2). Major trends emphasized the importance of Mexico City's growth and migration to the Mexico-U.S. borderlands region.

Among urban centers in Mexico, Mexico City was dominant. Alba (1984) pointed out that "all other cities and country as a whole gravitate around it. It is clearly a classical primary city." As shown in more detail in Chapter 5, beginning in the 1970s, much of the population of the Federal District began to overflow into nearby municipios of the State of Mexico (Van Arsdol et al., 1977).

Urbanization Between 1930 and 1990

Between 1930 and 1990, urbanization increased in all Mexican states. An average coefficient of variation (CV) of 35 for urbanization change 1930-90 also demonstrates that urbanization change varied moderately for the Mexican states between 1950 and 1990, even though the urban ratio more than doubled (see Table 2.2). As shown on Map 2.2, the greatest increase in urbanization, however, took place in the State of Mexico, with the urban ratio increasing by 0.58. The gain in urban population was from 368,000 in 1950 to a population of 8.3 million persons in 1990. Large population increases and urbanization also took place in the other nearby states, including Queretaro and Tlaxcala, undoubtedly over spill from the emerging Mexico Megacity. The lowest rate of urbanization during this era was for the Federal District; however, since it already was 94.6 percent urbanized in 1950, little more urbanization could occur. Urbanization, fueled by tourism, also grew sharply in the states of Baja California Sur and Quintana Roo.

States with the lowest urbanization rates were Campeche, Aguascalientes, Chiapas, Oaxaca, and Zacatecas. Except for Aguascalientes, these states in 1990 all lacked cities in Mexico's top twenty in population.

Urban Population in 1990

In 1990, the least urbanized states were the same as at earlier dates, except for Queretaro. Queretaro, undoubtedly, was becoming more urbanized as a result of overflow from the greater Mexico City complex (see Map 2.3). At an urban percent of 71.3, the country's population distribution was becoming concentrated in urban places (see Table 2.2).

States with the largest absolute urban population size were Mexico and the Federal District, followed by Jalisco, Veracruz, and Nuevo Leon. Unlike these other states, Veracruz did not contain any of the Mexico's largest cities but had several large cities. The least urban states in 1990 were the poorer and agriculturally oriented states of Oaxaca, Chiapas, Hidalgo, and Zacatecas. These states combined contained only two of the largest 59 cities in Mexico. The Pacific South and Gulf states were the least urbanized. The Gulf region in 1990 approximated the extent of urbanization that the rest of the country reached in 1950.

Analytically, urbanization in 1990 is associated with economic prosperity indicators, and inversely related with marginality and rural indicators. (Pick and Butler, 1994) Urbanization is substantially associated with higher levels of education, literacy, vehicle ownership, and telephones. Also, there are substantial relationships with high monthly income, tertiary employment, professional/technical, administrative/managerial, and service occupations, female economic activity, and number of corporations. On the other hand, urbanization varies inversely with the dependency ratio, annual fertility rate, literacy change between 1950-1990, as well as with households with low incomes, households without toilets and electricity, and no meat or eggs (1970). Home ownership also varied opposite to urbanization in Mexico. i.e. in Mexico urban residents tend to be renters rather than home owners.

Table 2.1 Historical Population Growth: Mexico, 1742-1996

Mexican Historical Development	Year	Mexico Population *
	1742	3,336
	1793	5,200
	1803	5,837
	1810	6,122
War of Independence	1823	6,800
	1838	7,044
Loss of half of territory to the U.S. by 1853	1855	7,853
	1862	8,397
Porfiero Diaz Dictatorship (1877-1911)	1877	9,389
	1884	10,448
	1900	13,607
Revolution (1910-1921)	1910	15,160
	1921	14,335
	1930	16,553
Land Reform (1934)	1940	19,649
Bracero Program (1942-1964)	1950	25,779
	1960	34,923
	1970	49,923
	1980	67,500
	1990	81,250
	1996	94,800

Sources: General Censuses of Mexico, Various dates; Unikel, 1977;
Wibel and de la Cruz, 1971; Population Reference Bureau, 1996.
* Thousands

Figure 2.1 Population Growth: Mexico, 1742 - 1996

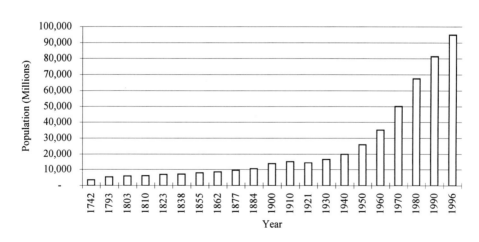

Note: Refer to Table 2.1.

Table 2.2 Urbanization in Mexico, 1930-1990

No.	State	1930		1950		1980		1990		Change Urbaniz. 1950-90
		Pop. Places 2500+	Urban Ratio	Pop. Places 2500+	Urban Ratio	Pop. Places 2500+	Urban Ratio	Pop. Places 2500+	Urban Ratio	
1	Aguascalientes		0.5473	103,262	0.5490	365,545	0.7037	550,697	0.7652	0.2162
2	Baja California		0.5435	146,391	0.6450	1,004,194	0.8525	1,509,794	0.9090	0.2640
3	Baja California Sur	16,979	0.3606	20,022	0.3290	149,973	0.6971	248,665	0.7825	0.4535
4	Campeche	38,155	0.4508	70,069	0.5739	292,006	0.6943	374,780	0.7003	0.1264
5	Coahuila	227,276	0.5208	413,978	0.5745	1,204,971	0.7738	1,697,321	0.8606	0.2861
6	Colima	27,402	0.4425	67,559	0.6015	258,586	0.7467	357,034	0.8332	0.2317
7	Chiapas	92,627	0.1748	209,133	0.2306	702,969	0.3372	1,296,742	0.4039	0.1733
8	Chihuahua	162,099	0.3296	373,357	0.4411	1,410,799	0.7035	1,889,766	0.7739	0.3328
9	Distrito Federal	1,135,123	0.9232	2,884,133	0.9455	8,831,079	1.0000	8,213,843	0.9973	0.0518
10	Durango	94,248	0.2331	180,486	0.2865	595,544	0.5037	774,417	0.5739	0.2874
11	Guanajuato	336,663	0.3408	552,516	0.4158	1,771,604	0.5893	2,525,533	0.6341	0.2183
12	Guerrero	97,336	0.1517	199,251	0.2167	883,394	0.4188	1,369,536	0.5226	0.3059
13	Hidalgo	114,933	0.1696	179,892	0.2115	506,275	0.3272	845,718	0.4479	0.2364
14	Jalisco	494,452	0.3939	836,124	0.4787	3,304,635	0.7559	4,340,432	0.8185	0.3398
15	Mexico	202,956	0.2050	367,679	0.2640	6,007,404	0.7942	8,285,207	0.8441	0.5801
16	Michoacan	275,330	0.2626	455,789	0.3204	1,530,083	0.5333	2,186,354	0.6162	0.2958
17	Morelos	33,219	0.2515	118,354	0.4338	699,331	0.7384	1,023,228	0.8562	0.4224
18	Nayarit	58,703	0.3500	99,008	0.3413	414,528	0.5709	511,731	0.6205	0.2792
19	Nuevo Leon	172,175	0.4124	413,911	0.5592	2,197,288	0.8744	2,850,657	0.9199	0.3607
20	Oaxaca	195,901	0.1806	293,953	0.2068	757,871	0.3199	1,191,303	0.3945	0.1877
21	Puebla	319,524	0.2777	539,233	0.3317	1,899,938	0.5675	2,652,779	0.6429	0.3112
22	Queretaro	46,276	0.1977	69,196	0.2417	350,623	0.4741	627,839	0.5972	0.3555
23	Quintana Roo	2,790	0.2627	7,247	0.2687	133,511	0.5908	364,374	0.7387	0.4700
24	San Luis Potosi	158,712	0.2737	260,452	0.3042	786,023	0.4696	1,105,023	0.5516	0.2474
25	Sinaloa	90,651	0.2291	177,522	0.2793	1,049,545	0.5674	1,412,447	0.6408	0.3615
26	Sonora	116,225	0.3675	231,424	0.4532	1,067,861	0.7054	1,443,067	0.7913	0.3381

Table 2.2 Urbanization in Mexico, 1930-1990 (Continued)

No.	State	1930 Pop. Places 2500+	1930 Urban Ratio	1950 Pop. Places 2500+	1950 Urban Ratio	1980 Pop. Places 2500+	1980 Urban Ratio	1990 Pop. Places 2500+	1990 Urban Ratio	Change Urbaniz. 1950-90
27	Tabasco	38,790	0.1732	79,558	0.2193	405,950	0.3819	745,718	0.4966	0.2773
28	Tamaulipas	147,367	0.4283	380,281	0.5295	1,445,960	0.7513	1,823,704	0.8107	0.2812
29	Tlaxcala	56,632	0.2756	110,315	0.3877	320,480	0.5758	582,351	0.7650	0.3773
30	Veracruz	392,926	0.2853	679,380	0.3330	2,743,286	0.5092	3,501,726	0.5622	0.2292
31	Yucatan	185,867	0.4814	285,567	0.5525	782,041	0.7352	1,071,618	0.7863	0.2338
32	Zacatecas	110,291	0.2403	166,678	0.2504	426,432	0.3751	586,317	0.4594	0.2090
	Urban Population	5,443,558		10,973,670		44,301,709		57,961,711		
	Total Population	16,552,722		25,779,254		66,846,833		81,249,645		
	Urban Ratio	0.3347		0.4260		0.6627		0.7134		0.2874
	Mean	175,599	0.3355	332,535	0.3993	1,342,476	0.6137	1,756,415	0.6912	0.2919
	Median	114,933	0.2815	199,251	0.3372	782,041	0.5901	1,191,303	0.7195	0.2836
	S.D.	214,420	0.1575	499,424	0.1676	1,776,572	0.1732	1,938,379	0.1605	0.1033
	C.V.	122.11	46.94	150.19	41.97	132.34	28.22	110.36	23.22	35.39
	Minimum	1,930	0.1517	1,950	0.2068	1,980	0.3199	1,990	0.3945	0.0518
	Maximum	1,135,123	0.9232	2,884,133	0.9455	8,831,079	1.0000	8,285,207	0.9973	0.5801

Definition: Urbanization is the ratio of population living in localities of the stated population total to the total population of the state.
Source: 1930 and 1950 Mexican Census of Population, Resumen General; 1980 Mexican Census of Population, Volume 2, Table 2, 1990 Mexican Census of Population, Resumen General, Table 3.

Map 2.1 Changes in Territory Between Mexico and the United States, 1836-1853

UNITED STATES

GUADALUPE HIDALGO TREATIES 1848

COLORADO RIVER

CLAIMED BY TEXAS AND NEW MEXICO 1836 TO 1850

RED RIVER

GADSEN PURCHASE 1853

TEXAS REPUBLIC 1836

BRAZOS RIVER

NUECES RIVER

RIO GRANDE

CLAIMED BY MEXICO AND TEXAS 1836 - 1848

MEXICO

Table 2.3 Urban and Mexico Megacity Population: 1900-1990

	1900	1910	1921	1930	1940	1950	1960	1970	1980	1990
Urban population*	10.5	11.7	14.7	17.5	20	28	36.5	44.3	66.3	71.3
Population of Mexico City urban area*	2.5	3.1	4.6	6.3	7.9	11.1	14.1	8.8	13.4	15.4
Population of Mexico City urban area as percent of urban population	24.1	26.4	31.8	36.3	39.7	39.8	36.9	19.9	20.2	21.6

Source: Unikel, 1977: 485, Mexican Censuses, various years.

* in millions

Figure 2.2 Urban and Rural Population, Mexico, 1900 - 1990

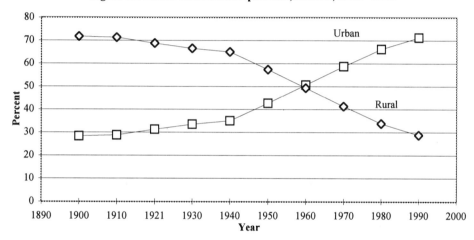

Supporting Data

Year	Urban	Rural
1900	28.3	71.7
1910	28.7	71.3
1921	31.2	68.8
1930	33.5	66.5
1940	35	65
1950	42.6	57.4
1960	50.7	49.3
1970	58.7	41.3
1980	66.3	33.7
1990	71.3	28.7

Source: *Estadisticas Historicas de Mexico,* 1985: INEGI, 1992a.

Map 2.2
Urbanization Change
in Mexico, 1950 - 1990

☐	0.0518 to 0.2172
⊠	0.2173 to 0.2623
⊡	0.2624 to 0.3007
◩	0.3008 to 0.3476
▨	0.3477 to 0.5801

Data Source: INEGI, 1950 and 1990 Mexican Censuses
Map Source: Butler/Pick Mexico Database Project

Map 2.3
Urbanization in Mexico, 1990

☐	0.3945 to 0.5371
⊠	0.5371 to 0.6273
⊡	0.6273 to 0.7651
◩	0.7651 to 0.8146
▨	0.8146 to 0.9973

Data Source: INEGI, 1990 Mexican Censuses
Map Source: Butler/Pick Mexico Database Project

Large Cities of Mexico

In 1990, there were three classes of cities as defined by the Mexican census (INEGI, 1993b): (1) the three largest cities -- Mexico City, Monterrey, and Guadalajara (*Area Metropolitana),* (2) M.U.s (*Mancha Urbana*) or urban grouping for cities in which there were several smaller places constituting a common urban unit, and (3) others. Official definitions of cities varied between 1980 and 1990 with some cities annexing areas of smaller nearby cities and there were other factors influencing political boundaries, so a longitudinal comparison of cities is subject to some variation as a result of these factors.

Urbanization between 1980 and 1990 increased by five percent. Almost half of the Mexican population in 1990 was concentrated in large cities -- cities with a population greater than 100,000. There were 59 such cities in 1990, with an increase of 13 of them since 1980 (see Table 2.4). The largest 59 cities grew faster than the national population. The 35 Mexican cities of 200,000 and more inhabitants are shown on Map 2.4. The twelve largest cities in 1990 contained 33 percent of the total national population -- over 26 million persons -- while a decade earlier they had nearly an identical one-third of the population. Thus, 1980s growth disproportionately took place in cities smaller than the top twelve, as well as in thirteen new large cities that emerged during the 1980s decade.

The next eleven largest cities grew during the 1980s by over 40 percent. Cities with the largest *relative* growth during the 1980s were Toluca, Mexico; Cuernavaca, Morelos; Tuxtla, Chiapas; Monclava, Coahuila; and Queretaro, Queretaro. All of these cities doubled in size during the 1980s. Three of them, Toluca, Cuernavaca, and Queretaro can be considered as being influenced by growth taking place in the greater Mexico Megacity region. Population growth between 1950 and 1990 for the four largest cities in Mexico is shown on Figure 2.3.

By far, the greatest relative growth took place in Toluca, located to the west of Mexico City and the capital of the State of Mexico. It grew by two and one-half times during the decade to reach a population of one-half million persons by 1990. Proximity to Mexico City likely favored Toluca's growth. Another major growth center was Tijuana, located on the Mexico-U.S. border, not far from San Diego, California. It grew by 63 percent during the decade to reach a population of almost 700,000. Along with San Diego, California, this conurbation makes up one of the largest bi-national cities in the world.

The spatial distribution of large cities in Mexico corresponds to the pattern of urbanization shown on earlier maps. Map 2.4 also showed the location of the largest 35 cities in 1990, all of which had more than 100,000 population. Numbering on the map is by rank order of city population size. Table 2.4 presents data for 1990 by rank order of city population size, the state of location, number of households, sex ratio, 1980 population, and percent population change between 1980 and 1990 for the largest 59 Mexican cities.

The major concentration of larger cities is across the central part of Mexico. Relatively near to Mexico City are the three large cities of Puebla -- the fourth largest city in the nation, located in the state of Puebla; Leon in the state of Guanajuato; and Toluca, Mexico. There are few large cities in the south and southeast regions, with the largest ones being Acapulco, Merida, and the city of Oaxaca in the state of Oaxaca.

Table 2.4 Large Cities, 1990

No.	City	State	1990 Pop.	1990 No. Households	1990 Sex Ratio	1980 Pop.	% Change 1980-1990
1	Mexico City AM	D.F./Mexico *	15,047,685	3,133,834	94.17	13,354,271	12.68
2	Guadalajara AM	Jalisco *	2,870,417	557,378	93.80	2,192,557	30.92
3	Monterrey AM	Nuevo Leon *	2,558,494	529,242	98.41	1,913,075	33.74
4	Puebla MU	Puebla *	1,157,386	238,388	92.31	772,908	49.74
5	Juarez	Chihuahua	789,522	176,902	98.02	544,496	45.00
6	Leon	Guanajuato *	758,279	128,951	94.93	593,002	27.87
7	Tijuana	Baja California	698,752	155,710	100.40	429,500	62.69
8	Torreon/G. P. MU	Coahuila/Durange	689,212	141,370	94.37	445,053	54.86
9	San Luis Potosi MU	San Lius Potosi *	613,181	122,928	92.31	471,047	30.17
10	Merida MU	Yucatan *	532,964	118,328	91.94	400,142	33.19
11	Toluca MU	Mexico *	517,150	103,102	93.05	199,778	158.86
12	Chihuahua	Chihuahua *	516,153	116,669	94.17	385,603	33.86
13	Acapulco de Juarez	Guerrero	515,374	109,144	93.05	301,902	70.71
14	Tampico/C. M. MU	Tamaulipas	490,003	112,556	92.68	400,401	22.38
15	Aguascalientes MU	Aguascalientes *	455,234	86,000	93.05	293,152	55.29
16	Veracruz MU	Veracruz	447,202	105,594	89.39	367,339	21.74
17	Cuernavaca MU	Morelos *	446,739	97,223	93.42	192,770	131.75
18	Saltillo MU	Coahuila *	441,739	89,842	97.63	284,937	55.03
19	Mexicali	Baja California *	438,377	99,140	98.02	341,559	28.35
20	Queretaro MU	Queretaro *	431,905	82,356	93.42	215,976	99.98
21	Morelia	Michoacan *	428,486	86,912	91.94	297,544	44.01
22	Culiacan	Sinaloa *	415,046	82,333	94.93	304,826	36.16
23	Hermosillo	Sonora *	406,417	86,769	98.41	297,175	36.76
24	Durango	Durango *	348,036	70,988	92.68	321,148	8.37
25	Oaxaca MU	Oaxaca *	295,658	49,761	89.04	154,223	91.71
26	Jalapa MU	Veracruz *	291,038	66,050	87.27	204,594	42.25
27	Tuxtla	Chiapas *	289,626	60,982	93.05	131,096	120.93
28	Matamoros	Tamaulipas	266,055	59,089	94.17	188,745	40.96
29	Reynosa	Tamaulipas	265,663	59,085	97.24	194,693	36.45
30	Irapuato	Guanajuato	265,042	49,549	92.68	170,138	55.78
31	Mazatlan	Sinaloa	262,705	56,331	95.31	199,830	31.46
32	Villahermosa/Centro	Tabasco *	261,231	57,531	93.42	158,216	65.11
33	Monclova MU	Coahuila	254,376	54,479	100.00	115,786	119.69
34	Cajeme/C. O.	Sonora	219,980	46,664	95.69	165,572	32.86
35	Nuevo Laredo	Tamaulipas	218,413	47,546	95.31	201,731	8.27
36	Celeya	Guanajuato	214,856	41,048	92.68	141,675	51.65
37	Tepic	Nayarit *	206,967	43,705	91.94	145,741	42.01
38	Coatzacoalcos	Veracruz	198,817	45,174	96.46	233,935	-8.50
39	Ciudad Victoria	Tamaulipas *	194,996	42,014	95.69	140,161	39.12
40	Uruapan	Michoacan	187,623	36,858	92.68	122,828	52.75
41	Orizaba MU	Veracruz	174,179	38,489	91.20	114,848	51.66
42	Pachuca	Hidalgo *	174,013	37,608	90.84	110,351	57.69
43	Ensenada	Baja California	169,426	40,694	97.24	120,483	40.62
44	Cancun	Q. Roo	167,730	39,832	108.33	**	**
45	Los Mochis/Ahome	Sinaloa	162,659	32,975	94.17	122,531	32.75
46	Poza Rica de Hidalgo	Veracruz	151,739	33,425	89.39	166,799	-9.03
47	Campeche	Campeche *	150,518	33,748	93.80	128,434	17.19
48	Cordoba MU	Veracruz	148,481	31,889	89.04	**	**
49	Zacatecas MU	Zacatecas *	146,484	29,309	93.80	**	**
50	Zamora MU	Michoacan	145,597	27,794	91.94	**	**

41

Table 2.4 Large Cities, 1990 (Continued)

No.	City	State	1990 Pop.	1990 No. Households	1990 Sex Ratio	1980 Pop.	% Change 1980-1990
51	Colima MU	Colima *	142,844	31,050	94.52	**	**
52	Minatitlan	Veracruz	142,060	31,032	94.17	**	**
53	Tehuacan	Puebla	139,450	27,236	92.68	**	**
54	Tapachula	Chiapas	138,858	29,541	91.20	**	**
55	La Paz	Baja Calif. Sur *	137,641	30,008	100.40	**	**
56	Salamanca	Guanajuato	123,190	23,649	94.55	**	**
57	Buenavista	Mexico	114,653	22,180	99.20	**	**
58	Cuautla	Morelos	110,242	23,555	91.20	**	**
59	Nogales	Sonora	105,873	22,797	101.61	**	**
	Total City Population		38,652,436			28,752,571	
	Population of Mexico		81,249,645			81,249,645	
	Proportion of Population in Cities		0.4757			0.3539	
	Mean City Population		655,126.0	136,175.2	94.4	625,055.9	49.02
	S.D.		1,949,754.6	405,166.8	3.5	1,937,721.0	33.03
	C.V.		297.62	297.53	3.73	310.01	67.38
	Minimum City Population		105,873	22,180	87.27	110,351	-9.03
	Maximum City Population		15,047,685	3,133,834	108.33	13,354,271	158.86

Note: Three state capitals are not populous enough to appear; Chilpancingo, Guerrero; Chetumal, Quintana Roo; and Tlaxcala, Tlaxcala.
AM = area metropolitana
MU = mancha urbana
G.P. = Gomez Palacio.
C.M. = Ciudad Madero.
C.O.= Ciudad Obregon.
* City is capital of state.
** Large city population data not avaliable for 1980.
Source: INEGI, 1993b; *Estadisticas Historicas de Mexico,* 1985.

Figure 2.3 Population of Mexico's Four Largest Cities, 1950-1990

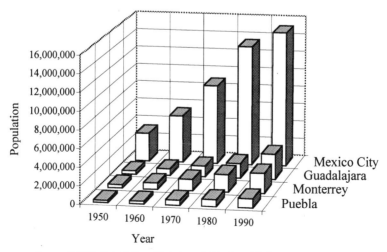

Source:INEGI: *Estadisticos Historicas de Mexico,* 1993.

42

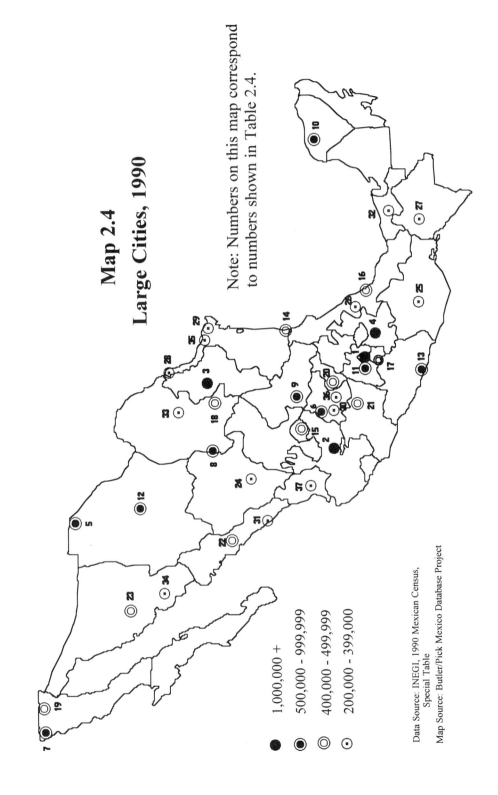

Map 2.4
Large Cities, 1990

Note: Numbers on this map correspond
to numbers shown in Table 2.4.

1,000,000 +

500,000 - 999,999

400,000 - 499,999

200,000 - 399,000

Data Source: INEGI, 1990 Mexican Census,
Special Table
Map Source: Butler/Pick Mexico Database Project

A System of Cities

The Mexico Population Council, i.e., Consejo Nacional de Población or CONAPO, is a unit of the federal government responsible for population planning and policy. One of the national goals advocated by CONAPO in the Salinas administration was to foster better balance of the national population in its distinctive regions: "One of the principal goals... [is] to reach a population distribution in the national territory that responds to the growth potential of distinct regions. In particular, it is essential to take decisive action to diminish the relative dominance of the great metropolitan zones and stimulate the growth of medium and small sized cities" (Fernando Gutiérrez Barrios, in CONAPO, 1991).

To research this goal, CONAPO sponsored a series of over twenty studies of the "systems and subsystems of cities of Mexico." These studies were held together by a theoretical base in central place theory and the theory of diffusion. It viewed the system of cities as a networking of human settlements connected by relationships including demographic, economic, cultural, commercial, and others, generally with dominance by large metropolitan centers.

A complex hierarchical system of cities of Mexico was constructed (CONAPO, 1991). It followed a gravity model based on the following characteristics: (1) economic activity in the locality, (2) volume of telephone calls, and (3) distance between pairs of cities. The gravity model outputs city "push" and "pull" values that allows assignment of cities to one of six ranks (see CONAPO, 1991). Ranked cities are then connected together in a complex hierarchy. The six ranks of cities are summarized in Table 2.5. Part of the hierarchical structure is shown in Map 2.5. In the map, the arrows point from cities of higher rank to those of lower rank. This map shows most of the cities of ranks 1-5, but only one city, Tepic, of rank 6. A full map would require a display of 79 cities instead of the 37 larger ones illustrated in Map 2.5.

The CONAPO studies examined many socioeconomic aspects of the hierarchical system of cities. These studies examined the system in the context of population, telephone flows, demographic carrying capacity, migration, potential to absorb and/or alter migration, and demographic development potential. The thrust of the studies was to examine the potential ways by which the historical trend to hyperconcentration in Mexico City could be altered and possibly reduced in the future.

CONAPO drew these studies together in a set of policy recommendations intended to deconcentrate the Megacity and divert demographic growth to medium sized cities. The recommendations may be grouped as demographic, economic/financial, infrastructure, and environmental. The demographic recommendation pointed to the problem of urban growth and suggested ways to focus it towards the middle sized cities. Economic/financial recommendations included enhancement of the labor force potential of middle sized cities, and greater financial investment and development of industrial and energy resources. The infrastructure recommendations were support and development in mid-sized cities of irrigation, communication networks, storage centers as well as facilities for health, education, and welfare. Environmental recommendations included solving ecological problems, introducing soil and water conservation practices, and bettering human settlements. The recommendations were linked back to the system of cities framework.

Although officially proposed in 1992 as the "100 cities" program and given attention in the 1994 presidential election, the program faltered in the early Zedillo administration (Vangas and Garcia, 1996). The reasons were the financial impacts of the economic crisis of 1995-96 leading to sharply reduced funding for the 100 cities program, as well as lack of political support, problems and delays in conversion of ejido land for the program, and lack of interest from international agencies.

The system of cities framework is important to this book in revealing a national awareness of Mexico City's hyperconcentration and over-enlarged primacy status. Mexico City dominates the urban system and absorbs national resources to such an extent that medium sized cities are unable to develop to their economic potential. At the same time, the over-expanded Megacity has developed many severe problems covered in this book including environment, provision of health services, and large poverty zones that point to the wisdom of the system of cities framework. Although the framework may have weaknesses in its detailed and highly structured hierarchy of city subsystems, nevertheless, it is useful in analyzing and assessing the national urban setting.

Table 2.5 Ranks of Cities in CONAPO's System of Cities

Rank	Definition	Cities
1	The Metropolitan Zone of Mexico City is the leader of the system of cities. A central place offering goods and services with a sphere of influence that affects, with greater or less intensity, all of the national territory. Known for enormous primacy.	Mexico City
2	A group of large metropolitan centers with great economic power, important service sectors, and large populations. Influential in a large regions extending to cities in neighboring states. Each center heads up a subsystem of dozens of cities.	Monterrey, Guadalajara, and Puebla
3	Cities with a great capacity to articulate with smaller cities usually in the same state. When extending into other states, these cities' influence diminishes with distance. They provide intergration and equilibrium in the national territory. Absent in certain parts of the nation.	Chihuahua, Tijuana, Hermosillo, Leon, Queretaro, Toluca, Cuernavaca, and Veracruz
4	Cities with minor influence on other cities in terms of distance. Generally tied only to cities in the same state.	Mexicali, Tampico, Gomerz Palacio, Ciudad Obregon, Culiacan, Morelia, San Luis Potosi, Xalapa, Coatzacoalcos, Villahermosa, Acapulco, and Merida
5	Smaller cities that serve smaller regions in the interior of states, although linked as distribution points nationally. Have a minor capacity to concentrate telephone call flows.	Matamoros, Reynosa, Nuevo Laredo, Ciudad Juarez, Ensenada, Mazatlan, Aguascalientes, Irapuato, Celaya, Guanajuato, Pachuca, Orizaba, Cordoba, Minatitlan, Tuxtla, Oaxaca, and Cancun
6	Smaller cities with reduced influence limited to nearby areas in the same state. Have specific and very diverse functions, with varying regional importance.	37 smaller regional cities.

Source: CONAPO: *Sistema de Ciudades y Distribucion Espacial de la Poblacion en Mexico,* 1991.

45

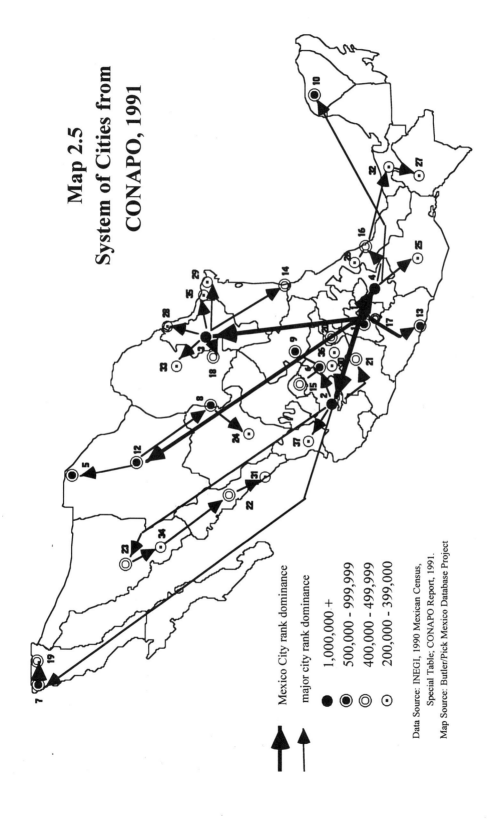

Map 2.5
System of Cities from
CONAPO, 1991

Mexico City rank dominance

major city rank dominance

1,000,000 +

500,000 - 999,999

400,000 - 499,999

200,000 - 399,000

Data Source: INEGI, 1990 Mexican Census,
　　　　　　 Special Table; CONAPO Report, 1991.
Map Source: Butler/Pick Mexico Database Project

United States-Mexican Border States and Cities[1]

A weakness in the CONAPO system of cities is that while Mexican border cities are tied hierarchically to larger Mexican cities and ultimately to Mexico City, the system ignores their strong linkages with bordering U.S. cities and states. This reflects the domestic concerns of CONAPO relating to deconcentration. This section highlights the Mexican border cities and states, and linkages with the U.S.

In the post-NAFTA era, border cities are key to development of free trade and maquila industry. Although the region has been overshadowed in importance in the history and development of Mexico, today border areas have emerged as vitally important economic, social, and political entities. Growth of the maquila sector in the 1980s and passage of the NAFTA agreement are key indicators of the vitality and importance of these cities. Examining their growth and development is essential to understanding Mexico City since the border cities, Monterrey, and Mexico City share the leadership as the most economically advanced areas of the nation (Pick and Butler, 1994). With the implementation of the free trade agreement, many co-production opportunities will become available for Mexico Megacity, although many of them will not be economically viable. Since the border cities and states led the nation in maquila development, Mexico City may borrow from them and adopt an increased co-production sector in the future.

Although border populations grew rapidly early in the century, since 1970, the portion of national population in the border region has remained constant. The proportion of national population in the border region was almost exact one sixth of national population from 1970 to 1990. Mexico's population in the border region between 1970 and 1990 is presented below.

State	1970 Pop.	1980 Pop.	1990 Pop.	% Growth 1970–1990	% Growth 1980–1990
Tamaulipas	1,457	1,924	2,250	54	17
Nuevo Leon	1,695	2,513	3,099	83	23
Coahuila	1,115	1,557	1,972	77	27
Chihuahua	1,613	2,005	2,442	51	22
Sonora	1,267	1,850	2,204	66	19
Baja California	870	1,178	1,661	91	41
Total Border Region	8,017	11,027	13,628	70	24
Nation	48,225	66,847	81,250	68	22
% in Border	0.166	0.165	0.168		

Note: The population figures are in thousands.
Source: INEGI, 1970-1990 Mexican Censuses of Population.

While the border region grew in the 70s and 80s at about the national rate within the region, Baja substantially exceeded the nation's growth, while Tamaulipas lagged the nation. Partly, this is explained by differences in regional economic partnerships with the U.S. While Tamaulipas is located along the south Texas border, an economically depressed region, Baja adjoins California, which during the 70s and 80s had a large and prosperous regional economy. Baja has also served as a major channel for large Mexican migration flows between Mexico and the U.S. (Lorey, 1990). This flow has implied an increase in temporary and longer term residence in Baja for migrants at various stages of their moves (see Pick et al., 1990a).

The border may also be conceived as a narrow band adjacent to the 2,000 mile U.S.-Mexican border. In such a view, the eight major metropolitan areas of twin U.S.-Mexican

---

[1] This section is slightly revised from Pick and Butler (1994).

cities rise in importance (see Map 2.6 and Table 2.6). In 1990, the twin cities had a bi-national population of 6.4 million persons, of which 2.9 million resided in Mexico and 3.5 million in the U.S.. These cities are developing into new urban and metropolitan forms that extend into economics, politics, and familial/social structure (Tamayo and Fernandez, 1983; Gonzalez-Arechiga and Ramirez, 1990; Arreola and Curtis, 1993). They are becoming important economic entities, since they are the loci for most of Mexico's maquiladora plants and offer unique international trade and commercial services.

Population figures referred to for the twin cities for the U.S. cities are based on the U.S. Census concept of urbanized area (U.S. Bureau of the Census 1992). An urbanized area includes the central city and any contiguous cities. It differs from a metropolitan area by not corresponding to county boundaries.

In the 1980s, both Mexican and U.S. border city components grew more rapidly than their respective nations. The Mexican component's growth rate of 42 percent was much higher than Mexico's 22 percent growth, while the U.S.'s border city component's growth of 25 percent exceeded U.S. decennial growth of 10 percent. However, Mexican population in border cities constituted 21 percent of the Mexican border region population, while the equivalent U.S. portion was only seven percent. This implies that Mexican border population is much more "bunched up" next to the border line, while in the U.S. the border region population is more spread out.

Twin cities show considerable variation (see Table 2.6). The largest twin city is the San Diego/Tijuana, with a 1990 population of 3.0 million. This twin city is a major North American metropolis. For example, its *combined* 1990 population total would rank it as the 12th largest metropolitan area in the United States, between Miami-Fort Lauderdale at 3.2 million and Atlanta at 2.8 million (U.S. Bureau of the Census, 1991) and second in size in Mexico after Mexico City. It holds nearly half of the border twin cities' population, and it is increasing its economic importance, both in North America and globally (Arreola and Curtis, 1993). Although Tijuana grew rapidly in the 80s, the population of this twin city is still nearly 80 percent U.S. citizens. Second in population size is Ciudad Juarez/El Paso, which had a combined population of 1.4 million in 1990, equivalent to about one quarter of the border twin cities' population. In contrast to San Diego/Tijuana, Ciudad Juarez/El Paso is about 60 percent Mexican citizens. Ciudad Juarez is roughly the size of Tijuana, but has the largest maquiladora sector in Mexico.

The twin city of Mexicali/Calexico had a population one sixth the size of San Diego/Tijuana. It is 96 percent Mexican citizens. This is due largely to the agricultural nature of Imperial County on the U.S. side, which so far has limited population growth. Mexicali/Calexico grew in the 80s at about 3/4 the rate of San Diego/Tijuana. The slower growth may be due to a hotter, inland location and less accessible transportation.

There are three twin cities in the east between the states of Texas, U.S., and Tamaulipas, Mexico. The two eastern ones, Matamoros/Brownsville and Reynosa/McAllen, are similar in many respects. They are fairly balanced between the two sides, with populations in the roughly half million range. They grew during the 1980s at about 30 percent, a rate about at average for border cities. These twin cities are not as prosperous as Tijuana/San Diego and Ciudad Juarez/El Paso, because south Texas is one of the poorest sections of the U.S. and Tamaulipas is only moderate in prosperity in Mexico. The third twin city of Nuevo Laredo/Laredo resembles the others although it is somewhat smaller at 1/3 million persons and grew more slowly in the 80s—by only 16 percent.

The smallest twin cities are Piedras Negras/Eagle Pass and Nogales/Nogales. Both are predominantly Mexican citizens in population. Nogales/Nogales grew rapidly in the 80s, in fact the most rapidly at 53 percent of the eight twin cities. This growth was due in large part to the influx of maquiladora industry into the city. By contrast, Piedra Negras

Negras/Eagle Pass grew at an average rate for twin cities.

Mexican portions of twin cities grew more rapidly in the 80s than the U.S. part. In particular, Mexican segments grew by 42 percent, while the U.S. growth was 25 percent. This differential reflects varying nationwide population growth rates in the two nations, as well as the build-up of maquiladora industry on the Mexican side of the border. Mexican cities of Nogales, Sonora, grew by 60 percent, and Tijuana grew by 63 percent, exceeding by far the Mexico City's growth rate of 13 percent or increased at about 2–1/2 times the rate of the border region as a whole.

The rapid growth of the Mexican border cities is largely based on proximity to the U.S. and its economic opportunities. It should be remembered that CONAPO's goal in the system of cities initiative was to divert growth from Mexico City into medium sized cities. The international economics of co-production seems to have determined in the 80s that Mexican border cities would seemingly meet this goal, regardless of federal policies.

The look at the border cities completes this chapter's overview of urbanization and city growth in Mexico. In subsequent chapters, our examination of Mexico City will be set in the broader context of the national urban system.

Table 2.6 U.S. - Mexico Twin Cities, 1990

No.	Twin City, State	Population	Twin Cities Population*	Percent	Twin Cities Pop. Growth 1980-90**
1	Matamoros, Tamaulipas	266,055	383,731	6.03	33.34
2	Brownsville, Texas, UA	117,676			
	Brownsville, Texas, City	98,962			
3	Reynosa, Tamaulipas	265,663	528,855	8.31	29.53
4	McAllen, Texas, UA	263,192			
	McAllen, Texas, City	84,021			
5	Nuevo Laredo, Tamaulipas	218,413	342,064	5.38	16.42
6	Laredo, Texas, UA	123,651			
	Laredo, Texas, City	122,899			
7	Piedras Negras, Coahuila	96,198	116,849	1.84	31.49
8	Eagle Pass, Texas, City	20,651			
9	Ciudad Juarez, Chihuahua	789,522	1,360,539	21.39	34.54
10	El Paso, Texas, UA	571,017			
	El Paso, Texas, City	515,187			
11	Nogales, Sonora	105,873	125,362	1.97	53.47
12	Nogales, Arizona, City	19,489			
13	Mexicali, Baja California	438,377	457,010	7.18	28.38
14	Calexico, California, City	18,633			
15	Tijuana, Baja California	698,752	3,047,169	47.90	38.59
16	San Diego, California, UA	2,348,417			
	San Diego, California, City	1,109,962			
	Total		6,361,579		34.15
	Mexico Total		2,878,853	45.25	41.52
	U.S. Total		3,482,726	54.75	24.75

Source: U.S. Census of Population, General Population Characteristics, CP-1, 1992; INEGI, 1992.
UA=urbanized area.
*   For U.S. component of twin cities, urbanized area population included where applicable, otherwise city population included.
** In 1980-90 growth calculations, for U.S. component, city populations used exclusively for consistency.

49

Map 2.6
United States–Mexican Border
Cities and States, 1990

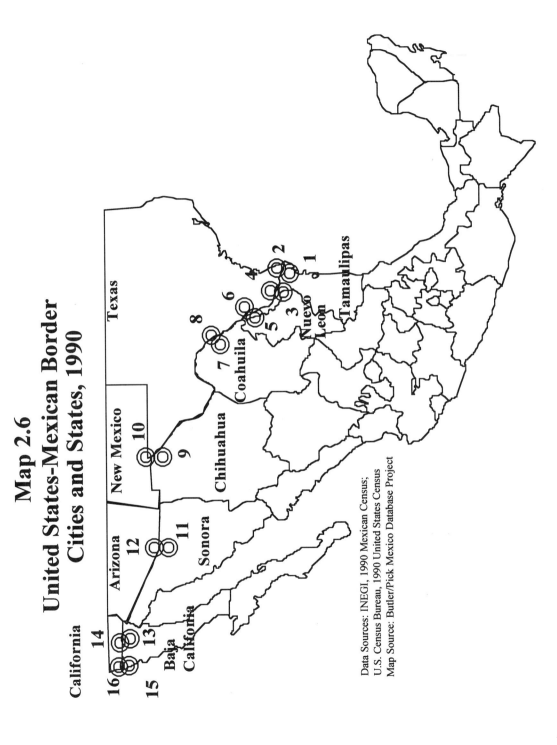

Data Sources: INEGI, 1990 Mexican Census;
U.S. Census Bureau, 1990 United States Census
Map Source: Butler/Pick Mexico Database Project

Future Urbanization in Mexico

Population forecasts strongly imply that urban concentration will continue in the future in Mexico and will exceed that of population growth. For instance, the UN projects that the national urban percent will increase from 72.6 percent in 1990 to 83.1 percent by the year 2015 (United Nations, 1995). However, there will be a deceleration in urban growth rate, i.e. the projected annual rate of change in the percent urban is projected to decline from 0.74 in the early 90s to 0.59 from 2015-19 (United Nations, 1995).

Another likely trend is a continuation of population loss in Mexico City. According to the UN, Mexico City's dominance as measured by proportion of national population will decrease from 25 percent in 1990 to 18 percent in 2015. Yet even at 18 percent, the city will remain dominant. It is likely Mexico City will continue to be the principal urban destination of internal migrants, but primarily their destination will be in municipios surrounding the Federal District, especially in the State of Mexico. Deconcentration of the national urban system hoped for in the early 1990s by CONAPO and the Salinas administration will only take place to a limited extent. The border urban region will continue to increase in economic and demographic importance; for instance, the UN projects Tijuana will increase by sixteen percent between 1990 and 2015 in national urban proportion.

3

Population of Mexico Megacity

Photo courtesy of Tomas Mojarro

Introduction

In 1994, Mexico City was the world's fourth most populated city according to the UN (United Nations, 1995). "Mexico City has been described repeatedly as an example of calamitous and pathological urban development" (Schteingart 1988:268). It has been thus described because of its hyperconcentration of population and associated problems (Butler and Pick, 1995). This chapter explores population dimensions, some of which contribute to the view of calamitous and pathological development. Subsequent chapters examine other aspects of Mexico Megacity that share this view but also present information implying that such a perspective misses many positive contributions of the city.

This chapter traces historical population growth of Mexico City, elaborates upon its being a primate city, examines various dimensions of its contemporary population, explores recent developments in the deconcentration of its central population, and presents a cluster analysis of some basic population dimensions. Among the dimensions explored are population size and density, population growth, age structure and dependency, and sex ratio. These dimensions are fundamental to understanding the expansion and changes of Mexico City elaborated in this book, since nearly every other city feature or characteristic is tied in one way or another to population. Analysis of many of these dimensions shows strong inter-relationships as well as high degree of stability in some features over time. The cluster analysis that concludes the chapter divides the city into population zones for 1990 that are meaningful on an historical as well as contemporary basis. It is likely that Mexico Megacity will continue its expansion in the future, with rapid population growth in some areas now classified as semi-urban while continuing the de-population of the core area. Understanding the process of build up of today's population will be helpful in anticipating future changes.

Historical Population Growth of Mexico Megacity

As noted in the last chapter, Mexico Megacity is the heart of the nation. It controls the economy, financial system, communication networks, and government of the nation. At the beginning of the twentieth century Mexico City was historically the most important city in Mexico (Schteingart, 1988: 269). In addition, it had the most sophisticated infrastructure in Mexico, the largest consumer market, and a concentration of the few existing industries in Mexico, and it was the site of the national government. Thus it was an ideal location for attracting migrants from other parts of Mexico and for fueling economic growth as the country began industrializing.

In 1900, Mexico City had 344,000 residents and was growing at an annual rate of 3.1 percent. As noted previously, part of the growth in the 1910s was fueled by internal conflict in Mexico as many ruralites sought refuge in cities, and especially in Mexico City. This growth slowed somewhat during the 1930s when agrarian reform was undertaken. However, during 1900 - 1970, there was a rather constant population buildup of Mexico City. The city experienced growth rates of 4.6 percent per year, doubling in population every fifteen years. Beginning around 1970 nearby municipios in the State of Mexico began to attract persons from the Federal District and migrants from other states in Mexico (Delgado, 1990). Thus, deconcentration, or urban sprawl, of the greater Mexico City area began in earnest. In the 1970s, population growth continued to be slightly over 5 percent per year.

The population percentage of the national population for the Federal District and the State of Mexico for 1895 to 1990 is shown on Figure 3.1. These data are from the *Historical Statistics of Mexico* (INEGI, 1994). Definitions of the metropolitan area of Mexico City changed several times from 1940 to 1990. The Federal District's proportion of the national population reached its peak in the 1960s and dropped after that date. In contrast, the State of Mexico's percentage of the national population accelerated during the 1960s and continued thereafter exceeding the Federal District's in the 1980s. By 1990, the growth rate of the State of Mexico appeared to have moderated. Figure 3.2 illustrates that the annual growth rate for the Federal District had already began to decline by 1950. The Federal District's growth rate declined from 4.61 between 1950-1960, to 3.44 between 1960-1970, 2.23 between 1970-1980, to a recorded negative rate between 1980-1990 (-0.01). During 1950-1960, the State of Mexico's growth rate was 8.08 which increased to 12.14 between 1960-1970. Its growth rate declined between 1970-1980 to 8.28 and further declined to 4.64 between 1980-1990. Thus, the growth rate for the State of Mexico increased through the 1960s but decelerated thereafter.

While the overall rate of population increase in the metropolitan complex was declining, overall population in absolute numbers was increasing. However, as shown on Figure 3.3, this overall population increase was associated with population growth in municipios of the State of Mexico included in Mexico Megacity since the Federal District actually declined in population between 1980 and 1990. In 1990, Mexico City had a population of 15,440,748. This population consists of the total population of the 16 delegations that make up the Federal District and 53 municipios in the State of Mexico shown in Chapter 1.

Figure 3.1 Megacity States as Percentage of National Population 1895-1990

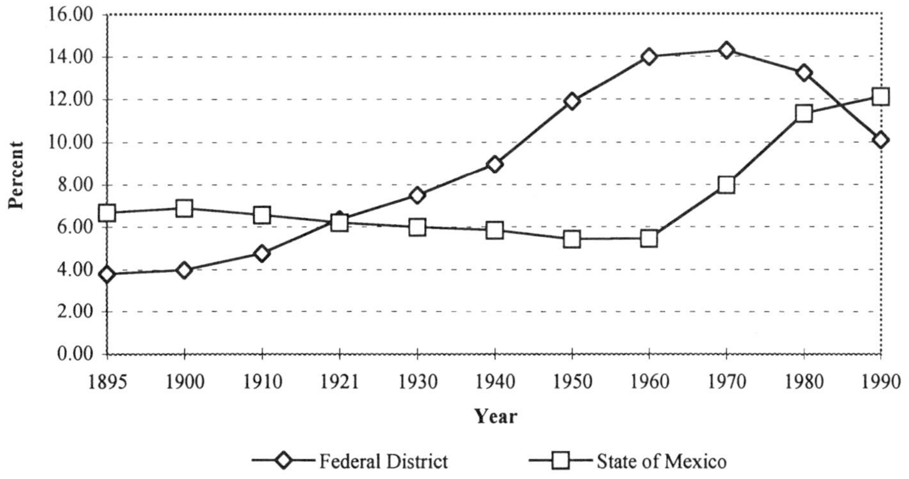

Federal District   State of Mexico

| Supporting Data | | |
Year	Federal District	State of Mexico
1895	3.77	6.66
1900	3.97	6.86
1910	4.75	6.53
1921	6.32	6.17
1930	7.48	5.98
1940	8.94	5.83
1950	11.90	5.40
1960	13.95	5.43
1970	14.25	7.95
1980	13.21	11.31
1990	10.10	12.10

Source: INEGI, *Estadisticas Historicas de Mexico,* 1994

54

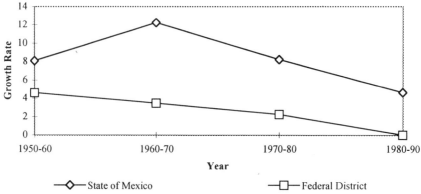

Figure 3.2 Annual Growth Rate, Mexico City and Metropolitan
State of Mexico, 1950-1990

Source: Atlas of Mexico City,1987: *Estadisticas Historicas de Mexico,* 1994

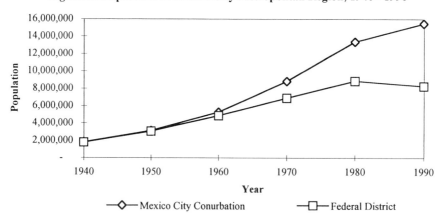

Figure 3.3 Population of Mexico City Metropolitan Region, 1940 - 1990

Population of Mexico City Metropolitan Region, 1940-1990

Year	Mexico City Conurbation	Federal District
1940	1,802,679	1,757,530
1950	3,137,599	3,050,442
1960	5,251,755	4,870,876
1970	8,799,939	6,874,165
1980	13,354,271	8,831,079
1990	15,440,746	8,235,744

Source: *Estadisticas Historicas de Mexico,* 1994
Note: Conurbation for 1940 - 1980 is based on the definition of the Mexico City Metropolitan Area in
Estadisticas Historicas de Mexico.

Mexico City as a Primate City

Mexico City in 1803 had a primacy index of 2.0, meaning that it was only two times larger than the next largest city which then was Puebla (Garza and Schteingart, 1978: 56). By the end of the century Mexico City had become 3.4 times larger then the next largest city, which then was Guadalajara. By 1950, the primacy index was 8.3. In 1990, the primacy index had lowered to 5.4. Mexico City has thus historically been a primate city in Mexico with the primacy index increasing greatly to mid century and decreasing since then. While primacy as thus described is measured by population size, Mexico City also has been primary in political, economic, and communication activities as well.

In 1990, Mexico City had a population of over 15 million persons, containing 18.5 percent of the total population of Mexico. Such a high proportion of population in one city in a country clearly categorizes it as a *primate city* (Jefferson, 1939; Berry, 1981). Because of this primacy, Mexico City exercises an ever-increasing share of the country's resources to meet the demands of its population (Unikel, 1977).

Mexico, to a large degree, does not fit Mehta's conclusion that primate cities are "to some significant extent a function of small area and population size" of a country (Mehta, 1964). He further concluded that primate cities do not appear to be a function of the level of economic development, industrialization, or urbanization. Mexico Megacity thus may be an anomaly in comparison to primate cities in other countries. In addition, it appears that Mexico City as primate city is not one in a transitional state unless one wants to consider a century or more as a transitional period (Smith, 1982). Undoubtedly Mexico Megacity will continue well into the future being the primary city in Mexico.

Mexico Megacity Population Characteristics

Population characteristics examined here by small area include population size, population growth, density, age structure, and sex ratio. They are summarized in Tables 3.1 and 3.2. Population growth is divided into absolute growth, i.e. the difference in population over a ten year inter-censal period, and relative growth, which is the ratio of population in a particular year to population at the prior census ten years earlier. The age structure is examined by dividing the population into three categories, the proportion of the population 0-17 years, 18-64 years, and 65 years and older. These categories may be viewed generally as children and adolescents, working age population, and elderly. The dependency ratio is defined as the ratio of the sum of population 0-17 and 65 and older to the population 18-64 years. Hence, it roughly indicates of the balance between the "dependent population" and the economically independent or working population (Shryock and Siegel, 1976). The sex ratio is defined as 100 times the ratio of the number of males to females.

The population characteristics are highly inter-related in particular ways that will be brought out in the chapter. The correlations between the population variables in this chapter are given in Table 3.3. The table is not discussed at this point, since each characteristic is discussed in the following sections.

Population Size

Population growth of the Megacity by delegation and municipio reveals detailed spatial trends over the four decades from 1950 to 1990. Three sequential absolute population size maps at two-decade intervals (Maps 3.1, 3.2, and 3.3) are keyed with the same mapping intervals, i.e. the break points for mapping shown in the legend remain the same for the three maps. These "standard break points" improve longitudinal comparisons.

All areas of the Megacity grew in population over the forty years with the exception of loss of population in Cuauhtemoc in the core of the old city center. The population buildup in the areas surrounding the top of the Federal District is dramatic over the forty years. In fact, these areas are transformed from low to moderate areas with populations of 5,000 to 50,000 into areas of great population concentration, in two instances exceeding a million population.

Within the Federal District, the northern half has been consistently more populous than the southern half. In 1990, even Milpa Alta in the south still had moderate population at 63,654. It will be seen later in the book that Milpa Alta is also the poorest of the Federal District delegations.

The Megacity periphery is seen to have increased in population extensively over the forty years. In 1950, the municipios in the northeastern, southeastern, and western semi-urban arms (see Map 3.1) had populations ranging from 700 to 14,999. By 1990, the municipio populations in these areas were mostly in the range of 15,000 to 49,999. Although the total numbers in 1990 are still not very high, these areas shared high growth rates with most of the rest of the Megacity. In 1950, many peripheral delegations and municipios with populations of 15,000 to 49,999 were ones that subsequently moved into the hundreds of thousands or millions. If historical tends hold true, 1990's semi-urban areas offer the potential in the future for considerable metropolitan expansion and growth. Delgado (1990) identified a group of municipios at the periphery, overlapping largely with our northeastern and southeastern semi-urban areas, that he termed "municipios for the rest of the Valley of Mexico," observing that they "can be considered as a territorial reserve in the medium term for the metropolitan zone of Mexico City."

Population Growth

From 1950 to 1990 the Megacity population grew by 12.3 million persons (see Figure 3.3). The sheer size of this increase underscores the impact of rural-to-urban inmigration combined with high to moderate fertility. These themes will be elaborated on more in Chapters 4, 5, and 13. The spatial distribution of this four decade increase is shown by the absolute and relative increases 1950-70 and 1970-90 in delegations and municipios (see Maps 3.4 through 3.7, which again have standard breakpoints).

In terms of absolute growth (Maps 3.4 and 3.5), in the 1950-70 period, the central delegation of Cuauhtemoc lost 79,673 population. Cuauhtemoc is an exception since only two other delegations/municipios lost population 1950-70 and each had tiny losses of less than 5,000. Cuauhtemoc's early population loss is a harbinger of population deconcentration of the central city area. This is consistent with the well known trend of central city deconcentration in U.S. cities in the mid 20th century (Frey, 1995). The explanations often point to metropolitan transportation and communication improvements as well as deteriorating conditions in the central city. For 1950-70, the rest of the central city showed large population increases. For instance, Benito Juarez and Miguel Hidalgo grew by nearly a half million. However, the Megacity's largest increases occurred in Gustavo Madero at 900,000 and Nezahualcoyotl at 600,000.

Surrounding the 1950-70 loss zone of Cuauhtemoc is a ring of 13 delegations and municipios, each of which had population gains 1950-70 of 150,000 or more. The total 1950-70 population gain of this ring was 4,820,678. We call this the 50-70 Expansion Ring. Ten of these delegations and municipios became incorporated in the 50s and 60s (Negrete, Graizbord, and Ruiz, 1993). Seven of these 13 municipios overlap with "contorno 1" and three with "contorno 2" in a recent study (Negrete, Graizbord, and Ruiz, 1993). Outside the 50-70 Expansion Ring is a second wider ring that stretches from the 50-70 Expansion Ring to the edges of the Megacity, with the exceptions of the northeast and southeast semi-urban arms. In this second expansion ring, populations increases per zone are in the range of 7,500 to 149,999.

The population growth 1970-90 continued some of the trends noted from 1950-70. However, there are also differences, which are reflected in non-significant correlation between absolute populations growth for the two periods. As seen in Map 3.5, the central area of population loss expanded and besides Cuauhtemoc included Azcapotzalco, Miguel Hidalgo, Venustiano Carranza, Benito Juarez, and Tlahuac. This central area experienced population loss of 1.16 million persons. Central city deconcentration is now established as a major trend. There is again an expansion ring of delegations/municipios with population gains of 150,000 or more apiece, but the ring moved outwards radially and now contains 14 municipios. Total population gain of this 70-90 Expansion Ring was 4,749,003. The 70-90 Expansion Ring overlaps substantially with "contornos 1 and 2" of Negrete et al. (1993).

Although the 70-90 Expansion Ring moved outwards, the two expansion rings overlap by about fifty percent. Altogether, the 50-70 and 70-90 rings account for population increase 1950-90 of 9,569,6781, equivalent to 78 percent of the city's increase over the forty years. To summarize, the population growth and change in the city over four decades is largely ascribed to increasing deconcentration of the old central city and huge population gains in expanding rings around the old central city.

Relative population growth is the ratio of the change over twenty years to the population at the start of the period. The maps for relative growth (Maps 3.6 and 3.7) are highly correlated with the absolute population growth for the same periods. There are two important patterns to note, however. One is the greater evenness of population growth for the entire conurbation, and especially so for 1970-90. In other words, population increased consistently, on a relative basis, throughout the Megacity. For the period 1970-90, population increases in the semi-urban periphery ranged from 60 to 120 percent, i.e. the semi-urban arms showed substantial demographic growth, although not in the ranges of the more central expansion rings.

Population Density

Population density also grew rapidly 1950 to 1990 in Mexico Megacity. The median density, in persons per square kilometer, for delegations/municipios in 1950 was 101. It grew to 234 in 1970 and to 791 in 1990. This eight fold increase is a consequence of the rapid population growth just examined. The density build-up over time is shown in Maps 3.8 and 3.9.

The spatial pattern of density remained very stable, as seen by the highly significant correlations between the 1950, 1970, and 1990 time points shown in Table 3.3.

It is important to point out that density and population are very highly correlated, ranging in value r = 0.97 for 1950 to r = 0.77 for 1990. As with population, a single delegation/municipio, Cuauhtemoc, lowered in density over the forty years. Its density dropped from 33,200 persons per square kilometer in 1950 to 18,900 in 1990. On the other hand, delegations and municipios with the greatest density increases 1950-1990 were the same as for population: Nezahualcoyotl (210 times density increase), Ecatepec (75 times increase), Coacalco (61 times increase), and Atizapan de Zaragoza (61 times increase), These areas all adjoin the northern Federal District in the State of Mexico. Over the forty years, they were transformed from moderate densities of 100 to 600 to densities ranging from 3,400 to over 20,000.

The density build-up decade by decade follows a similar pattern of expanding rings pointed out for population. It is important also to note the elevating density in the semi-urban areas. The density of these areas in 1990 resembles that of municipios just north of the Federal District in 1950.

Age Structure

A city's age structure is crucial in determining everything from labor force potential to schooling needs to medical/health care. Mexico Megacity underwent patterns of major changes in age structure from 1970 to 1990. The large extent of change is seen in the following table.

Percent of The Population of Mexico Megacity

	1970	1990
Age 0-17	50.1	39.9
Age 18-64	46.7	54.6
Age 65+	3.2	5.5

Source: INEGI, Population Censuses of 1970 and 1990.

Not only did proportion of children drop, but the elderly component, although small, nearly doubled.

The shape of change in age structure is displayed graphically in Figure 3.4. Comparing the age structures for the Federal District in 1970 and 1990, the 1970 age structure resembles a smooth pyramid. It reflects the consistently high post World War II fertility, as will be discussed more in Chapter 4. On the other hand, in 1990, the fertility lowering starting in the 1970s is reflected in reduced numbers of children and adolescents aged 0-19. The curtailment of fertility in the Federal District was greater than for the nation, which is reflected in the sharper reduction in age groups 0-19 for the Federal District versus the nation.

By contrast, the Megacity's outlying areas have much younger age structures (see Maps 3.10 - 3.12). In particular, the disadvantaged zone to the east of the Federal District as well as the semi-urban peripheral areas have 1990 age structures that resemble the Federal District twenty years earlier. Typical of these age structures is that of Chalco (see Figure 3.4). It is a smooth pyramid with a large proportion under age 20.

The proportion of elderly population varies considerably, with high proportions in the traditional city center but also in the semi-urban peripheral areas. This partly reflects inmigration, since inmigrants tend to be young adults and children. This is seen by looking ahead to Map 5.7 of inmigrants 1985-90. The inmigration pattern is the opposite of the elderly in 1990. This is further confirmed by the significant inverse association between these two dimensions of r = -0.24.

Dependency Ratio

Paralleling age structure changes, dependency ratio lowered from 1970 to 1990 (see Maps 3.13 and 3.14). As seen in Figure 3.5, the drop was consistent for the nation, Federal District, and State of Mexico. The Federal District is about one quarter lower in dependency ratio than the nation or State of Mexico. The reduction over time has ramifications for the economy, education, and social welfare. It implies a lowering of the economic burden on the active labor force to support dependents. At the same time, the moderate geographical differences in dependency imply there are spatial differences in family economic burdens as well as need of the government to provide health and social welfare benefits. The latter topic will be discussed more in Chapter 6. The highest dependency ratios are located in the northwest, Chalco, the southeast and northeast peripheral areas. The dependency ratio pattern is strongly opposite to total population and population density, i.e. non-populous and non-dense areas have high dependency ratios.

Sex Ratio

Figure 3.6 illustrates that the sex ratio for the nation and State of Mexico for 1940-1990 was substantially the same and with almost exact convergence in 1990. On the other hand, the Federal District has consistently had a lower sex ratio than the nation and State of Mexico but with an increase during the 1940s through 1970s and with a slightly lower ratio beginning in the 1980s and continuing through 1990. The data conclusively support the fact that the Federal District had and continues to have a surplus of female residents (see Table 3.4).

In 1990, this sex ratio difference of the Federal District from the nation and State if Mexico was about 5 percent. The Federal District's sex ratio of 92 implies eight percent fewer males than females. The cause of this long-term structural difference in spatial gender balance has not been determined. However, it may be linked to greater opportunities for employment of women in the city center versus periphery and to much higher proportions of divorced and separated women in the Federal District than in other city areas (see Map 4.6).

Maps 3.15 and 3.16 show the distribution of sex ratios by delegations and municipios of Mexico Megacity for 1950 and 1990. While there have been some changes, basically all delegations in the Federal District have had low sex ratios while peripheral areas have had higher sex ratios. The sex ratios for 1950, 1970 (not shown in a map) and 1990 are significantly correlated with each other (see Table 3.3). Table 3.4 presents the 1990 male, female, and sex ratios for the delegations and municipios that make up Mexico Megacity. Map 3.16 shows the distribution of sex ratios in 1990. The only delegation in the Federal

District with a near average sex ratio is Milpa Alta (bottom right of the district map), with all other delegations continuing to have a low sex ratio. The highest sex ratios in 1990, as in past years, were located on the periphery, especially in the northwest, northcentral, and northeast. Municipios located in the southeast have mixed sex ratios, some very high – Chalco, Temamatla, Ayapango, Tepetlixpa, Tenango del Aire, and Ecatzingo; two very low -- Amecameca and Ozumba; and several others in the middle range.

Table 3.1 Population and Density of Mexico City, 1950-1990

Area	1950	1970	1990	Relative Population Growth 1950-70	Relative Population Growth 1970-90	Density 1950	Density 1990
Acolman	9,422	20,964	43,276	1.2250	1.0643	179.6	824.8
Alvaro Obregon	133,200	456,707	642,753	2.4287	0.4074	1,422.0	6,861.9
Amecameca	13,519	21,945	36,321	0.6233	0.6551	80.2	215.4
Atenco	5,424	10,616	21,219	0.9572	0.9988	38.8	151.9
Atizapan de Zaragoza	5,133	44,322	315,192	7.6347	6.1114	68.5	4,205.4
Atlautla	8,920	11,831	18,993	0.3263	0.6054	66.1	140.8
Axapusco	7,595	9,256	15,803	0.2187	0.7073	26.7	55.5
Ayapango	1,839	2,263	4,239	0.2306	0.8732	32.0	73.8
Azcapotzalco	199,732	534,554	474,688	1.6764	-0.1120	5,787.7	13,755.1
Benito Juarez	356,531	617,682	407,811	0.7325	-0.3398	14,967.7	17,120.5
Chalco	23,421	41,450	282,940	0.7698	5.8261	85.6	1,034.2
Chiautla	3,867	7,266	14,764	0.8790	1.0319	154.7	590.8
Chicoloapan	3,431	8,750	57,306	1.5503	5.5493	53.9	899.5
Chiconcuac	4,520	8,399	14,179	0.8582	0.6882	258.4	810.7
Chimalhuacan	7,814	21,485	242,317	1.7496	10.2784	232.0	7,194.7
Coacalco	2,462	13,197	152,082	4.3603	10.5240	54.7	3,381.9
Cocotitlan	3,052	4,996	8,068	0.6370	0.6149	174.5	461.3
Coyoacan	73,020	339,446	640,066	3.6487	0.8856	1,233.7	10,813.8
Coyotepec	4,471	8,888	24,451	0.9879	1.7510	99.4	543.7
Cuajimalpa	10,293	36,200	119,669	2.5170	2.3058	141.2	1,642.0
Cuauhtemoc	1,049,079	969,406	595,960	-0.0759	-0.3852	33,188.2	18,853.5
Cuautitlan	5,106	11,499	48,858	1.2521	3.2489	192.9	776.6
Cuautitlan Izcalli	9,350	31,898	326,750	2.4116	9.2436	192.9	4,427.7
Ecatepec	16,242	216,408	1,218,135	12.3240	4.6289	128.7	9,654.7
Ecatzingo	2,405	3,637	5,808	0.5123	0.5969	43.8	105.7
Gustavo A. Madero	308,002	1,186,107	1,268,068	2.8510	0.0691	3,367.6	13,864.7
Huehuetoca	4,198	7,958	25,529	0.8957	2.2080	28.2	171.7
Huixquilucan	14,315	33,527	131,926	1.3421	2.9349	130.2	1,200.1
Isidro Fabela	2,482	2,598	5,190	0.0467	0.9977	42.3	88.4
Ixtapaluca	11,481	36,722	137,357	2.1985	2.7405	55.7	666.4
Iztacalco	39,529	477,331	448,322	11.0755	-0.0608	1,809.9	20,527.6
Iztapalapa	78,624	522,095	1,490,499	5.6404	1.8548	631.7	11,975.7
Jaltenco	2,767	4,738	22,803	0.7123	3.8128	71.4	588.8
Jilotzingo	4,512	4,240	9,011	-0.0603	1.1252	31.4	62.7
Juchitepec	5,619	8,301	14,270	0.4773	0.7191	84.9	215.5
Magdalena Contreras	23,343	104,591	195,041	3.4806	0.8648	375.3	3,136.2
Melchor Ocampo	4,928	10,834	26,154	1.1985	1.4141	151.7	805.2
Miguel Hidalgo	445,566	633,134	406,868	0.4210	-0.3574	9,438.0	8,618.3
Milpa Alta	19,322	33,694	63,654	0.7438	0.8892	71.9	237.0
Naucalpan	31,884	382,184	786,551	10.9867	1.0580	205.8	5,077.8
Nextlalpan	2,611	4,360	10,840	0.6699	1.4862	52.3	216.9
Nezahualcoyotl	5,990	610,268	1,256,115	100.8811	1.0583	96.6	20,259.9
Nicolas Romero	24,781	47,504	184,134	0.9170	2.8762	120.2	893.3
Nopaltepec	2,931	2,681	5,234	-0.0853	0.9523	90.2	161.1
Otumba	8,407	12,349	21,834	0.4689	0.7681	41.0	106.6
Ozumba	6,355	11,026	18,052	0.7350	0.6372	121.1	344.0
Papalotla	706	1,088	2,387	0.5411	1.1939	80.8	273.1
Paz, La	4,463	32,258	134,782	6.2279	3.1783	120.9	3,650.7
San Martin de las P.	4,718	7,242	13,563	0.5350	0.8728	80.3	231.0
Tecamac	9,666	20,882	123,218	1.1604	4.9007	70.3	896.7
Temamatla	1,474	2,421	5,366	0.6425	1.2164	30.3	110.1

Table 3.1 Population and Density of Mexico City, 1950-1990 (Continued)

Area	1950	1970	1990	Relative Population Growth 1950-70	Relative Population Growth 1970-90	Density 1950	Density 1990
Temascalapa	8,191	8,892	19,099	0.0856	1.1479	56.5	131.8
Tenango del Aire	2,357	3,600	6,207	0.5274	0.7242	38.5	101.4
Teoloyucan	7,446	15,477	41,964	1.0786	1.7114	212.9	1,199.7
Teotihuacan	8,348	16,283	30,486	0.9505	0.8723	121.5	443.7
Tepetlaoxtoc	5,373	7,068	16,120	0.3155	1.2807	22.9	68.6
Tepetlixpa	4,555	8,216	12,687	0.8037	0.5442	43.9	122.4
Tepotzotlan	10,703	21,902	39,647	1.0463	0.8102	44.4	164.4
Texcoco	32,265	65,628	140,368	1.0340	1.1388	64.1	278.8
Tezoyuca	2,532	4,770	12,416	0.8839	1.6029	144.8	709.9
Tlahuac	20,720	62,419	206,700	2.0125	2.3115	234.4	2,338.0
Tlalmanalco	13,840	20,655	32,984	0.4924	0.5969	85.2	203.1
Tlalnepantla	31,002	366,935	702,807	10.8358	0.9153	376.0	8,524.0
Tlalpan	34,843	130,719	484,866	2.7517	2.7092	112.5	1,565.5
Tultepec	5,517	11,480	47,323	1.0808	3.1222	245.3	2,104.2
Tultitlan	9,823	52,317	246,464	4.3260	3.7110	102.1	2,562.3
Venustiano Carranza	398,045	782,762	519,628	0.9665	-0.3362	11,431.5	14,923.3
Xochimilco	49,991	116,498	271,151	1.3304	1.3275	371.5	2,014.8
Zumpango	17,498	36,105	71,413	1.0634	0.9779	83.9	342.3
Mean	52,329	131,297	217,618	3.4455	1.9402	1,304.0	3,381.0
Median	8,270	20,769	48,091	0.9619	1.0613	100.8	790.9
S.D.	152,509	251,645	336,008	12.3079	2.2722	4,701.3	5,456.8
C.V.	291.44	191.66	154.40	357.22	117.11	360.52	161.39
Minimum	706	1,088	2,387	-0.0853	-0.3852	22.9	55.5
Maximum	1,049,079	1,186,107	1,490,499	100.8811	10.5240	33,188.2	20,527.6

Sources: INEGI: Population Censuses 1950, 1970, and 1990.

Table 3.2 Age Structure, 1990

No.	Area	Age 0 - 17		Age 18 - 64		Age 65+		Dependency Ratio	Total Population
		Population	Ratio	Population	Ratio	Population	Ratio	Ratio	Population
1	Acolman	19,391	0.4481	22,043	0.5094	1,769	0.0409	0.9599	43,276
2	Alvaro Obregon	247,770	0.3855	365,508	0.5687	27,532	0.0428	0.7532	642,753
3	Amecameca	16,534	0.4552	18,009	0.4958	1,731	0.0477	1.0142	36,321
4	Atenco	9,590	0.4520	10,747	0.5065	849	0.0400	0.9713	21,219
5	Atizapan De Zaragoza	139,438	0.4424	167,163	0.5304	6,940	0.0220	0.8757	315,192
6	Atlautla	9,195	0.4841	8,785	0.4625	938	0.0494	1.1534	18,993
7	Axapusco	7,664	0.4850	7,237	0.4580	892	0.0564	1.1823	15,803
8	Ayapango	2,017	0.4758	2,024	0.4775	197	0.0465	1.0939	4,239
9	Azcapotzalco	170,883	0.3600	278,123	0.5859	24,470	0.0515	0.7024	474,688
10	Benito Juarez	113,449	0.2782	254,229	0.6234	35,888	0.0880	0.5874	407,811
11	Chalco	144,750	0.5116	132,254	0.4674	5,560	0.0197	1.1365	282,940
12	Chiautla	6,667	0.4516	7,447	0.5044	634	0.0429	0.9804	14,764
13	Chicoloapan	28,274	0.4934	27,648	0.4825	1,325	0.0231	1.0706	57,306
14	Chiconcuac	6,316	0.4454	7,254	0.5116	597	0.0421	0.9530	14,179
15	Chimalhuacan	126,219	0.5209	111,798	0.4614	4,149	0.0171	1.1661	242,317
16	Coacalco	63,907	0.4202	83,571	0.5495	4,040	0.0266	0.8130	152,082
17	Cocotitlan	2,806	0.3478	4,093	0.5073	1,166	0.1445	0.9704	8,068
18	Coyoacan	230,260	0.3597	377,222	0.5893	29,730	0.0464	0.6892	640,066
19	Coyotepec	12,050	0.4928	11,617	0.4751	778	0.0318	1.1042	24,451
20	Cuajimalpa	50,964	0.4259	65,283	0.5455	3,336	0.0279	0.8318	119,669
21	Cuauhtemoc	192,951	0.3238	352,195	0.5910	44,768	0.0751	0.6750	595,960
22	Cuautitlan	21,552	0.4411	25,834	0.5288	1,436	0.0294	0.8898	48,858
23	Cuautitlan Izcalli	146,831	0.4494	171,740	0.5256	6,748	0.0207	0.8943	326,750
24	Ecatepec	551,624	0.4528	638,397	0.5241	26,764	0.0220	0.9060	1,218,135
25	Ecatzingo	3,063	0.5274	2,461	0.4237	258	0.0444	1.3495	5,808
26	Gustavo A. Madero	475,985	0.3754	633,199	0.4993	157,623	0.1243	1.0006	1,268,068
27	Huehuetoca	12,649	0.4955	12,208	0.4782	650	0.0255	1.0894	25,529
28	Huixquilucan	57,251	0.4340	70,741	0.5362	3,494	0.0265	0.8587	131,926
29	Isidro Fabela	2,367	0.4561	2,576	0.4963	224	0.0432	1.0058	5,190
30	Ixtapaluca	66,393	0.4834	67,475	0.4912	3,366	0.0245	1.0338	137,357
31	Iztacalco	165,231	0.3686	262,055	0.5845	20,672	0.0461	0.7094	448,322

Table 3.2 Age Structure, 1990 (Continued)

No.	Area	Age 0 - 17 Population	Ratio	Age 18 - 64 Population	Ratio	Age 65+ Population	Ratio	Dependency Ratio	Total Population
32	Iztapalapa	628,752	0.4218	812,587	0.5452	46,110	0.0309	0.8305	1,490,499
33	Jaltenco	10,922	0.4790	11,176	0.4901	555	0.0243	1.0269	22,803
34	Jilotzingo	4,049	0.4493	4,090	0.4539	852	0.0946	1.1983	9,011
35	Juchitepec	6,756	0.4734	6,855	0.4804	568	0.0398	1.0684	14,270
36	Magdalena Contreras	78,066	0.4003	109,601	0.5619	7,154	0.0367	0.7775	195,041
37	Melchor Ocampo	12,123	0.4635	13,061	0.4994	946	0.0362	1.0006	26,154
38	Miguel Hidalgo	128,107	0.3149	244,677	0.6014	29,961	0.0736	0.6460	406,868
39	Milpa Alta	27,499	0.4320	33,496	0.5262	2,445	0.0384	0.8940	63,654
40	Naucalpan	319,174	0.4058	441,247	0.5610	24,004	0.0305	0.7777	786,551
41	Nextlalpan	5,348	0.4934	5,108	0.4712	380	0.0351	1.1214	10,840
42	Nezahualcoyotl	532,533	0.4240	683,502	0.5441	35,580	0.0283	0.8312	1,256,115
43	Nicolas Romero	86,981	0.4724	91,864	0.4989	4,992	0.0271	1.0012	184,134
44	Nopaltepec	2,425	0.4633	2,495	0.4767	303	0.0579	1.0934	5,234
45	Otumba	10,566	0.4839	10,147	0.4647	1,075	0.0492	1.1472	21,834
46	Ozumba	8,546	0.4734	8,642	0.4787	825	0.0457	1.0844	18,052
47	Papalotla	1,061	0.4445	1,215	0.5090	107	0.0448	0.9613	2,387
48	Paz, La	63,516	0.4712	67,790	0.5030	3,257	0.0242	0.9850	134,782
49	San Martin De Las P.	6,136	0.4524	6,746	0.4974	671	0.0495	1.0090	13,563
50	Tecamac	57,368	0.4656	62,076	0.5038	3,609	0.0293	0.9823	123,218
51	Temamatla	2,521	0.4698	2,648	0.4935	191	0.0356	1.0242	5,366
52	Temascalapa	9,144	0.4788	8,850	0.4634	1,089	0.0570	1.1563	19,099
53	Tenango Del Aire	2,745	0.4422	3,166	0.5101	288	0.0464	0.9580	6,207
54	Teoloyucan	20,410	0.4864	20,194	0.4812	1,327	0.0316	1.0764	41,964
55	Teotihuacan	14,193	0.4656	15,094	0.4951	1,190	0.0390	1.0191	30,486
56	Tepetlaoxtoc	7,685	0.4767	7,706	0.4780	717	0.0445	1.0903	16,120
57	Tepetlixpa	5,800	0.4572	6,182	0.4873	698	0.0550	1.0511	12,687
58	Tepotzotlan	18,707	0.4718	19,607	0.4945	5,554	0.1401	1.0202	39,647
59	Texcoco	61,818	0.4404	73,159	0.5212	5,306	0.0378	0.9175	140,368
60	Tezoyuca	5,641	0.4543	6,240	0.5026	523	0.0421	0.9878	12,416
61	Tlahuac	91,829	0.4443	108,597	0.5254	6,113	0.0296	0.9019	206,700
62	Tlalmanalco	14,014	0.4249	17,564	0.5325	1,359	0.0412	0.8753	32,984
63	Tlalnepantla	283,842	0.4039	395,311	0.5625	174,496	0.2483	0.7748	702,807

Table 3.2 Age Structure, 1990 (Continued)

No.	Area	Age 0 - 17		Age 18 - 64		Age 65+		Dependency Ratio	Total Population
		Population	Ratio	Population	Ratio	Population	Ratio		
64	Tlalpan	193,478	0.3990	272,484	0.5620	16,345	0.0337	0.7700	484,866
65	Tultepec	22,864	0.4831	23,236	0.4910	1,173	0.0248	1.0345	47,323
66	Tultitlan	114,430	0.4643	126,341	0.5126	5,023	0.0204	0.9455	246,464
67	Venustiano Carranza	186,248	0.3584	302,554	0.5823	30,461	0.0586	0.7163	519,628
68	Xochimilco	112,179	0.4137	148,737	0.5485	10,024	0.0370	0.8216	271,151
69	Zumpango	34,335	0.4808	34,382	0.4815	2,633	0.0369	1.0752	71,413
Total		6,295,852		8,409,363		846,428		0.8493	15,440,746
Mean		92,301	0.4426	123,343	0.5128	12,421	0.0471	0.9576	226,433
Median		25,182	0.4526	26,741	0.5034	2,088	0.0394	0.9836	53,082
S.D.		138,231	0.0495	184,814	0.0410	29,446	0.0352	0.1532	339,215
C.V.		149.76	11.18	149.84	7.99	237.06	74.81	16.00	149.81
Minimum		1,061	0.2782	1,215	0.4237	107	0.0171	0.5874	2,387
Maximum		628,752	0.5274	812,587	0.6234	174,496	0.2483	1.3495	1,490,499

Definition: Dependency ratio is the population age 0-17 and age 65+ to age 18-64.

Source: INEGI, 1990 Mexican Census of Population, Resumen General, Table 2.

Table 3.3 Correlation Matrix of Population Variables

	Pop. 1950	Pop. 1970	Pop. 1990	Rel. Pop. Growth 50-70	Rel. Pop. Growth 70-90	Density 1950	Density 1990	Pop. Age 0-17	Pop. Age 18-64	Pop. Age 65+	Dependency Ratio 1970	Dependency Ratio 1990	Sex Ratio 1950	Sex Ratio 1990
Pop. 1970	.768***													
Pop. 1990	.356**	.772***												
Rel. Pop.Growth 50-70	-.055	.281*	.495***											
Rel. Pop. Growth 70-90	-.271*	-.307*	-.003	.001										
Density 1950	.972***	.672***	.255*	-.054	-.250*									
Density 1990	.621***	.879***	.772***	.464***	-.120	.601***								
Pop. Age 0 - 17	-.528***	-.658***	-.465***	-.106	.330**	-.500***	-.614***							
Pop. Age 18 - 64	.524***	.638***	.526***	.180	-.144	.510***	.691***	-.805***						
Pop. Age 65+	.233	.328**	.150	-.037	-.380**	.200	.195	-.706***	.149					
Dependency Ratio 1970	-.771***	-.728***	-.438***	.040	.272**	-.743***	-.645***	.643***	-.734***	-.180				
Dependency Ratio 1990	-.497***	-.613***	-.523***	-.189	.121	-.480***	-.663***	.791***	-.996***	-.132	.705***			
Sex Ratio 1950	-.568***	-.521***	-.282*	.008	.254*	-.543***	-.464***	.395***	-.459***	-.102	.526***	.436***		
Sex Ratio 1990	-.617***	-.630***	-.384***	-.048	.167	-.608***	-.625***	.640***	-.775***	-.127	.707***	.750***	.608***	
Immigration 1985 - 90	-.088	-.083	.145	.123	.700***	-.074	.029	.121	.028	-.240*	.165	-.048	.218	.001

Note: Significance Levels

*   .05
** .01
*** .001

Map 3.1
Population, 1950

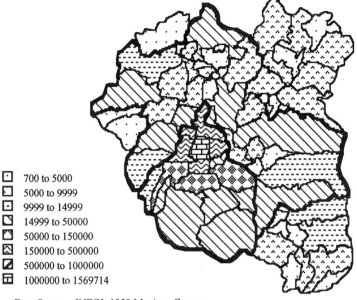

⊡	700 to 5000
⊟	5000 to 9999
⊡	9999 to 14999
◩	14999 to 50000
◮	50000 to 150000
◪	150000 to 500000
◩	500000 to 1000000
⊞	1000000 to 1569714

Data Source: INEGI, 1950 Mexican Census
Map Source: Butler/Pick Mexico Database Project

Map 3.2
Population, 1970

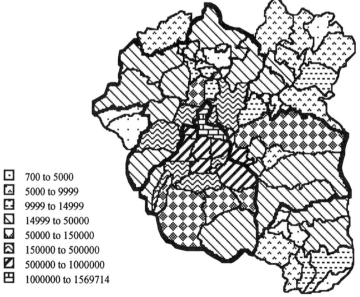

⊡	700 to 5000
◩	5000 to 9999
⊟	9999 to 14999
◩	14999 to 50000
◪	50000 to 150000
◪	150000 to 500000
◩	500000 to 1000000
⊞	1000000 to 1569714

Data Source: INEGI, 1970 Mexican Census
Map Source: Butler/Pick Mexico Database Project

Map 3.3
Population, 1990

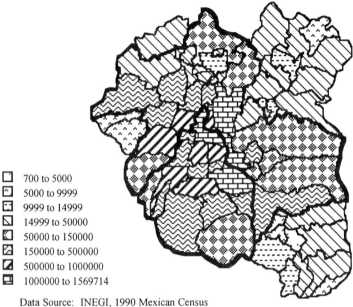

☐ 700 to 5000
▣ 5000 to 9999
▣ 9999 to 14999
◩ 14999 to 50000
◪ 50000 to 150000
▨ 150000 to 500000
◪ 500000 to 1000000
▥ 1000000 to 1569714

Data Source: INEGI, 1990 Mexican Census
Map Source: Butler/Pick Mexico Database Project

Map 3.4
Absolute Growth, 1950-1970

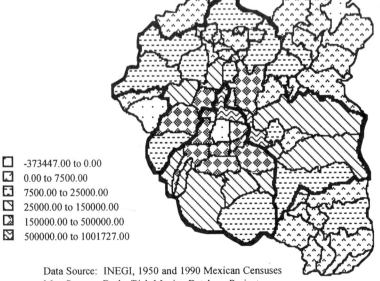

☐ -373447.00 to 0.00
◪ 0.00 to 7500.00
▣ 7500.00 to 25000.00
◩ 25000.00 to 150000.00
▨ 150000.00 to 500000.00
▨ 500000.00 to 1001727.00

Data Source: INEGI, 1950 and 1990 Mexican Censuses
Map Source: Butler/Pick Mexico Database Project

Map 3.5
Absolute Growth, 1970-1990

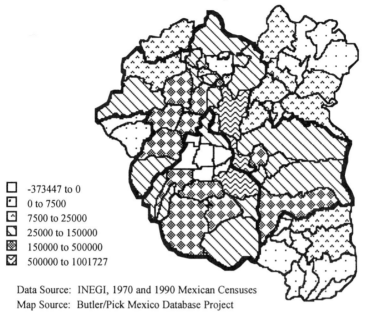

- -373447 to 0
- 0 to 7500
- 7500 to 25000
- 25000 to 150000
- 150000 to 500000
- 500000 to 1001727

Data Source: INEGI, 1970 and 1990 Mexican Censuses
Map Source: Butler/Pick Mexico Database Project

Map 3.6
Relative Growth, 1950-1970

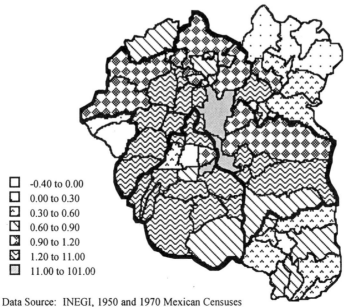

- -0.40 to 0.00
- 0.00 to 0.30
- 0.30 to 0.60
- 0.60 to 0.90
- 0.90 to 1.20
- 1.20 to 11.00
- 11.00 to 101.00

Data Source: INEGI, 1950 and 1970 Mexican Censuses
Map Source: Butler/Pick Mexico Database Project

Map 3.7
Relative Growth, 1970-1990

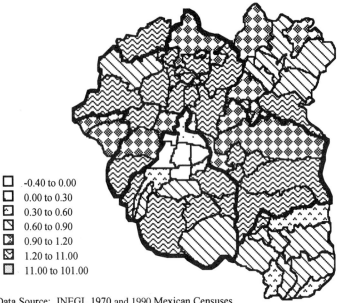

☐ -0.40 to 0.00
☐ 0.00 to 0.30
☒ 0.30 to 0.60
☒ 0.60 to 0.90
☒ 0.90 to 1.20
☒ 1.20 to 11.00
☒ 11.00 to 101.00

Data Source: INEGI, 1970 and 1990 Mexican Censuses
Map Source: Butler/Pick Mexico Database Project

71

Map 3.8
Density, 1950

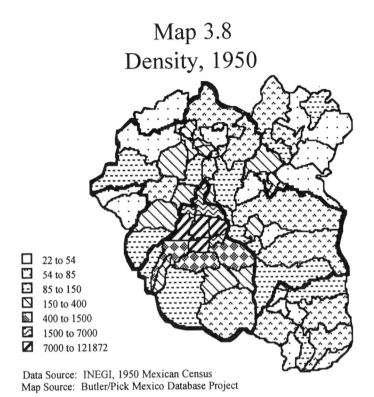

☐	22 to 54
⊡	54 to 85
⊡	85 to 150
◩	150 to 400
▩	400 to 1500
▨	1500 to 7000
◪	7000 to 121872

Data Source: INEGI, 1950 Mexican Census
Map Source: Butler/Pick Mexico Database Project

Map 3.9
Density, 1990

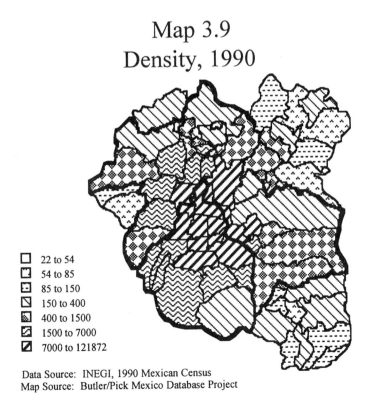

☐	22 to 54
⊡	54 to 85
⊡	85 to 150
◩	150 to 400
▩	400 to 1500
▨	1500 to 7000
◪	7000 to 121872

Data Source: INEGI, 1990 Mexican Census
Map Source: Butler/Pick Mexico Database Project

72

Figure 3.4 Age, Sex Structures for the Nation, Federal District, and Chalco

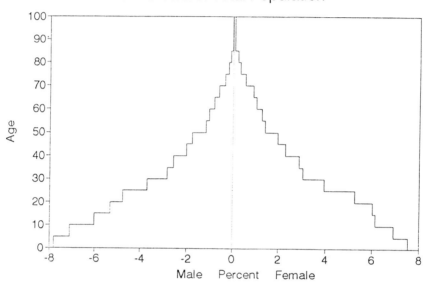

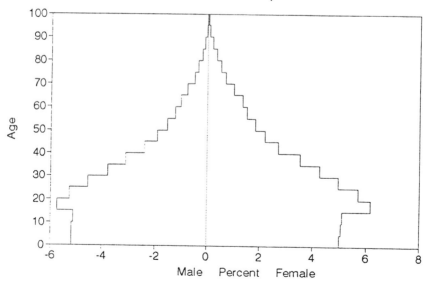

Source: INEGI: 1990 Mexican Census

Figure 3.4 Age, Sex Structures for the Nation, Federal District, and Chalco (Continued)

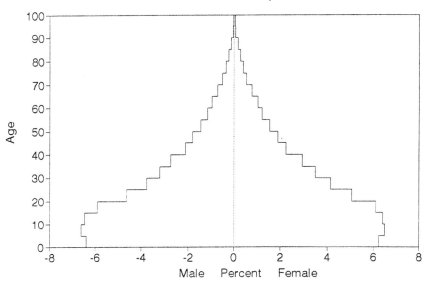

Nation of Mexico, 1990
3. Percent of Total Population

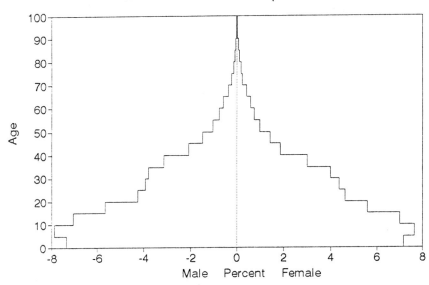

CHALCO, 1990
3. Percent of Total Population

Source: INEGI: 1990 Mexican Census

Map 3.10
0 to 17 Years of Age, 1990

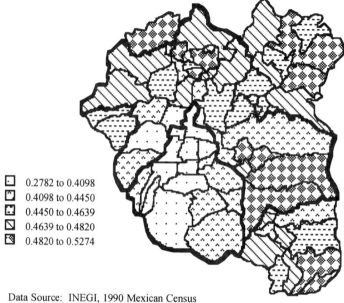

0.2782 to 0.4098
0.4098 to 0.4450
0.4450 to 0.4639
0.4639 to 0.4820
0.4820 to 0.5274

Data Source: INEGI, 1990 Mexican Census
Map Source: Butler/Pick Mexico Database Project

Map 3.11
18 to 64 Years of Age, 1990

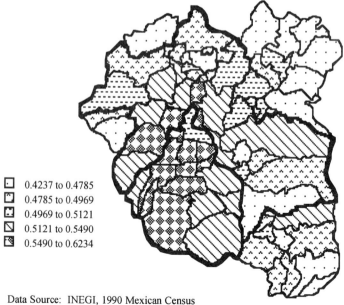

0.4237 to 0.4785
0.4785 to 0.4969
0.4969 to 0.5121
0.5121 to 0.5490
0.5490 to 0.6234

Data Source: INEGI, 1990 Mexican Census
Map Source: Butler/Pick Mexico Database Project

Map 3.12
65 Years and Older, 1990

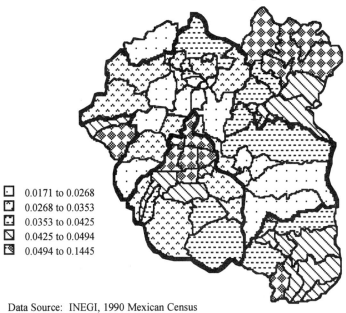

▫	0.0171 to 0.0268
▣	0.0268 to 0.0353
▣	0.0353 to 0.0425
◪	0.0425 to 0.0494
▨	0.0494 to 0.1445

Data Source: INEGI, 1990 Mexican Census
Map Source: Butler/Pick Mexico Database Project

Map 3.13
Dependency Ratio, 1970

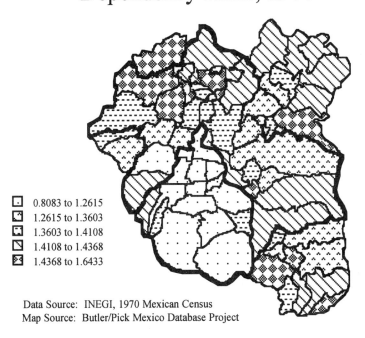

▫	0.8083 to 1.2615
▣	1.2615 to 1.3603
▣	1.3603 to 1.4108
◪	1.4108 to 1.4368
▨	1.4368 to 1.6433

Data Source: INEGI, 1970 Mexican Census
Map Source: Butler/Pick Mexico Database Project

Map 3.14
Dependency Ratio, 1990

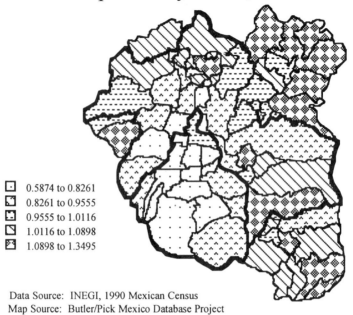

	0.5874 to 0.8261
	0.8261 to 0.9555
	0.9555 to 1.0116
	1.0116 to 1.0898
	1.0898 to 1.3495

Data Source: INEGI, 1990 Mexican Census
Map Source: Butler/Pick Mexico Database Project

Figure 3.5 Dependency Ratio, Nation, Federal District, State of Mexico, 1970 - 1990

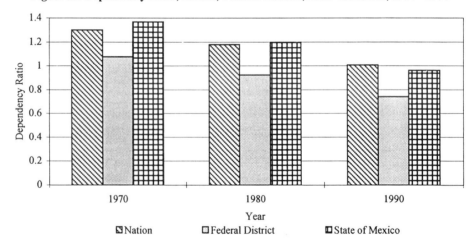

Supporting Data

Year	Nation	Federal District	State of Mexico
1970	1.297	1.0753	1.3643
1980	1.177	0.9216	1.1955
1990	1.007	0.7394	0.9597

Source: *Estadisticas Historicas de Mexico*, 1994

Table 3.4 Sex Ratio, 1990

No.	Area	Male Population	Female Population	Sex Ratio
1	Acolman	20,937	22,339	0.9372
2	Alvaro Obregon	307,118	335,635	0.9150
3	Amecameca	17,683	18,638	0.9488
4	Atenco	10,585	10,634	0.9954
5	Atizapan De Zaragoza	154,321	160,871	0.9593
6	Atlautla	9,386	9,607	0.9770
7	Axapusco	7,905	7,898	1.0009
8	Ayapango	2,120	2,119	1.0005
9	Azcapotzalco	228,420	246,268	0.9275
10	Benito Juarez	179,713	228,098	0.7879
11	Chalco	141,527	141,413	1.0008
12	Chiautla	7,252	7,512	0.9654
13	Chicoloapan	28,294	29,012	0.9753
14	Chiconcuac	6,868	7,311	0.9394
15	Chimalhuacan	120,940	121,377	0.9964
16	Coacalco	74,063	78,019	0.9493
17	Cocotitlan	4,000	4,068	0.9833
18	Coyoacan	302,047	338,019	0.8936
19	Coyotepec	12,158	12,293	0.9890
20	Cuajimalpa	58,333	61,336	0.9510
21	Cuauhtemoc	277,812	318,148	0.8732
22	Cuautitlan	24,081	24,777	0.9719
23	Cuautitlan Izcalli	160,693	166,057	0.9677
24	Ecatepec	600,410	617,725	0.9720
25	Ecatzingo	2,891	2,917	0.9911
26	Gustavo A. Madero	612,459	655,609	0.9342
27	Huehuetoca	12,660	12,869	0.9838
28	Huixquilucan	62,406	69,520	0.8977
29	Isidro Fabela	2,595	2,595	1.0000
30	Ixtapaluca	68,533	68,824	0.9958
31	Iztacalco	215,749	232,573	0.9277
32	Iztapalapa	730,466	760,033	0.9611
33	Jaltenco	11,306	11,497	0.9834
34	Jilotzingo	4,601	4,410	1.0433
35	Juchitepec	7,057	7,213	0.9784
36	Magdalena Contreras	93,603	101,438	0.9228
37	Melchor Ocampo	12,955	13,199	0.9815
38	Miguel Hidalgo	184,949	221,919	0.8334
39	Milpa Alta	31,710	31,944	0.9927
40	Naucalpan	387,272	399,279	0.9699
41	Nextlalpan	5,327	5,513	0.9663
42	Nezahualcoyotl	615,947	640,168	0.9622
43	Nicolas Romero	91,328	92,806	0.9841
44	Nopaltepec	2,697	2,537	1.0631
45	Otumba	10,945	10,889	1.0051
46	Ozumba	8,755	9,297	0.9417
47	Papalotla	1,173	1,214	0.9662
48	Paz, La	66,515	68,267	0.9743
49	San Martin De Las P.	6,807	6,756	1.0075
50	Tecamac	60,886	62,332	0.9768
51	Temamatla	2,684	2,682	1.0007
52	Temascalapa	9,625	9,474	1.0159
53	Tenango Del Aire	3,086	3,121	0.9888
54	Teoloyucan	20,830	21,134	0.9856

Table 3.4 Sex Ratio, 1990 (Continued)

No.	Area	Male Population	Female Population	Sex Ratio
55	Teotihuacan	15,063	15,423	0.9767
56	Tepetlaoxtoc	8,080	8,040	1.0050
57	Tepetlixpa	6,390	6,297	1.0148
58	Tepotzotlan	19,661	19,986	0.9837
59	Texcoco	70,834	69,534	1.0187
60	Tezoyuca	6,152	6,264	0.9821
61	Tlahuac	102,060	104,640	0.9753
62	Tlalmanalco	16,287	16,697	0.9754
63	Tlalnepantla	343,974	358,833	0.9586
64	Tlalpan	234,335	250,531	0.9354
65	Tultepec	23,266	24,057	0.9671
66	Tultitlan	121,678	124,786	0.9751
67	Venustiano Carranza	247,458	272,170	0.9092
68	Xochimilco	133,679	137,472	0.9724
69	Zumpango	35,398	36,015	0.9829
Total		7,488,798	7,951,948	0.9418
Mean		108,533	115,246	0.9673
Median		24,081	24,777	0.9753
S.D.		163,422	172,712	0.1233
C.V.		150.5732	149.8639	12.7427
Minimum		1,173	1,214	0.7879
Maximum		730,466	760,033	1.0631

Definition: Sex Ratio is the male population to the female population

Source: INEGI, 1990 Mexican Census of Population, Resumen General, Table 2.

Figure 3.6 Sex Ratio, Nation, Federal District, State of Mexico, 1940 - 1990

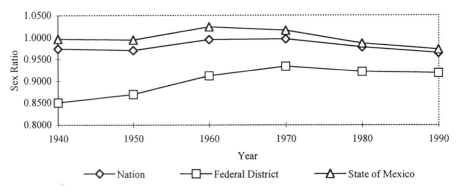

Supporting Data

Year	Nation	Federal District	State of Mexico
1940	0.9737	0.8501	0.9960
1950	0.9697	0.8690	0.9939
1960	0.9947	0.9117	1.0235
1970	0.9961	0.9336	1.0154
1980	0.9773	0.9213	0.9862
1990	0.9643	0.9180	0.9722

Source: Mexican Population Censuses, 1940-1990

Note: Sex ratio = male population/female population

Map 3.15
Sex Ratio, 1950

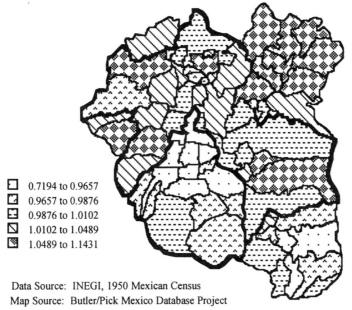

0.7194 to 0.9657
0.9657 to 0.9876
0.9876 to 1.0102
1.0102 to 1.0489
1.0489 to 1.1431

Data Source: INEGI, 1950 Mexican Census
Map Source: Butler/Pick Mexico Database Project

Map 3.16
Sex Ratio, 1990

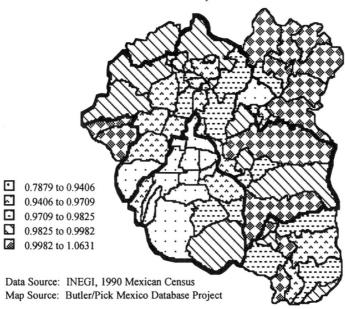

0.7879 to 0.9406
0.9406 to 0.9709
0.9709 to 0.9825
0.9825 to 0.9982
0.9982 to 1.0631

Data Source: INEGI, 1990 Mexican Census
Map Source: Butler/Pick Mexico Database Project

Cuauhtemoc, Nezahualcoyotl, and Mexico City's Most Populated Areas

Figure 3.7 shows population change for Cuauhtemoc (Federal District) and Nezahualcoyotl (State of Mexico immediately adjacent to the Federal District) for 1950 and 1990. The year 1950 was chosen as a starting point since Neza had virtually no population at that date while Cuauhtemoc had a population of well over one million persons. Subsequently, Neza's population began growing in the 1960s and passed Cuauhtemoc's population during the 1970s. Thus Neza's population increased from virtually zero to a peak of 1,256,115 recorded in 1980. In contrast, Cuauhtemoc's population of 1,049,079 in 1950 began declining beginning in the 1950s and continued to do so through 1990 with a population of 595,960.

Cuauhtemoc and Nezahualcoyotl summarize many aspects of the population transformation of Mexico Megacity since mid-century. Trends include (1) a growing population deconcentration of the old central core, (2) rapid population growth in areas adjoining the (northern) Federal District, some of which were former ejido areas and (3) huge density increases in the northeast Federal District and adjoining municipios.

Growth in periphery expansion rings is further emphasized by considering the historical growth of Mexico Megacity's most populated areas in 1990 of Gustavo Madero and Iztapalapa, in the eastern Federal District, and Nezahualcoyotl and Ecatepec in the State of Mexico (see Figure 3.8). Map 3.17 shows that all four areas are located adjacent to each other and accounted in 1990 for 5,252,817 persons, or 34 percent of the total city population. The areas followed each other by a decade or two in transformation and seemed to grow until carrying capacity or other limits were attained at about a million and a half, at which point the growth slowed or declined. Ecatepec in 1990 still appears to be in a growth phase. It is important to note the most populated areas have developed in a different region than the old city center, in particular to the northeast; the populous areas do not coincide with the city's huge industrial complex, which is centered somewhat to its west (see Map 9.2).

Figure 3.7 Population Change in Nezahualcoyotl and Cuauhtemoc, 1950-1990

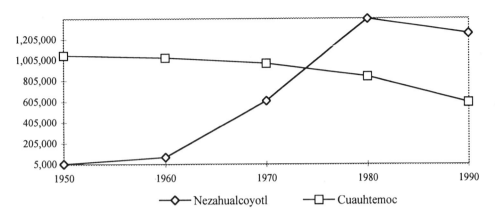

Supporting Data

Year	Nezahualcoyotl	Cuauhtemoc
1950	5,990	1,049,079
1960	69,297	1,024,389
1970	610,268	969,406
1980	1,396,854	843,283
1990	1,256,115	595,960

Source: INEGI: Population Censuses, 1950-1990.

Figure 3.8 Population of Mexico City's Most Populated Municipios. 1940 - 1990

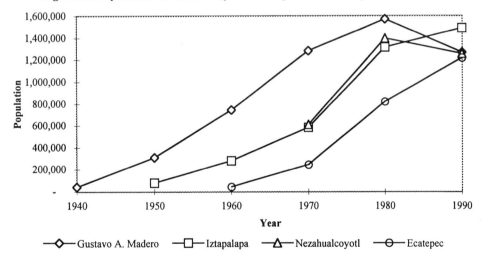

Supporting Data

Year	Gustavo A. Madero	Iztapalapa	Nezahualcoyotl	Ecatepec
1940	41,567			
1950	308,002	78,624		
1960	743,043	280,625		43,764
1970	1,282,280	582,197	610,268	244,647
1980	1,569,714	1,315,063	1,396,854	819,478
1990	1,268,068	1,490,499	1,256,115	1,218,135

Source: INEGI: Population Censuses, 1940-1990.

Map 3.17
Mexico Megacity's Most
Populated Areas

Data Source: INEGI, 1990 Mexican Census
Map Source: Butler/Pick Mexico Database Project

Population Cluster Analysis

A separate cluster analysis was performed for the five population characteristics shown in the overall set of variables in Table 1.2: log of total population, relative population growth 1970-90, log of population density, sex ratio, and inmigration in the past five years. As mentioned in Chapter 1, the purpose of the special cluster analyses by the six groups, is to illustrate that spatial differences may vary among variable groups. We expect that performing the cluster analyses for the variable groups will reveal spatial features helpful in understanding the complex and multi-dimensional socioeconomic context of the Megacity. This population cluster analysis is the first of six cluster analyses by variable set. The others are urbanism/familism (in chapter 4), housing (in chapter 7), social rank (in chapter 8), economic (in chapter 9), and race/ethnicity (in chapter 12). In chapter 12, several of them are compared and contrasted, and they are summarized in chapter 13.

The population cluster analysis reveals distinctive core, intermediate, and peripheral areas. The ten clusters are displayed in Map 3.18, with the means for the cluster variables summarized in Table 3.5. The central core has a large population that has undergone deconcentration of about thirty percent 1970-90. It is characterized by a very low sex ratio (0.87) and a low 1985-90 inmigration rate. With the net population loss, this implies a high outmigration rate. Population density of the core is exceptionally high at 15,000 persons per square kilometer. Immediately surrounding the core is a ring of four populous delegations, which, have a modest population increase of about 30 percent over twenty years. The sex ratio is low at 0.92, and inmigration is low and the population density is greatly reduced at about 2,000. Surrounding these two core clusters is Cluster 3. It has the highest total population, lower population density at about 350 and a higher sex ratio of 0.96. It had moderate inmigration 1970-90 and over doubling of size. Its delegations and municipios became incorporated in the 50s, 60s, and 70s (Negrete et al., 1993).

Cluster 4 is the populous delegation of Ecatepec. It is distinguished as a unique delegation by its very high inmigration rate 1970-90 of 15 percent and its rapid population growth of nearly five fold 1970-90. The high inmigration rate points to continuing growth in the 1990s. Such growth is encouraged by the still low 1990 density of 129. Clusters 5, 6, and 7 include municipios and delegations to the north, east, and southwest of the core and its two surrounding rings. These clusters have a total population of 1.7 million. They have moderate to low population density and moderate to high sex ratios. They differ from each other most markedly in their growth profiles. Cluster 7, consisting of Atizapan de Zaragoza, Chalco, Chicoloapan, and Tecamac, had very high growth of 10-fold in the 70s and 80s. These areas tend to be located on former ejido land that has been transformed by urbanization. Another consequence of the rapid growth is the young age structures for these municipios with the exception of Tecamac (see Figure 3.4 for Chalco). Cluster 8 contains one delegation and 18 municipios that tend to have low population size, modest growth, and low population density. The sex ratios are moderately high at 99. This large cluster is largely peripheral encompassing much of the semi-urban arms and other peripheral areas. Clusters 9 and 10 are also largely peripheral. Cluster 10 consists of seven municipios that have tiny populations, very low population density, low growth and high sex ratios. It is important to note also that these municipios are mostly very limited in land area. These are the least urbanized yet may have potential for rapid urbanization in the future.

Comparing our population clusters with the "contornos" of Negrete et al. (1993), there is a similarity between our and their core. Also our ring clusters 2 and 3 resemble somewhat their "contorno 1." However, our clusters divide up the intermediate areas and periphery entirely differently, which is due to a more complex set of population characteristics in differentiating zones.

Map 3.18
Population Clusters

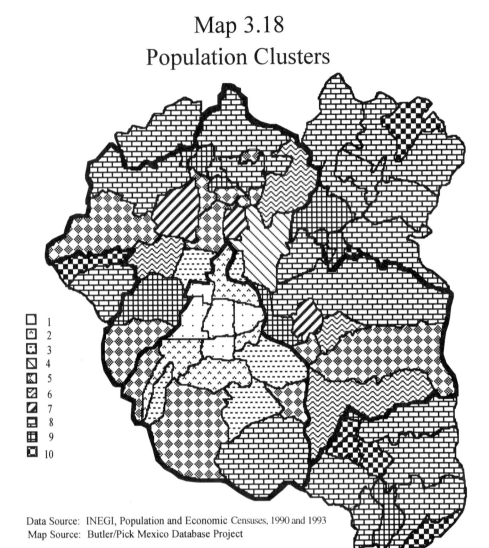

Data Source: INEGI, Population and Economic Censuses, 1990 and 1993
Map Source: Butler/Pick Mexico Database Project

85

Table 3.5 Population Cluster Means

Variable / Cluster No.	1	2	3	4	5	6	7	8	9	10	Mexico City
Total Population 1990	2,404,955	2,999,209	4,702,164	1,218,135	203,324	778,656	721,149	613,841	203,324	34,431	15,440,746
Population 1990	480,991	749,802	783,694	1,218,135	22,592	194,664	240,383	32,307	22,592	4,920	223,779
Population Growth 1970-1990	-0.31	0.33	1.18	4.63	1.17	5.60	10.02	0.97	1.17	0.94	1.92
Population Density 1990	14,926.6	1,958.3	342.8	128.7	166.4	69.6	159.9	59.2	166.4	51.1	1,305.7
Sex Ratio	0.866	0.918	0.958	0.972	0.967	0.978	0.971	0.993	0.967	1.002	0.967
Inmigration 1985-1990	0.046	0.035	0.059	0.151	0.031	0.117	0.137	0.043	0.031	0.039	0.059

Note: Values for Population 1990 are cluster totals. All other values are cluster means.
For population and population density, natural log values used in cluster analysis.

Cluster 1	Cluster 2	Cluster 3	Cluster 4	Cluster 5	Cluster 6	Cluster 7	Cluster 8	Cluster 9
Azcapotzalco	Alvaro Obregon	Iztapalapa	Ecatepec	Cuajimalpa	Atizapan de Zaragoza	Chimalhuacan	Amecameca	Acolman
Benito Juarez	Coyoacan	Magdalena Contreras		Cuautitlan	Chalco	Coacalco	Atenco	Chiautla
Cuauhtemoc	Gustavo A. Madero	Naucalpan		Huixquilucan	Chicoloapan	Cuautitlan Izcalli	Atlautla	Chiconcuac
Miguel Hidalgo	Iztacalco	Nezahualcoyotl		Ixtapaluca	Tecamac		Axapusco	Cocotitlan
Venustiano Carranza		Tlalnepantla		Jaltenco			Huehuetoca	Coyotepec
		Xochimilco		Nicolas Romero			Jilotzingo	Melchor Ocampo
				Paz, La			Juchitepec	Ozumba
				Tlahuac			Milpa Alta	Teoloyucan
				Tlalpan			Nextlalpan	Tezoyuca
				Tultepec			Otumba	
				Tultitlan			San Martin de las P.	
							Temascalapa	
							Teotihuacan	
							Tepetlaoxtoc	
							Tepetlixpa	
							Tepotzotlan	
							Texcoco	
							Tlalmanalco	
							Zumpango	

Cluster 10
Ayapango
Ecatzingo
Isidro Fabela
Nopaltepec
Papalotla
Temamatla
Tenango del Aire

Future Population Growth of Mexico Megacity

While population projections for Mexico City vary, all of them differ only slightly in anticipation that the Mexico Megacity will continue to be among the largest in the world. Mexico is projected to have a population of 124 million persons and Mexico Megacity a population of 19 million in year 2015 (UN, 1995). The concentration of population in the metropolitan area is expected to continue at present ratio of one out of every six persons in Mexico will be residing in Mexico Megacity.

In an alternative projection shown below, the Federal District has been projected to contain over 12 million persons by 1995 and by the year 2010 to have over 15 million persons -- approximately the total population for Mexico Megacity in 1990! The State of Mexico was projected to have a population of over 13 million by 1995 and grow to over 21 million by 2010 (FEMAP 1987). While not all population growth in the State of Mexico will be in the metropolitan or conurbation area, a substantial portion of it will be adjacent to or in areas of the expanding Megacity. Garza and Schteingart (1978: 54) assumed that Mexico City in the year 2000 would have a population of over 28 million or 30 million, depending upon the definition utilized. The FEMAP and Garza/Schteingart projections are too high in lieu of continuing fertility declines. They are presented for illustration and historical reasons.

Projected Population by FEMAP[1]		
Year	Federal District	State of Mexico
1995	12,173,441	13,281,347
2000	13,206,095	15,723,288
2005	14,272,708	17,704,875
2010	15,359,383	21,440,888

The central core undoubtedly will continue to lose population although it will continue to contain a huge population living under extremely dense conditions. Areas adjacent to the old core but in the Federal District will continue to grow in population size. However, the major anticipated population growth will be in many peripheral areas of the State of Mexico which will expand to the geographical limits of Mexico Megacity and thus ensure that it will be among the largest metropolitan complexes in the world. Undoubtedly, most of this population growth will first take place along major transportation arteries and later fill in interstitial areas. Thus, to a large degree the location of population growth within the complex can be predicted.

---

[1] Additional projections are shown in Chapter 13.

4

Marriage, Fertility, and Family

Photo courtesy of Tomas Mojarro

Introduction

This chapter examines the marital, fertility, and familial dimensions of Mexico Megacity. These dimensions are important for several reasons. The family unit is the major economic unit of the Megacity. It is a repository of the cultural and social values of the Megacity. It is influential in determining population and urban growth. In this chapter the fertility component of urban change will be particularly examined.

Marriage rates in Mexico City have been steady in rate over time and not varied much spatially. This steadiness reflects consistent social mores for marriage. By contrast divorce and separation have increased substantially since the 1970s. Both show widely varying aerial patterns. About one eighteenth of the metropolitan population is in a free union, a proportion much lower than that reported for Mexican rural areas (Goldman and Pebley, 1981; Pick, Butler, and Lanzer, 1989). There is a gradation in the linkage of these marital statuses to social rank. Marriage and separation are unrelated to social rank. This implies that these statuses are independent of social level, but relate to other factors such as family structure, location of residence, etc. On the other hand, free union and divorce are strongly associated with social rank -- free union with low rank and divorce with high rank.

Fertility has been the largest component of population change in Mexico Megacity over the past half century, even though its level is considerably lower than for the nation and has decreased consistently since the sixties (Partida Bush, 1987). Although fertility has little spatial variation, it is influential nonetheless in determining differential metropolitan population growth and distribution. Fertility is important at the family level because of its impacts in the family unit on standards of living, housing, educational opportunities, and schooling.

The Urbanism/Familism variable group is a composite of marital, fertility, and female labor force factors. The pattern of urbanism/familism clusters divide the Megacity into several rings, as well as impoverished areas characterized by high fertility, high free union, and low female labor force participation. Cluster boundaries are nearly identical to those for social rank except in the far west. This is not surprising, given the strong bivariate associations between variables in the urbanism/familism and social rank variable groups. The general modified ring cluster structure for urbanism/familism may reflect the historical expansion population thrusts of the metropolis, which in turn resulted from distinctive historical family patterns of migration and fertility (Graizbord and Salazar, 1987; Negrete et al., 1993).

Marriage and Free Union

The marriage rate for Mexico Megacity in 1990 was 7.2 marriages per 1,000 population. This was thirteen percent lower than the national mean of 8.3 percent (Pick and Butler, 1994). As seen in Figure 4.1, 1990 marriage rates are similar for the Federal District and from 1940-1980, the marriage rate for the State of Mexico was lower than the Federal District's. Since studies of Mexico and other nations consistently indicate that higher rates of marriage are linked to lower socioeconomic status, the lower rates for the Megacity are plausible (Quilodrán, 1991, chapter 25; McLanahan and Casper, 1995).

The proportion of population married in 1990 was 44 percent. There is a slight variation in percent married, as seen in a CV of eleven (see Table 4.1). Other marital dimensions considerably exceed this CV value, and most have high values of over 100. Marriage likely shows little variation due to consistency in the social expectation of marriage that extends across social classes (Quilodrán, 1991). The pattern of marriage (see Map 4.1) indicates that there are high rates in the north and northwest, i.e. in the range of

46 to 51 percent, while the lowest proportions are located in the oldest central delegations in the Federal District (Benito Juarez, Cuauhtemoc, and Miguel Hidalgo), in Milpa Alta in the southeastern Federal District, and in the metropolitan extensions to the northeast and southeast.

This pattern for marriage is somewhat reflected in the map of 1970 married population given in Map 4.2. Although the low marriage proportion areas are similar, the areas of high marriage in the north were shifted somewhat to the east and there is a strong reversal to high percent married in Milpa Alta in 1970   The correlation of marriage proportions between 1970 and 1990 is not significant at p = 0.05 level.

The proportion married is not correlated with the other marital/fertility variables (Table 4.2), nor with the selected socioeconomic variables in Table 4.3, with one exception. The only significant association is an opposite one with Free Union (r = -0.26). Examining the entire set of variables in the book, marriage is generally unrelated to social rank variables, although it is positively associated with literacy (r = 0.22). Overall, it is surprisingly unrelated to social rank, since studies generally ascribe marriage to higher rank (Quilodrán, 1991).

Married population is related to inmigration and demographic growth, as seen by significant correlations with relative population growth 1970-90 (r = 0.36), inmigration 1985-90 (r = 0.36), and population native to state (r = -0.37). These results likely relate to higher proportion of married population inmigrating to population growth areas, perhaps seeking better economic conditions and/or housing.

Free union, sometimes called common law marriage, has been prevalent in Mexico for generations. Free union as a percent of all unions in Mexico in the 1969 PECFAL survey was estimated at 32 percent (Goldman and Pebley, 1981). It is often the first form of union. It is not as lasting as marriage, and usually results within ten years in legal marriage or in dissolution (Goldman and Pebley, 1981). In Mexico, formation of free union is associated with younger age of union, lower education, and non-Catholic religion (Goldman and Pebley, 1981). These factors also are associated with somewhat higher rates of legalization of free unions (Goldman and Pebley, 1981).

Six percent of the adult Megacity population had the status of free union, a proportion much higher than either divorce or separation. Overall marriage predominates as a form of union. It must be emphasized that Mexican family institutions in the 1990s remain tradition-bound stemming from the predominant Catholic religion. There are indications that alternatives to marriage are becoming more prevalent (Quilodrán, 1991), but in 1990 they were slight including free union. The level of free union is low in the Megacity compared to the rest of the nation (Pick and Butler, 1994, Table 4.2).

Comparing the 1990 Megacity's rate with the 1990 United States rates of cohabitation, the proportion is considerably higher in Mexico. According to 1990 U.S. Census results, 3.4 percent of unmarried males and 5.6 percent of unmarried females cohabited (McLanahan and Casper, 1995). However, for the adult population as a whole, U.S. rates would be under two percent.

As seen in Table 4.2, free union is significantly inversely associated with marriage and divorce (r = -0.26 and -0.51), although it has no association with separation. This may stem from free union being an alternative to marriage, so areas with a high number of free unions have a lower number of marriages. The spatial pattern of free union (see Map 4.3) is strongly opposite to the patterns for population and population density (Maps 3.3 and 3.10). Free union is very significantly related to social status, women's labor force, and population variables as seen in the correlations in Table 4.3. Free union increases with lower social status and reduced proportion of women in the labor force. In the Megacity, free union is more characteristic of the lower ranks of society. This may be due to its greater flexibility and more temporary nature, compared to marriage. Lower social status partners may not be willing to make the long-term economic commitments of marriage. The fertility in free unions tends to be roughly equivalent to that in civil marriages (Quilodrán, 1991). The traditional, low status free union in Mexico may be contrasted with "cohabitation" in the U.S., which increased in the 70s and 80s, and does not vary much by social rank indicators (McLanahan and Casper, 1995).

Figure 4.1 Marriage, Nation,
Federal District, State of Mexico 1940-1990

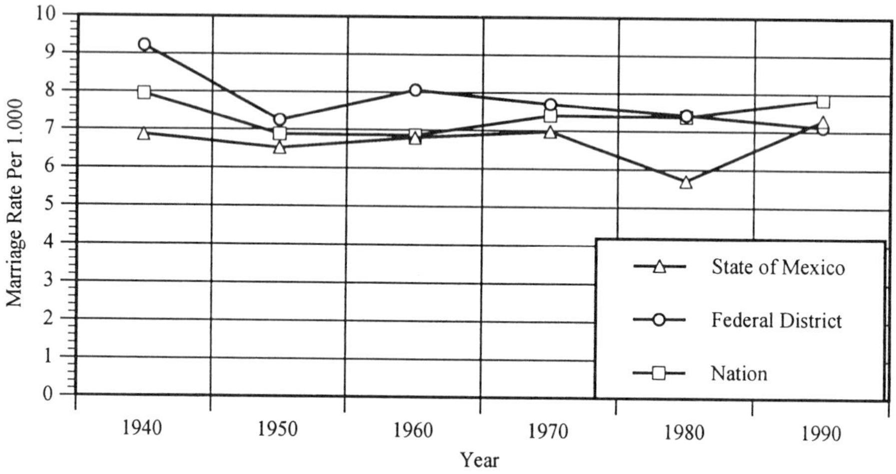

Note: Marriage rates per 1,000
Source: *Estadisticas Historicas de Mexico,* 1994.

Table 4.1 Marital Status, 1990

No.	Area	Married Population	Percent Married	Population in Free Union	Percent in Free Union	Divorced Population	Percent Divorced	Separated Population	Percent Separated
1	Acolman	13,268	0.4345	2,876	0.0942	147	0.0048	383	0.0125
2	Alvaro Obregon	211,034	0.4381	31,279	0.0649	6,113	0.0127	7,239	0.0150
3	Amecameca	11,261	0.4444	2,267	0.0895	148	0.0058	388	0.0153
4	Atenco	6,959	0.4626	988	0.0657	48	0.0032	172	0.0114
5	Atizapan de Zaragoza	107,807	0.4878	14,455	0.0654	2,007	0.0091	2,441	0.0110
6	Atlautla	5,485	0.4305	1,351	0.1060	52	0.0041	260	0.0204
7	Axapusco	4,473	0.4167	1,219	0.1136	41	0.0038	135	0.0126
8	Ayapango	1,254	0.4318	325	0.1119	16	0.0055	41	0.0141
9	Azcapotzalco	158,932	0.4353	18,516	0.0507	4,986	0.0137	5,782	0.0158
10	Benito Juarez	138,671	0.4187	10,216	0.0308	11,202	0.0338	5,462	0.0165
11	Chalco	80,408	0.4429	24,957	0.1375	792	0.0044	2,485	0.0137
12	Chiautla	4,521	0.4375	781	0.0756	38	0.0037	147	0.0142
13	Chicoloapan	17,123	0.4456	3,951	0.1028	180	0.0047	536	0.0139
14	Chiconcuac	4,519	0.4494	766	0.0762	22	0.0022	118	0.0117
15	Chimalhuacan	70,195	0.4519	18,878	0.1215	528	0.0034	1,873	0.0121
16	Coacalco	55,352	0.5018	4,304	0.0390	1,071	0.0097	1,313	0.0119
17	Cocotitlan	2,433	0.4232	613	0.1066	26	0.0045	102	0.0177
18	Coyoacan	219,428	0.4433	22,813	0.0461	8,847	0.0179	7,309	0.0148
19	Coyotepec	7,869	0.4842	1,221	0.0751	66	0.0041	211	0.0130
20	Cuajimalpa	39,404	0.4583	5,833	0.0678	641	0.0075	1,166	0.0136
21	Cuauhtemoc	176,780	0.3805	33,737	0.0726	10,906	0.0235	9,823	0.0211
22	Cuautitlan	16,082	0.4680	2,344	0.0682	224	0.0065	437	0.0127
23	Cuautitlan Izcalli	115,560	0.5083	11,785	0.0518	1,868	0.0082	2,391	0.0105
24	Ecatepec	398,491	0.4694	66,697	0.0786	5,510	0.0065	11,384	0.0134
25	Ecatzingo	1,533	0.4147	535	0.1447	14	0.0038	66	0.0179
26	Gustavo A. Madero	420,466	0.4373	56,241	0.0585	11,456	0.0119	15,405	0.0160
27	Huehuetoca	7,779	0.4665	1,768	0.1060	68	0.0041	210	0.0126
28	Huixquilucan	42,244	0.4487	6,291	0.0668	731	0.0078	1,027	0.0109
29	Isidro Fabela	1,478	0.4072	385	0.1061	17	0.0047	17	0.0047
30	Ixtapaluca	41,210	0.4483	10,277	0.1118	556	0.0060	1,315	0.0143
31	Iztacalco	147,282	0.4304	21,545	0.0630	4,274	0.0125	5,877	0.0172
32	Iztapalapa	475,860	0.4417	16,720	0.0155	9,376	0.0087	84,523	0.0785

Table 4.1 Marital Status, 1990 (Continued)

No.	Area	Married Population	Percent Married	Population in Free Union	Percent in Free Union	Divorced Population	Percent Divorced	Separated Population	Percent Separated
33	Jaltenco	7,309	0.4742	1,244	0.0807	83	0.0054	179	0.0116
34	Jilotzingo	3,005	0.4875	506	0.0821	21	0.0034	36	0.0058
35	Juchitepec	3,871	0.3954	1,676	0.1712	28	0.0029	139	0.0142
36	Magdalena Contreras	63,918	0.4414	9,897	0.0684	1,782	0.0123	2,293	0.0158
37	Melchor Ocampo	8,365	0.4629	1,477	0.0817	57	0.0032	228	0.0126
38	Miguel Hidalgo	131,000	0.4061	14,805	0.0459	6,867	0.0213	5,829	0.0181
39	Milpa Alta	14,671	0.3243	4,510	0.0997	175	0.0039	610	0.0135
40	Naucalpan	257,577	0.4468	40,704	0.0706	5,773	0.0100	7,116	0.0123
41	Nextlalpan	2,945	0.4099	942	0.1311	17	0.0024	848	0.1180
42	Nezahualcoyotl	404,872	0.4459	942	0.0010	6,239	0.0069	94	0.0001
43	Nicolas Romero	58,265	0.4618	11,108	0.0880	574	0.0045	1,267	0.0100
44	Nopaltepec	1,358	0.3740	645	0.1776	15	0.0041	36	0.0099
45	Otumba	6,312	0.4296	1,654	0.1126	61	0.0042	161	0.0110
46	Ozumba	5,379	0.4371	1,112	0.0904	55	0.0045	217	0.0176
47	Papalotla	677	0.4011	140	0.0829	11	0.0065	23	0.0136
48	Paz, La	40,795	0.4391	8,919	0.0960	502	0.0054	1,445	0.0156
49	San Martin de las P.	4,338	0.4538	697	0.0729	47	0.0049	80	0.0084
50	Tecamac	37,622	0.4399	8,397	0.0982	519	0.0061	1,122	0.0131
51	Temamatla	1,700	0.4668	320	0.0879	23	0.0063	56	0.0154
52	Temascalapa	5,406	0.4191	1,716	0.1330	41	0.0032	154	0.0119
53	Tenango del Aire	1,774	0.4002	560	0.1263	15	0.0034	61	0.0138
54	Teoloyucan	13,254	0.4675	2,060	0.0727	92	0.0032	324	0.0114
55	Teotihuacan	9,211	0.4359	1,980	0.0937	111	0.0053	298	0.0141
56	Tepetlaoxtoc	4,841	0.4428	999	0.0914	49	0.0045	102	0.0093
57	Tepetlixpa	3,804	0.4331	1,174	0.1337	31	0.0035	125	0.0142
58	Tepotzotlan	12,293	0.4563	2,287	0.0849	107	0.0040	324	0.0120
59	Texcoco	44,994	0.4467	6,395	0.0635	737	0.0073	1,174	0.0117
60	Tezoyuca	3,845	0.4371	742	0.0844	28	0.0032	97	0.0110
61	Tlahuac	65,050	0.4443	2,066	0.0141	849	0.0058	13,331	0.0910
62	Tlalmanalco	10,879	0.4520	2,249	0.0934	152	0.0063	367	0.0152
63	Tlalnepantla	234,259	0.4507	32,850	0.0632	5,304	0.0102	6,678	0.0128

Table 4.1 Marital Status, 1990 (Continued)

No.	Area	Married Population	Percent Married	Population in Free Union	Percent in Free Union	Divorced Population	Percent Divorced	Separated Population	Percent Separated
64	Tlalpan	159,604	0.4455	24,327	0.0679	4,593	0.0128	5,533	0.0154
65	Tultepec	15,436	0.4885	2,442	0.0773	118	0.0037	310	0.0098
66	Tultitlan	84,795	0.5048	10,430	0.0621	1,110	0.0066	1,931	0.0115
67	Venustiano Carranza	167,792	0.4212	25,593	0.0642	6,067	0.0152	7,596	0.0191
68	Xochimilco	89,222	0.4524	16,665	0.0845	1,623	0.0082	2,726	0.0138
69	Zumpango	5,865	0.1214	4,388	0.0908	189	0.0039	568	0.0118
	Total	4,991,464	0.4421	644,552	0.0571	126,036	0.0112	233,516	0.0207
	Mean	73,209	0.4374	9,436	0.0843	1,851	0.0072	3,428	0.0168
	Median	15,054	0.4431	2,316	0.0819	178	0.0054	487	0.0135
	S.D.	110,789	0.0494	13,403	0.0328	3,104	0.0054	10,552	0.0178
	C.V.	151.33	11.30	142.03	38.93	167.64	75.87	307.78	105.48
	Minimum	677	0.1214	140	0.0010	11	0.0022	17	0.0001
	Maximum	475,860	0.5083	66,697	0.1776	11,456	0.0338	84,523	0.1180

Definition: Married Status for Population (Age 12+).

Source: INEGI, 1990 Census of Population.

Map 4.1
Married, 1990

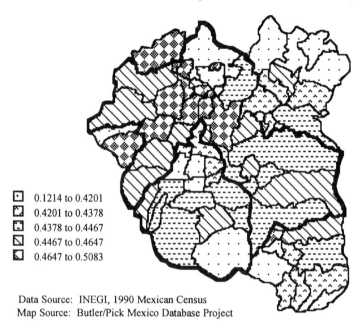

⊡	0.1214 to 0.4201
▨	0.4201 to 0.4378
⊟	0.4378 to 0.4467
◰	0.4467 to 0.4647
▧	0.4647 to 0.5083

Data Source: INEGI, 1990 Mexican Census
Map Source: Butler/Pick Mexico Database Project

Map 4.2
Married, 1970

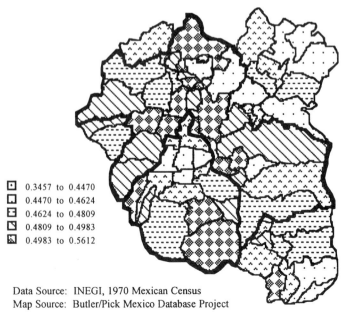

⊡	0.3457 to 0.4470
▢	0.4470 to 0.4624
⊟	0.4624 to 0.4809
◰	0.4809 to 0.4983
▧	0.4983 to 0.5612

Data Source: INEGI, 1970 Mexican Census
Map Source: Butler/Pick Mexico Database Project

Map 4.3
Free Union, 1990

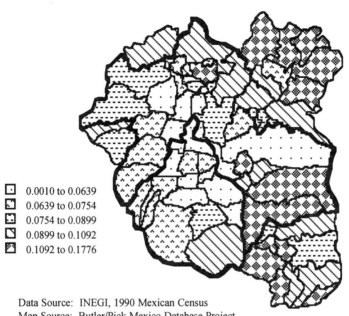

0.0010 to 0.0639
0.0639 to 0.0754
0.0754 to 0.0899
0.0899 to 0.1092
0.1092 to 0.1776

Data Source: INEGI, 1990 Mexican Census
Map Source: Butler/Pick Mexico Database Project

96

Table 4.2 Correlation Matrix of Marital Status and Fertility Variables

	Married	Divorced	Separated	Free union	Children born	Fertility ages 20-29
Divorced	-.025					
Separated	-.062	.000				
Free union	-.263*	-.511***	-.111			
Children born	-.131	-.748***	-.025	.701***		
Fertility ages 20 -29	.007	-.721***	.024	.539***	.780***	
Fertility ages 45 and older	.034	-.642***	-.014	.352**	.584***	.545***

Note: Significance Levels   *   .05
                             **   .01
                            ***   .001

**Table 4.3 Correlation Matrix Between Marital Status/Fertility Variables
and Socioeconomic/Population Variables**

	Married	Divorced	Separated	Free union	Children born	Fertility ages 20-29	Fertility ages 45 and older
Economically active women	-.000	.793***	.085	-.584***	-.817***	-.735***	-.519***
Professional and technical	.111	.897***	-.005	-.634***	-.852***	-.793***	-.610***
Primary educated	.129	.814***	.060	-.736***	-.905***	-.824***	-.571***
Earn 5 times minimum wage	.172	.758***	.080	-.535***	-.746***	-.603***	-.479***
Home ownership	.101	.789***	-.062	.442***	.649***	.634***	.500***
Population 1990	.118	.595***	.071	-.621***	-.728***	-.540***	-.397***

Note: Significance Levels   *   .05
                             **   .01
                            ***   .001

Separation and Divorce

As Mexican society gradually modernizes and outgrows somewhat its Spanish, Catholic social traditions, there are indicators of emerging forms of family structure. Separation has increased over the past several decades, resulting in a 1990 separation proportion rate of 2.1 percent and a separated population of 234,000. As seen in Figure 4.2, the divorce rate rose rapidly in the Megacity since the 1950s. For instance in the State of Mexico it increased from 3.23 per 100,000 persons in 1950 to 32.59 in 1990, a fifteen fold increase. Likewise rates in the Federal District at least doubled. Since there was almost no divorce in 1950, this large relative increase resulted four decades later in only a small proportion divorced. In 1990, there were 126,000 divorced people in the giant city.

Marital separation proportion in the Megacity has a wide range varying from nearly zero (0.0001) in Nezahualcoyotl to nearly 12 percent in Nextlalpan. It has a high CV of 105. The geographic pattern for separated persons is seen in Map 4.4. This pattern shows high separation in Nextlalpan municipio to the north, the northern Federal District and southeastern semi-urban metropolitan extension. There are low proportions separated in the most of the northern half of the metropolis outside of the Federal District and Nextlalpan.

Separation is not correlated with the other urbanism/familism variables nor with the selected socioeconomic ones (see Tables 4.2 and 4.3). Examining the full set of dimensions covered in the book, separation has almost no significant correlations and none that appears meaningful. It is a surprisingly unique spatial characteristic. This uniqueness stems from its common high prevalence in two areas which usually are contrasting, i.e. the Federal District and the far southeast. Since separation appears more characteristic of higher status areas, the surprising results are high levels for the far southeast, which is largely an impoverished semi-urban area.

The spatial patterns of divorced population are shown in Maps 4.5 and 4.6 for 1970 and 1990. The spatial pattern of divorce for 1990 resembles closely that of population, and in fact they are correlated at the 0.05 level. Divorce has significant opposite association with fertility (see Table 4.2). This reflects mostly the higher social rank of divorced persons, which would tend to lower fertility, since the social status is known from numerous studies to be associated with higher fertility (Kasarda, Billy, and West, 1986; Rubin-Kurtzman, 1987). This is further corroborated by examining the correlations in Table 4.3. Divorce is highly related to all the social rank dimensions. This underscores that divorce is inversely associated with home ownership, and positively associated with population.

Reflecting the rise in divorce, the proportion divorced in 1990 is about fifty percent higher than for 1970. The spatial patterns are highly correlated ($r = 0.62$) over the two decades (compare Maps 4.5 and 4.6). The main difference is the higher relative proportion divorced in the inner areas of the semi-urban "arms" extending to the northeast and southeast. It should be noted that the absolute proportion of divorced population in those areas remained stable over the twenty years, while divorce in the rest of the metropolitan area increased substantially.

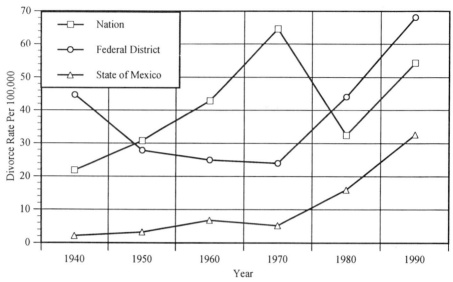

**Figure 4.2 Divorce, Nation,
Federal District, State of Mexico 1940-1990**

Note: Divorce rates per 100,000
Source: Estadisticas Historicas de Mexico, 1994

Map 4.4
Separated, 1990

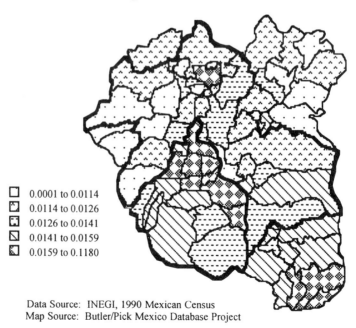

☐ 0.0001 to 0.0114
▣ 0.0114 to 0.0126
▦ 0.0126 to 0.0141
◨ 0.0141 to 0.0159
▨ 0.0159 to 0.1180

Data Source: INEGI, 1990 Mexican Census
Map Source: Butler/Pick Mexico Database Project

Map 4.5
Divorced, 1970

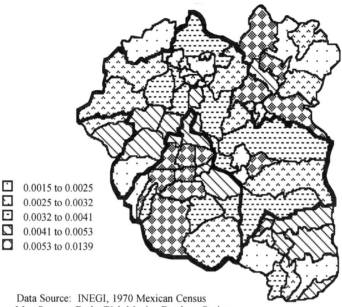

	0.0015 to 0.0025
	0.0025 to 0.0032
	0.0032 to 0.0041
	0.0041 to 0.0053
	0.0053 to 0.0139

Data Source: INEGI, 1970 Mexican Census
Map Source: Butler/Pick Mexico Database Project

Map 4.6
Divorced, 1990

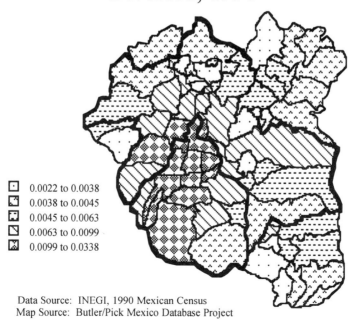

	0.0022 to 0.0038
	0.0038 to 0.0045
	0.0045 to 0.0063
	0.0063 to 0.0099
	0.0099 to 0.0338

Data Source: INEGI, 1990 Mexican Census
Map Source: Butler/Pick Mexico Database Project

Fertility

Mexican fertility lowered substantially since the 1970s (Alba, 1984; Figueroa Campos, 1989; Pick and Butler, 1994). In 1994, the national crude fertility rate was 28 per 1,000 and the total fertility rate was 3.2 (United Nations, 1994). This compares to 1994 U.S. crude fertility rate of 9 per 1,000 and total fertility rate of 2.1 (United Nations, 1994). The results of the twentieth century drop is reflected in Mexico's age-adjusted fertility rates lowering to levels about 50 percent higher than the U.S.

The average decennial crude fertility rates for the Mexico City metropolis designated by Garza as the ZMCM (consisting of the Federal District plus fifteen adjacent municipios in the State of Mexico) were 44.7 in the 50s, 41.4 in the 60s and 37 in the 70s (See Table 4.4). The rate for the single year of 1990 is 28 (estimated from INEGI, 1992). This reflects a drop in crude fertility rate of nearly forty percent over three decades. This decrease has contributed to a lowering of the rate of population increase in the conurbation, from about five percent annually at mid-century to about one percent today.

A full century plot of fertility decline (Figure 4.3) contrasts the Federal District, State of Mexico, and nation. The national pattern reflects low rates in the first two decades of the century followed by a sharp increase in the 20s after the revolutionary period; high rates in the 30s through 60s; and substantial decline from 1960 to 1990. The Federal District and State of Mexico differ from the national pattern, especially prior to 1960. The two states were higher than the nation in 1900 and lower in 1922. In 1930, the State of Mexico was exceptionally high, which may reflect errors in the vital registration system. The pre-1940 fluctuations in the State of Mexico may reflect its highly rural status, which was impacted in 1922 by the revolution but returned to characteristically high rural fertility level by 1930. The Federal District was lower than the nation in the 40s and 50s, before converging to the national pattern. Although these patterns are not consistent, it is clear that the entire set of fertility rates declined substantially since 1960, with the exception of a modest uptick for the State of Mexico in the 80s.

The crude fertility rates for the decades of the 50s, 60s, and 70s (Table 4.5 and Maps 4.7 - 4.9) reveal highly consistent spatial patterns even though the crude fertility rate dropped substantially. Results for the three years are significantly intercorrelated. The spatial pattern consists of low values in the old areas of the Federal District of Benito Juarez and Cuauhtemoc as well as in Chalco, Iztapalapa, and several adjacent municipios. The highest fertility is in the northern section of the ZMCM especially Cuautitlan Izcalli and Tecamac as well as in the western municipios of Huixquilucan, Cuajimalpa and Magdalena Contreras. These correspond to many of the zones of population expansion (see Maps 3.5 and 3.7 of relative growth 1950-90). Presumably the other expansion zones tended to grow more through migration than fertility.

Cumulative fertility indicates fertility rates relative to childbearing women in the population. Children ever born to women 12 years and older (Table 4.6 and Map 4.10) reveals a ring-like pattern with higher fertility at the periphery and lower fertility in the center. Cumulative fertility may be further disaggregated by age group of women, which reflects cohorts, i.e. generations, of childbearing. Generational differences are so great that fertility for young women age 20-29 is uncorrelated with that for older women age 45+. Older women account for more childbearing due to both higher fertility rates and longer exposure periods. Older women's geographic pattern resembles that for children ever born (r = 0.58), with a ring effect and higher levels at the periphery. For younger women with an average childbearing of only 1.3, the pattern is quite different, with high values in the southern Federal District and far parts of the northeast and southeast metropolitan "arms."

In 1990, there is more consistency between the cohorts. Both younger and older 1990 fertility patterns include the ring already noted for children ever born for 1970 and 1990 and for fertility of older women in 1970 (see Maps 4.11 - 4.14). These rates are all significantly correlated, for instance, the fertility for women 20-29 and 45+ is correlated at   r =   0.55. The divergent pattern for younger women in 1970 may relate to the great changes in contraceptive practice that were taking place at that time, so the geographic pattern of early childbearing was inconsistently altered, but returned after completed fertility to the normative ring-like pattern (i.e. as reflected in women 45+ in 1990 in Map 4.14.)

There are remarkably strong correlations between the "normative" pattern of fertility and social rank/population variables (see Table 4.3). In fact, there are significant correlations with every social rank and population variable. The direction of correlations indicates that lower fertility is associated with higher social rank, higher female labor force participation, and higher population and population density. In other words, areas of the conurbation that have dense, well-off population with women working have lower fertility and vice versa. The close correspondence of fertility with social rank and women's labor force participation is well known in numerous literature studies in Mexico as well as many other nations (Rubin-Kurtzman, 1989; Holian, 1983; Kasarda, Billy, and West, 1986). Fertility reduction with higher population and density reflects a broader literature finding that higher urbanization leads to lower fertility. In this case, the general finding can be extrapolated to Megacity, where more dense parts of the Megacity have lower fertility.

Table 4.4 Population of Mexico Metropolis, Rates of Growth, and Components of Change, 1940-1990

Year	Population	Decennial Population Increase	Average Annual Rate of Population Increase	Average Decennial Crude Mortality Rate**	Average Decennial Crude Fertility Rate**	Federal District Average Decennial Net Migration Rate**
1940	1,802,679	1,334,920	5.54			
1950	3,137,599	2,114,356	5.15	12.9	44.7	14.1
1960	5,251,955	3,547,984	5.16	9.7	41.4	5.4
1970	8,799,939	4,554,332	4.17	7.3	37.0	8.2
1980	13,354,271	2,086,475	1.45	5.6	30.1	-13.6
1990	15,440,746					
1970-1990			2.81	NA	NA	-2.9

*	Annual percent rate of population increase averaged for the decade.
**	Per thousand
Note:	The decade starts in the year on the left. For each column except Population, the value applies to the whole decade and is listed for the year that begins the decade, e.g. average rate of population increase for the 1940s is listed under the year 1940.
Note:	The mortality and fertility rates listed for the year, i.e. for the 1980's, are the average rates for the two metropolitan states, hence they only approximate Mexico City's vital rates.

Source: Modified from Garza, 1987 and INEGI, 1992.

**Figure 4.3 Crude Fertility Rate, Federal District,
State of Mexico, and Nation, 1900 - 1990**

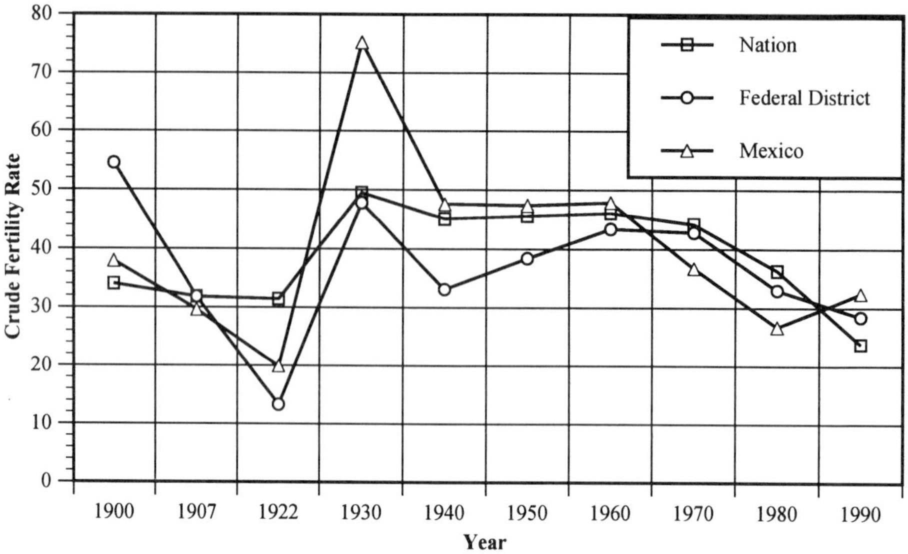

Source: INEGI: *Estadisticas Historicas de Mexico*, Vol 1, 1994

Table 4.5 Crude Fertility, 1950-1980

No.	Area	Crude Fertility Rate 1950-1960	Crude Fertility Rate 1960-1970	Crude Fertility Rate 1970-1980
2	Alvaro Obregon	46.7	43.0	37.5
5	Atizapan de Zaragoza	47.6	37.9	35.4
9	Azcapotzalco	48.0	44.5	38.8
10	Benito Juarez	39.0	37.5	32.6
11	Chalco	45.8	37.4	35.0
13	Chicoloapan	45.8	37.4	35.0
15	Chimalhuacan	45.8	37.4	35.0
16	Coacalco	47.9	42.0	39.3
18	Coyoacan	44.9	41.9	36.5
20	Cuajimalpa	52.8	49.2	42.9
21	Cuauhtemoc	52.8	35.8	31.1
22	Cuautitlan	52.6	46.4	43.4
23	Cuautitlan Izcalli	52.6	46.4	43.4
24	Ecatepec	51.7	41.1	38.5
26	Gustavo A. Madero	47.9	44.9	39.1
28	Huixquilucan	54.6	47.7	44.6
30	Ixtapaluca	45.8	37.4	35.0
31	Iztacalco	47.9	43.9	38.2
32	Iztapalapa	45.7	46.1	40.2
36	Magdalena Contreras	50.8	47.9	41.7
38	Miguel Hidalgo	41.4	40.3	35.1
39	Milpa Alta	45.7	42.9	37.4
40	Naucalpan	43.8	38.2	35.7
43	Nicolas Romero	47.6	37.9	35.4
48	Paz, La	45.8	37.3	35.0
50	Tecamac	52.6	46.4	43.4
61	Tlahuac	50.9	44.4	38.7
63	Tlalnepantla	45.5	41.8	39.1
64	Tlalpan	42.8	41.0	35.7
66	Tultitlan	51.1	43.6	40.8
67	Venustiano Carranza	47.4	42.4	36.9
68	Xochimilco	45.0	41.9	36.5
Mean		47.8	42.0	37.9
Median		47.6	42.0	37.5
S.D.		3.7	3.8	3.4
C.V.		7.77	9.13	8.94
Minimum		39.0	35.8	31.1
Maximum		54.6	49.2	44.6

Definition: Crude fertility rate is the ratio of births averaged for the decade to the
population at the midpoint of the decade.

Source: Garza, *Atlas of Mexico City,* 1987.

104

Map 4.7
Crude Fertility Rate, 1950-1960

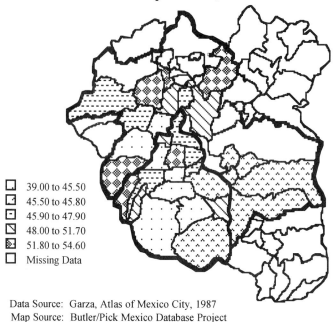

39.00 to 45.50
45.50 to 45.80
45.90 to 47.90
48.00 to 51.70
51.80 to 54.60
Missing Data

Data Source: Garza, Atlas of Mexico City, 1987
Map Source: Butler/Pick Mexico Database Project

Map 4.8
Crude Fertility Rate, 1960-1970

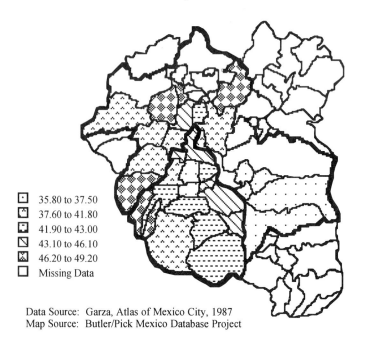

35.80 to 37.50
37.60 to 41.80
41.90 to 43.00
43.10 to 46.10
46.20 to 49.20
Missing Data

Data Source: Garza, Atlas of Mexico City, 1987
Map Source: Butler/Pick Mexico Database Project

Map 4.9
Crude Fertility Rate, 1970-1980

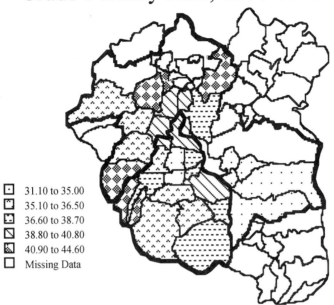

31.10 to 35.00
35.10 to 36.50
36.60 to 38.70
38.80 to 40.80
40.90 to 44.60
Missing Data

Data Source: Garza, Atlas of Mexico City, 1987
Map Source: Butler/Pick Mexico Database Project

106

Table 4.6 Cumulative Fertility, 1990

No.	Area	Ages 20 -29	Ages 45+
1	Acolman	1.3634	5.0134
2	Alvaro Obregon	0.0640	4.7299
3	Amecameca	1.4362	5.1268
4	Atenco	1.7394	6.0026
5	Atizapan de Zaragoza	1.2269	5.0913
6	Atlautla	1.8486	6.1199
7	Axapusco	1.6903	7.0658
8	Ayapango	1.6067	6.0427
9	Azcapotzalco	0.8803	4.6524
10	Benito Juarez	0.5586	3.0269
11	Chalco	1.8336	5.7148
12	Chiautla	1.3898	5.5771
13	Chicoloapan	1.5801	5.7899
14	Chiconcuac	1.2698	5.6979
15	Chimalhuacan	1.8197	5.9555
16	Coacalco	1.0897	4.9022
17	Cocotitlan	1.3016	5.5548
18	Coyoacan	0.7828	4.1654
19	Coyotepec	1.6403	6.3593
20	Cuajimalpa	1.1676	5.6711
21	Cuauhtemoc	0.8597	3.3247
22	Cuautitlan	1.2822	5.7398
23	Cuautitlan Izcalli	1.2488	5.2737
24	Ecatepec	1.3100	5.6264
25	Ecatzingo	2.1422	6.4120
26	Gustavo A. Madero	0.9558	4.8621
27	Huehuetoca	1.6963	6.6637
28	Huixquilucan	1.1407	5.0876
29	Isidro Fabela	1.3225	5.5494
30	Ixtapaluca	1.6171	6.0341
31	Iztacalco	0.9193	4.8953
32	Iztapalapa	1.1731	5.2011
33	Jaltenco	1.4645	5.7857
34	Jilotzingo	1.5744	5.4452
35	Juchitepec	0.8328	5.9068
36	Magdalena Contreras	0.5050	4.9404
37	Melchor Ocampo	1.4462	5.9451
38	Miguel Hidalgo	0.7343	3.5842
39	Milpa Alta	1.3312	4.7502
40	Naucalpan	1.1051	4.8119
41	Nextlalpan	1.7039	6.0199
42	Nezahualcoyotl	1.1449	5.7446
43	Nicolas Romero	1.4868	5.9689
44	Nopaltepec	1.7089	6.6613
45	Otumba	1.6119	0.8740
46	Ozumba	1.5506	5.7687
47	Papalotla	1.1151	5.2881
48	Paz, La	1.4228	6.0197
49	San Martin de las P.	1.3809	5.9276
50	Tecamac	1.4256	6.0497
51	Temamatla	1.5566	5.7425
52	Temascalapa	1.6817	6.3728
53	Tenango del Aire	1.4545	5.5773
54	Teoloyucan	1.5685	6.7557

Table 4.6 Cumulative Fertility, 1990 (Continued)

No.	Area	Ages 20 -29	Ages 45+	
55	Teotihuacan	1.4571	5.9154	
56	Tepetlaoxtoc	1.4561	5.9590	
57	Tepetlixpa	1.6098	5.4214	
58	Tepotzotlan	1.4762	6.0645	
59	Texcoco	1.2768	5.5705	
60	Tezoyuca	1.3981	5.3236	
61	Tlahuac	1.2949	5.2521	
62	Tlalmanalco	0.5620	5.4765	
63	Tlalnepantla	1.0527	5.1954	
64	Tlalpan	1.0168	4.4682	
65	Tultepec	1.5625	5.9518	
66	Tultitlan	1.3951	5.5629	
67	Venustiano Carranza	0.9311	4.4223	
68	Xochimilco	1.1762	4.7399	
69	Zumpango	1.5012	6.1661	
Mean		1.3178	5.4255	
Median		1.3898	5.5773	
S.D.		0.3630	0.9316	
C.V.		27.5447	17.1716	
Minimum		0.0640	0.8740	
Maximum		2.1422	7.0658	

Definition: Cumulative fertility is defined as the number of children
ever born to women in a designated age group to the total number of
women in that age group.

Source: INEGI, 1990 Census of Population, Resumen General, Table 24.

Map 4.10
Children Ever Born to Women
12 Years and Older, 1990

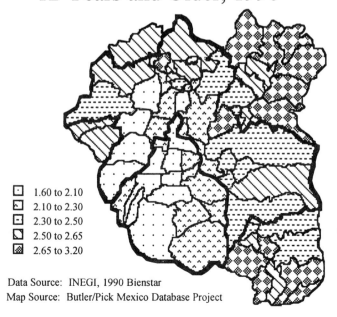

⊡	1.60 to 2.10
⊡	2.10 to 2.30
⊡	2.30 to 2.50
◩	2.50 to 2.65
▨	2.65 to 3.20

Data Source: INEGI, 1990 Bienstar
Map Source: Butler/Pick Mexico Database Project

108

Map 4.11
Cumulative Fertility of Women
Age 20 - 29, 1970

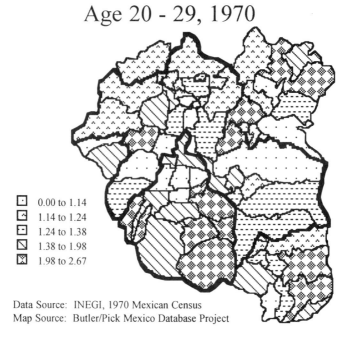

- 0.00 to 1.14
- 1.14 to 1.24
- 1.24 to 1.38
- 1.38 to 1.98
- 1.98 to 2.67

Data Source: INEGI, 1970 Mexican Census
Map Source: Butler/Pick Mexico Database Project

Map 4.12
Cumulative Fertility of Women
Age 20 - 29, 1990

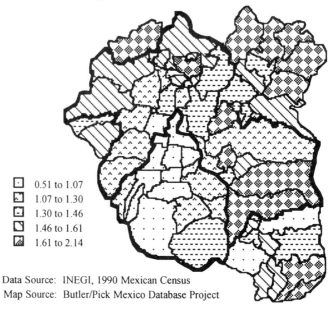

- 0.51 to 1.07
- 1.07 to 1.30
- 1.30 to 1.46
- 1.46 to 1.61
- 1.61 to 2.14

Data Source: INEGI, 1990 Mexican Census
Map Source: Butler/Pick Mexico Database Project

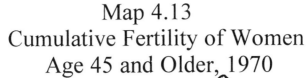

Map 4.13
Cumulative Fertility of Women
Age 45 and Older, 1970

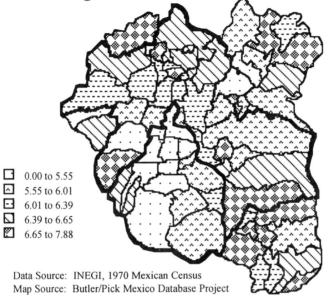

- 0.00 to 5.55
- 5.55 to 6.01
- 6.01 to 6.39
- 6.39 to 6.65
- 6.65 to 7.88

Data Source: INEGI, 1970 Mexican Census
Map Source: Butler/Pick Mexico Database Project

Map 4.14
Cumulative Fertility of Women
Age 45 and Older, 1990

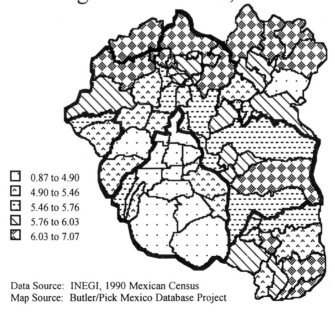

- 0.87 to 4.90
- 4.90 to 5.46
- 5.46 to 5.76
- 5.76 to 6.03
- 6.03 to 7.07

Data Source: INEGI, 1990 Mexican Census
Map Source: Butler/Pick Mexico Database Project

Urbanism/Familism Cluster Analysis

The dimensions of marriage, fertility, and family are brought together through a cluster analysis of Urbanism/Familism. The urbanism/familism variable group consists of cumulative fertility to women age 20-29, percent of persons in a free union, percent separated and divorced, and the ratio of women economically active (see Table 1.2). These variables encompass many aspects of fertility and marriage already discussed in this chapter. In addition, the dimension of women economically active is introduced. The definition of ratio of women economically active is economically active female population age 12+ divided by total economically active population age 12+. The variable is discussed in depth in Chapter 10 under "economic activity."

Economic activity of women is highly relevant to urbanism/familism, since economic activity is an important factor in family dynamics, fertility, and childbearing (Kasarda et al., 1986) and influenced by marital status (Kasarda et al., 1986; Quilodrán, 1991). Kasarda et al. provide a series of alternative models that interrelate all or some of the variables of female employment, fertility, contraception, age at marriage, and education. They consider cause and effect, intermediate factors, and explanation of effects. Fundamental to their theories are that higher status, greater education, and higher female labor force participation are linked to lower fertility in a wide variety of models and circumstances. This interrelatedness of the urbanism/familism variables justifies its adoption for cluster grouping. Also, as mentioned in Chapter 1 and discussed in greater depth in Chapter 12, urbanism/familism is recognized as a fundamental cornerstone of social area analysis (Shevky and Bell, 1955).

The results of the cluster analysis for urbanism/familism point to the traditional urban ring theory modified somewhat. As seen in Map 4.15 and Table 4.7, there is an urban core, which consists of three adjacent clusters, a tight inner ring, a broader ring that intermixes two clusters, and the semi-urban periphery consisting of transition zones and fringe zones. There is a resemblance in general form to the overall cluster pattern discussed in Chapter 1.

The cluster zones show remarkable differentiation. As seen in Table 4.4, the three central zones (Zones 1, 2, and 3) have common low fertility and one or more of other "modern" urbanism/familism features. They are very populous, having a combined population of 5.6 million, i.e. about a third of the Megacity. The most "modern" cluster zone is Zone 1, consisting of the old central districts of Cuauhtemoc, Miguel Hidalgo, and Coyoacan. Although old, these districts encompass the heart of the business downtown areas of the metropolis, as well as some wealthy residential areas. On our urbanism/familism gradient, Zone 1 has very low fertility (40 percent below the Megacity mean), very high proportions of population in free union and separated/divorced status (24 and 62 percent above the mean respectively), and very high female economic activity (56 percent elevated). These dramatic extremes in urbanism/familism are at levels that almost resemble advanced nations such as the United States. This makes sense because families living in this zone are largely affluent and have often adopted life styles conforming to advanced countries.

The other two central cluster zones (Zone 2 and Zone 3) are predominantly in the northern and central Federal District surrounding Zone 1. These two zones have some "modern" urbanism/familism features, but not uniformly. For instance, Zone 2 in the northern Federal District has a high proportion in free union and fairly low fertility. By contrast, Zone 3 in the central Federal District has the lowest fertility of any zone, in particular under half of the Megacity fertility mean. Together, these zones constitute a "core" characterized by "modern" family life including low fertility and greater marital alternatives although still low by comparison with advanced nations. A visitor from the U.S. middle class to a typical family in the core zones might feel a sense of familiarity.

The distinctive inner ring (Zone 4) encompasses eleven delegations and municipios in the Federal District and State of Mexico to the north. The inner ring is very populous with 5.7 million persons or about 40 percent of the Megacity. It may be characterized as "modal," with fertility, marital status, and women work parameters about equal to the Megacity means. The modal characteristic implies family and fertility values and norms standard for the Megacity. It is important to point out that "modal" for Mexico City implies "modern" urbanism/familism relative to Mexico as a whole (see Table 4.4).

One can view a more irregular outer semi-circle (termed "outer ring") that is mostly located to the north of the inner ring, but with two delegations wrapping around to the southeast in the Federal District (Xochimilco and Iztacalco). The populous outer ring contains 3.05 million residents (one fifth of the total). It includes two contiguous zones (5 and 6). They are fairly modal, with one exception -- the economic activity of women is quite low. In particular, it is one third lower than the Megacity average. The lowering of women's economic activity is consistent with a gradation of zones from central core to inner ring to outer ring.

The last three cluster zones (7, 8, and 10) predominantly consist of the semi-rural extensions to the northeast and southeast, as well as fringe area due west. These zones also include the interior municipios of Chalco, Chimalhuacan, Atenco, and Nextlalpan. The largely fringe areas are relatively unpopulated with 1.03 million persons. These areas have the highest fertility that increases moving outward. At the extreme in Ecatzingo (Zone 10), with a fertility rate of 2.14, i.e. 63 percent elevated above the mean. It truly is the periphery and verges on some rural qualities. The high fertility approaches rural levels.

At the same time in these outer zones, the progression of female economic activity is from the lowest economic activity in the "transition zone" (Zone 8) of about half the Megacity mean to somewhat higher but still very low values at the extremes. Reversal of economic activity progression in these outer zones versus what one would expect from modernization may relate to particular forms of employment located in the "transition zone" versus the extreme fringe. By contrast, marital status indicators are consistently modal for the two outermost zones and reduced from the mean for the "transition zone." Overall, these three outer zones are "backward" in urbanism/familism, and do not follow a systematic progression as they move outwards. The lesser modernity must be put in the context of the nation as a whole, for which these zones would appear more rather than less advanced.

Table 4.7 Urbanism/Familism Cluster Means

Variable / Cluster No.	1	2	3	4	5	6	7	8	9	10	Mexico City
Total Population 1990	1,642,894	2,710,706	1,278,589	5,713,245	2,103,505	950,165	641,974	379,590	14,270	5,808	15,440,746
Cumulative Fertility to Women, 20-29	0.79	0.92	0.57	1.23	1.31	1.45	1.75	1.59	0.83	2.14	1.33
Free Union	0.1031	0.1030	0.0706	0.0807	0.0987	0.0706	0.0843	0.0782	0.1311	0.0821	0.0844
Separated and Divorced	0.0389	0.0303	0.0319	0.0265	0.0238	0.0171	0.0284	0.0173	0.0171	0.0216	0.0239
Ratio of Economically Active Women	0.3694	0.2704	0.2601	0.2145	0.1573	0.1488	0.1520	0.1253	0.0624	0.1851	0.1798

Note: Values for Population 1990 are cluster totals. All other values are cluster means.

Cluster 1	Cluster 2	Cluster 3	Cluster 4	Cluster 5	Cluster 6	Cluster 7	Cluster 8	Cluster 9	Cluster 10
Coyoacan	Azcapotzalco	Alvaro Obregon	Atizapan de Zaragoza	Acolman	Amecameca	Atenco	Ayapango	Juchitepec	Ecatzingo
Cuauhtemoc	Gustavo A. Madero	Benito Juarez	Coacalco	Chiautla	Jaltenco	Atlautla	Chicoloapan		
Miguel Hidalgo	Iztacalco	Magdalena Contreras	Cuajimalpa	Chiconcuac	Melchor Ocampo	Axapusco	Coyotepec		
	Venustiano Carranza	Tlalmanalco	Huixquilucan	Cocotitlan	Nicolas Romero	Chalco	Ixtapaluca		
			Iztapalapa	Cuautitlan	Paz, La	Chimalhuacan	Jilotzingo		
			Naucalpan	Cuautitlan Izcalli	Tecamac	Huehuetoca	Otumba		
			Nezahualcoyotl	Ecatepec	Tenango del Aire	Nextlalpan	Ozumba		
			Papalotla	Isidro Fabela	Teotihuacan	Nopaltepec	Temamatla		
			Tlalnepantla	Milpa Alta	Tepetlaoxtoc	Temascalapa	Teoloyucan		
			Tlalpan	San Martin de las P.	Tepotzotlan		Tepetlixpa		
			Xochimilco	Texcoco	Tezoyuca		Tultepec		
				Tlahuac	Tultitlan				
					Zumpango				

Map 4.15
Urbanism/Familism Clusters

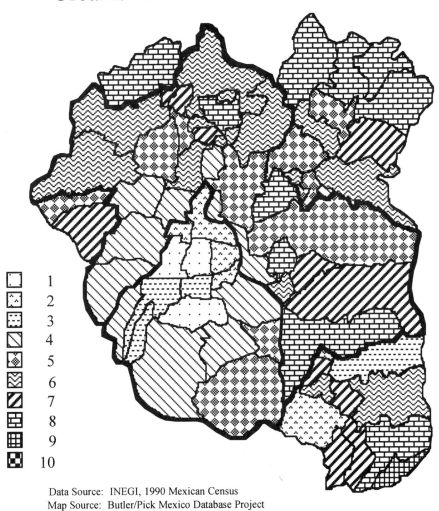

Data Source: INEGI, 1990 Mexican Census
Map Source: Butler/Pick Mexico Database Project

Conclusions

Marital status, fertility, and family are crucial dimensions for Mexico Megacity in both micro and macro aspects. People of the Megacity live in the behavioral environment of the family and respond to these dimensions as cornerstones of socialization. In a macro sense, the dimensions are important in encompassing the fertility component of change. That component of change has been one of the two principal factors in melding historical population growth and re-distribution of the metropolis.

The Megacity historically experienced lower marriage rates and proportions than the nation as a whole. This is logical, since traditional marriage would be expected to diminish somewhat in the most urban and modernized location. Free union as a marital form takes on special significance and greater prevalence in Latin America. It is generally limited in duration leading to civil marriage or dissolution. Marital alternatives of divorce and separation have been on the increase in the metropolis since 1970 and continue upward. However, their prevalence is still low, since the starting point in the 1970s was extremely low, due partly to the strength of the Catholic tradition.

Marital dimensions are mostly inter-correlated. Free union and divorce are closely related to social status. Marriage and free union are opposite of each other which makes sense since couples in union are in one or the other statuses. Marriage, and especially separation, are much less correlated with socioeconomic dimensions. This may be due to local marriage customs within the Megacity creating unique geographical patterns.

Fertility has decreased in Mexico Megacity since 1960. The crude fertility rate has been stable geographically over the past thirty years, while decreasing substantially in level. In 1990, it was highest to the immediate north and west of the Federal District. One explanation for the elevation is the high marriage rates in those areas.

By contrast, cumulative fertility in 1990 reveals a concentric pattern with lower cumulative fertility in the core radiating out to higher cumulative fertility at the metropolitan fringe. Chalco and other selected municipios also have heightened cumulative fertility. In 1990, the cumulative fertility for younger and older childbearing women are highly correlated.

The reason that the crude and cumulative fertility spatial patterns differ relates to differences in the age structure. Examining Map 3.10, the younger population shows a consistent concentric pattern with older population in the center and younger population on the periphery, except in the southwest. The age structure explains differences between crude and cumulative fertility patterns, since cumulative fertility encompasses age. It is important to note that the pattern of higher cumulative fertility in the outer periphery of the metropolis differs from U.S. large cities, in which fertility is high in core areas particularly those of predominant Hispanic and black ethnicity and low in the outlying "suburbs."

Urbanism/familism blends several dimensions of family, fertility, and female economic activity. It reflects a major construct of social area analysis. Our findings show that the Megacity groups into very distinctive zones based on urbanism/familism. The pattern of clusters resembles classic ring theory, modified in terms of Latin America (Griffin and Ford, 1983). In particular, the more "modern" urbanism/familism zones are in the central core and more "traditional" zones on the periphery. Cluster analysis reveals that only certain components change between zones, but overall a concentric pattern is present. The results for Mexico Megacity must be qualified since parts of the metropolis that appear very old and traditional in urbanism/familism are actually average or better based on the nation as a whole.

5

Migration

Introduction

Migration has been a major component of change in the population growth and development of Mexico City. In the second half of the twentieth century, fertility has lowered substantially and net migration has changed from inflow to outflow. The reversal of net migration is the result of over-urbanization and environmental degradation of the metropolis (Tudela, 1991; Mumme, 1991; WHO, 1992; Ezcurra and Mazari-Hiriat, 1996).

Early in the century, migration contributed to population build-up of the central core of Mexico City, including the original core in the delegations of Miguel Hidalgo, Cuauhtemoc, and Benito Juarez that now contain the city's cultural and governmental hub. Migration continued to be very large into the Federal District past mid-century and into the 70s but reversed in the 80s. Enlargement of the metropolitan area is reflected in over spill of the Federal District into the surrounding State of Mexico starting in the 60s. In the 70s and 80s, about five million people migrated on a net basis into the State of Mexico.

The expansion of the Megacity from the Federal District outward included substantial flows directly from the Federal District into the State of Mexico. Many of these migrants sought land on which to construct housing, since land was increasingly a scarce and precious commodity in the Federal District. Less well off migrants often simply claimed land that was abandoned or unoccupied in the nearby State of Mexico municipios (Lourdes Vega, 1991; Hiernaux Nicolas, 1991; Schteingart, 1991). Housing developers built up areas for better off migrants (Schteingart, 1991). The size of this migration stream is reflected in the dominance for Mexico as a whole of the Federal District-to-State of Mexico migration stream. In the late 70s and late 80s, it was by far the largest interstate migration stream for all of Mexico, exceeding other streams by a factor of 5 to 6 times.

Mexico City has a low proportion born in the metropolis. This reflects high inmigration rates over the past century. It corresponds to other regions in Mexico that have had substantial inflow of migrants, such as the Baja California, Colima, and Quintana Roo (Pick and Butler, 1994). Within the Megacity, the more rapidly growing areas north of the Federal District have the lowest native to state, often less than half native.

The foreign born population averages about a quarter of one percent in Mexico City, which may be surprising for the nation's most cosmopolitan location. The low proportion reflects restrictive immigration and naturalization policies in this century as well as economic barriers to migration from less developed nations. Not surprisingly, foreign born population is more concentrated in the wealthy metropolitan center and much sparser on the periphery.

The bi-directional flows from the Federal District to the State of Mexico and vice versa have been influential in determining population and housing build-up and de-concentration. The pattern of migration into the State of Mexico is highly consistent over the past quarter century. It has been most heavily concentrated on the municipios to the north of the Federal District in a rapidly growing and now very large industrial zone. Large migration flows have also existed to municipios surrounding the Federal District to the northwest and east. The much smaller volume of migrants in the opposite stream have tended to locate in the northwestern Federal District.

In the late 80s inmigration to the Megacity was concentrated in State of Mexico municipios surrounding the Federal District, with especially high inmigration into the growing industrial zone north of the Federal District.

Major regions sending migrants to Mexico City have been the rest of the Central regions, Veracruz, Puebla, and the South region. Although they vary a little, immigration patterns by different origin region resemble each other and the overall pattern of inmigration. Thus, region of origin does not appear important in differentiating inmigration patterns.

The spatial patterns of migration are linked to many other dimensions covered in this volume, especially to population and density, good quality of housing, and economic prosperity.

In summary, migration has been a huge component of growth and change in Mexico City in the second half of the century. Although it lowered in recent decades, it remains a large force. It has been more important than the other major change component of fertility in determining metropolitan settlement patterns, since fertility has much less spatial variation. The areas of the largest inmigration have moved outward from the center of the metropolis over time. This largely reflects the desire of central residents to seek more affordable housing and better living conditions further outwards.

Correlations of Migration Characteristics

This chapter focuses on migration variables available in the 1990 Mexican Census (INEGI, 1992). These variables are defined in Table 5.1 and values for most of them appear in Table 5.2. These nine variables do not include outmigration, since the 1990 population census did not include questions on municipio or delegation of prior residence.

Migration dimensions are strongly related to each other and moderately related to the overall set of cluster variables. It is plausible that migration dimensions are related, since they all reflect inmigration to Mexico City, either recently or from time of birth. However, the strong intercorrelations of the migration set confirms that inflow patterns have been consistent, whether by time of migration, gender of migrant, place of origin, or native-born versus foreign born status. Consistency among migration variables is supported by other cross-sectional and longitudinal studies of Mexican migration (Butler et al., 1987; Pick et al., 1990; Butler, Pick, and Fukurai, in press).

As seen in Table 5.3, inmigration variables are intercorrelated with only a few exceptions. The largest exception is the lack of correlation for the sex ratio of inmigration. In fact, it is related to only two of the ten other migration variables. The association with male inmigration in the last five years is inherent in the definition of inmigration sex ratio, which has male inmigration in the numerator. The inverse relation of sex ratio and foreign inmigration is unexplained. Another variable with fewer migration intercorrelations is foreign inmigration. The lack of association overall may be the result of the small proportion of foreign inmigrants relative to all inmigrants and to the total population. For instance, on the average foreign born population accounts for only 0.26 percent of the population and one percent of the non-native population. The small size reduces the absolute impacts of the foreign born dimension on other migration variables.

The migration dimensions include inmigration from the major sending places of the Central remainder region, Veracruz, Puebla, and South region. These factors are highly interrelated (see Table 5.3), with the exception of the non-significant correlation for inmigration of the Central remainder region and Puebla (however, that correlation is close to significant at $r = 0.210$ with $p = 0.08$). The conclusion is that the place of origin of migrants to the Megacity has little influence on the spatial patterning of inmigration.

Migration variables have weaker and less constant associations with the cluster set of variables. They are related to population size and density, population growth 1970-90, and to income, but inversely with factors of poor housing (see Table 5.4). This underscores that inmigrants are attracted to the more built-up sections of Mexico City and less to the sparsely populated periphery. For one thing, there are more jobs and economic opportunities in the built-up core and fewer in the periphery. The association of migration with income at destination is one noted in several Mexican migration studies (e.g.,   Greenwood and

Ladman, 1978). The inverse relationship with poor housing is not surprising. Housing has been a critical dimension in determining the growth and evolution of many areas within the Megacity (Schteingart, 1991; Tudela, 1991), including Nezahualcóyotl (Lourdes Vega, 1991), Chalco (Hiernaux Nicolas, 1991), and others. Often the economic improvement of areas has been tied to the evolution of housing improvements (Schteingart, 1991). Inmigrants likely consider Mexico City housing quality in deciding on destination zone and on settlement after arrival.

Inmigration variables are not related to population growth 1950-70. This reflects major changes in population growth patterns between the 50s/60s and 70s/80s that were discussed in Chapters 2 and 3. The lack of association with indigenous language may reflect the small indigenous proportion of the population (one percent on average), so that ethnicity is less of a determinant of destination choice than other socioeconomic dimensions.

Table 5.1 Definitions of Migration Variables

Name Variable	Definition of Variable
Population Native to State	The ratio of population born in the state to all population for a small area
Foreign Born Population	The ratio of population born in a foreign country to the total population for a small area
Inmigration in Past Five Years	The ratio of inmigrants to an area in the past five years to the total population for a small area
Sex Ratio of Inmigration	The ratio of male inmigrants to female inmigrants in the past five years
Region-Specific Inmigration	The ratio of population born in a designated region or state to the total population for a small area

Table 5.2 Migration Characteristics of Migration Variables

Area	Population Native to State	Population Foreign Born	Immigration 1965-70	Immigration 1985-90	Sex Ratio 1985-90	Immigration from Puebla 1985-90	Immigrants from Cent. Rem 1985-90	Immigration from S. Region 1985-90	Immigration from Veracruz 1985-90
Acolman	0.76280	0.00074	0.13027	0.04021	0.88316	0.00199	0.00342	0.00166	0.00270
Alvaro Obregon	0.76055	0.00774	0.09830	0.03459	0.65864	0.00402	0.00470	0.00491	0.00268
Amecameca	0.90653	0.00058	0.03017	0.02335	0.97275	0.00176	0.00328	0.00176	0.00091
Atenco	0.89288	0.00019	0.02289	0.02022	0.89399	0.00146	0.00203	0.00127	0.00066
Atizapan de Zaragoza	0.44401	0.00549	0.37038	0.11220	0.93551	0.00385	0.00659	0.00607	0.00414
Atlautla	0.93382	0.00153	0.00642	0.02011	0.89309	0.00126	0.00290	0.00079	0.00042
Axapusco	0.81067	0.00006	0.03436	0.03487	0.97097	0.00051	0.00063	0.00070	0.00063
Ayapango	0.85162	0.00071	0.01856	0.04293	0.89541	0.00236	0.00495	0.00047	0.00024
Azcapotzalco	0.76917	0.00170	0.10526	0.03175	0.40687	0.00184	0.00426	0.00383	0.00314
Benito Juarez	0.67452	0.02471	0.09802	0.05856	0.73323	0.00517	0.00772	0.00822	0.00491
Chalco	0.50557	0.00056	0.05175	0.16259	0.99794	0.00944	0.00568	0.01241	0.00516
Chiautla	0.85830	0.00108	0.01858	0.03868	0.94895	0.00318	0.00433	0.00115	0.00224
Chicoloapan	0.51028	0.00047	0.14446	0.10275	0.97178	0.00553	0.00513	0.00459	0.00405
Chiconcuac	0.94767	0.00000	0.01607	0.01213	0.80381	0.00176	0.00282	0.00127	0.00049
Chimalhuacan	0.53936	0.00033	0.06158	0.08377	1.00232	0.00775	0.00518	0.01270	0.00425
Coacalco	0.27951	0.00155	0.47117	0.17022	0.99279	0.00279	0.00560	0.00337	0.00320
Cocotitlan	0.92972	0.00012	0.01902	0.01512	0.75549	0.00050	0.00112	0.00062	0.00099
Coyoacan	0.73247	0.00965	0.11535	0.04037	0.70908	0.00388	0.00530	0.00762	0.00195
Coyotepec	0.86107	0.00020	0.02925	0.03182	1.06995	0.00155	0.00556	0.00168	0.00192
Cuajimalpa	0.79771	0.00655	0.06956	0.03442	0.67679	0.00315	0.00404	0.00334	0.00194
Cuauhtemoc	0.69994	0.00412	0.11368	0.04796	0.97985	0.00343	0.00560	0.00688	0.00477
Cuautitlan	0.61206	0.00227	0.43482	0.10440	0.92870	0.01531	0.00612	0.00268	0.00594
Cuautitlan Izcalli	0.40590	0.00184	0.15675	0.15592	0.99728	0.00279	0.00590	0.00149	0.00401
Ecatepec	0.34427	0.00067	0.38792	0.15102	0.97770	0.00451	0.00747	0.00544	0.00420
Ecatzingo	0.96815	0.00000	0.00715	0.00430	0.67266	0.00034	0.00172	0.00086	0.00034
Gustavo A. Madero	0.75116	0.00215	0.10550	0.03488	0.89671	0.00279	0.00545	0.00412	0.00320
Huehuetoca	0.59517	0.00055	0.08369	0.19460	0.95615	0.00227	0.01018	0.00274	0.00376
Huixquilucan	0.54812	0.01825	0.18179	0.10564	0.74716	0.00684	0.00772	0.00772	0.00342
Isidro Fabela	0.90983	0.00000	0.00693	0.02408	1.04918	0.00019	0.00077	0.00135	0.00058
Ixtapaluca	0.54559	0.00076	0.13066	0.11646	0.04741	0.00817	0.00498	0.00748	0.00371

Table 5.2 Migration Characteristics of Migration Variables (Continued)

Area	Population Native to State	Population Foreign Born	Immigration 1965-70	Immigration 1985-90	Sex Ratio 1985-90	Inmigration from Puebla 1985-90	Inmigrants from Cent. Rem 1985-90	Inmigration from S. Region 1985-90	Inmigration from Veracruz 1985-90
Iztacalco	0.77142	0.00173	0.10273	0.02825	0.86407	0.00297	0.00521	0.00564	0.00248
Iztapalapa	0.73807	0.00126	0.10238	0.03667	0.96687	0.00462	0.00407	0.00721	0.00301
Jaltenco	0.49656	0.00057	0.02976	0.13726	0.97614	0.00219	0.00574	0.00206	0.00039
Jilotzingo	0.82366	0.00033	0.02075	0.04095	0.93286	0.00089	0.00189	0.00211	0.00178
Juchitepec	0.94954	0.00000	0.02180	0.01233	0.67498	0.00063	0.00301	0.00035	0.00035
Magdalena Contreras	0.77989	0.00736	0.05437	0.03369	0.66507	0.00446	0.00732	0.00497	0.00271
Melchor Ocampo	0.77919	0.00038	0.05963	0.03923	0.97606	0.00134	0.00719	0.00306	0.00157
Miguel Hidalgo	0.70624	0.03150	0.11807	0.06315	0.68790	0.00573	0.00728	0.00760	0.00466
Milpa Alta	0.89289	0.00039	0.02659	0.02118	0.89718	0.00228	0.00330	0.00368	0.00204
Naucalpan	0.46184	0.00733	0.35062	0.08508	1.09110	0.00558	0.00773	0.01036	0.00811
Nextlalpan	0.77841	0.00065	0.06445	0.06255	0.86664	0.00129	0.00867	0.00268	0.00424
Nezahualcoyotl	0.39814	0.00078	0.33456	0.07878	0.95440	0.00465	0.00391	0.00679	0.00335
Nicolas Romero	0.68641	0.00040	0.08606	0.04814	0.96413	0.00215	0.00322	0.00285	0.00249
Nopaltepec	0.88384	0.00000	0.02275	0.03095	0.89534	0.00076	0.00611	0.00096	0.00038
Otumba	0.88852	0.00032	0.02616	0.03307	0.94125	0.00096	0.00536	0.00115	0.00110
Ozumba	0.93192	0.00033	0.03492	0.01501	0.93654	0.00138	0.00266	0.00105	0.00011
Papalotla	0.81818	0.00293	0.05882	0.05111	0.93793	0.00042	0.00880	0.00084	0.00168
Paz, La	0.52836	0.00071	0.31264	0.07456	1.00311	0.00716	0.00482	0.00855	0.00519
San Martin de las P.	0.89597	0.00044	0.02265	0.02676	0.98705	0.00111	0.00553	0.00111	0.00118
Tecamac	0.49981	0.00144	0.12197	0.09207	1.05746	0.00437	0.00977	0.00441	0.00371
Temamatla	0.69866	0.00056	0.05204	0.09411	1.22376	0.00559	0.01249	0.00969	0.00335
Temascalapa	0.87507	0.00068	0.01046	0.03702	0.92229	0.00110	0.00759	0.00152	0.00068
Tenango del Aire	0.90978	0.00016	0.01389	0.02529	1.07788	0.00048	0.00097	0.00032	0.00064
Teoloyucan	0.79635	0.00024	0.04161	0.03336	0.96648	0.00131	0.00448	0.00238	0.00212
Teotihuacan	0.79958	0.00098	0.08856	0.03926	1.03249	0.00331	0.00456	0.00423	0.00233
Tepetlaoxtoc	0.86439	0.00149	0.01104	0.04001	0.87067	0.00378	0.00416	0.00242	0.00217
Tepetlixpa	0.91692	0.00047	0.03518	0.02231	0.92470	0.00142	0.00552	0.00142	0.00063
Tepotzotlan	0.71786	0.00091	0.07196	0.05544	0.91128	0.00303	0.00439	0.00293	0.00267
Texcoco	0.74891	0.00410	0.07471	0.06683	1.39898	0.00444	0.00770	0.00578	0.00475
Tezoyuca	0.74340	0.00048	0.03040	0.05686	0.96758	0.00362	0.00427	0.00217	0.00234
Tlahuac	0.79159	0.00062	0.06309	0.02934	0.92526	0.00345	0.00371	0.00505	0.00049

Table 5.2 Migration Characteristics of Migration Variables (Continued)

Area	Population Native to State	Population Foreign Born	Immigration 1965-70	Immigration 1985-90	Sex Ratio 1985-90	Inmigration from Puebla 1985-90	Inmigrants from Cent. Rem 1985-90	Inmigration from S. Region 1985-90	Inmigration from Veracruz 1985-90
Tlalmanalco	0.90877	0.00012	0.02774	0.02189	1.02802	0.00203	0.00161	0.00212	0.00136
Tlalnepantla	0.42770	0.00217	0.31462	0.08404	0.94713	0.00349	0.00654	0.00496	0.00485
Tlalpan	0.73012	0.00766	0.10632	0.04823	0.93308	0.00484	0.00902	0.00869	0.00488
Tultepec	0.62929	0.00040	0.04416	0.10733	0.95829	0.00342	0.00727	0.00323	0.00391
Tultitlan	0.42326	0.00075	0.28851	0.14853	0.95714	0.00296	0.03029	0.00526	0.00374
Venustiano Carranza	0.77419	0.00183	0.10590	0.02975	0.94495	0.00299	0.00351	0.00441	0.00294
Xochimilco	0.80671	0.00253	0.05433	0.03284	1.00870	0.00370	0.00394	0.00625	0.00357
Zumpango	0.83440	0.00073	0.06163	0.04148	0.98898	0.00238	0.00025	0.00011	0.00171
Mean	0.72832	0.00261	0.10128	0.05905	0.90854	0.00323	0.00543	0.00391	0.00261
Median	0.77142	0.00071	0.06163	0.04021	0.94495	0.00296	0.00513	0.00306	0.00249
S.D.	0.17291	0.00536	0.11165	0.04384	0.17540	0.00249	0.00388	0.00301	0.00169
C.V.	23.74	205.21	110.25	74.23	19.31	77.23	71.39	77.09	64.79
Minimum	0.27951	0.00000	0.00642	0.00430	0.04741	0.00019	0.00025	0.00011	0.00011
Maximum	0.96815	0.03150	0.47117	0.19460	1.39898	0.01531	0.03029	0.01270	0.00811

Source: INEGI, Censuses of Population, 1970 and 1990 Note: Cent. Rem = Central Remainder of Region

122

Table 5.3 Correlation Matrix of Migration Variables

	Immigration 1985-90	Sex Ratio of Inmigrants 1985-90	Inmigration from Puebla 1985-90	Immigration from Cent. Rem 1985-90	Inmigration from S. Region 1985-90	Immigration from Veracruz 1985-90	Immigration 1965-70	Population Native to State
Sex Ratio of Inmigrants 1985-90	.117							
Inmigration from Puebla 1985-90	.480***	-.071						
Inmigration from Cent. Rem 1985-90	.516***	.112	.210					
Inmigration from S. Region 1985-90	.396***	-.004	.683***	.325**				
Inmigration from Veracruz 1985-90	.577***	.098	.708***	.401***	.731***			
Immigration 1965-70	.590***	.054	.523***	.332**	.390***	.647***		
Population Native to State	-.871***	-.086	-.545***	-.451***	-.566***	-.708***	-.796***	
Population Foreign Born	.060	-.266*	.298**	.163	.407***	.362**	.150	-.148

Note: Cent. Rem = Remainder of Central Region

Note: Significance Levels
* .05
** .01
*** .001

Table 5.4 Correlation Matrix of Migration and Dependent Variables

	Immigrants 1985-90	Sex Ratio of Immigrants 1985-90	Immigration from Puebla 1985-90	Immigration from Cent. Rem 1985-90	Immigration from S. Region 1985-90	Immigration from Veracruz 1985-90	Immigration 1965-70	Population Native to State	Population Foreign Born
Unemployment	-.112	.102	-.275*	-.161	-.238	-.201	-.239*	.196	-.219
Post Primary Education	.131	-.130	.286*	.215	.410***	.485***	.428***	-.351**	.567***
Earn 5x Min. Wage	.319**	-.151	.331**	.257*	.443***	.537***	.404***	-.470***	.770***
Owner/Employer Salaried Workers	.218	.085	.148	.069	.188	.264*	.253*	-.289*	.164
Home Ownership	.028	.139	-.306**	-.136	-.451***	-.469***	-.241*	.176	-.555***
Fertility Ratio, Women 20 - 29	.010	.211	-.139	-.050	-.252*	-.274*	-.256*	.111	-.536***
Ratio Econ. Active Women	.005	-.236	.369**	.187	.528***	.518***	.204	-.219	.666***
Indigenous Language	-.121	.076	.026	-.043	.127	.102	-.027*	.066	.182
Log of Pop. 1990	.311*	-.121	.462***	.192	.670***	.641***	.555***	-.590***	.371**
Relative Pop Growth 1950-70	.326**	.111	.237	.118	.335**	.273*	.471***	-.477***	-.127
Relative Pop Growth 1970-90	.700***	.170	.357**	.209	.294*	.326**	.443***	-.684***	.137
Crowded Housing	.591***	-.120	-.252*	-.381***	-.161	-.513***	-.618***	.666***	-.186
No Toilet	-.389***	.074	-.491***	-.262**	-.516***	-.544***	-.503***	.561***	-.306**

Note: Significance Levels

*	.05
**	.01
***	.001

Native and Foreign Born Population

Nativity

The percent native to state is the ratio of people born in the state (either Federal District or State of Mexico) to the population of the zone. It reflects the rootedness of population. The mean nativity is 0.728, which is eleven percent lower than the national average of 0.815. As seen in Map 5.1, the lowest nativity is in the populous and industrialized zone to the north of the Federal District, as well as in areas to the east of the upper Federal District and the impoverished municipio of Chalco. The explanations are different for these areas. The rapidly growing northern area of business development is less "rooted" because of economic-based mobility. To the east, the municipio of Nezahualcoyotl had the most rapid population growth rates, 1970-1990, of any municipio in the metropolis, leading to very low nativity of forty percent. This startling growth is explained by unique political events in Nezahualcoyotl, including politically-based changes in water coverage of portions of this area (Lourdes Vega, 1991). For Chalco, low nativity is explained by inmigration over the past 40 years of impoverished and often indigenous people, as well as outmigration of some native population due to the increasing impoverishment in the zone (Hiernaux Nicolas, 1991). There were ten zones having under half of the population native to state, with the lowest of 28 percent located in the industrial area of Coacalco directly north of the tip of the Federal District.

Nativity is significantly inversely related to population, density, and relative and absolute population growth, as well as to many indicators of in-migration. The highest nativity (90 percent or higher) is located in the semi-urban peripheral parts of the State of Mexico, while at the same time the lowest regions of nativity are in the areas of high growth in the 80s surrounding the northern Federal District.

Percent Foreign Born

There was slight foreign born population in Mexico Megacity, with a mean of 0.3 percent. This is much higher than the mean percent foreign born in Mexico. By comparison, percent foreign born in the U.S. in the decade 1981-90 was 8.0 percent (Chiswick and Sullivan, 1995). The percent foreign born in the U.S. urban states in 1990 was even higher, with sixteen percent of residents of New York and 22 percent of California residents of foreign birth (Chiswick and Sullivan, 1995). The difference stems from much more restrictive migration policies in Mexico versus the U.S. as well as reduced economic incentives in the 70s and 80s.

As seen in Map 5.2, foreign born population is concentrated in the middle and eastern Federal District and adjacent municipios to the east. The histogram illustrating number of delegations and municipios with people foreign born (see Figure 5.1) reveals a skewed distribution mostly concentrated under 0.25 percent, with three extreme outlier values. Foreign born residents were highest in the old, city center delegations of Miguel Hidalgo (3.2 percent) and Benito Juarez (2.5 percent), as well as in the eastern delegation of Huixquilucan (1.8 percent). The outliers of Miguel Hidalgo and Benito Juarez are wealthy corporate and residential districts, containing high density of multinational corporations (see Chapter 11) and governmental/diplomatic offices and centers, while Huixquilucan is a residential section attracting foreigners and foreign-born. Generally the highest proportions of foreign born are in the Federal District, State of Mexico areas to the northwest, Texcoco, and two adjacent municipios.

There are much lower proportions in the semi-rural peripheral areas, with the exception of a large concentration in the far southeastern municipio of Atlautla. Generally there is a very high association between foreign-born population and social rank. For instance, there are highly significant correlations with high earners (r = 0.77), professional / technical / managerial workforce (0.75), and primary education (0.57). The overall positive correlation with social rank may reflect the tendency of mostly highly educated and skilled foreign population to settle in urban zones of higher social rank. Most high social rank foreign-born population had migrated from Europe. Exceptional low social rank destinations for foreign inmigrants are Texcoco, Papalotla, Chiautla, Tepetlaoxtoc, and Atlautla that may reflect inmigration of lower social rank population, from Central American nations.

Foreign born population is correlated with the urbanism/familism variables. This is plausible since the urbanism/familism group is strongly related to the social rank group (see Chapter 8). The explanations are similar to those for social rank.

The proportion foreign born is also 'associated with population size and density, although more so to population size. This reflects the configuration of the Megacity (see Chapters 3 and 12) with the more populous and denser parts also being the wealthier and more prosperous. Most foreign born population, especially that from Europe, would be more attracted to these areas.

Figure 5.1 Foreign Born by Spatial Unit, 1990

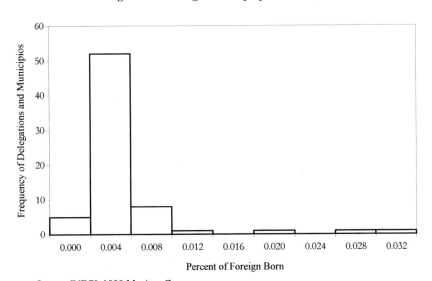

Source: INEGI, 1990 Mexican Census

Map 5.1
Native to State,1990

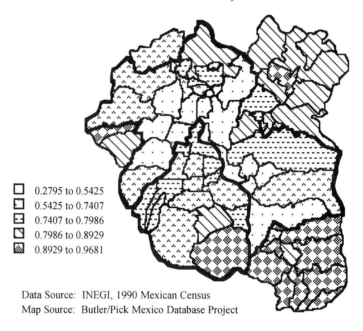

- ☐ 0.2795 to 0.5425
- ☑ 0.5425 to 0.7407
- ⊟ 0.7407 to 0.7986
- ◩ 0.7986 to 0.8929
- ▦ 0.8929 to 0.9681

Data Source: INEGI, 1990 Mexican Census
Map Source: Butler/Pick Mexico Database Project

Map 5.2
Foreign Born, 1990

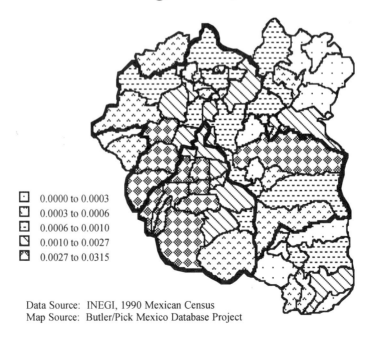

- ⊡ 0.0000 to 0.0003
- ☑ 0.0003 to 0.0006
- ⊟ 0.0006 to 0.0010
- ◩ 0.0010 to 0.0027
- ▨ 0.0027 to 0.0315

Data Source: INEGI, 1990 Mexican Census
Map Source: Butler/Pick Mexico Database Project

Inmigration Flows Between the Two Megacity States

Mexico City was originally located entirely in the Federal District. For instance, in 1900, Mexico City had 344,000 population located within the Federal District (INEGI, 1902). The national dominance of the Federal District as a destination state is reflected in rapid growth of the Federal District in the 30s and 40s. As seen in Table 5.5, in these decades the Federal District grew at an average decennial growth rate of 4.5 percent, versus a much lower growth rate of 1.7 percent for the State of Mexico. The ratio of population for the two states (shown in the right hand column in Table 5.5) peaked in favor of the Federal District in 1950, with a lowering ratio ever since. This population dominance of the Federal District over the State of Mexico in the 1930-90 period has several explanations. First, in the period 1930-1950, the metropolitan industrial base, largely located at that time in the Federal District, grew rapidly. Garza (1985) points out that the non-durable goods industry increased the most rapidly 1930-1950. A second "push" factor in migration to the Federal District, 1930-1950, was the high growth rates for rural population in Mexico. As seen in Figure 2.2, the urban population grew rapidly for the first time in the 1940s. Rapid urban increase has continued in the four decades since then.

A finer grained view of the influence of net migration on the two central states is seen in Figure 5.2. This graph reveals a major reversal in volume of net migration for the Federal District from consistent inmigration during the span 1933-1980 to a very large net outmigration of about 1.35 million persons for the decade of the 80s. By contrast, the State of Mexico had very little net migration centering on zero for the period 1933-1960. However starting in the 60s and increasing in the 70s and 80s there were major new inmigration flows by millions of persons. This fine grained view accounts for a good part of the State of Mexico's high growth 1960-1990 and also explains the dampening to around one percent of the Federal District's growth rates for the period 1970-1990. The dramatic reversal of about 1.6 million in the Federal District's net migration between the 70s and 80s is a key turning point in the migration history of Mexico City. It reflects a new trend towards *deconcentration* of the central part of the metropolis. In many developed nations, such as the United States, such deconcentration effects have been noted in the late 20th century, even more noticeably than in Mexico City. For the Megacity in the 80s, the deconcentration effect was moderated because natural increase was much higher than in U.S. metropolitan areas as a result of high fertility.

Migration flows between the core and more peripheral parts of the Megacity can be examined through the spatial patterning of inmigration into Federal District delegations from the State of Mexico and into State of Mexico municipios from the Federal District. Table 5.6 and Maps 5.3 through 5.6 show these spatial patterns for the periods 1965-70 and 1985-90. For the second half of the 60s, there was heavy migration from the Federal District into the State of Mexico adjoining areas to the north, while migrants from the State of Mexico tended to enter the northern Federal District. There was relatively little migration flow from the semi-urban northeast and southeast or from the southern Federal District.

The volume of inmigration in the later 60s was already shifting towards the State of Mexico. In particular, the mean Federal District-to-Mexico inmigration was 0.051, while the opposite Mexico-to-Federal District inmigration flow was 0.011. These figures further reflect a migration flow shift in the 60s seen in Figure 5.2. The shift in balance toward the State of Mexico is evident starting in the 60s. By the late 80s, the respective percentages are 0.046 and 0.009, i.e. the State of Mexico inmigration remained high, but reverse inflow into the Federal District has slowed to a trickle. This is seen in terms of net migration in Figure 5.2, which shows in the 80s over one million net population leaving the Federal District.

128 Migration

In the late 80s, the migration pattern had shifted (see Maps 5.5 and 5.6). Migration inflows to the Federal District have shifted from the north to the west and northwest. On the other hand, the inmigration patterns into the State of Mexico remain similar to the late 60s, except that the inmigration has moved further north to such municipios as Huehuetoca and Jaltenco. Also, in the far northeast, inmigration in some municipios increased to moderate levels.

The spatial pattern of inmigration is confirmed to have remained consistent between the late 60s and late 80s for the State of Mexico but shifted for the Federal District. This is reflected in correlations between the spatial patterns over the 20 year period. The correlation between inmigration to the State of Mexico 1965-70 and 1985-90 is 0.404 (p = 0.003), whereas the same correlation for the Federal District between the two periods is 0.361 (p = 0.170). The State of Mexico inmigration patterns are correlated longitudinally, whereas the Federal District patterns are not.

Table 5.5 Population of the Federal District and State of Mexico, 1930-1990

Year	Population of Federal District (1)	Ave. 20 Year Growth Rate	Population of State of Mexico (2)	Ave. 20 Year Growth Rate	Population Ratio of (1) to (2)
1930	1,229,576		990,112		1.24
1950	3,050,442	4.54	1,392,623	1.71	2.19
1970	6,874,165	4.06	3,833,185	5.06	1.79
1990	8,235,744	0.09	9,815,795	4.70	0.84

Source: INEGI, *Estadisticas Historicas de Mexico*, 1994

Table 5.6. Migration Rates Between Federal District and State of Mexico, 1965-1970 and 1985-1990

Federal District / Delegation	Inmigration 1965-70	Inmigration 1985-90	State of Mexico / Municipio	Inmigration 1965-70	Inmigration 1985-90	State of Mexico / Municipio	Immigration 1965-70	Immigration 1985-90
Alvaro Obregon	0.01474	0.00844	Acolman	0.05834	0.02489	Naucalpan	0.20390	0.03906
Azcapotzalco	0.01303	0.01127	Amecameca	0.00952	0.01297	Nextlalpan	0.02202	0.04022
Benito Juarez	0.00951	0.01004	Atenco	0.00706	0.01197	Nezahualcoyotl	0.18776	0.05359
Coyoacan	0.01189	0.00717	Atizapan de Zaragoza	0.22454	0.07763	Nicolas Romero	0.03983	0.03009
Cuajimalpa	0.02022	0.01309	Atlautla	0.00177	0.01295	Nopaltepec	0.00448	0.02140
Cuauhtemoc	0.01019	0.01086	Axapusco	0.00421	0.01677	Otumba	0.00615	0.02230
Gustavo A. Madero	0.00978	0.01063	Ayapango	0.01326	0.03232	Ozumba	0.00744	0.00864
Iztacalco	0.01135	0.00794	Chalco	0.01677	0.12171	Papalotla	0.01654	0.02681
Iztapalapa	0.01077	0.01046	Chiautla	0.00729	0.23341	Paz, La	0.17645	0.04229
Magdalena Contreras	0.00743	0.00633	Chicoloapan	0.06103	0.07703	San Martin de las P.	0.00939	0.01298
Miguel Hidalgo	0.00983	0.01600	Chiconcuac	0.00798	0.00367	Tecamac	0.04961	0.06115
Milpa Alta	0.00991	0.00644	Chimalhuacan	0.03388	0.04640	Temamatla	0.02726	0.04957
Tlahuac	0.00793	0.00800	Coacalco	0.33129	0.14430	Temascalapa	0.00607	0.02325
Tlalpan	0.00939	0.00877	Cocotitlan	0.01201	0.01078	Tenango del Aire	0.00111	0.02094
Venustiano Carranza	0.00939	0.00877	Coyotepec	0.00686	0.01472	Teoloyucan	0.00963	0.01854
Xochimilco	0.01023	0.00798	Cuautitlan	0.10575	0.07598	Teotihuacan	0.02156	0.01909
			Cuautitlan Izcalli	0.03812	0.01273	Tepetlaoxtoc	0.00241	0.02401
			Ecatepec	0.23408	0.12086	Tepetlixpa	0.00256	0.01222
			Ecatzingo	0.00110	0.00086	Tepotzotlan	0.02014	0.03377
			Huehuetoca	0.01244	0.16542	Texcoco	0.02539	0.02691
			Huixquilucan	0.12748	0.06315	Tezoyuca	0.01761	0.03987
			Isidro Fabela	0.00077	0.01580	Tlalmanalco	0.01176	0.01152
			Ixtapaluca	0.04874	0.08602	Tlalnepantla	0.18059	0.05431
			Jaltenco	0.00781	0.12165	Tultepec	0.01786	0.07979
			Jilotzingo	0.00920	0.02896	Tultitlan	0.18698	0.12048
			Juchitepec	0.00735	0.00708	Zumpango	0.01908	0.00015
			Melchor Ocampo	0.02141	0.01977			

Sources: INEGI Censuses of Population, 1970 and 1990.

Map 5.3
Inmigration to Federal District from State of Mexico, 1965-70

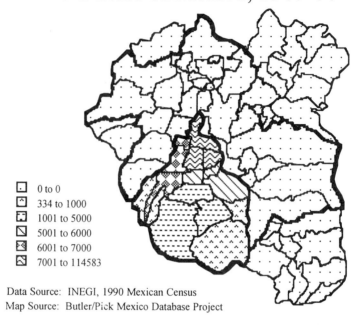

☐	0 to 0
⊡	334 to 1000
⊡	1001 to 5000
◫	5001 to 6000
⊠	6001 to 7000
◪	7001 to 114583

Data Source: INEGI, 1990 Mexican Census
Map Source: Butler/Pick Mexico Database Project

Map 5.4
Inmigration to State of Mexico from Federal District, 1965-70

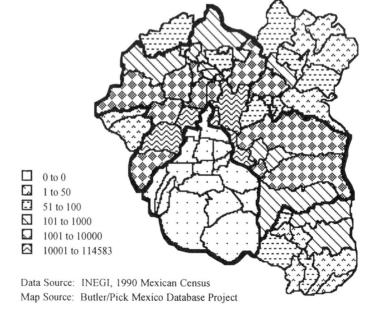

☐	0 to 0
⊡	1 to 50
⊡	51 to 100
◫	101 to 1000
⊡	1001 to 10000
◪	10001 to 114583

Data Source: INEGI, 1990 Mexican Census
Map Source: Butler/Pick Mexico Database Project

Map 5.5
Inmigration to Federal District From State of Mexico for the Past Five Years, 1990

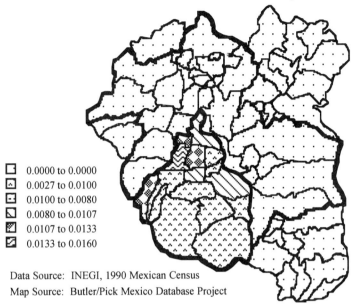

☐	0.0000 to 0.0000
◪	0.0027 to 0.0100
▣	0.0100 to 0.0080
◩	0.0080 to 0.0107
▨	0.0107 to 0.0133
▨	0.0133 to 0.0160

Data Source: INEGI, 1990 Mexican Census
Map Source: Butler/Pick Mexico Database Project

Map 5.6
Inmigration to State of Mexico From Federal District for the Past Five Years, 1990

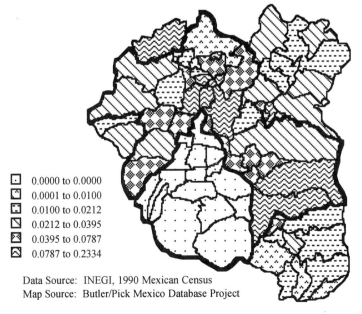

☐	0.0000 to 0.0000
▣	0.0001 to 0.0100
▣	0.0100 to 0.0212
◩	0.0212 to 0.0395
▨	0.0395 to 0.0787
▨	0.0787 to 0.2334

Data Source: INEGI, 1990 Mexican Census
Map Source: Butler/Pick Mexico Database Project

132

Figure 5.2
Net Intercensal Migration, 1930 - 1990,
Federal District

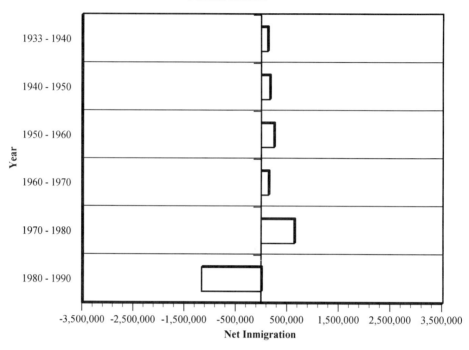

State of Mexico

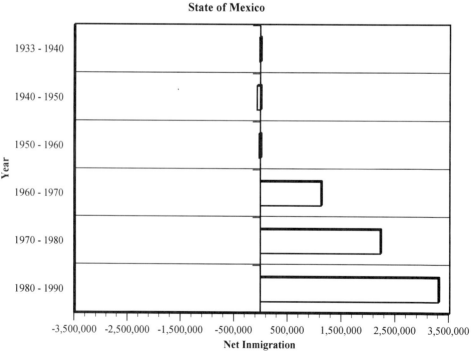

Source: INEGI: *Estadisticas Historicas de Mexico,* Vol 1, 1994

Inmigration in the Past Five Years

Inmigration to Mexico Megacity in the late 80s was average compared to the nation. The average inmigration was 0.059, nearly identical to the statewide mean of 0.058 (Pick and Butler, 1994). The State of Mexico inmigration exceeds the nation (0.092), but the Federal District inmigration is below average (0.041). The State of Mexico joined other areas as the Baja Californias and Quintana Roo to form the high migration regions, i.e. the "sunbelts" of Mexico. The low inmigration value for the Federal District reflects its situation in the 80s of net outmigration, with the largest stream going to the State of Mexico.

Past five year inmigration for the period 1985-90 (see Map 5.7) confirms a number of the trends noted earlier. The much greater migration to the State of Mexico versus the Federal District for the late 80s is evident. The areal pattern also reflects migratory contributions to the two metropolitan "arms" of population growth, i.e. one to the northwest and a second to the east. In addition, the pattern reveals a high rate of migratory growth in the impoverished zones of Chalco and Ixtapaluca. The lowest rates of 5 year inmigration are in the nine southeastern municipios, areas characterized by reduced population and low SES. There is dramatic difference between the very high Chalco/Ixtapaluca in-migration and very low in-migration in neighboring areas to the southeast. This great contrast calls for detailed investigation into political and economic causes.

The sex ratio is defined as the ratio of male population to female population Thus, the sex ratio of inmigrants is the ratio of male inmigrants to female inmigrants. The histogram of sex ratio of inmigrants given in Figure 5.3 shows that sex ratios are mostly concentrated in a bimodal pattern between 0.68 and 1.07. These sex ratios are low on a national basis and reflect the high proportion of women in the metropolis. There are four extreme values that range from 0.06, i.e. nearly all women arriving, to 1.31, i.e. a strong preponderance of males. The pattern shown in Map 5.8 differs from patterns for total population, population density, SES, and inmigration. Areas with a preponderance of male inmigrants are located mostly in scattered locations around the circumference of the State of Mexico. An exception of high male inmigration in the Federal District delegation of Xochimilco.

It is interesting to compare the sex ratio of inmigrants in the late 80s to the sex ratio of resident population in 1990 (see Map 3.16). The more male areas of 1990 resident population are in a broad half circle in the outer ring of municipios in the State of Mexico, while more female areas are located in the Federal District and several adjacent municipios to the northwest. There is moderate correlation between sex ratios of resident population and sex ratios of inmigrants. The main conclusion point is that high male areas for both resident population and inmigrants tend to be in State of Mexico municipios. The gender-based pattern for inmigration appears to be very specific and requires unique explanations for the high sex ratio as well as low sex ratio municipios. These differences may reflect familial considerations in in-migration, as well as the occupational structure of receiving areas.

134

Map 5.7
Inmigration in the
Past Five Years, 1990

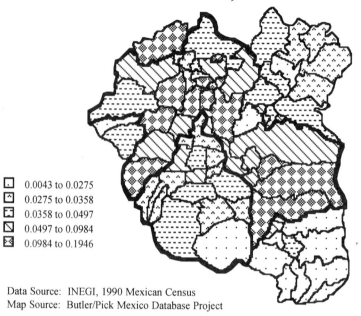

- 0.0043 to 0.0275
- 0.0275 to 0.0358
- 0.0358 to 0.0497
- 0.0497 to 0.0984
- 0.0984 to 0.1946

Data Source: INEGI, 1990 Mexican Census
Map Source: Butler/Pick Mexico Database Project

Map 5.8
Sex Ratio of Inmigrants in the
Past Five Years, 1990

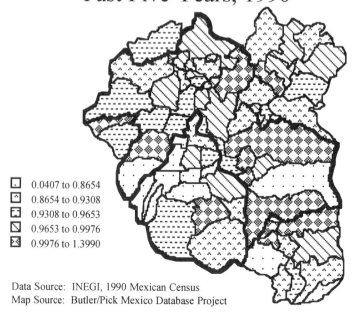

- 0.0407 to 0.8654
- 0.8654 to 0.9308
- 0.9308 to 0.9653
- 0.9653 to 0.9976
- 0.9976 to 1.3990

Data Source: INEGI, 1990 Mexican Census
Map Source: Butler/Pick Mexico Database Project

135

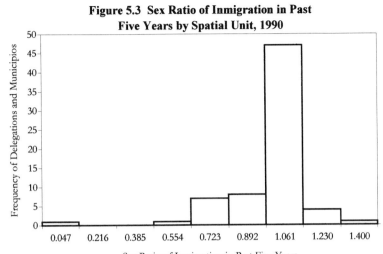

Figure 5.3 Sex Ratio of Inmigration in Past Five Years by Spatial Unit, 1990

Sex Ratio of Inmigration in Past Five Years
Source: INEGI, 1990 Mexican Census

Inmigration from Major States and Regions

It is important to know whether differences in sending state/region are reflected in the areal patterns of inmigrants. Patterns are shown for inmigration from four major sending states or regions to Mexico City (see Maps 5.9 - 5.12). Major sending states/regions are Veracruz, remainder of Central Region (i.e. excluding the Federal District and State of Mexico), Puebla, and Pacific South region. These correspond to many of the major interstate migration streams presented later in Table 5.7. It is clear that patterns for Puebla and the South region are very highly correlated. These inflows are higher in the Federal District and eastern State of Mexico municipios including Chalco/Ixtapaluca and moderate to low in the northern third of the Megacity. Migrants from Puebla and the South tend to migrate to older areas of the Federal District or to eastern impoverished as well as middle class areas. This areal selectivity probably relates to the presence in receiving areas of resident population from the South or Puebla. This would be especially important for migrants from the South, since they tend to be poorer and more indigenous, and may be more attracted to areas with South-origin residents.

As seen in Map 5.11, migrants from the Central remainder region tend to select northern municipios to a much greater extent. They are less attracted to the Federal District, although exceptions are the high inmigration rates for Benito Juarez and Tlalpan. This inmigration is correlated with only a few socioeconomic factors, primarily housing as well as economic activity and high income. Thus, inmigration of central remainder migrants appears associated more directly with destination housing than migration from other areas. The reason is uncertain.

Migrants from the remainder of the Central remainder tend to move into higher SES and newer areas of the metropolis. This may reflect more educated and skilled migrants who select more economically advanced parts of the metropolitan region.

Finally, the inmigration pattern from Veracruz tends to fall in-between those for the Puebla/South region and the Central remainder region (see Map 5.12). These migrants may be intermediate in SES and seek newer areas of Mexico City.

Only a few differences in the inmigration destination patterns by sending place are apparent, so region of origin must be viewed as a small influence in migrants' choice of destination within the Megacity.

Table 5.7 Major Migration Streams to and from Federal District and State of Mexico

	Major Migration Streams, 1965-70				Major Migration Streams, 1985-90		
Stream Rank	State of Origin	State of Destination	Stream Size	Stream Rank	State of Origin	State of Destination	Stream Size
1	Distrito Federal	Mexico	365,951	1	Distrito Federal	Mexico	548,975
2	Michoacan	Distrito Federal	87,885	2	Mexico	Distrito Federal	80,905
3	Mexico	Distrito Federal	79,662	3	Distrito Federal	Puebla	38,213
4	Puebla	Distrito Federal	67,520	4	Distrito Federal	Jalisco	37,330
5	Guanajuato	Distrito Federal	64,559	5	Distrito Federal	Guanajuato	35,766
6	Oaxaca	Distrito Federal	61,939	6	Distrito Federal	Michoacan	35,528
7	Veracruz	Distrito Federal	53,565	7	Distrito Federal	Veracruz	34,876
8	Hidalgo	Distrito Federal	49,615	8	Puebla	Mexico	34,199
9	Michoacan	Mexico	48,012	9	Veracruz	Mexico	32,795
10	Guerrero	Distrito Federal	42,009	10	Distrito Federal	Morelos	32,463
11	Guanajuato	Mexico	41,248	11	Puebla	Distrito Federal	31,200
12	Jalisco	Distrito Federal	30,889	12	Hidalgo	Mexico	29,191
13	Puebla	Mexico	29,594	13	Distrito Federal	Hidalgo	28,686
14	Hidalgo	Mexico	26,374	14	Veracruz	Distrito Federal	28,355
15	Oaxaca	Mexico	23,850	15	Distrito Federal	Queretaro	27,553
				16	Oaxaca	Mexico	26,573

Note: The stream rank only refers to migration streams to and from the Federal District and State of Mexico

Source: INEGI, 1972 and 1992

Map 5.9
Inmigration from Puebla in
the Past Five Years, 1990

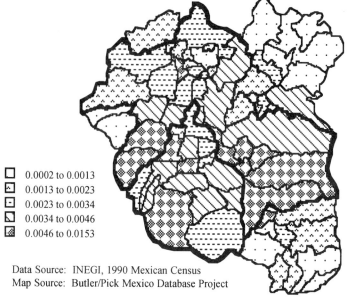

0.0002 to 0.0013
0.0013 to 0.0023
0.0023 to 0.0034
0.0034 to 0.0046
0.0046 to 0.0153

Data Source: INEGI, 1990 Mexican Census
Map Source: Butler/Pick Mexico Database Project

Map 5.10
Inmigration from the South Region
in the Past Five Years, 1990

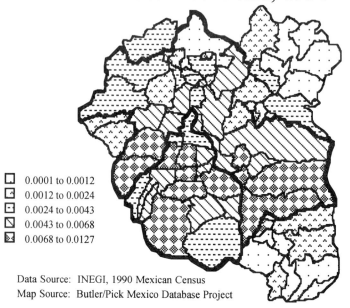

0.0001 to 0.0012
0.0012 to 0.0024
0.0024 to 0.0043
0.0043 to 0.0068
0.0068 to 0.0127

Data Source: INEGI, 1990 Mexican Census
Map Source: Butler/Pick Mexico Database Project

139

Map 5.11
Inmigration from Remainder of the Central Region in the Past Five Years, 1990

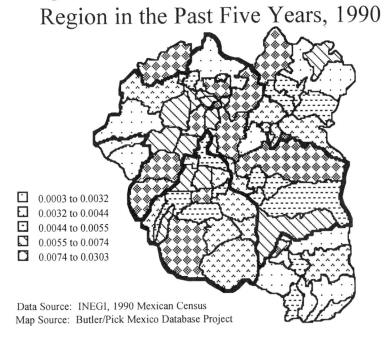

0.0003 to 0.0032
0.0032 to 0.0044
0.0044 to 0.0055
0.0055 to 0.0074
0.0074 to 0.0303

Data Source: INEGI, 1990 Mexican Census
Map Source: Butler/Pick Mexico Database Project

Map 5.12
Inmigration from Veracruz in the Past Five Years, 1990

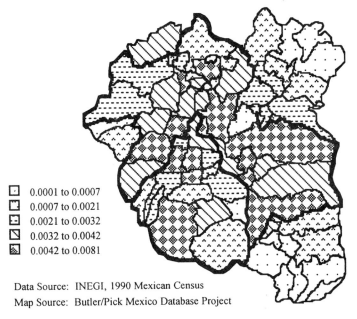

0.0001 to 0.0007
0.0007 to 0.0021
0.0021 to 0.0032
0.0032 to 0.0042
0.0042 to 0.0081

Data Source: INEGI, 1990 Mexican Census
Map Source: Butler/Pick Mexico Database Project

Inmigration Streams Into and Out of the Megacity

The Mexican Census of Population has a standard question that enables compilation of 992 interstate migration streams. Whetten and Burnight (1956) studied the 29 largest streams for 1945-1950 *for non-contiguous states*. They chose non-contiguous because they were more interested in long distance migration. Results showed that about two thirds of the largest non-contiguous streams were to the Federal District. Besides number of streams, non-contiguous streams into the Federal District were also considerably larger in volume of migrants, accounting for over 90 percent of the volume of migrants for non-contiguous streams.

Table 5.7 and Maps 5.13 and 5.14 illustrate the major interstate migration streams to and from the Federal District and State of Mexico for 1965-70 and for 1985-90. In contrast to Whetten's study, these streams include both contiguous and non-contiguous states.

The two most important streams are those between the two states comprising the Megacity. Corresponding to the much higher growth rate 1970-90 in the State of Mexico versus the Federal District, by far the largest stream both in the late 60s and late 80s was migration from the Federal District to the neighboring State of Mexico. The preponderance of this growth may be viewed as migration from the older central part of the metropolis, i.e. Federal District, to newer areas in the State of Mexico. This large net annual flow of about 94,000 persons per year in the late 80s and 56,000 persons per year in the late 60s between the two states is mostly explained by the increasing overpopulation of the center, as reflected in the 185,000 annual net population increase in the Federal District over the twenty years.

Examining major stream flows other than those between the two central states, it is clear from Table 5.7 and Maps 5.13 and 5.14 that two major shifts taking place between the late 60s and late 80s were a trend towards reduced major streams into the Federal District and increased major streams out of the Federal District. For example, in the 1965-1970 period, the flows next in importance (under rank 1) were seven flows from populous states into the Federal District that totaled 464,745, exceeding the stream flow from the Federal District to the State of Mexico. By contrast for annual flows in the period 1985-1990, the next five ranked flows (under rank 1 and 2) were from the Federal District into populous states across the whole middle flank of the nation. A portion of this outflow from the Federal District may be interpreted as return migration in fact many outflow streams reverse the inflow streams of the late 60s. The middle-flank states were more slowly growing demographically in the 80s. These flows had an average volume of 36,343 for the 1985-1990 period, which is one third of the average Federal District-State of Mexico stream. Further research beyond the census information is needed to determine more specifically the proportion of return migrants in these flows and length of stay of the return migrants.

Another trend apparent in comparing the major interstate streams of the late 60s and the late 80s is that major streams not involving Mexico City increased in number and volume. Data for non-Mexico City streams are not shown on Table 5.7. There was eight non-Mexico-City stream in the top 23 in 1965-70 and seven non-Mexico-City streams in the top 23 for 1985-90. The total volume of these major streams for other parts of the nation remained stable , i.e. 224,866 in 1965-70 and 217,195 in 1985-90. The total volume of all 23 major streams was nearly identical at 1.3 million in the late 60s and late 80s. One might expect an increasingly mobile population, such as took place in the U.S. throughout the twentieth century. However, Mexico has a traditional residential rootedness (Pick and Butler, 1994) that is reflected in the lack of change in overall levels of large stream mobility during this two decade period.

In conclusion, analysis of major interstate migration streams in the late 40s, late 60s, and late 80s reveals major changes. The transition is from strong inflows from the State of Mexico and other states into the Federal District in the 40s, to a reversal of major outflow from the Federal District to the State of Mexico while continuing other inflows to the Federal District in the 60s and to outflows to the State of Mexico as well as to major populous states in the nation's central flank in the 80s. The 80s trends reflect both Mexico City intrametropolitan expansion to the periphery as well as some tendency for return migration to other central states.

142

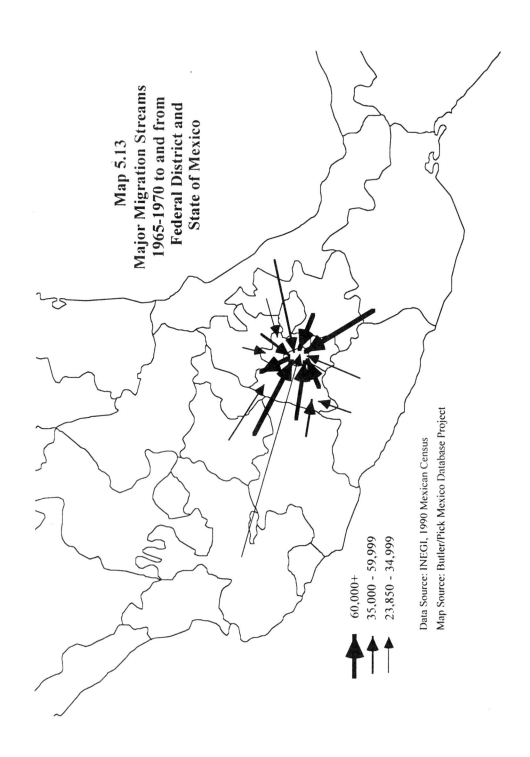

Map 5.13
Major Migration Streams
1965-1970 to and from
Federal District and
State of Mexico

60,000+

35,000 - 59,999

23,850 - 34,999

Data Source: INEGI, 1990 Mexican Census

Map Source: Butler/Pick Mexico Database Project

143

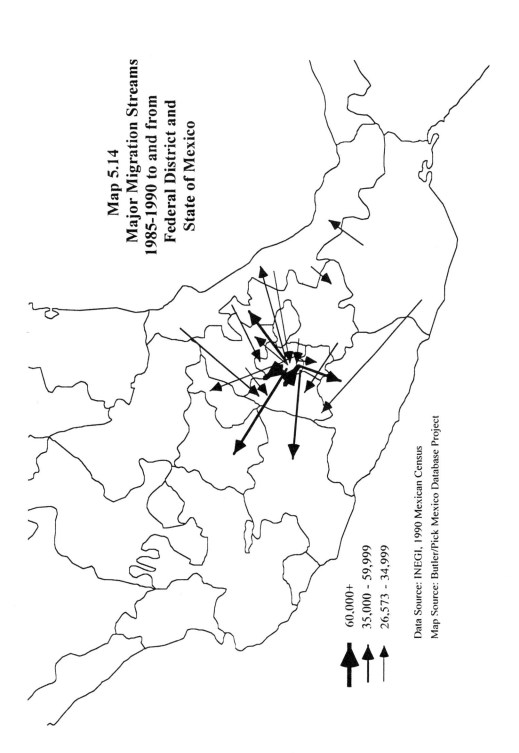

Map 5.14
Major Migration Streams
1985-1990 to and from
Federal District and
State of Mexico

60,000+

35,000 - 59,999

26,573 - 34,999

Data Source: INEGI, 1990 Mexican Census

Map Source: Butler/Pick Mexico Database Project

Conclusions

In gross terms, migration has been very large in Mexico City in this century. Over the decades, millions of people have moved into the city and millions moved away. Migration has had major impact. It is largely studied through census of population data for 1970 and 1990. This source provides migration stream data at the state level and inmigration and place of origin data at the local level. GIS analysis tools are useful in displaying migration trends and patterns.

The city was built up early in the century through inmigration into the old city core. In recent decades migration inflows have moved outward from the core into surrounding areas in the State of Mexico. Trends in interstate migration reveal former strong inflows into the Federal District changing in the 80s to strong flows into the State of Mexico and out of the Federal District into surrounding states such as Guerrero, Jalisco, Zacatecas, and others. This points to a future pattern of an enlarged megalopolis, perhaps encompassing parts of four or five states.

The Megacity has had much higher mobility in recent decades than the nation as a whole. Its migration rates approximate those of 80s growth states. At the same time, Mexico City's migration rates are much lower than rates in the largest U.S. cities. This reflects a nation that is much more geographically stable than the U.S.

A number of conclusions are drawn on migration patterns. For instance, the sex ratio of migrants tends to be higher on the periphery and lower in the center. This pattern cumulatively over time may have contributed to the Megacity's much higher sex ratio in the periphery. Another example is that place of origin is not important in determining the spatial patterns on inmigration.

Migration variables have moderate association with cluster variables. Housing, and population, density stand out as especially strong correlates of migration. Inmigrants tend to be associated with better housing, more population/density, and higher income. In other words, they locate themselves more centrally. For some variables, however, migration is higher in the band surrounding the Federal District and almost always very little in the semi-urban bands.

In the future, the migration and mobility of the Mexico City population should continue to be high. It is expected that the spatial patterns of inflows and outflows to the city's regions and small areas will continue to shift and change.

6

Mortality and Health

Photo courtesy of Tomas Mojarro

Introduction

Mortality dropped in Mexico during the second half of the twentieth century. This was due to several causes including improved public health, better medical services, and improved sanitation. Mexico Megacity stands out as an advanced area within Mexico from mortality and health standpoints.

Important influences on the geographic pattern of mortality in the Megacity are population concentration and age distribution. In zones with large numbers of elderly people, deaths as well as demand for health services are much higher. This chapter also examines the effect of gender distribution on mortality, since women are known to have lower mortality rates than men (Preston, Keyfitz and Schoen, 1972).

Although there has been criticism of the quality of Mexican mortality registration and vital records, in recent years studies have shown that the death registration system has become more complete and accurate (Garcia y Garma, 1988). In this chapter, most mortality data refer to the residential location of the affected individual, although some data refer to the location of health institutions such as hospitals.

The chapter begins with an overview of mortality changes from 1930 to the 1990s. The changes reflect substantial improvement in mortality in the twentieth century, as well as convergence in mortality rates between Mexico Megacity and the rest of the nation.

This chapter turns to causes of death in the Megacity. Since small area data are not available, this section looks into five causes of death in Mexico City versus the remainder of the nation. Chronic disease causes of cardiovascular and cancer are higher in the Federal District and lower in the State of Mexico than in non-Megacity states. Trauma is low in the Federal District and high in the State of Mexico versus the nation remainder. Not surprisingly, respiratory disease mortality is much higher in the Megacity than states elsewhere.

Diet is discussed in historical context, referring to data from the 1970 census of population. There was sharp contrast in diet patterns of the semi-urban fringe versus the central city that mirrors rural-urban differences of the nation.

The geographical distribution of mortality in Mexico City is examined for the period 1950-1993. The pattern of infant mortality reveals large variation in the Federal District in 1991. Longitudinally there is a lowering of crude mortality to the north in the State of Mexico and increase in the northern Federal District.

The relationships of mortality rates and other mortality dimensions are studied through correlation analysis. Association of 1993 mortality rates with key cluster dimensions indicates many significant relationships. Mortality is associated with older population (65+) and varies opposite with population growth 1970-90, among other significant results. These associations are discussed in the context of others' findings.

The spatial pattern of medical and health care in the Megacity shows large differences in medical center treatment volume, medical attention for fatal diseases, and federal government medical benefits. In the Federal District there are differences in patterns of medical services for categories of government medical services including Departmento Del Distrito Federal (DDF) and ISSTE. Generally, the highest capacity of medical services is in the prosperous northern part of the Federal District.

Historical Mortality Change

The mortality of Mexico City improved significantly in the twentieth century. At the same time, some measures of mortality were affected by improvements in the vital records system for registering deaths (Cardenas, 1995). In the 80s and early 90s, for instance, the quality of mortality data by subregistration and response errors improved significantly (Cardenas, 1995). The proportion of deaths without medical certificates dropped from 12.1 percent in 1980 to 2.4 percent 1993. Likewise, the percent of deaths caused by "signs, symptoms, and morbid states poorly defined" decreased from 6.7 percent in 1980 to 1.9 percent in 1993 (Cardenas, 1995). Mortality discussions concern both age adjusted measures (life expectancy and infant mortality) and age unadjusted measures (crude mortality). It is important to point out that unadjusted measures are responsive to changes in the population age distribution. On the other hand, crude measures reflect the true impact of mortality on the population (Shryock and Siegel, 1976; Smith, 1992). The problem of subregistration was worse earlier in the century and for infant mortality versus adult mortality (see Rabell et al., 1986). However, longitudinal trends discussed in this section probably would have showed even greater lowering, if registration could be accurately adjusted, since rates earlier in the century would be even higher with adequate registration.

The age-standardized measure of life expectancy has shown dramatic increase for the nation in the 20th century. As seen in Figure 6.1, life expectancy increased by 89 percent from 1930 to 1993. The increase was greater for women, which is apparent in the figure indicating a gender gap increasing over two-thirds of a century. The gender gap is in line with most nations during this century (UN, 1994).

Crude mortality is the total number of deaths divided by population. As seen in Figure 6.2, it dropped by about 90 percent during the twentieth century. There was an increase during the 1920s which may reflect the social instability following the Mexican Revolution. The Federal District had higher crude mortality than either the State of Mexico or nation at the turn of the century, but had dropped to levels approximating the nation by 1930 and has remained at those levels. On the other hand, the State of Mexico was elevated in crude mortality from 1930 to 1960, after which it converged to approximate the nation. Currently, the Federal District, State of Mexico, and nation are nearly identical in crude mortality.

Infant mortality is the ratio of infant deaths to births multiplied by 1,000. Infant deaths are defined as deaths to children under one year of age (Shryock and Siegel, 1976). Infant mortality is particular subject to subregistration (Shryock and Siegel, 1976), so official data presented must be considered as a significant underestimate of actual infant mortality. Infant mortality is not discussed in this volume for the small areas of Mexico City due to the problems in subregistration compounded by random errors in registration by sub-areas.

Infant mortality is seen in Figure 6.3 to have dropped substantially during the entire century with the exception of the 30s and 60s. In the past two decades, infant mortality has dropped by two thirds according to official figures. The rate estimated by the UN and taking into account subregistration was 36 (UN, 1994). An alternative 1994 estimate is 35 (Population Reference Bureau, 1994).

Infant mortality is sometimes taken as an indicator of health levels for nations. This puts Mexico in the middle range worldwide above the U.S. and Europe with average infant mortality rates of 8 and 11; comparable to the Central American rate of 39; and lower than the South American rate of 53.

Concomitant with the drop in infant mortality is a rise in the proportion of deaths for older ages, i.e. age fifty or more. As seen in Figure 6.4, this proportion increased in the Federal District from 47 to 67 percent over the sixteen years from 1976 to 1992. In the

State of Mexico, the proportion of older deaths was much lower, increasing from 31 to 50 percent over the same period. By contrast rates for the remainder of the nation were in between. Using this as a rough gauge for the change from communicable to noncommunicable diseases that characterizes the epidemiological transition, it would appear that Mexico has undergone rapid transition and especially so in the Federal District, i.e. the older and more central part of Mexico City. These rates exceed the average of 50 percent for Latin America (Heligman et al., 1993). Heligman et al. predict that Latin America will reach an average level of 70 percent in the period 2010-2015, a level already approximated by Mexico City in 1992.

There are large socioeconomic differences in mortality with higher socioeconomic status generally implying lower mortality rates (Preston and Taubman, 1994). In Mexico, a number of studies have supported these conclusions. For instance, Rutstein (1992) analyzed Mexican mortality rates per thousand for children under five for the period 1979-1987; rates were as follows:

Mother's Education	Mortality Rate for Children Under 5
None	112
1-3 years	91
4-6 years	54
7-11 years	29

Source: Rutstein, 1992

This study revealed a nearly fourfold difference in mortality rate based on educational level. An implication is that the Federal District's lower rates earlier in the century for crude and infant mortality were due to its higher socioeconomic status. The convergence of rates for the Federal District may imply opposite differentials due to other causes such as environmental degradation. The socioeconomic differences will be examined further for small area data.

In the twentieth century, mortality rates have improved greatly in the nation and Mexico City. As elsewhere in the world, causes of death are shifting as disease prevention and health programs change (Martin and Preston, 1993). The drop in mortality rates earlier in the century was largely due to control of communicable diseases through improved sanitation, water quality, quality of nutrition, antibiotics and other public health and medical measures. The drop in recent decades is increasingly due to improvements related to chronic and noncommunicable diseases such as heart disease, cancer, and accidents (Martin and Preston, 1993). There has been convergence in overall mortality between Mexico City, Federal District, and the nation-remainder, i.e. non-Megacity states. This convergence may represent compensating geographical patterns favoring improved mortality in more rural and less prosperous regions. However, the inner Megacity differs in its increased older mortality, versus the nation.

Figure 6.1 Life Expectancy at Birth, Mexico, 1930-1993, By Gender

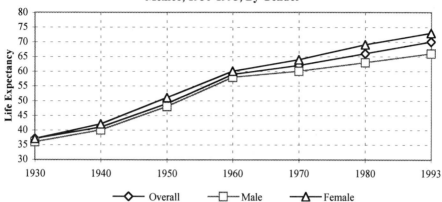

Overall —◇—   Male —□—   Female —△—

Supporting Data

Year	Overall	Male	Female
1930	37	36	37
1940	41	40	42
1950	49	48	51
1960	59	58	60
1970	62	60	64
1980	66	63	69
1993	70	66	73

Sources: CEED, 1981; Rabell et al., 1986; *Population Reference Bureau*, 1993

Figure 6.2 Mortality Rate, Federal District, State of Mexico, and Nation, 1900 -1990

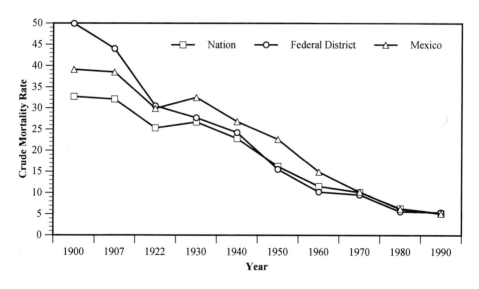

Source: INEGI: *Estadisticas Historicas de Mexico*, Vol 1, 1994

150

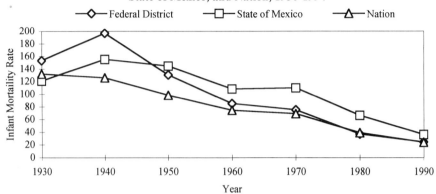

**Figure 6.3 Infant Mortality Rate, Federal District,
State of Mexico, and Nation, 1930-1994**

Infant Mortality Rate

Year	Federal District	State of Mexico	Nation
1930	152.8	120.6	131.6
1940	196.3	154.8	125.7
1950	130.2	144.6	98.2
1960	85.1	107.9	74.2
1970	74.7	109.6	68.5
1980	37.0	66.3	38.8
1990	24.2	35.9	23.9

Sources: INEGI: *Estadisticas Historicas de Mexico,* 1994;

UN: *World Population,* 1994;

INEGI: *Defunciones en Los Estados Unidos Mexicanos,* 1994.

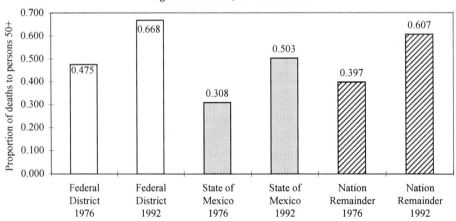

**Figure 6.4 Proportion of Deaths to Persons
Age 50 or Older, 1976 and 1992**

Source: INEGI, *Defunciones en Los Estados Unidos Mexicanos, 1994.*

Causes of Death

Causes of death are important to examine, since aggregated together they account for overall mortality. Since there are considerable differences in death causes nationally, it is important to examine causes of death nationally, prior to examining them for the two Megacity states.

From a national perspective, the effects of the epidemiological transition stages are apparent (Pick and Butler, 1994, 1995). Cause of death can be studied by age-standardizing the mortality rates. This is necessary to adjust for differences in the age structure between states. The method used is indirect standardization (Keyfitz and Flieger, 1971). The standard population selected is the nation of Mexico, 1990. The method adjusts the cause-specific mortality rate for each state by a factor d/Summation (M_aP_a), where d represents the total cause-specific deaths in the state, M_a is the age-cause-specific death rate for the nation and P_a is the population of a five-year age group for the state. It is important to mention that, since the age distribution of the population has small variation among states, indirect standardization in this case has only a modest effect on values.

The leading cause-specific mortality rates for the nation in 1990 are shown in Table 6.1 and Figure 6.5. Nationally, these causes accounted for two thirds of deaths. It is also clear that the cause of death profile differs considerably in the Megacity states. In our analysis, we refer to the cause of death category of nutritional, metabolic, endocrine, and immunity diseases as NMEI. For the leading chronic diseases of cardiovascular, NMEI, and cancer, the Federal District is significantly higher than the State of Mexico and the nation-remainder. This agrees with a growing consensus that cardiovascular and cancer mortality and morbidity are inversely related to prosperity and advanced nation lifestyle (Gribble and Preston, 1993, see Introduction). The reason is ascribed mainly to diet, nutrition, environmental degradation, and stress factors. On the other hand mortality from respiratory disease is highest by far in the State of Mexico followed by the Federal District and nation-remainder. This may relate to cumulative patterns of air pollution, discussed in Chapter 7, which may have greater impact on mortality in the State of Mexico. Particulates and nitrogen dioxide in particular have been more concentrated in the State of Mexico and may impact respiratory disease, although the research on health impacts is inconclusive. Finally, trauma mortality is much higher in the State of Mexico, exceeding the Federal District by 62 percent. The reason may be a cumulation of different types of trauma in the State of Mexico. Felony sentences are shown in Chapter 8 to be very high in the populous municipios of Nezahualcoyotl, Tlalnepantla, and Naucalpan that adjoin the northern part of the Federal District (see Map 8.16). Overall, there is a higher felony as well as homicide sentencing rate in the Federal District. They must be viewed cautiously, since homicide sentencing rate is a weak proxy for homicide rate. Accident mortality is higher in the State of Mexico as are industrial accident rates. Overall, the State of Mexico is not a safe area for trauma, especially in the populous areas immediately adjoining the northern Federal District.

It is revealing to examine in more depth the pattern for cardiovascular mortality, the leading cause of death nationally in 1990, accounting for 21 percent of deaths in the nation (Pick and Butler, 1994). Cardiovascular standardized mortality (see Map 6.1) is seen to be roughly twice as high in the northern border states than in the far south. Mexico City, as reflected in the Federal District level of 1.18 and State of Mexico value of 1.01, is intermediate in value, close to the national mean of 1.08. Mexico Megacity's middle position is due to countervailing reasons. On the one hand, it has among the best medical/health care system in the nation. On the other, the cardiovascular risk factors of age, diet, nutrition, stress, and lack of exercise are assumed to be higher in the metropolitan center. As discussed in the next section, the diet factor is historically confirmed to be much less favorable in the center. We postulate there is lack of access to exercise because of urban sprawl and the center's urban stress level is high. The age risk factor is important since the Federal District has a substantially older population than the State of Mexico. Fine-grained age differences were noted in Chapter 3. It is clear from Map 3.12 that the very populous northern Federal District has a high proportion of elderly, which contrasts with much lower proportion in many of the populous municipios to the north.

It is important to emphasize that Mexico Megacity resides at an intermediate levels of cause-specific mortality on a national basis. For non-communicable diseases, the northern border states are worse off. For communicable diseases, the south far exceeds the Megacity. Internally the Megacity to a certain extent reflects the national cause-specific patterns (Pick and Butler, 1995). A recent study has pointed out on a national basis that the most important predictors of cause-specific mortality are crowding, housing characteristics, marriage/divorce, and manufacturing (Pick and Butler, 1995). These factors may have a strong influence within the Megacity in small area patterns, since they vary by zone so greatly.

Although the cause-specific data for small areas are not used in this research, it is possible to compare more detailed causes of death for the Federal District (central Megacity) and State of Mexico. Since the State of Mexico consists 69 percent of Megacity and the rest in non-Megacity, the State of Mexico only roughly reflects the Megacity periphery.

The nine leading causes of death in 1993 are shown in Figure 6.6. For the Federal District, the chronic and noncommunicable diseases dominate. Among leading causes, cardiovascular, cancer, diabetes, and liver diseases, and kidney diseases accounted for 55 percent of the deaths. Cardiovascular dominates with about a quarter of deaths. By contrast in the State of Mexico, among leading causes, noncommunicable diseases accounted for 40 percent of deaths, with cardiovascular responsible for one sixth. By contrast, accidents, homicides, pneumonia/influenza, and prenatal diseases are substantially higher. It is interesting that accidents and homicides accounted for a sixth of deaths about equivalent to cardiovascular. The more detailed comparison further substantiates the conclusion that the central Megacity has a more advanced profile of mortality causation while the periphery has higher trauma and certain infectious diseases.

Table 6. 1 Standardized Cause-Specific Mortality Rates, 1990

| | Standardized Cause - Specific Mortality Rate | | | | |
	Nation-Remainder	Federal District	State of Mexico	Number of Deaths Nation	Percent of Deaths Nation
Cardiovascular Diseases	1.08	1.18	1.01	88,982	21.0
Trauma	0.73	0.53	0.86	58,094	13.7
NMEI Diseases	0.52	0.68	0.62	45,575	10.8
Respiratory Diseases	0.47	0.59	0.86	44,277	10.5
Cancer	0.52	0.59	0.47	42,017	9.9
Other				143,858	34.0
TOTAL				422,803	

Source: INEGI, *1991 Anuario Estadistico.*

Map 6.1
Standardized Mortality Rate from Cardiovascular Diseases, Mexico, 1990

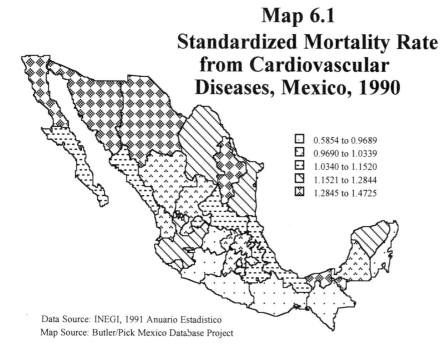

	0.5854 to 0.9689
	0.9690 to 1.0339
	1.0340 to 1.1520
	1.1521 to 1.2844
	1.2845 to 1.4725

Data Source: INEGI, 1991 Anuario Estadistico
Map Source: Butler/Pick Mexico Database Project

**Figure 6.5 Standardized Mortality Rates
Nation-Remainder, Federal District,
and State of Mexico, 1990**

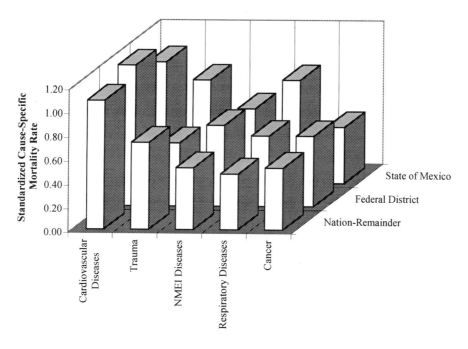

Source: INEGI, *1991 Anuario Estadistico.*

154

Figure 6.6 Leading Causes of Death, Federal District and State of Mexico, 1993

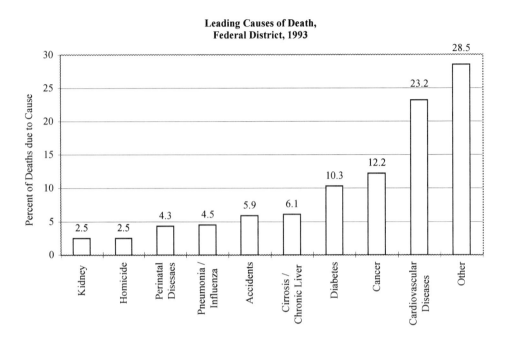

Leading Causes of Death, Federal District, 1993

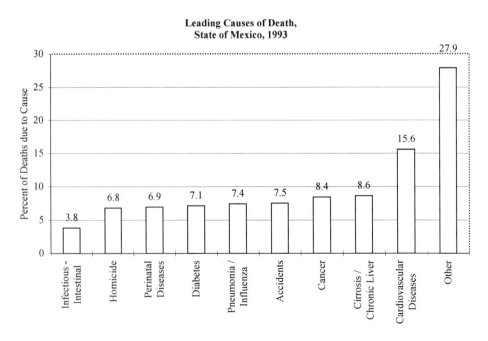

Leading Causes of Death, State of Mexico, 1993

Source: INEGI: *Anuario Estadistico,* 1995.

Diet

Diet is an important factor in death and disease in Mexico City because of the prominence of cardiovascular disease, where diet is a well known risk factor (Black, 1992). It is also viewed as a risk factor for cancer (Roberts, 1984, Henderson, Ross, and Pike, 1991), although dietary effects vary by type of cancer (Henderson, Ross, and Pike, 1991).

The Mexican census historically allowed study of diet through questions regarding meat and egg consumption by children that were included from mid-century up to 1980. In 1980, the Federal District was the highest of any state in meat and egg consumption by children and the State of Mexico was above average. This is born out in more detail by examining the historical geographical patterns for children consuming no meat and children consuming no eggs in 1970 (see Maps 6.2 and 6.3). In both cases, the proportion of children with no meat and no eggs is much higher in the semi-urban zones to the northeast, southeast, and west, while the populous center in the northern Federal District has very low proportions. The differences are quite large as seen in the ranges for the upper and lower quintiles.

The information is limited by its age of twenty five years and by the limitation to children. However, it does provide some albeit limited support for dietary factors that encourage improved cardiovascular and cancer risks in the city periphery versus the center (Roberts, 1984; Henderson, Ross, and Pike, 1991; Black, 1992). It is hoped that more detailed dietary information will become available by small area that would inform future research on mortality and health factors.

Map 6.2
No Meat, 1970

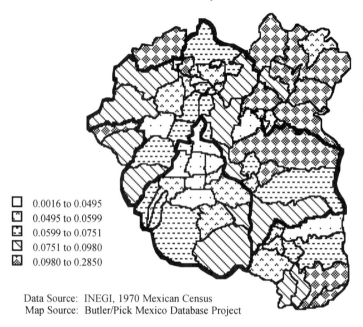

☐	0.0016 to 0.0495
▤	0.0495 to 0.0599
▥	0.0599 to 0.0751
▧	0.0751 to 0.0980
▩	0.0980 to 0.2850

Data Source: INEGI, 1970 Mexican Census
Map Source: Butler/Pick Mexico Database Project

Map 6.3
No Eggs, 1970

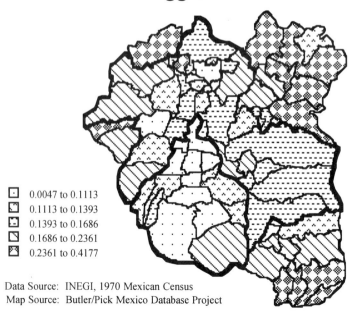

▫	0.0047 to 0.1113
▤	0.1113 to 0.1393
▥	0.1393 to 0.1686
▧	0.1686 to 0.2361
▨	0.2361 to 0.4177

Data Source: INEGI, 1970 Mexican Census
Map Source: Butler/Pick Mexico Database Project

Megacity Patterns of Mortality

The spatial patterns of crude mortality and their causes can be studied over the second half of this century. Although data earlier in the century were subject to under-registration, and random fluctuations, the series is nevertheless worthwhile examining for the years 1950 to 1980 (Partida Bush, 1987). It is also important to point out that the data from 1950 to 1980 reflect the location the death certificate was filled out, rather than the place of habitual residence of the decedent (Partida Bush, 1987). This is in contrast to the crude mortality data for 1993, which is for place of habitual residence (INEGI, *Anuarios Estadisticos*, 1995). Thus the earlier 1950-80 series tends to overestimate mortality rates in the delegations that have major medical centers and hospitals, namely, Benito Juarez, Cuautémoc, Miguel Hidalgo, and Venustiano Carranza, while underestimating mortality rates in other areas.

Mortality rates for a decade are computed by totaling mortality over the decade and dividing by an estimate of the mid-decade population (Partida Bush, 1987). The time series 1950-70 seen in Maps 6.4, and 6.5 reflect generally high mortality in a group of adjoining municipios to the north of the tip of the Federal District that include Cuautitlan Izcalli, Tultitlan, Coacalco, and Tecamac. The most important tendency over time is a reversal of mortality for the old central business district delegations, from a low level in the 50s to a high level in the 70s. Partida Bush regarded this a puzzling change, since elevated city center rates would have been expected over the whole period for the aforementioned reason of medical center/hospital locations. Part of the puzzle may be answered by a longitudinal shift in age structure leading to an increase in elderly population in the city center. In the 50s, the city center's greater youth contributed to offsetting the presence of medical centers and hospitals. Also, we postulate that those centers and hospitals were smaller and not able to support the greater numbers of patients of subsequent decades. There may well be other explanations as well. It is important to note in this time series that the baseline level of mortality was reduced greatly each decade (see Figure 6.2).

The crude mortality rate for 1993 reflects 1993 death registration and 1990 population (see Map 6.7). Hence, it somewhat underestimates values, since population may have increased by approximately five percent (Population Reference Bureau, 1994). However, the error is considered small for examining spatial differences. The pattern reflects higher mortality in the central delegations of Miguel Hidalgo, Cuautémoc, and Benito Juarez, a trend consistent with changes in the central delegations 1950-80. The semi-urban periphery has elevated mortality, which likely reflects elevated proportions of elderly (see Map 3.12). Zones adjoining the semi-urban periphery also show higher mortality, which partly reflects age structure transition. There is heightened mortality in Nextlalpan that is unexplained since it has fewer elderly. It is curious that the lowest mortality rate of 1.8 is Jaltenco that Nextlalpan surrounds.

Although there are several outliers, the spatial distribution of crude mortality in 1993 shows modest variation (CV = 23). This reflects a certain underlying uniformity of health risk factors and health services in different parts of the Megacity. The amount of uniformity may reflect underlying uniformities in age distribution. For health planning purposes, it would be essential to examine age standardized measures. An especially valuable one would be life expectancy, although migration and random fluctuations in mortality might preclude its use. With standardized measures, health planners could better plan for greater equity of services in the Megacity (Bobadilla and Possas, 1993).

158

Map 6.4
Crude Mortality Rate, 1950-1960

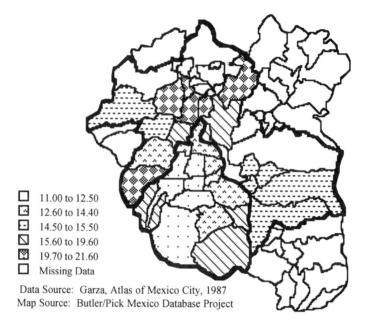

☐ 11.00 to 12.50
▣ 12.60 to 14.40
▣ 14.50 to 15.50
◩ 15.60 to 19.60
▨ 19.70 to 21.60
☐ Missing Data

Data Source: Garza, Atlas of Mexico City, 1987
Map Source: Butler/Pick Mexico Database Project

Map 6.5
Crude Mortality Rate, 1960-1970

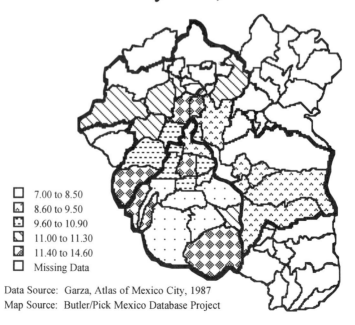

☐ 7.00 to 8.50
▣ 8.60 to 9.50
▣ 9.60 to 10.90
◩ 11.00 to 11.30
▣ 11.40 to 14.60
☐ Missing Data

Data Source: Garza, Atlas of Mexico City, 1987
Map Source: Butler/Pick Mexico Database Project

Map 6.6
Crude Mortality Rate, 1970-1980

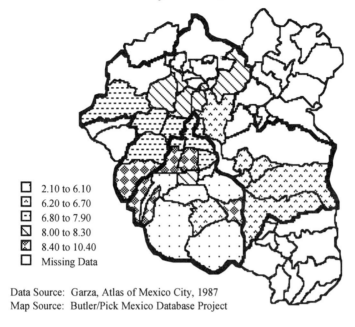

2.10 to 6.10
6.20 to 6.70
6.80 to 7.90
8.00 to 8.30
8.40 to 10.40
Missing Data

Data Source: Garza, Atlas of Mexico City, 1987
Map Source: Butler/Pick Mexico Database Project

Map 6.7
Crude Mortality Rate, 1993

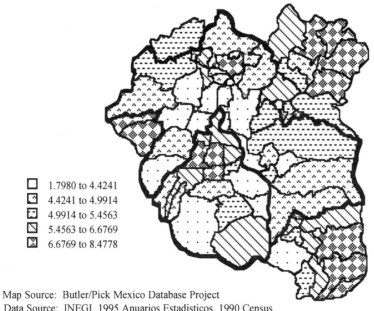

1.7980 to 4.4241
4.4241 to 4.9914
4.9914 to 5.4563
5.4563 to 6.6769
6.6769 to 8.4778

Map Source: Butler/Pick Mexico Database Project
Data Source: INEGI, 1995 Anuarios Estadisticos, 1990 Census

Mortality Correlation Analysis

Mortality and health variables may be related to each other as well as to key cluster dimensions of the larger study. The interrelationships between mortality and health attributes are examined first, followed by exploring how crude mortality may be related to other cluster dimensions.

A constraint of applying correlation methodology to mortality/health variables is that some variables are limited to a portion of the sample. This includes the crude mortality for the 50s, 60s, and 70s, as well as medical care and health service attributes. The 1991 data on federal government health care, limited to the Federal District, are excluded from the correlations. The common sample size is 32 small areas including the 16 Federal District delegations as well as 16 municipios in the State of Mexico. The preponderance of populous zones of the Megacity is included in this sample, with the exception of Nezahualcoyotl.

Crude mortality is significantly related between the 50s and 60s and 60s and 70s, but not between the 50s and 70s implying longer term changes already noted (see Table 6.2). The 50s and 60s crude mortality are inversely related to population, which may be a definitional artifact, since population is in the rate denominator. Since the 1993 crude mortality registration keyed to residence (versus place of death record) as explained earlier, its lack of association with 50s, 60s, and 70s crude mortality is not surprising. Historical and 1993 crude mortality have little association with health care and benefit variables. This underscores that the provision of health care and benefits may be less important for mortality than other factors. The 1993 mortality is not associated with elderly population for the sample ($N = 32$), although they are associated for the larger sample ($N = 69$).

Health care and benefits variables have strong inter-correlation (see Table 6.2). The percent of adult deaths lacking federal medical benefits is associated with deaths having no prior medical attention ($r = 0.67$) and inversely with percent of adult deaths from communicable diseases and from non communicable diseases in medical centers ($r = -0.39$ and $r = -0.38$ respectively). These relationships underscore that lack of federal benefits is strongly associated with lack of access to medical personnel and centers, i.e. that federal benefits have substantial health care impacts. Decedents lacking prior medical attention are inversely related to deaths taking place in medical centers for both communicable and non communicable diseases. This has obvious explanation of the presence of medical attention in hospitals. The percent of deaths in medical centers has extremely high correlation between communicable and non-communicable diseases ($r = 0.93$). Zones have high health center-based mortality regardless of class of diseases. Hence, we will only discuss further this attribute for communicable diseases, with results carrying over to the non-communicable category.

Crude mortality in 1993 was compared with the overall cluster dimensions introduced in Chapter 1. This was done to explore relationships of mortality with other crucial dimensions for this book.

As seen in Table 6.3, there is a set of significant relationships with demographic attributes. Crude Mortality in 1993 is associated with population density ($r = 0.35$) and elderly population ($r = 0.26$) and inversely related to population log ($r = -0.35$), population growth 1950-70 ($r = -0.54$) and inmigration ($r = -0.54$). The relationship with density is not surprising, since mortality tends to fall off away from the city center with the exception of the rural periphery. Associations with population growth and inmigration are explicable since high growth/inmigration areas also tend to have younger and healthier population, i.e. migrants tend to be young adults and children. The association of mortality with the aged was explained earlier. The opposite association with log of population has partly to do with population deconcentration of the Megacity center as well as many other population features.

Also evident in the correlations are inverse relationships with dimensions of economic prosperity, for instance with high income (r = -0.24), and owners/employers/salaried workers (r = -0.30). These results correspond to most economic studies reported in the literature (Preston and Taubman, 1994), although a recent study of Mexican states found mixed associations with economic prosperity (Pick and Butler, 1995). There are strong associations with measures of lower quality of housing, for instance with housing lacking a toilet (r = 0.54) and with households using firewood or coal (r = 0.57). These housing associations are opposite to findings at the state level for cancer although for other mortality causes the study was inclusive (Pick and Butler, 1995). Finally, there are weak inverse relationships for some indigenous language attributes, in particular Mixteco and indigenous language remainder.

In summary, correlations confirm that crude mortality is closely related over time and that the health care/benefit variables are tightly related in expected ways but lack associations with mortality. Crude mortality in 1993 has associations with elderly population and low quality housing and inverse associations with population growth, migration, and economic prosperity.

Table 6.2 Correlation Matrix of Mortality Variables

	Natural Log of Population 1990	Mortality 1950-60	Mortality 1960-70	Mortality 1970-80	Mortality 1993	Deaths Lacking Prior Government Benefits	No Prior Medical Attention	Medical Center Deaths - Non Communic.	Medical Center Deaths - Communic.
Mortality 1950-60	-.559***								
Mortality 1960-70	-.482***	.693***							
Mortality 1970-80	-.048	.325**	.558***						
Mortality 1993	.094	-.461***	-.009	-.041					
Deaths Lacking Prior Government Benefits	-.238	-.180	-.167	-.133	.131				
No Prior Medical Attention	-.150	.069	-.022	.095	-.033	.666***			
Medical Center Deaths - Non Communic.	.345**	-.341**	-.263*	-.090	.060	-.384***	-.437***		
Medical Center Deaths - Communic.	.399***	-.366**	-.319**	-.135	.055	-.388***	-.421***	.930***	
Percent of Population 65+	.385***	-.077	-.002	-.072	.268*	-.184	-.246*	-.073	.022

Note: Significance Levels   N=32

*   .05
**   .01
***   .001

Table 6.3 Correlations of Crude Mortality in 1993 with Overall Cluster Variables

Cluster Variable	Correlation Coefficent
Population	-.212
Density	.351 **
Log of Population	-.353 **
Log of Density	.150
Relative Pop. Growth 70-90	-.535 ***
Mortality 93	1.000 ***
Percent 65+	.262 *
Inmigraton 1985-90	-.536 ***
Sex Ratio	-.065
No Running Water	.016
Housing with 1 Room	-.023
No Septic Tank	-.006
No Toilet	.535 ***
Percent Wood or Coal	.565 ***
Crowded Housing	-.142
Economic Activity	-.226
Unemployed	.180
Owners/Employed/Salaried	-.296 **
Wholesale Revs.	-.043
Metal/Machinery Revs.	-.235
Prof/Tech. Svcs. Revs.	.113
Prof/Tech/Mgr	-.146
Prim Educ.	-.22
High Income	-.238
Tenure	-.152
Cum Fert. 20-29	.121
Free Union	.062
Separated/Divorced	.090
Fem. Econ. Activity	.113
Indig. Lang.	-.213
Mixteco Speaking	-.253 **
Nahautl Speaking	-.038
Otomi Speaking	-.195
Zapotec Speaking	-.204
Indig. Lang. Remainder	-.253 **

Note: Significance Levels	*	.05
	**	.01
	***	.001

Medical and Health Care and Benefits

Provision of medical and health care is critical for the huge city. Policies have been put in place to provide services for population dispersed spatially in a variety of Megacity areas and locales. The federal government hospital and medical services infrastructure is looked at first, followed by examining several medical services and benefits attributes.

The federal government in Mexico is responsible for most health services, both through the social security system and health ministry (Bobadilla and Possas, 1993). The main other source of health care for the populace is through private sources, although it is more costly. Government medical centers and services for the Megacity are located mainly in the six delegations of Alvaro Obregon, Benito Juarez, Cuauhtemoc, Gustavo Madero, Miguel Hidalgo, and Venustiano Carranza. These delegations were in mid-century the most populous, but have undergone population deconcentration, so that today the most populous zones besides Gustavo Madero are to the northeast in Iztapalapa, Nezahualcoyotl, and Ecatepec (see Map 3.3). The major health care complex was built up in the mid-century in the then heart of the city, but is not ideally located today. A constraint with this complex is transportation access, since it is difficult to reach from outlying areas including populous ones to the north and northeast. It is even difficult to reach from populous Nezahualcoyotl and Chimalhuacan to the east.

The following table shows the percent of Federal District medical/health resources located in these six municipios.

Medical Health Resource	Percent Located in the Six Delegations
Medical Services Provided by the Federal Government	65.3
Federal Government Medical Centers	54.8
Federal Government Hospital Beds	63.5
DDF Medical Center Personnel	67.3

Alvaro Obregon, Benito Juarez, Cuauhtemoc, Gustavo Madero,
Miguel Hidalgo, and Venustiano Carranza.
Source: INEGI: 1991 *Anuario Estadistico.*

Even after calculating on a per capita basis, the federal medical resources are concentrated in the northern part of the Federal District. As seen in Maps 6.8 - 6.11, the highest per capita concentrations are in the six municipios, with the addition of Milpa Alta. It is important to note the high variation for the health resources in the Federal District. In Tables 6.4, and 6.5, the CV's are high, ranging from 60 to over 200. This reflects large disparities in the availability of health care services cited as a weakness in the Mexican system (Bobadilla and Possas, 1993).

Another set of data refers to the provision of health services to adults (Luna Santos, 1995). Luna Santos obtained data from examination of death certificates for entries on presence or absence of health benefits, medical center location at death, medical attention for last illness, and location of death in hospital, home, or other. This entire section cites the data source collected by Luna Santos and incorporated into her research (Luna Santos, 1995).

Many adults die in the Megacity without prior federal government medical benefits. As seen in Map 6.12, decedents without medical benefits are not located in the Federal District except for Xochimilco, but tend to be located in the far north, east, and in Huixquilucan in the west. These areas tend to be less economically prosperous ones (compare with Map 10.7). The highest areas lacking benefits are Xochimilco (69 percent), Chimalhuacan (64 percent), Nextlalpan (57 percent), and Chalco (54 percent). These are all areas that are associated with poverty. It is particular surprising that Xochimilco located in the central Federal District near the major medical complex would have such lack of medical benefits. The overall pattern reinforces the need to plan better for more equitable distribution of government health benefits (Bobadilla and Possas, 1993).

The proportion of adult deaths in medical centers from communicable diseases (Map 6.13) reveals a high proportion of medical center deaths in Coyoacan and Iztapalapa. Rates are lower throughout the State of Mexico. Overall, there is a relatively small proportion of adult deaths in federal government medical centers. This may reflect the limited capacity and crowded nature of the centers (Bobadilla and Possas, 1993), especially the more sophisticated tertiary centers.

The percent of adult deaths having received no prior medical attention for the final illness (see Map 6.14) is highest in the far north municipios in the State of Mexico, as well as in Nezahualcoyotl and Chimalhuacan (Luna Santos, 1995). The far north lack of medical attention is linked to the lack of government medical benefits. Another reason is difficulty in transportation access to the major central medical complex. The lack of medical attention in Nezahualcoyotl and Chimalhuacan may derive from their rapid population growth, which has not been accompanied by needed equivalent growth in medical services. The levels of this variable are generally low in the Federal District, which makes sense because of the high density of government and private medical services available.

Map 6.8
Medical Services Provided by
Government Per Capita, 1992

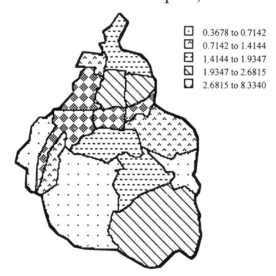

□	0.3678 to 0.7142
▨	0.7142 to 1.4144
▤	1.4144 to 1.9347
▨	1.9347 to 2.6815
▢	2.6815 to 8.3340

Data Source: 1991 Anuario Estadistico of the Federal District
Map Source: Butler/Pick Mexico Database Project

Map 6.9
Government Medical Centers, 1992
Per 100,000

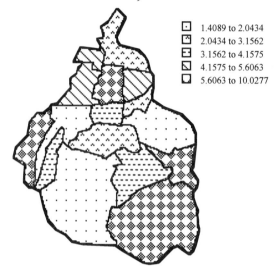

1.4089 to 2.0434
2.0434 to 3.1562
3.1562 to 4.1575
4.1575 to 5.6063
5.6063 to 10.0277

Data Source: 1991 Anuario Estadistico of the Federal District
Map Source: Butler/Pick Mexico Database Project

Map 6.10
Government Hospital Beds, 1992
Per 10,000

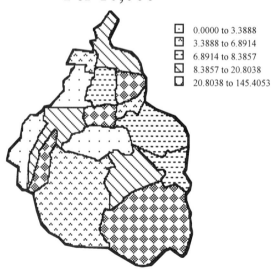

0.0000 to 3.3888
3.3888 to 6.8914
6.8914 to 8.3857
8.3857 to 20.8038
20.8038 to 145.4053

Data Source: 1991 Anuario Estadistico of the Federal District
Map Source: Butler/Pick Mexico Database Project

Map 6.11
DDF Medical Center Personnel, 1992
Per 100,000

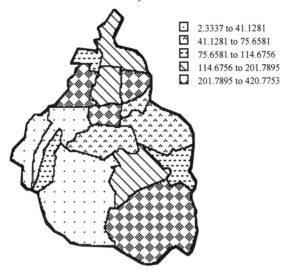

2.3337 to 41.1281
41.1281 to 75.6581
75.6581 to 114.6756
114.6756 to 201.7895
201.7895 to 420.7753

Data Source: 1991 Anuario Estadistico of the Federal District
Map Source: Butler/Pick Mexico Database Project

Map 6.12
Percent of Adult Deaths with No Prior
Federal Government Medical Benefits, 1992

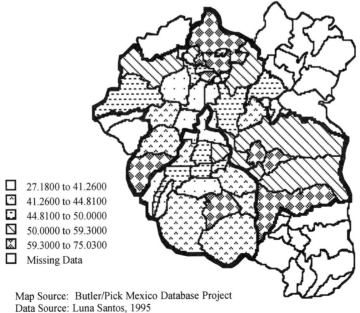

27.1800 to 41.2600
41.2600 to 44.8100
44.8100 to 50.0000
50.0000 to 59.3000
59.3000 to 75.0300
Missing Data

Map Source: Butler/Pick Mexico Database Project
Data Source: Luna Santos, 1995

168

Map 6.13
Percent of Adult Deaths in Medical Centers from Communicable Diseases, 1992

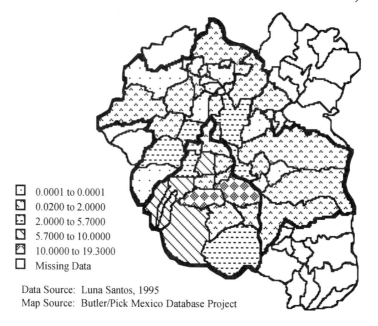

- 0.0001 to 0.0001
- 0.0200 to 2.0000
- 2.0000 to 5.7000
- 5.7000 to 10.0000
- 10.0000 to 19.3000
- Missing Data

Data Source: Luna Santos, 1995
Map Source: Butler/Pick Mexico Database Project

Map 6.14
Percent of Deaths in Adults who Received No Prior Medical Attention, 1992

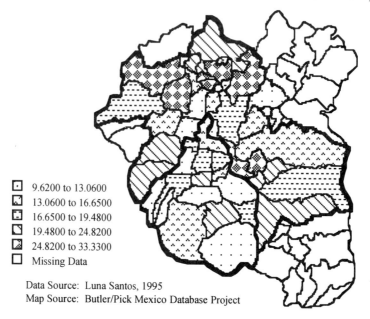

- 9.6200 to 13.0600
- 13.0600 to 16.6500
- 16.6500 to 19.4800
- 19.4800 to 24.8200
- 24.8200 to 33.3300
- Missing Data

Data Source: Luna Santos, 1995
Map Source: Butler/Pick Mexico Database Project

Table 6.4 Government Hospitals and Medical Services, 1992

No.	Area	Medical Services Provided by Government	Medical Services Provided by Government Per Capita	Government Medical Centers	Government Medical Centers Per 100,000 Population	Government Hospital Beds	Government Hospital Beds Per 10,000 Population
1	Alvaro Obregon	2,672,701	4.16	11	1.71	629	9.79
2	Azcapotzalco	605,046	1.27	20	4.21	148	6.24
3	Benito Juarez	3,398,687	8.33	13	3.19	807	25.01
4	Coyoacan	939,665	1.47	20	3.12	108	3.37
5	Cuajimalpa	57,003	0.48	12	10.03	0	0.00
6	Cuauhtemoc	1,436,527	2.41	55	9.23	263	8.24
7	Gustavo A. Madero	2,063,115	1.63	30	2.37	643	8.53
8	Iztacalco	1,677,713	3.74	10	2.23	98	4.37
9	Iztapalapa	2,028,175	1.36	21	1.41	816	7.99
10	Magdalena Contreras	143,294	0.73	8	4.10	1,418	145.41
11	Miguel Hidalgo	1,201,338	2.95	22	5.41	2,122	62.23
12	Milpa Alta	153,402	2.41	6	9.43	87	27.34
13	Tlahuac	143,406	0.69	12	5.81	104	7.55
14	Tlalpan	178,333	0.37	9	1.86	110	3.40
15	Venustiano Carranza	1,165,195	2.24	24	4.62	1,084	31.29
16	Xochimilco	398,212	1.47	10	3.69	300	16.60
	Total	18,261,812	2.22	283	3.44	8,737	10.61
	Mean	1,141,363	2.23	18	4.53	546	22.96
	Median	1,052,430	1.55	13	3.89	282	8.39
	S.D.	960,141	1.97	12	2.81	614	36.19
	C.V.	84.12	88.21	69.76	62.05	112.35	157.63
	Minimum	57,003	0.37	6	1.41	0	0.00
	Maximum	3,398,687	8.33	55	10.03	2,122	145.41

Source: Luna Santos, 1995.

Table 6.5 DDF Hospitals and Medical Services, 1992

No.	Area	Medical Services Provided by DDF	Medical Services Provided by DDF Per Capita	DDF Hospital Beds	DDF Hospital Beds Per 10,000 Population	DDF Medical Center Personnel	DDF Medical Center Personnel Per 100,000
1	Alvaro Obregon	33,939	0.05	0	0.00	15	2.33
2	Azcapotzalco	282,182	0.59	148	3.12	495	104.28
3	Benito Juarez	425,123	1.04	213	5.22	954	233.93
4	Coyoacan	189,547	0.30	108	1.69	310	48.43
5	Cuajimalpa	27,387	0.23	0	0.00	20	16.71
6	Cuauhtemoc	320,710	0.54	228	3.83	756	126.85
7	Gustavo A. Madero	870,706	0.69	439	3.46	1,586	125.07
8	Iztacalco	1,600,818	3.57	98	2.19	314	70.04
9	Iztapalapa	623,926	0.42	375	2.52	995	66.76
10	Magdalena Contreras	143,294	0.73	1,418	72.70	171	87.67
11	Miguel Hidalgo	561,449	1.38	410	10.08	1,712	420.78
12	Milpa Alta	121,812	1.91	87	13.67	235	369.18
13	Tlahuac	143,406	0.69	52	2.52	168	81.28
14	Tlalpan	106,135	0.22	55	1.13	164	33.82
15	Venustiano Carranza	754,162	1.45	542	10.43	1,849	355.83
16	Xochimilco	223,450	0.82	150	5.53	460	169.65
	Total	6,428,046	0.61	4,323	5.25	10,204	123.90
	Mean	401,753	0.92	270	8.63	638	144.54
	Median	252,816	0.69	149	3.29	387	95.98
	S.D.	410,666	0.87	348	17.53	612	131.46
	C.V.	102.22	94.76	128.72	203.08	95.98	90.95
	Minimum	27,387	0.05	0	0.00	15	2.33
	Maximum	1,600,818	3.57	1,418	72.70	1,849	420.78

Source: Luna Santos, 1995.

Conclusions

This chapter examined mortality and health services in Mexico City. Viewed historically, there has been great improvement in mortality and morbidity in the twentieth century. The center of Mexico City has a more advanced mortality profile than the periphery, but the Megacity center is less advanced than the northern border region. Infant mortality also dropped very sharply in the century reflecting great improvement in the health system. The proportion of deaths of older ages increased substantially over the past decade and a half which indicates that Mexico City has been undergoing the epidemiological transition, i.e. a shift from communicable to non-communicable and chronic diseases. This shift is likely to continue in the future, raising new challenges in health planning for the metropolis as well as the nation.

Causes of death vary between Megacity center, periphery, and the rest of the nation. The city center is more characterized by cardiovascular, cancer, and diabetes, while the periphery has somewhat reduced levels for them and increased infectious and trauma causes. In the trauma category, both homicides and accidents are higher in the periphery than in the center.

Dietary factors are difficult to examine except historically. There is some indication that diet factors contribute to reduced cardiovascular mortality in the periphery.

The mortality dimensions relate to each other. Crude mortality in 1993 varies with population density, elderly population, and economic prosperity and oppositely with population growth, inmigration, and quality of housing. These relationships are understandable in terms of the rest of this book and mortality literature, with the exception of lack of explanation for housing.

Medical resources are concentrated in the traditional city center of the northern Federal District, a zone that depopulated in the 70s and 80s. The centralization of health services leads to spatial inequities, since newer parts of the city have not been able to develop comparable resources. Health benefits available from the federal government appear to conform to the pattern of poverty versus prosperity in the city discussed more in detail in Chapter 9. Overall, health care services appear to need improved planning for the larger and more spread out metropolis of the future.

7

Environment And Housing

Early the next day we left Iztapalapa . . . [now part of the Federal District of Mexico City] and followed the causeway, which is eight yards wide and goes straight. I do not think it curves at all. . . . With such wonderful sights to gaze on we did know what to say, if this was real that we saw before our eyes. On the land side there were great cities, and on the lake side many more. The lake was crowded with canoes. At intervals along the causeway there were many bridges and before us was the great city of Mexico (Diaz ca. 1400).

A newcomer today is more apt to arrive by air, and before he even glimpses the dried-up bed of Lake Texcoco, now edged with miles of slum hovels, the first thing he sees is an almost perpetual blanket of smog that shrouds the entire city. It is an ugly grayish brown. There is something strangely sinister about it -- a cloud of poison. The pilot orders the seat belts tightened and announces an imminent descent into the murk and filth (Friedrich 1984).

Introduction

As a result of the massive upheaval of the land, many of the world's megacities are beset by environmental problems and Mexico Megacity is no exception. Mexico Megacity is located in an environment that has been described as "a topographical error" (UN, 1992) or as a capital of pollution and slums (Friedrich, 1984, quoting Carlos Fuentes). The city sits in a high altitude basin, surrounded by mountains. Two corridors located to the northeast and northwest funnel air to the center and to the southwest of the city. Much of the city is located upon a former lake which makes parts of the city particularly susceptible to land subsidence and to earthquake damage (NRC/AIC/ANI, 1995).

Huge urban development such as in Mexico Megacity alters large areas of the earth's surface. In Mexico Megacity hillsides have been cut, land surfaces have been reshaped, soil eroded, and the level of water aquifer lowered. The creation of the Megacity has transformed the entire environment of the Valley of Mexico and has impacted regions far beyond the Megacity.

Mexico Megacity has a number of serious environmental problems. For example, *UnoMasUno* (1983) pointed out that the "Valley of Mexico has lost 99 percent of its lakes, 75 percent of its woodlands, and 71 percent of all land is in an advanced process of degradation. In the Federal District, the fauna has been devastated and the biological equilibrium altered such that plagues occasionally arise."

Without question then, Mexico Megacity has a number of serious problems related to an interaction of its environmental conditions and huge population living in the basin. Among the more prominent problems are (1) land use/housing, (2) transportation, (3) pollution, (4) financing urban development, (5) spatial segregation by social class, (6) intergovernmental coordination, (7) water supply, (8) waste disposal and (9) land subsidence (Cornelius, 1976). Marginality of the population has been reviewed in another paper (Butler and Pick, 1995).[1] In this chapter, we examine housing and neighborhood deficits, and then devote special attention to water waste and disposal, and air pollution. All of these enigmas undoubtedly are linked to ill health and premature death caused by biological agents in

---

[1] Only briefly examined in that paper are nutritional deficits; for an extended analysis of nutrition in some areas of the Federal District, see Spring (1991).

water, food, air, and soil (Hardoy et al., 1993). While not explored in this volume, it also should be recognized that Mexico Megacity also has a great potential for *natural disasters* -- for instance another major earthquake like the one that took place in September 1985 (Garza, 1987).

Neighborhoods and housing in Mexico Megacity are of particular interest because of a longtime continuing existence of housing deficits and deteriorating neighborhoods, extensive squatter settlements, and unauthorized subdivisions, especially on the edge of the city in former *ejido* areas (Varley, 1987; Frieden, 1965). Land now filled with middle- and upper-class neighborhoods, sites with private industrial enterprises, and middle-class housing projects were formerly *ejido* land holdings, swamp land, or mountain sides.

In the 1930s Mexico City became a place with families living in old buildings that had been divided into *vecindades* (Lewis, 1961; 1974) with perhaps a half-million people in 1935 living in *tugarios*, neighborhoods of *vecindades* (Frieden, 1965). Subsequently, *jacales*, or temporary shacks, were built on empty lots, especially in fringe areas of the complex; an estimated 315,000 people lived in *jacales*. Areas with a concentration of slums were being built in locations that lacked basic urban services of water, electricity, drainage, and paved streets. Nezahualcoyotl fit the profile in the late 50s/early 60s (see Figure 3.7) as Chalco did more recently. Well over a half-million squatters, or *paracaidistas*, were living in *colonias proleterias* by 1952 and by 1955 an estimated 750,000. *Colonias proleterias* in outlying areas reduced pressure for housing in the city center and as a result there has been a migration of families from tenements to the periphery (see Chapter 5; Pick and Butler, 1994).

In 1970, it was estimated that there was a 43.6 percent housing deficit in the Federal District which included overcrowding (6.3 persons per household), a population with no place to live, and deteriorated housing; overall there was a reported 47.6 percent deficit in the State of Mexico, but Amecameca and Texcoco, which later became part of the Megacity, had deficits of 63.0 and 49.6 percent, respectively (Garza and Schteingart, 1978). Another analysis of 1970 housing reported that 11.3 percent of housing in the urban region of the Federal District was totally deteriorated and that 3.4 percent was without basic services (water, drainage, and electricity). In rural areas, 21.4 percent were considered as totally deteriorated and 12.2 percent were without basic services (COPLAMAR, 1983: 272-273).[2]

Neighborhood and housing conditions in Mexico Megacity have improved over the past several decades. However, there are still many areas with substantial housing and service deficits; generally these areas are located on the periphery. More than half of the housing in the city has been financed by low-income groups and much of it remains on land of uncertain ownership (U.N., 1991).

Housing and neighborhood components examined in this paper include measures of (1) crowding, (2) using kitchen as a bedroom, and (3) use of firewood and coal for heating and cooking, (4) lack of electricity, (5) no running water, (6) no toilet, and (7) inadequate drainage. While this chapter addresses several different kinds of environmental problems in Mexico Megacity, clearly many other problems that have been identified and worthy of examination are not examined in this chapter.

---

[2]   In 1970, it was estimated that 70 percent of housing in Guadalajara had at least one housing deficiency (Walton 1976), so Mexico City was not the only Mexican city having extensive neighborhood and housing deficits.

Correlations of Neighborhood and Housing Dimensions

Correlations among housing dimensions are shown in Table 7.1. Housing dimensions by delegation and municipio are reported in Table 7.2 and Table 7.3. All of these dimensions are strongly interrelated and also strongly linked to population. This confirms that the housing attributes have similar spatial patterns, for example deteriorated plumbing implies other housing features are deteriorated. Because of its very strong links to other attributes, housing without drainage is not mapped. Instead, refer to the map for no toilet, which is correlated r = 0.82 with housing without drainage.

It is clear from the correlations that housing attributes are strongly and positively linked to population and social rank (see Table 7.1). Higher quality housing is located in populous and high social rank areas. The latter relationship is consistent with many other nations including the U.S. The former relationship is not present for advanced nations, but is supported conceptually by Griffin and Ford's (1983) theory of Latin American cities. They theorized that elite residential neighborhoods would be in or very near the populous city center, with low quality housing located on the periphery.

Table 7.1 Correlations of Housing Variables with Each Other and with Selected Cluster Variables.

	Crowded Housing	One Room	No Electricity	No Running Water
One Room	.528 ***			
No Electicity	.528 ***	.463 ***		
No Running Water	.341 **	.648 ***	.469 ***	
No Toilet	.493 ***	.196	.773 ***	.276 *
Wood or Coal	.610 ***	.102	.701 ***	.242 *
Log Pop. 1990	-.330 **	-.209	-.592 ***	-.160
Pop. Growth 70-90	-302 **	.127	.062	.213
Primary Education	-.533 ***	-.546 ***	.791 ***	-.503 ***
Home Ownership	.255 *	.248 *	.574 ***	.432 ***

	No Toilet	Wood or Coal	Log Pop. 1990	Pop. Growth 70-90	Primary Education
Wood or Coal	.777 ***				
Log Pop. 1990	-.697 ***	-.534 ***			
Pop. Growth 70-90	-.281 *	-.243 *	.209		
Primary Education	-.764 ***	-.646 ***	.691 ***	-.025	
Home Ownership	.530 ***	.446 ***	-.519 ***	.306 **	-.676 ***

Note: Significance Levels   *   .05
                               **   .01
                               *** .001

Table 7.2 Housing Dimensions, 1990

No.	Area	Population with Crowded Housing	Percent Population with Crowded Housing	Total Number of Housing Units	Housing Units with One Room	Percent Housing Units with One Room	Average Number of Rooms per Housing Unit
1	Acolman	3,095	38.88	7,961	525	6.60	1.50
2	Alvaro Obregon	32,509	24.27	133,937	10,313	7.70	1.20
3	Amecameca	1,947	28.89	6,739	667	9.90	1.70
4	Atenco	1,431	38.73	3,695	200	5.40	1.60
5	Atizapan De Zaragoza	15,518	24.05	64,529	5,162	8.00	1.20
6	Atlautla	1,041	32.73	3,181	274	8.60	2.10
7	Axapusco	864	29.06	2,973	285	9.60	1.70
8	Ayapango	186	22.91	812	129	15.90	1.80
9	Azcapotzalco	24,130	23.40	103,130	4,538	4.40	1.20
10	Benito Juarez	13,606	11.93	114,002	3,078	2.70	0.80
11	Chalco	11,727	21.72	53,980	11,336	21.00	2.00
12	Chiautla	935	35.91	2,604	255	9.80	1.60
13	Chicoloapan	3,211	29.91	10,737	1,149	10.70	1.60
14	Chiconcuac	1,034	47.89	2,159	84	3.90	1.60
15	Chimalhuacan	11,704	26.63	43,944	7,734	17.60	2.00
16	Coacalco	8,462	26.57	31,843	478	1.50	1.00
17	Cocotitlan	407	27.15	1,499	169	11.30	1.80
18	Coyoacan	31,401	22.03	142,533	7,697	5.40	1.20
19	Coyotepec	1,656	40.51	4,088	352	8.60	1.80
20	Cuajimalpa	7,388	31.54	23,422	2,225	9.50	1.40
21	Cuauhtemoc	22,975	14.63	157,079	7,069	4.50	1.00
22	Cuautitlan	2,781	28.74	9,678	513	5.30	1.30
23	Cuautitlan Izcalli	18,531	27.42	67,582	2,365	3.50	1.10
24	Ecatepec	66,767	28.04	238,117	21,192	8.90	1.40
25	Ecatzingo	240	23.88	1,005	69	6.90	2.20
26	Gustavo A. Madero	68,444	26.03	262,905	14,986	5.70	1.20
27	Huehuetoca	620	12.81	4,839	247	5.10	1.50
28	Huixquilucan	1,535	6.08	25,259	2,551	10.10	1.10
29	Isidro Fabela	311	33.44	930	83	8.90	1.80
30	Ixtapaluca	6,818	25.85	26,377	3,324	12.60	1.60
31	Iztacalco	23,910	25.49	93,815	5,629	6.00	1.20
32	Iztapalapa	81,079	27.51	294,738	25,053	8.50	1.30
33	Jaltenco	2,734	62.42	4,380	153	3.50	1.20
34	Jilotzingo	457	26.11	1,750	130	7.40	1.70
35	Juchitepec	678	25.54	2,655	372	14.00	1.90
36	Magdalena Contreras	9,644	23.96	40,247	4,025	10.00	1.20
37	Melchor Ocampo	1,680	36.54	4,598	368	8.00	1.60
38	Miguel Hidalgo	17,714	18.07	98,051	4,314	4.40	0.90
39	Milpa Alta	3,429	27.97	12,258	1,471	12.00	1.60
40	Naucalpan	40,011	25.20	158,779	14,131	8.90	1.20
41	Nextlalpan	686	34.66	1,979	148	7.50	1.50
42	Nezahualcoyotl	74,376	31.18	238,508	19,319	8.10	1.40
43	Nicolas Romero	10,570	30.52	34,635	3,325	9.60	1.60
44	Nopaltepec	300	28.93	1,037	90	8.70	1.50
45	Otumba	1,239	30.48	4,065	378	9.30	1.70
46	Ozumba	1,018	33.78	3,014	289	9.60	1.90
47	Papalotla	146	34.11	428	41	9.60	1.60
48	Paz, La	7,956	31.62	25,160	3,371	13.40	1.60
49	San Martin De Las P.	805	31.02	2,595	244	9.40	1.60
50	Tecamac	7,073	29.42	24,040	1,971	8.20	1.40

Table 7.2 Housing Dimensions, 1990 (Continued)

No.	Area	Population with Crowded Housing	Percent Population with Crowded Housing	Total Number of Housing Units	Housing Units with One Room	Percent Housing Units with One Room	Average Number of Rooms per Housing Unit
51	Temamatla	292	27.47	1,063	105	9.90	1.50
52	Temascalapa	1,305	35.74	3,651	453	12.40	1.80
53	Tenango Del Aire	323	27.12	1,191	133	11.20	1.70
54	Teoloyucan	2,703	36.71	7,363	582	7.90	1.60
55	Teotihuacan	1,854	32.53	5,699	502	8.80	1.50
56	Tepetlaoxtoc	1,585	54.64	2,901	252	8.70	1.70
57	Tepetlixpa	648	28.19	2,299	271	11.80	1.90
58	Tepotzotlan	2,264	29.49	7,676	583	7.60	1.50
59	Texcoco	7,755	29.95	25,892	1,735	6.70	1.40
60	Tezoyuca	762	32.79	2,324	230	9.90	1.60
61	Tlahuac	11,897	30.26	39,311	3,813	9.70	1.50
62	Tlalmanalco	1,724	26.53	6,499	526	8.10	1.50
63	Tlalnepantla	3,705	2.57	144,014	10,513	7.30	1.20
64	Tlalpan	22,100	21.43	103,137	10,004	9.70	1.10
65	Tultepec	2,715	30.14	9,008	793	8.80	1.50
66	Tultitlan	13,410	26.99	49,693	2,683	5.40	1.30
67	Venustiano Carranza	24,879	21.15	117,640	5,647	4.80	1.20
68	Xochimilco	14,096	26.61	52,966	5,614	10.60	1.40
69	Zumpango	4,648	38.49	12,075	785	6.50	1.60
Total		765,444	23.98	3,192,673	239,097	592	103
Mean		11,093	28.77	46,271	3,465	8.57	1.49
Median		2,781	28.19	9,678	667	8.70	1.50
S.D.		17,886	9.01	69,276	5,334	3.33	0.29
C.V.		161.2342	31.3345	149.7184	153.9321	38.7972	19.3044
Minimum		146	2.57	428	41	1.50	0.80
Maximum		81,079	62.42	294,738	25,053	21.00	2.20

Source: INEGI, 1990 Population Census, 1990 *Bienstar*

Table 7.3 Housing Variables, 1990

	No Electricity	No Toilet	Percent No Drainage	Percent No Running Water
Acolman	0.0191	0.2294	35.4	9.1
Alvaro Obregon	0.0098	0.0894	4.2	3.2
Amecameca	0.0304	0.1503	25.3	4.3
Atenco	0.0517	0.2122	37.5	14.9
Atizapan de Zaragoza	0.0399	0.0855	17.2	14.4
Atlautla	0.0588	0.3867	62.7	14.6
Axapusco	0.0531	0.5193	57.2	10.5
Ayapango	0.0751	0.1379	42.6	8.6
Azcapotzalco	0.0022	0.1056	1.9	1.2
Benito Juarez	0.0012	0.0200	1.4	1.1
Chalco	0.0525	0.1718	76.3	71.4
Chiautla	0.0419	0.2803	42.5	10.3
Chicoloapan	0.0195	0.1019	39.9	5.2
Chiconcuac	0.0259	0.1746	16.9	6.4
Chimalhuacan	0.1129	0.1399	57.2	15.8
Coacalco	0.0092	0.0179	2.3	2.8
Cocotitlan	0.0440	0.2522	48	8.6
Coyoacan	0.0026	0.0579	5.7	1.2
Coyotepec	0.0634	0.3253	33.7	8.9
Cuajimalpa	0.0152	0.1562	11.4	5.9
Cuauhtemoc	0.0021	0.0362	2.1	1.4
Cuautitlan	0.0231	0.0855	8.5	2.9
Cuautitlan Izcalli	0.0155	0.0553	8.8	3.4
Ecatepec	0.0306	0.0743	14.3	11.4
Ecatzingo	0.1333	0.6109	84.9	15.2
Gustavo A. Madero	0.0041	0.0823	2.8	2.2
Huehuetoca	0.0380	0.2238	40.6	6.8
Huixquilucan	0.0363	0.1825	21.1	11.1
Isidro Fabela	0.1312	0.6462	76.6	22
Ixtapaluca	0.0910	0.1504	41.2	28.8
Iztacalco	0.0031	0.0903	1.8	1.3
Iztapalapa	0.0134	0.0862	11	6
Jaltenco	0.0180	0.1005	14.8	2.7
Jilotzingo	0.0703	0.4880	60.4	20.1
Juchitepec	0.0437	0.2350	43.1	20.2
Magdalena Contreras	0.0110	0.1150	6.3	3.9
Melchor Ocampo	0.0352	0.2047	29.2	6
Miguel Hidalgo	0.0021	0.0864	2.3	1.4
Milpa Alta	0.0572	0.2190	36.9	17.6
Naucalpan	0.0100	0.1133	3.8	2
Nextlalpan	0.0541	0.2996	54.6	6.3
Nezahualcoyotl	0.0039	0.1031	1.9	3.1
Nicolas Romero	0.0368	0.1984	28.5	17.1
Nopaltepec	0.1234	0.6480	73.4	11.5
Otumba	0.0871	0.5124	56	12.9
Ozumba	0.0544	0.1788	47.1	12.3
Papalotla	0.0257	0.2687	29.9	8.4
Paz, La	0.0529	0.1246	19.8	12.2
San Martin de las P.	0.0393	0.3152	37.8	6
Tecamac	0.0304	0.1313	21.9	11.9
Temamatla	0.0263	0.2098	29.4	3.4
Temascalapa	0.0748	0.5412	65.2	11.1
Tenango del Aire	0.0579	0.2914	42.1	7.6

Table 7.3 Housing Variables, 1990 (Continued)

	No Electricity	No Toilet	Percent No Drainage	Percent No Running Water
Teoloyucan	0.0276	0.2830	39.8	12.5
Teotihuacan	0.0237	0.2323	27.7	16.1
Tepetlaoxtoc	0.0534	0.4519	52.3	10.9
Tepetlixpa	0.0500	0.2862	70.8	18.7
Tepotzotlan	0.0508	0.2478	29.9	12.5
Texcoco	0.0261	0.2207	24.6	8.3
Tezoyuca	0.0340	0.1876	34.5	14.7
Tlahuac	0.0208	0.1012	23.2	6.1
Tlalmanalco	0.0225	0.1494	19.1	9.9
Tlalnepantla	0.0045	0.0967	4.1	2.5
Tlalpan	0.0131	0.0833	15.8	14.4
Tultepec	0.0282	0.1442	23	5.5
Tultitlan	0.0171	0.0791	17.9	11.9
Venustiano Carranza	0.0021	0.0741	1.5	1.3
Xochimilco	0.0284	0.0977	19.4	9.6
Zumpango	0.0332	0.2703	29.2	4.8
Mean	0.0377	0.2077	30.00	9.98
Median	0.0304	0.1718	28.50	8.60
S.D.	0.0309	0.1509	22.00	9.57
C.V.	81.98	72.69	73.34	95.97
Minimum	0.0012	0.0179	1.40	1.10
Maximum	0.1333	0.6480	84.90	71.40

Source: INEGI, 1990 Population Census, 1990 *Bienstar*

Neighborhood and Housing Dimensions

Crowding

This chapter examines two measures of crowding: (1) crowded housing defined as housing units with three or fewer rooms and six or more occupants and (2) housing units with one room.

As shown on Map 7.1, housing units with only one room in 1990 were concentrated primarily in the State of Mexico, especially in the mid-east and south. However, two southern delegations in the Federal District -- Milpa Alta and Xochimilco -- also are characterized as having a much higher than average number of housing units with only one room; the range is from less than one percent to a high of 21 percent. Interestingly, housing units with one room are located primarily in the southeastern section of the Megacity. Crowding in the highest quintile of housing units ranges from 10 to 21 percent.

The percent of crowded housing units has a different spatial arrangement than housing units with one room (see Map 7.2). The range varies from a maximum of over 62 percent to a low of around 2.5 percent. None of the delegations in the Federal District is considered as having an inordinate number of crowded housing units. Areas of the Megacity with the most crowded housing are in the West-central, Northeast, and Southeast. There is very little crowding by room in the Federal District. Thus, the most crowded housing exists outside of the Federal District -- core city -- in outlying areas. The approximately one-fifth of municipios with the highest percentage of crowding have over one-third of crowded housing units, with a high of over 62 percent.

Housing Without Electricity

Installed electrical generating capacity in the Megacity is minimal at 1,348 megawatts (INEGI, 1995). Most electricity is transmitted to the city from hydroelectric plants in the southern region of Mexico, including as far away as Chiapas (INEGI, 1995). There are twelve municipios in which around six to thirteen percent of housing units do not have electricity. As reported in Table 7.3 and shown on Map 7.3, twelve of these municipios are scattered throughout the State of Mexico, with only one delegation in the Federal District having a similar deficit -- Milpa Alta. The heaviest concentration is in the northeast and southeast regions with generally 4 to 13 percent of the housing units not having electricity.

Housing Without Running Water

It has been estimated that over 400,000 persons in the Federal District do not have access to potable water and for those who do there is great variation in consumption patterns. For example, in Lomas de Chapultepec per capita consumption is 450 liters per day while residents of Nezahualcoyotl consume only 30 liters per day (Spring, 1991). A second area of scrutiny is the quality of water that is considered potable. Waterborne contamination can result in cholera, diarrheal diseases, fevers, various worm diseases, infective jaundice, and polio. Other water-related diseases and problems are scabies, typhus, malaria, etc. (Hardoy et al., 1993: 39).

Map 7.4 shows that the concentration of households without running water are scattered throughout the metropolitan complex but with a concentration in the southeast and west, slightly to the north. Within the Federal District, the same delegation with the least electricity -- Milpa Alta -- also has the highest proportion of housing units without running water (18 percent). The range of housing units without running water is one percent to over 71 percent (see Table 7.3). There is substantial correspondence of housing without running water to those without electricity ($r = 0.47$), and to those with a single room ($r = 0.65$).

Housing Without Toilet and Drainage

Mexico Megacity has substantial deficits in its ability to process sewage and the 1985 earthquake damaged part of the system making the situation even worse. Most housing not hooked up to a sewer is located in peripheral areas, (see Table 7.3). In some of these areas raw sewage is discharged into river beds or seeps into the ground polluting underground aquifers (U.N., 1991).

Aguas negras, black waters, are a result of poor drainage and contain such contaminants as lead, zinc, and arsenic (Spring, 1991:61). Housing units without adequate drainage are located substantially in the same areas that lack a toilet (see Map 7.5) and they are highly correlated (r = 0.84). At the upper end of the spectrum, over 50 percent of the housing units in some municipios do not have adequate drainage (Table 7.3). These deficit areas are spread throughout the periphery, but the most prominent areas are in the far northeast, far southeast, and two municipios in the mid-west. Chalco (76 percent) and Chimalhuacan (85 percent) are high extremes. These areas were converted from ejido land and lack a utilities infrastructure. In the State of Mexico, Isidro Fabela, Ecatzingo, and Nopaltepec, all on the extreme periphery, have over 60 percent of their housing units without a toilet. Delegations, with the exception of Milpa Alta, have average or better percentage of housing units with a toilet (see Map 7.5).

Use of Firewood and Coal for Heating and Cooking

The use of firewood and coal for heating continues in the Megacity which undoubtedly contributes to air pollution. However, their use also has other consequences. For example, coal must be transported to the city from some distance contributing to pollutants engendered by combustion engines. In addition, there is little firewood readily accessible in the Valley, thus it also must be transported to the city from a distance and requires the destruction of forest reserves.

There are two areas of concentration in which firewood and coal are used for heating – peripheral areas of the northeast and southeast. In addition, two municipios in the west mid-section are substantially higher in their use than the rest of the city.

There is substantial relationship of the use of firewood and coal with other housing deficits. Housing in which firewood or coal are used for cooking and/or heating have a distribution substantially similar to those of household crowding (r = 0.61) and lack of toilet (r = 0.78); that is, the far northeast and far southeast, plus a fringe area on the mid-west. Virtually no one in the old core of the city in the Federal District uses firewood and coal but over 82 percent of the housing residents of Ecatzingo use firewood and/or coal for cooking and/or heating and there are other areas with 25 percent or more using firewood or coal for cooking and/or heating!

Map 7.1
Housing Units with
Only One Room, 1990

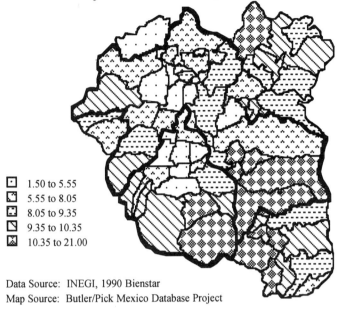

▫	1.50 to 5.55
▣	5.55 to 8.05
▣	8.05 to 9.35
◩	9.35 to 10.35
▨	10.35 to 21.00

Data Source: INEGI, 1990 Bienstar
Map Source: Butler/Pick Mexico Database Project

Map 7.2
Crowded Housing Units, 1990

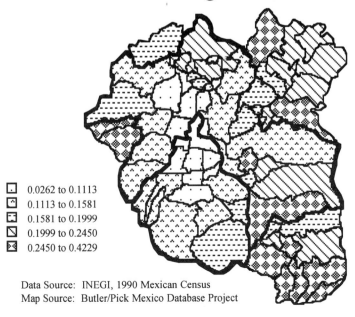

▫	0.0262 to 0.1113
▣	0.1113 to 0.1581
▣	0.1581 to 0.1999
◩	0.1999 to 0.2450
▨	0.2450 to 0.4229

Data Source: INEGI, 1990 Mexican Census
Map Source: Butler/Pick Mexico Database Project

Map 7.3
No Electricity, 1990

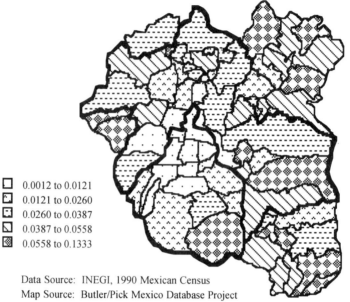

□	0.0012 to 0.0121
▨	0.0121 to 0.0260
▦	0.0260 to 0.0387
◩	0.0387 to 0.0558
▧	0.0558 to 0.1333

Data Source: INEGI, 1990 Mexican Census
Map Source: Butler/Pick Mexico Database Project

Map 7.4
Housing Units
Without Running Water, 1990

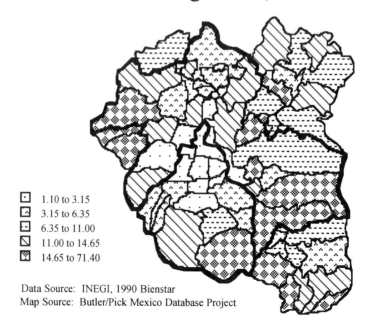

▣	1.10 to 3.15
◪	3.15 to 6.35
⊟	6.35 to 11.00
◩	11.00 to 14.65
▨	14.65 to 71.40

Data Source: INEGI, 1990 Bienstar
Map Source: Butler/Pick Mexico Database Project

Map 7.5
No Toilet, 1990

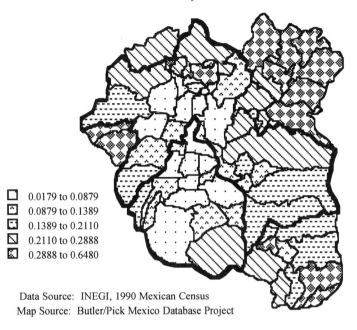

0.0179 to 0.0879
0.0879 to 0.1389
0.1389 to 0.2110
0.2110 to 0.2888
0.2888 to 0.6480

Data Source: INEGI, 1990 Mexican Census
Map Source: Butler/Pick Mexico Database Project

Map 7.6
Firewood or Coal, 1990

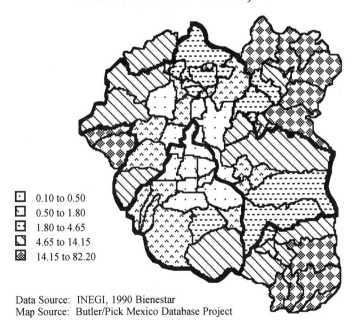

0.10 to 0.50
0.50 to 1.80
1.80 to 4.65
4.65 to 14.15
14.15 to 82.20

Data Source: INEGI, 1990 Bienestar
Map Source: Butler/Pick Mexico Database Project

Municipios with the Most Neighborhood and Housing Deficits

All Mexico Megacity areas with the most housing and neighborhood deficits are located in the State of Mexico, although there are delegations in the Federal District with some major deficits.

Table 7.4 reports housing and neighborhood deficiencies for the four delegations or municipios with the most deficits: (1) Chimalhuacan -- five deficits, (2) Ecatzingo, -- five (3) Jilotzingo -- five, and (4) Temascalapa -- seven.[3] Note that these four municipios with the most deficits are located in all four regions -- north, south, east, and west. Map 7.7 shows housing deficits throughout the city.

Table 7.4 Megacity Areas with the Most Neighborhood and Housing Deficits, 1990

Deficit	Temascalapa	Ecatzingo	Chimalhuacan	Jilotzingo	Total Deficits
Crowded HU	X				1
One Room HU	X		X		2
Kit/Bedroom	X		X		2
No Electricity	X	X	X	X	4
No Toilet	X	X		X	3
No Drainage	X	X	X	X	4
No Running Water		X	X	X	3
Wood/Coal	X	X		X	3
Totals	7	5	5	5	22

In Ecatzingo, over 80 percent of the households use wood/coal for heating and cooking, by far the highest percentage in Mexico Megacity! Over 13 percent of the households have no electricity, about two thirds do not have a toilet, and over 34 percent use their kitchen as a bedroom. However, only eight percent of the housing units reported as lacking adequate sewage disposal.

Over 28 percent of the households in Jilotzingo use wood/coal for heating and cooking. Over seven percent of the households do not have electricity, about half do not have a toilet, and almost half of the households use their kitchen as a bedroom. Over 33 percent of the households lack adequate sewage disposal.

Over 17 percent of the households in Temascalapa use wood/coal for heating and cooking. Seven percent have no electricity, over 54 percent do not have a toilet, and over 72 percent use their kitchen as a bedroom. Over 17 percent of the housing units lack adequate sewage disposal.

While Chimalhuacan has a number of neighborhood and housing deficits, it is extremely low (0.8%) in households that use wood/coal for cooking. Over 11 percent of the households do not have electricity, almost 14 percent do not have a toilet, and over one-third use their kitchen as a bedroom. About one-fifth of the households have a sewage deficit.

---

[3] Spring (1991) analyzes in detail Iztapalapa, Alvaro Obregon, and Tlahuac in respect to marginality and housing.

Table 7.5 presents a summary of housing and neighborhood deficits in Mexico Megacity.[4] Each checked column contains only those areas which had the greatest deficit for each particular housing dimension. As shown on Map 7.7, regions with the most housing deficits are peripheral areas in the far northeast, far southeast, and a smaller concentration of two municipios in the west mid-section. Only one of these areas, Chimalhuacan, is an area of the highest level population density.

Information presented here confirms that as of 1990 there remains substantial housing deficits in Mexico Megacity. We have shown that housing and related problems are scattered throughout the city but the most severe conditions are concentrated in certain regions. Areas with the most deficits are on the periphery of the city, depending upon which dimensions are being examined. In the future, there will have to be concern with all of the environmental deficits acknowledged in this chapter. It is problematic given the current economic situation in Mexico if any of these environmental problems will be overcome in the near future. Even further environmental difficulties will ensue if the population continues to increase in Mexico Megacity -- as it is projected to do! Thus, housing and neighborhood deficits described here are substantial and are likely to increase with an increasing rural to urban migration.

Clearly many other housing problems that have been identified and worthy of examination were not discussed in this section. Given the magnitude of the housing and neighborhood problems shown here, it would be easy to become resigned to the fact that these problems will continue to exist in the future and most likely will become even more intense than they are currently. On the other hand, the first step to overcoming these and other problems of the city are to recognize them and to begin to concentrate resources in overcoming them. Not an easy thing to do, especially given the current economic conditions in Mexico.

Finally, we have generally ignored the problems of squatters, ejido lands, and community action groups.[5] The conflict and uncertainty of *ejido* land rights are of relevance, especially in light of the presumed inability of these rights to be sold, rented, or mortgaged. The process of 'normalizing property rights' was a goal of the Salinas administration which possibly could have enhanced the projected deficit for 30 million persons needing houses in 1995 (Presidencia, 1990). In addition, it was proposed to expand the electricity grid for millions of residents. It remains to be seen if these lofty goals will be achieved during the current Zedillo administration.

---

[4] For an extended analysis of neighborhood and housing deficiencies in Cuauhtemoc, Venustiano Carranza, and Gustavo A. Madero in, 1970 and 1980, see Connolly et al., (1991).

[5] For an example of these kinds of problems and reactions of local residents, see Pezzoli (1985) who studied an area of Tlalpan, Pedregal in Ajusco.

Table 7.5 Summary of Mexico Megacity: Neighorhood and Housing Deficits, 1990

No.	Area	Crowding	One Room	Kitchen as Bedroom	Electricity	Running Water	No Toilet	Drainage	Wood/Coal	Total Deficits
1	Acolman									0
2	Alvaro Obregon									0
3	Amecameca								X	1
4	Atenco	X				X				2
5	Atizapan de Zaragoza									0
6	Atlautla			X	X					2
7	Axapusco		X	X	X					3
8	Ayapango						X	X	X	3
9	Azcapotzalco									0
10	Benito Juarez									0
11	Chalco		X	X		X				3
12	Chiautla							X		1
13	Chicoloapan		X	X						2
14	Chiconcuac	X								1
15	Chimalhuacan		X	X	X	X		X		5
16	Coacalco									0
17	Cocotitlan									0
18	Coyoacan									0
19	Coyotepec	X					X			2
20	Cuajimalpa									0
21	Cuauhtemoc									0
22	Cuautitlan									0
23	Cuautitlan Izcalli									0
24	Ecatepec									0
25	Ecatzingo				X	X	X	X	X	5
26	Gustavo A. Madero									0
27	Huehuetoca									0
28	Huixquilucan				X	X	X	X	X	5
29	Isidro Fabela									0
30	Ixtapaluca		X	X	X	X				4
31	Iztacalco									0
32	Iztapalapa									0
33	Jaltenco	X								1
34	Jilotzingo				X	X	X	X	X	5
35	Juchitepec		X	X		X				3

Table 7.5 Summary of Mexico Megacity: Neighorhood and Housing Deficits, 1990 (Continued)

No.	Area	Crowding	One Room	Kitchen as Bedroom	Electricity	Running Water	No Toilet	Drainage	Wood/Coal	Total Deficits
36	Magdalena Contreras									0
37	Melchor Ocampo	X								1
38	Miguel Hidalgo									0
39	Milpa Alta		X		X	X				3
40	Naucalpan									0
41	Nextlalpan	X					X			2
42	Nezahualcoyotl									0
43	Nicolas Romero					X				1
44	Nopaltepec				X		X	X	X	4
45	Otumba				X		X	X	X	4
46	Ozumba	X								1
47	Papalotla	X								1
48	Paz, La		X	X						2
49	San Martin de las P.						X			1
50	Tecamac									0
51	Temamatla									0
52	Temascalapa	X	X	X	X		X	X	X	7
53	Tenango del Aire		X	X	X		X			4
54	Teoloyucan	X								1
55	Teotihuacan					X				1
56	Tepetlaoxtoc	X					X	X	X	4
57	Tepetlixpa		X			X		X	X	4
58	Tepotzotlan									0
59	Texcoco									0
60	Tezoyuca									0
61	Tlahuac									0
62	Tlalmanalco									0
63	Tlalnepantla									0
64	Tlalpan									0
65	Tultepec									0
66	Tultitlan									0
67	Venustiano Carranza									0
68	Xochimilco		X							1
69	Zumpango	X								1
	Total	12	12	10	12	12	12	11	10	91

Map 7.7

Mexico Megacity: Municipios
with the Most Housing Deficits, 1990

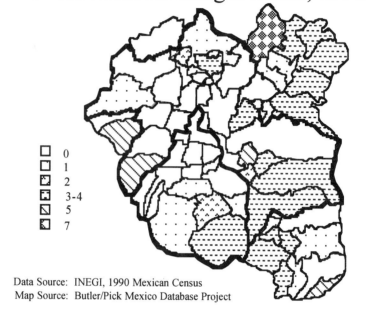

0
1
2
3-4
5
7

Data Source: INEGI, 1990 Mexican Census
Map Source: Butler/Pick Mexico Database Project

Housing Cluster Analysis

There are nine housing clusters that are based on six housing attributes. The general spatial pattern (see Map 7.8) reveals a core with northward offshoots, a partially surrounding "ring," an incomplete "outer ring," Chalco a distinctive area, several areas adjoining Chalco, and three peripheral zones and the unique area of Ecatzingo. Table 7.6 presents the unique characteristics that distinguish each cluster and lists the delegations and municipios in each cluster.

Ninety five percent of the Megacity population is contained in clusters 1-4. These areas have generally more favorable housing characteristics, with better housing quality, and are located near the center. Cluster 1 encompasses the traditional Central Business District and northward delegations that include the most prosperous parts of the Megacity, as well as four municipios that are located to the north of the CBD. There is a strong contrast within these clusters in population growth and migration. Whereas the delegations in these clusters tended to lose population from 1970-90, the northern municipios were gainers (see Map 3.5). The contrast is also seen for inmigration 1985-90, for which the cluster's municipios grew rapidly while the delegations were nearly stagnant (see Map 5.7). The explanation is that the central delegations contain the better housing as predicted in the theory of Latin American cities (Griffin and Ford, 1983); since the northern municipios have grown rapidly with large inmigration, there is an implied housing buildup, presumably involving construction of some new housing, which we surmise brought up the overall level of housing quality. The core has the best housing quality, far exceeding the Megacity average.

The "inner ring," i.e. Cluster 2, isn't a true ring since it surrounds the delegations but not the municipios of Cluster 1. We, nevertheless, refer to it here as the "inner ring." It has the next best housing quality substantially exceeding the Megacity means on plumbing and firewood/coal. It includes some areas of rapid growth in the 70s and 80s.

The "outer ring" consists of Clusters 3 and 4. As a "ring," it is somewhat incomplete, especially in the southeast and southwest. Overall housing quality is average, although the two clusters differ for specific housing parameters, for instance Cluster 3 has a much higher average lack of running water than Cluster 4, while the opposite is true for no tioliet.

Chalco stands out as a unique housing cluster. The uniqueness is most evident for housing with one room (21 percent) and lack of running water (71 percent). On the other hand it has low firewood/coal and moderate crowding. It may be regarded as a zone in transition, i.e. changing from its original "slum pioneer" stage to a below average status with improvement in some aspects of housing. Cluster 6 consists of three municipios surrounding Chalco. Generally, this cluster is below average in housing, especially in crowding and 1-room housing.

Clusters 7-10 are located in the periphery. Ecatzingo stands out as the cluster with the worst housing. Nearly two thirds lack a toilet; fifteen percent lack running water, and 24 percent are overcrowded. The other peripheral clusters vary by characteristics but overall have low housing quality. Clusters 7 and 8 have the worst crowding, while clusters 5 and 6 are among the worst in lacking running water. The periphery has not experienced population growth and re-development of its old and substandard housing. This may happen in the future if the Megacity continues its historical outward expansion.

Map 7.8
Housing Clusters

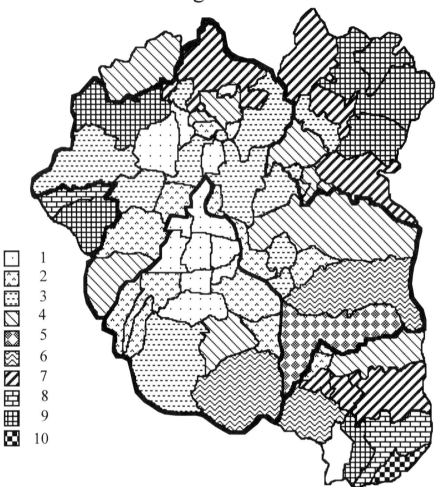

Data Source: INEGI, Population and Economic Censuses, 1990 and 1993
Map Source: Butler/Pick Mexico Database Project

Table 7.6 Housing Cluster Means

Variable	Cluster No. 1	2	3	4	5	6	7	8	9	10	Mexico City
Total Population 1990	5,311,904	5,510,130	3,094,840	793,039	282,940	215,281	120,000	24,183	82,621	5,808	15,440,746
Household Crowding	0.2566	0.2582	0.2992	0.2774	0.2172	0.2645	0.3440	0.3308	0.2942	0.2388	0.2074
Housing with One Room	4.3100	9.0100	9.2600	7.9800	21.0000	12.8700	10.8700	8.7500	9.4000	6.9000	8.5725
Lack of Running Water	1.9100	4.2500	13.8300	8.1200	71.4000	22.2000	8.2000	18.3000	14.3300	15.2000	9.9754
No Toilet	0.0677	0.1197	0.1599	0.2195	0.1718	0.2145	0.3162	0.5165	0.4388	0.6109	0.2077
Septic Tank or Open Flow	0.0499	0.1560	0.1838	0.2227	0.1272	0.1425	0.1237	0.1500	0.1684	0.0836	0.1509
Firewood or Coal	0.4417	0.9800	2.7000	4.3500	3.3000	8.6700	13.8700	46.2000	26.9800	82.2000	8.2696

Cluster 1	Cluster 2	Cluster 3	Cluster 4	Cluster 5	Cluster 6	Cluster 7	Cluster 8	Cluster 9	Cluster 10
Azcapotzalco	Alvaro Obregon	Atenco	Acolman	Chalco	Ixtapaluca	Amecameca	Atlautla	Axapusco	Ecatzingo
Benito Juarez	Chicoloapan	Atizapan de Zaragoza	Chiautla		Juchitepec	Ayapango	Isidro Fabela	Jilotzingo	
Coacalco	Cuajimalpa	Chimalhuacan	Chiconcuac		Milpa Alta	Coyotepec		Nopaltepec	
Coyoacan	Iztapalapa	Ecatepec	Cocotitlan			San Martin de las P.		Otumba	
Cuauhtemoc	Magdalena Contreras	Nicolas Romero	Huehuetoca			Temascalapa		Ozumba	
Cuautitlan	Naucalpan	Paz, La	Huixquilucan			Tenango del Aire			
Cuautitlan Izcalli	Nezahualcoyotl	Tecamac	Melchor Ocampo			Tepetlaoxtoc			
Gustavo A. Madero	Temamatla	Teoloyucan	Nextlalpan			Tepetlixpa			
Iztacalco	Tlahuac	Teotihuacan	Papalotla						
Jaltenco	Tlalnepantla	Tepotzotlan	Texcoco						
Miguel Hidalgo	Tultepec	Tezoyuca	Tlalmanalco						
Venustiano Carranza		Tlalpan	Xochimilco						
		Tultitlan	Zumpango						

Water

Mexico City's water supply is based on the huge Mexico City aquifer under the metropolitan area, and on imported water. Historically, all the city's water was provided by freshwater lakes and springs. This was supplemented later by drilling wells into the aquifer. At the beginning of the century, however, the lowering of the groundwater level became noticeable and land subsidence of Mexico City started. By 1960, due to rapid population growth, it became necessary to import surface water from other water basins, a practice that has grown to now account for about twenty six percent of the Megacity water supply (Ezcurra and Mazari-Hiriart, 1996). This section discusses the city's water supply situation, wastewater system, water quality, and health impacts of deteriorating water.

As seen in Table 7.7, currently the Megacity's water use is 60.3 cubic meters per second (NRC/AIC/ANI, 1995; DDF, 1992). This grew from a water use of 1.7 cubic m/s in 1910 and 11.0 cubic m/s in 1950 (Ezcurra and Mazari-Hiriart, 1996). The bulk of this supply comes from wells located throughout the city. There are currently 1,189 registered wells in the city, plus many unregistered wells especially in the State of Mexico (NRC/AIC/ANI, 1995). The Mexico City aquifer was recently estimated at 1.2 trillion cubic feet (Herrera et al., 1994). The net groundwater loss to the aquifer is estimated at 3.5-5.6 billion cubic meters per year. Thus, the annual draw down of the aquifer averages 0.38 percent per year.

Besides well pumping, there are minor water supply sources inside Mexico City consisting of springs and streams, the Magdalena River and the Madin Dam that account for 1.4 percent of the water supply. The outside water supply comes from the neighboring water basins of Cutzamala to the west and Lerma to the northwest (see Map 7.9). Imported water sources have grown rapidly since 1960 and continue to increase (Ezcurra and Mazari-Hiriart, 1996). The expanding reliance on distant natural resources parallels other long-term shifts away from the city's inherent resource base to dependency on other parts of the nation. Another example is the city's energy supply, which today mostly comes from the state of Chiapas.

There are environmental problems with all of these water sources. The groundwater situation is close to a crisis state. Because of heavy dependence on wells, groundwater levels have been lowering. As groundwater levels lowered, land subsidence tended to occur. In fact, Mexico City land subsidence was estimated at 7 meters from 1940 to 1985 (Ortega et al., 1993). Land subsidence in turn leads to aggravated problems in flooding during the rainy season. Flooding in turn leads to potentially dangerous overflows of the wastewater system. Another problem of flooding is injury to the city's physical infrastructure. Another impact is that lowering of the groundwater level threatens subsurface water contamination, since the subsurface layers may weaken causing shedding in the groundwater of inorganic contaminants (NRC/AIC/ANI. 1995). The natural springs, albeit minor, increasingly present the problem of contamination from subsurface contamination.

The water supply from outside the Mexico City water basin has its pluses and minuses. A plus is that the original water sources have fair water quality that can be improved by water treatment plants located near the source. Disadvantages include the extra cost of pumping long distances and uphill, risks of water leakages over long distance, and negative impacts on sending water basins. For instance, Chapala Lake, the largest freshwater lake in Mexico, has dropped in recent decades presumably due to the water diversion of the Cutzamala River (Ezcurra and Mazari-Hiriart, 1996).

The water distribution system serves a large land area totaling 3,373 square kilometers in Mexico City. This analysis is based on a smaller sized metropolitan definition (NRC/AIC/ANI, 1995: DDF, 1992). Much of Mexico City's land area is not served by the current water distribution and wastewater systems; the proportion not served approaches 3/4 in the State of Mexico. However, many areas not served are remote and sparsely populated.

It is also clear that the city has high daily water use for a developing nation. The average of 304 liters per day is higher than for most developing nations, although about fifty percent of the U.S. average daily use of 660 liters. It is also seen in Table 7.8 that the largest category of water is domestic followed by industrial and commercial.

Another serious problem to the water supply is the growing volume of hazardous waste in the Megacity. This does not stem from lack of regulations but from lack of enforcement. Ninety percent of the hazardous waste is dropped into the sewage system.

The increasing urbanization of the Mexico City basin (see Chapter 3) further threatens this precarious situation. This is especially true of the southern Federal District and adjoining southeastern municipios. Here, greater urbanization threatens the capacity to recharge the aquifer, as well threatening its quality, since soils in those areas are more permeable (Mazari and Mackay, 1993).

Wastewater for Mexico Megacity is disposed of through an open sewage canal, termed the Grand Canal, and by a deep transmission system, termed Emisor Central (NRC/AIC/ANI, 1995). The Grand Canal runs from many inflow points in the Federal District past the border and into the state of Hidalgo (see Map 7.9). Sewage in the Grand Canal is completely untreated. At its destination, it is used as fertilizer to irrigate 5,500 hectares in Chiconautla in the State of Mexico and 60,000 hectares in the state of Hidalgo (Ezcurra and Mazari-Hiriart, 1996). The strategy is that the control of this contaminated sewage is achieved not by water treatment but by carefully regulated uses of the Hidalgo crops growing from the sewage effluent.

The Emisor Central was built in 1960 to provide a needed second wastewater effluent channel. It was especially justified, since the Grand Canal was sinking in the Federal District, so the incline needed for gravity flow was disrupted. Today, the Grand Canal and Federal District are at about the same level, so it has become necessary (and more expensive) to pump the wastewater in the canal (DDF, 1990).

Of 23 water treatment plants for which data are available, 19 use secondary treatment and 4 use tertiary treatment (DDF, 1992; State of Mexico, 1993). A hazardous aspect is that the sewage sludge is fed back into the sewage system without any treatment.

As seen in Map 7.10, there are several areas in the eastern Federal District and nearby that were not in compliance with federal water quality standards. The populous delegation of Iztapalapa is by far the worst, not meeting water standards for three out of four contaminant groups. The problem stems largely from too many groundwater wells and too much pumping leading to weakening of subsurface soil layers and to contamination.

Water reuse, instituted in Mexico City in 1984, is utilized to a limited basis. One promising program is for Lake Texcoco. The plan calls for lowering the water level and creation of smaller ponds within the huge lake bed. Certain areas were designated for drying and use for urban and industrial purposes. Some pond water as well as storm water will be treated for reuse (Espino et al., 1987).

Direct potable use of reclaimed water is controversial, since there are possibly traces of presently unknown organic compounds in the water that cannot be removed today in treatment.

There are major potential public health problems with use of waste ditches to carry untreated waste. According to the Federal District, more than 90 percent of industrial liquid wastes are discharged into the sewer system without treatment (DDF, 1992; Ezcurra and Mazari-Hiriart, 1996). There is a very large network carrying wastes which has potential for losses. Another grave problem is the potential underground leakage of the recent system of deep drainage.

The high concentration of the nation's industrial production in Mexico Megacity (see Chapter 10) presents an enhanced problem of hazardous wastes. "The amount of hazardous waste generated in the Federal District is about 3 million metric tons per year, of which more than 95 percent are process effluents or treated effluents discharged to the municipal sewage system. The remainder, or some 150,000 tons, are solids, most of which are sent to municipal waste dumps or to illegal dumps." (NRC/AIC/ANI, citing work of National Institute of Nuclear Investigations, 1992). Unfortunately, there are no studies of whether or not the aquifer is contaminated by industrial waste. A problem with the large volume of solid wastes generated is that today there is not one study of the impact of industrial contaminants on the aquifer (NRC/AIC/ANI, 1996). Another problem is lack of control over pesticides, which potentially could find their way into the aquifer.

There are serious potential human health problems arising from the lowered water and wastewater quality. These include diarrhea, especially that of infants, cholera, and diseases triggered by exposure to toxic wastes (NRC/AIC/ANI, 1996). Some of the latter effects such as cancer are long term ones.

Table 7.7 Water Supply Sources to Mexico Megacity

Source	Federal District	17 Municipios in Metropolitan State of Mexico	Total
Inside Mexico City Water Basin			
Well Fields	22.7	20.3	43.0
Springs/streams	0.5	0.2	0.7
Magdalena River	0.2	0.0	0.2
Madin Dam	0.0	0.5	0.5
Outside Mexico City Water Basin			0.0
Cutzamala River	7.6	3.0	10.6
Lerma Well Fields	4.3	1.0	5.3
Total	35.3	25.0	60.3

Note: all figures are in cubic meters per second.
Source: NRC/AIC/ANI, 1995; DDF, 1992.

Table 7.8 Water Use and Category of Use in Federal District and Municipios in State of Mexico, 1992

	Federal District	17 Municipios in Metropolitan State of Mexico
Percent of land area served by water distribution and wastewater disposal systems	44.3	27.3
Daily water use per capital (in liters)	364	230
Water use by category (in percent)		
domestic	67	80
industrial	17	17
commercial and urban services	16	3

Source: NRC/AIC/ANI, 1995; DDF, 1992.

Map 7.9 The Water Flows into and out of Mexico City

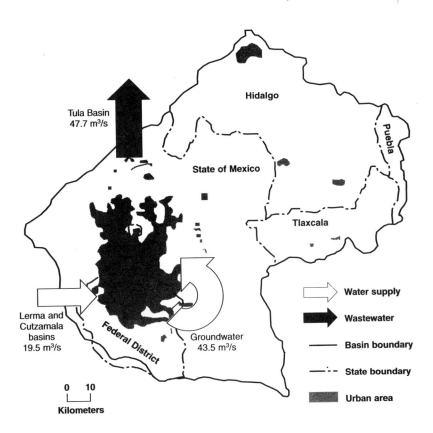

Source: National Research Council, Acadmia de la Investigacion Cientifica,
Academia Nacional de Ingeniera, 1995. By permission of Heldref Publications.

198

Map 7.10 Well Field Areas Where Water Quality is Not in Compliance To Standards

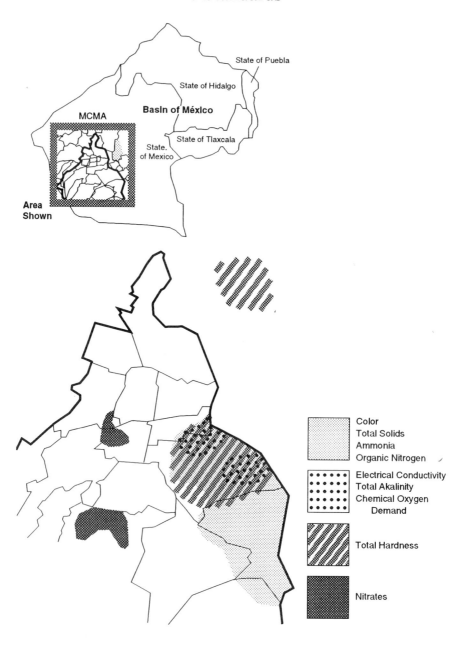

Source: National Research Council, Acadmia de la Investigacion Cientifica,
Academia Nacional de Ingeniera, 1995. Reprinted with permission from
Mexico City's Water Supply. Copyright 1995 by National Academy of Sciences.
Courtesy of National Academy Press, Washington, D.C.

Solid Waste

Solid waste generation and disposal present challenges to Mexico City and federal government planners. In 1992, 8,273 tons of solid waste were generated per day in the Federal District (INEGI, 1994). This constituted 14 percent of the national solid waste total of 60,185 tons per day. However, we estimate the entire Megacity generated about a quarter of the national total.

Tons of garbage go uncollected and of the garbage that is collected, at least 25 percent of it is placed in illegal barrancas and uncovered landfills at the city's edge. Particulates from the dumps become airborne as winds sweep across the uncovered waste (Mumme, 1991). Finally, there is extensive air contamination by fecal matter in the air and 308,000 tons annually from land erosion, especially from the northeast of the Federal District (Spring, 1991: 61).

Solid wastes fall into many categories including a small category of dangerous ones, which is not publicly reported. The composition of solid wastes for metropolitan Mexican City, with percentages in parentheses, were: food waste (43), paper (16), agricultural/gardening (9), diapers (5), transparent glass (5), cardboard (4), colored glass (3), rigid plastic (3), and other (12) (INEGI, 1994). This is comparable to rates for the nation, except food wastes and paper are higher and agricultural/gardening are lower in the Megacity.

Solid waste generation has increased in Mexico City, although it falls short of the level of advanced nations. Mexico City solid waste was 370 grams per capita in 1950. The level for the Federal District in 1992 was 1,019 grams per day (INEGI, 1994). For Mexico City, INEGI estimates the total volume of solid wastes will increase from 19 million tons per day in 1993 to 25 million tons per day in year 2000, about equally divided between the Federal District and State of Mexico (INEGI, 1994).

The challenge for the future is to provide adequate size and quality of landfill to accommodate this huge volume of solid waste. As seen in Table 7.9 and Map 7.11, in 1994 there were 286 hectares of landfill area in the Megacity, of which 85 percent was sanitary. The 43 hectares of non-sanitary landfill were entirely in the State of Mexico. The largest landfill location of 104 hectares is located in Venustiano Carranza, in the northeastern Federal District (INEGI, 1995). Generally, large landfills are concentrated in eastern Federal District municipios or adjoining State of Mexico municipios, especially Venustiano Carranza, Iztapalapa, Nezahualcoyotl, and Chimalhuacan, and in Naucalpan. Smaller landfills are mostly in the State of Mexico to the north and northwest.

Some open air landfills have been closed in the recent past. The largest was the old Santa Cruz Meyehualco landfill consisting of 150 hectares at the time of closure, followed by Santa Fe at 60 hectares. The closure program in the Federal District has led to recuperation of 230 hectares for greenbelts and parks. In the metropolitan parts of the State of Mexico, many open air landfills have been closed and sanitary landfills opened (INEGI, 1994). There is also a program of developing treatment plants for solid wastes, although it has gotten off to a slow start (INEGI, 1994). In 1992, the Megacity had only a single solid waste treatment plant, which treated 225 tons per day, equivalent to 2.7 percent of Federal District and about 1.5 percent of total city solid waste accumulation.

The future trend should be to locate landfills in northern metropolitan municipios, since population and industry are moving in that direction and there is open space available. New landfills will likely adhere to higher sanitary standards, helping to alleviate the potential contributions of uncovered and untreated solid wastes to air and water pollution.

Table 7.9 Landfill Area, Mexico City, 1994
(in Hectares)

	Sanitary Landfill Area	Non-Sanitary Landfill Area	Total Landfill Area
Federal District			
Iztapalapa	32		32
Venustiano Carranza	104		104
State of Mexico			
Atizapan de Zaragoza		5.7	5.7
Coacalco	4		4
Chicoloapan	1		1
Chimalhuacan		17	17
Ecatepec	3		3
Huehuetoca		4	4
Huixquilucan	1		1
Jaltenco		1.5	1.5
Melchor Ocampo		1	1
Naucalpan	40		40
Nezahualcoyotl	30		30
Nicolas Romero	3		3
Otumba		1	1
Ozumba		1	1
Tecamac	2		2
Temascalapa		1	1
Tenango del Aire		1	1
Tepetlaoxtoc		2	2
Tepetlixpa		1.5	1.5
Tlalmanalco		2	2
Tlalnepantla	9		9
Tultepec		1.5	1.5
Tultitlan	7		7
Zumpango		2.5	2.5
Cuautitlan Izcalli	7		7
Total	243	42.7	285.7
Mean	19	3	4
Median	7	2	0
S.D.	29	4	14
C.V.	154.56	138.88	345.95
Minimum	1	1	0
Maximum	104	17	104

Source: INEGI, *Anuarios Estadisticos,* 1995.

Map 7.11
Solid Waste Landfill Area, 1994
(in Hectares)

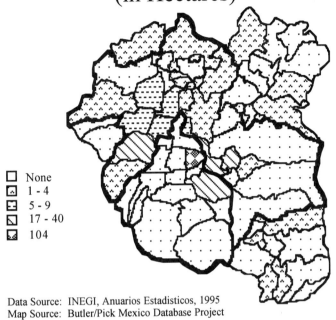

None
1 - 4
5 - 9
17 - 40
104

Data Source: INEGI, Anuarios Estadisticos, 1995
Map Source: Butler/Pick Mexico Database Project

Air Pollution

Introduction

Notwithstanding very serious neighborhood and housing deficits, water, and solid waste problems, Mexico Megacity's most serious problem may be air pollution. Air pollutants affect the health of the population via pollutants from firewood, coal, oil combustion, and gas leakages. Mexico Megacity's air contains virtually all major categories of air pollution -- smoke/suspended particulates, sulfur dioxide, sulfuric acid, hydrocarbons, nitric oxide, nitrogen dioxide and ozone, partial oxidation products, and lead.

As shown in Figure 7.1, the U.N.'s assessment of air quality in the world's major megacities indicates that Mexico Megacity has one of the worst air quality problems among all of these cities. The actual extent of the air pollution problem was shown in 1985 when birds fell from the sky in midflight and one-third of the trees in the city died from air pollution (Schteingart, 1988). Mortality also was excessively high during this episode (Spring, 1991). Another indication of the problem is that 36 percent of the trees in Desierto de los Leones park see, Map 1.4, one of the few forests left in the Valley, were damaged and had to be chopped down (Doremus, 1988).

Topography of the valley is conducive to developing and maintaining pollution in the Valley. The city is 2,240 meters (7,350 feet) above sea level, surrounded by mountains, with winds blowing during the day primarily from the northeast (see Map 7.12), and has abundant sunshine -- one of the key elements in producing photochemical smog. At night winds typically reverse and blow northeast but with a continuation of some winds blowing inward from the northeast (Lacy, 1993). Winds rarely blow with enough force to clear the city's air. Thermal inversion layers trap pollution in the city, especially during 7 or 8 months of the year; June, July, August, and September are months with the fewest inversion layers, while the layers begin to build up in October (Alvarez et al., 1986). Atmospheric conditions are such that at times pollution is trapped for several days in the Valley's airshed. There is substantial variation in pollution by month, day of week, and hour of the day (see Alvarez et al., 1986; Lawrence, 1971; Lacy, 1993).

Mexico Megacity air contains all traditional air pollutants but also there has been a growth in toxic and carcinogenic chemicals such beryllium, cadmium, mercury, lead, etc. Undoubtedly, all of these emissions and pollutants have an impact upon health and mortality (see Pick and Butler, 1995). Air pollution adversely effects human health, animals, flora and fauna, ground water and aquifers, and works of art and buildings. For humans, the impact may be by direct inhalation but may also be indirect via contamination of drinking-water and food and skin transfer.

Sources of Air Pollution

The main source of air pollution in most megacities is from industry and vehicles and Mexico Megacity is no exception. However, a recent study also points to liquefied natural gas (LNG) as a major source of ozone pollution (Blake and Rowland, 1995). Between 36 and 44 percent of the national product, 46 percent of the industrial product, and consumption of 17 percent of the country's energy production takes place in the metropolitan complex (Spring, 1991). In addition industries and 12,000 service facilities are located in the Valley. Over 4,000 industries use combustion or transformation processes generating major atmospheric emissions.

The over 2.5 million vehicles in Mexico Megacity account for nearly half of the energy consumed in the city. It has been estimated that they burn 40,000 barrels of diesel fuel and one million barrels of leaded gasoline each day (U.N., 1994). Spring (1991) says that 5,170,000 tons of contaminants are generated yearly by vehicles, primarily carbon monoxide (4,60,000 tons) and that there are 35,000 industries producing 385,000 tons of particulates and other contaminants. Most of these pollutants are generated by automobiles (DDF, 1996).

Few vehicles in the city are equipped with emission control devices and because of its high altitude and consequent lack of oxygen, automobile engines produce nearly twice as much carbon monoxide and hydrocarbon pollution as they would at lower altitudes.

One estimate places transport vehicles as producing 76 percent of all contaminants released into the city's atmosphere (Presidencia, 1992). Consumption of gasoline grew almost constantly between 1987 up until 1992 when it dropped slightly (Lacy, 1993). During this same period, there was some growth in the use of unleaded gas. However, unless the use of unleaded gas increases dramatically, it also can be anticipated that the number of transport vehicles in the region will continue to grow and air pollution will not abate without further use of unleaded gasoline and other emission controls.

Recently, liquefied petroleum gas has been identified as the probable major source of ozone pollution in Mexico City (Blake and Rowland, 1995). Most house heating in Mexico City is by liquefied petroleum gas. It has the advantages of low cost and easy transport. As a result, approximately 200,000 LPG deliveries are made daily in Mexico City (Cone, 1995). LPG is used instead of natural gas from pipelines principally because of the grave threat of earthquakes, which would break lines. Leakages of LPG are postulated in the delivery and home storage stages. Unburned LPG gases, leaked to the atmosphere, are converted through a series of chemical reactions into ozone (Blake and Rowland, 1993). Because of the recency of this discovery, there are no regulations on LPG transport and storage. Possible government control measures might include restrictions on amount of particular LPG hydrocarbon components and anti-leakage regulations (Blake and Rowland, 1995).

Secondary sources of air pollution up until recently were an oil refinery, power and cement plants, and some 35,000 factories. In addition, 4,000 factories use combustion or transformation processes generating atmospheric emissions. However, as a result in 1991 of closing an oil refinery and two power plants switching to natural gas, there has been a reduction in sulfur emissions.

Air Quality Monitoring

Air pollution monitoring in Mexico City began in the 1950s. As shown on Map 7.13, monitoring consists of a manual network of 16 stations and an automatic network (Red Automatica -- RAMA) established in 1985 (Lacy, 1993).[6] The automatic network, however, consists of only five full capability stations; one in each quadrant and one located at the center of the city. Stations measure SO_2 (sulfur dioxide), CO (carbon monoxide), O_3 (ozone), NO_x (oxides of nitrogen), HCNM (non-methane hydrocarbons); particulates, and other pollutants. Lead pollution is not currently systematically monitored by the government and lead pollution has been a serious problem (Ezcurra and Mazari - Huriart, 1996). However, since 1986 Pemex reduced the lead content of its gasoline and lead pollution has declined dramatically.

The closure of the oil refinery and the switching by power plants to natural gas in 1991 reduced sulfur dioxide emissions around 30 percent. Current sulfur dioxide pollution is primarily from industries and services with some contribution by suburban buses and diesel trucks (Environment, 1994). Overall, sulfur dioxide remains of the major pollutants in the city. Of lesser importance are oxides of nitrogen; major contributors are all transport

---

6 Note that Lacy's metropolitan area is more restricted than ours (see his Map 1).

One of the major air pollutants in Mexico Megacity is carbon monoxide. Because of the high altitude, the city has a relatively low oxygen content in its atmosphere. A result is to increase CO emissions because of incomplete fuel combustion (WHO/UN, 1992). Closure of the oil refinery and converting the power plants to natural gas, while reducing emissions of sulfur dioxide, had negligible impact upon the extent of carbon monoxide in the city. Over 95 percent of carbon monoxide is from transport vehicles, primarily private cars, taxis, and combis/minibuses. Private automobiles account for almost half of the carbon monoxide emitted in the city (WHO/UN, 1992).

Non-methane hydrocarbons are the second major pollutant currently measured in the city. Main sources are gasoline powered automobiles and trucks, combis and minibuses and industry. Suspended particulate matter is primarily derived from environmental erosion degradation. However, an unmeasured source of pollutants may be the burning of firewood and coal for cooking and heating.

Not considered in this chapter is lead pollution. Limited research has shown that lead in blood in Mexico City is substantially higher than for six other cities in Mexico. This holds for both sexes and whether or not they are smokers. Further, there is variation among respiratory infections within the city which also may be related to air and lead pollution (Sector Salud, 1987, Table 1). However, lead pollution levels have declined greatly since 1986 (WHO/UN, 1992).

Distribution of Air Pollution

According to Lacy's (1993) analysis, SO_2 is the most pervasive geographically distributed air pollutant being strong in all areas of the city except the oldest areas. Carbon monoxide, on the other hand, is concentrated in older areas, as well as in other areas. The central area of Merced (#13 on Map 7.12) has the greatest range of air pollutants but two other areas designated as central have low levels. Of the other five areas with highest levels of pollutants, one each is located in the southwest (Pedregal, #14) and southeast (Ciudad de la Estrella, #15). One is located in the northwest (Tlalnepantla, #11) and two are in the northeast (Hangares, #17 and Xalostoc, #12). Generally, then, air pollution, as measured by RAMA, is highly variable in the District with the major pollutants of SO_2, O_3, and CO being most widely distributed. A broader view of air pollutants by region is shown on Maps 7.13 and 7.14. The values in these maps are in IMECA units. IMECA (Indice Metropolitano de la Calidad del Aire) is an index that scales each pollutant concentration from 0 (best) to 500 (worst). Each pollutant's scale converts to chemical concentration (INEGI, 1994: Table 94).

CO at the Merced station was high all day but peaked between 7:00 A.M. and 9:30 A.M. (Lacy 1993). On the other hand, ozone peaked later in the day at both the Merced and Pedregal, from around 9:00 A.M. until around 4:00 P.M.; there was a very strong correspondence of Ozone buildup with solar radiation. An analysis of CO by day of week for several of the stations with the highest levels showed a consistent buildup from the lowest levels on Sunday to a peak on Friday which then receded on Saturday and then to the lowest levels on Sunday.

Ozone levels are highest in the southwest and lowest in the northeast. Based on new research on LPG leakages (Blake and Rowland, 1995), we postulated that ozone would be produced from leaking gases in the most populated sections of the Megacity and then be blown toward the southwest during the day by prevailing northeast winds (see Figure 7.2). The actual ozone dispersion mechanism is expected to be elaborated on soon in the growing research studies. Particulates had a clear, higher concentration in the northeast and declining basically toward the southwest probably illustrating the importance of prevailing winds, especially during the night hours (see Figure 7.2).

205

Figure 7.1 Air Pollution in the World's Twenty Largest Megacities

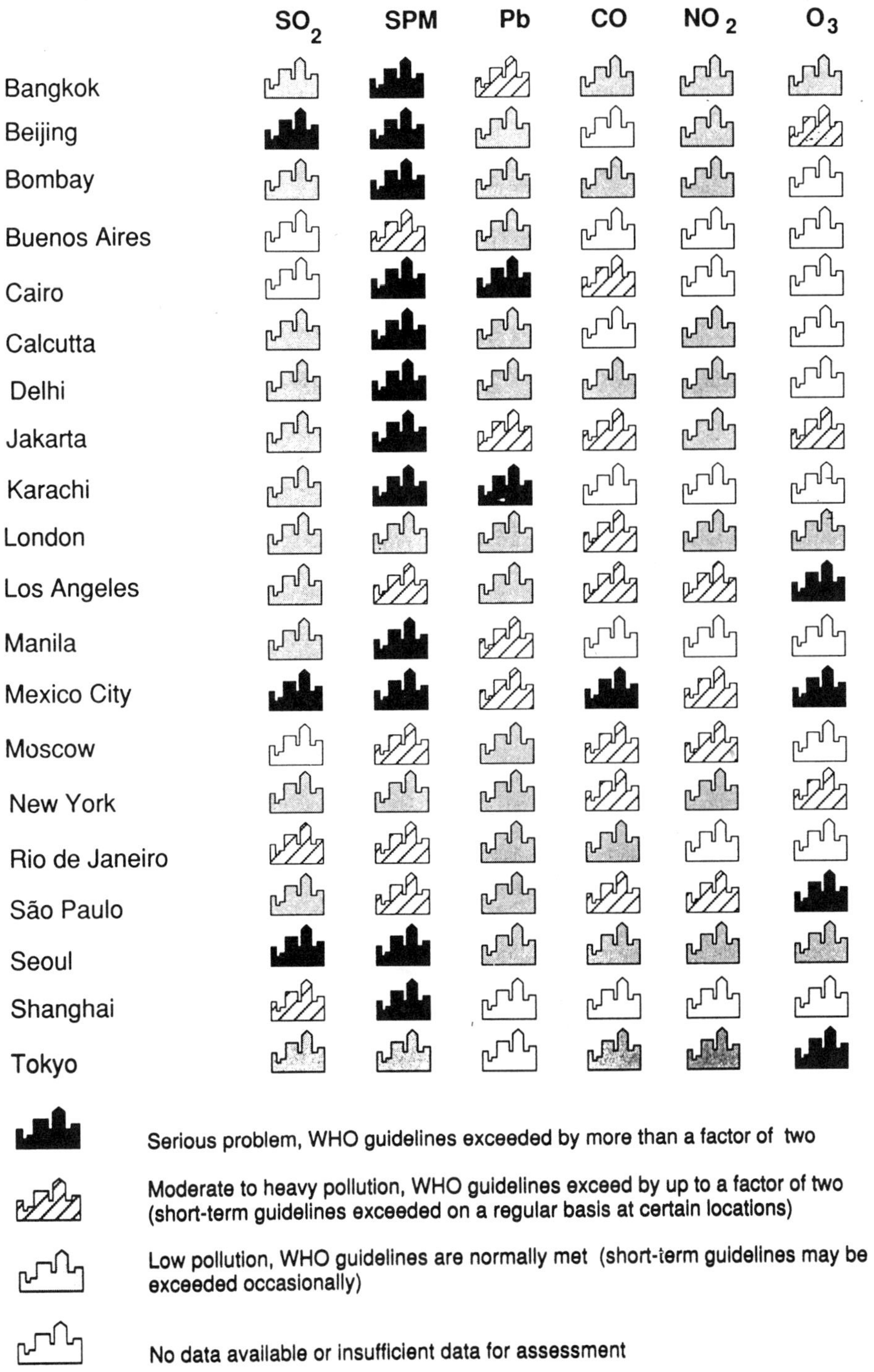

Source: United Nations, 1994. By permission of United Nations Enviroment Programme.

Figure 7.2 Direction of Wind,
Night and Day, in Mexico City

Day

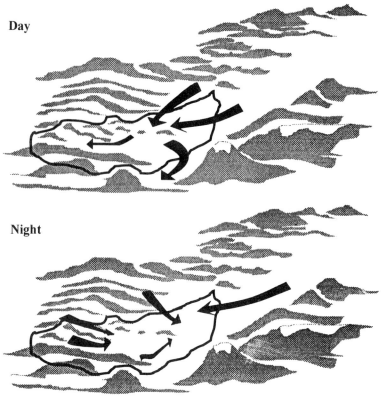

Night

Source: Departmento del Distrito Federal. By permission of El Colegio de Mexico.

Figure 7.3 Air Pollution
Impacts Breathing in Mexico City

Map 7.12 Air Quality Monitoring Stations in Mexico City

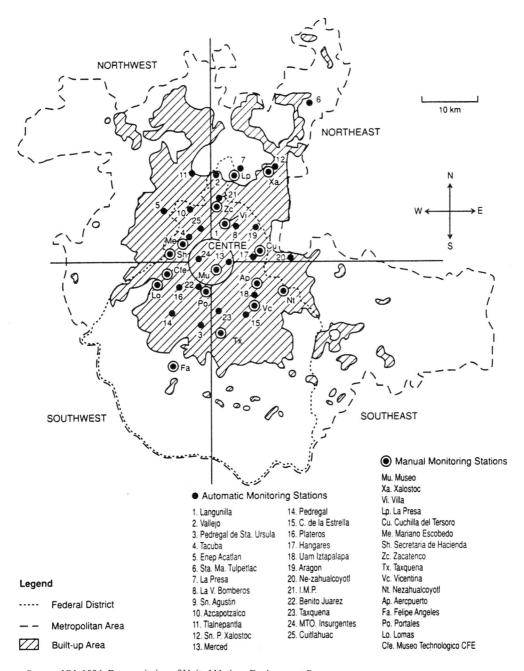

NORTHWEST

NORTHEAST

N

W ← → E

S

10 km

CENTRE

SOUTHWEST

SOUTHEAST

◉ Manual Monitoring Stations

Mu. Museo
Xa. Xalostoc
Vi. Villa
Lp. La Presa
Cu. Cuchilla del Tersoro
Me. Mariano Escobedo
Sh. Secretaria de Hacienda
Zc. Zacatenco
Tx. Taxquena
Vc. Vicentina
Nt. Nezahualcoyotl
Ap. Aercpuerto
Fa. Felipe Angeles
Po. Portales
Lo. Lomas
Cfe. Museo Technologico CFE

● Automatic Monitoring Stations

1. Langunilla	14. Pedregal
2. Vallejo	15. C. de la Estrella
3. Pedregal de Sta. Ursula	16. Plateros
4. Tacuba	17. Hangares
5. Enep Acatlan	18. Uam Iztapalapa
6. Sta. Ma. Tulpetlac	19. Aragon
7. La Presa	20. Ne-zahualcoyotl
8. La V. Bomberos	21. I.M.P.
9. Sn. Agustin	22. Benito Juarez
10. Azcapotzalco	23. Taxquena
11. Tlalnepantla	24. MTO. Insurgentes
12. Sn. P. Xalostoc	25. Cuitlahuac
13. Merced	

Legend

----- Federal District

— — Metropolitan Area

▨ Built-up Area

Source: UN, 1994. By permission of United Nations Environment Programme.

208

Map 7.13   Sulfur Dioxide, Nitrogen Dioxide, and Carbon Monoxide Air Pollution, 1991, in IMECA Units

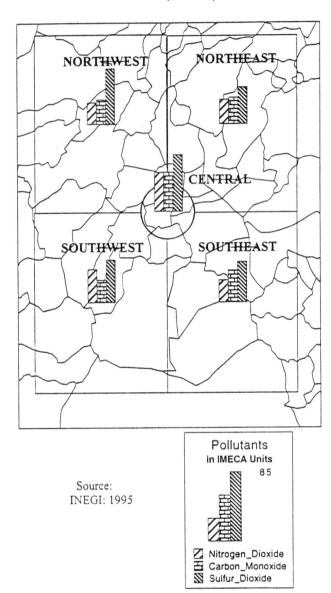

Source:
INEGI: 1995

Map 7.14. Ozone and Particulate Air
Pollution, 1991, in IMECA Units

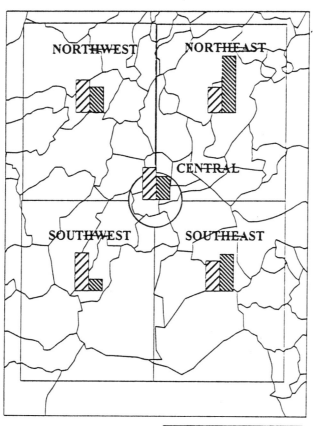

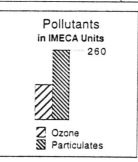

Source:
INEGI: 1995

Air Pollution Control Strategies

Mexico has developed control strategies in attempts to control chronic air pollution, while other strategies are contingency plans for high pollution episodes. Chronic air pollution control strategies have been to lower the sulfur content of fuel oil and diesel fuel; retrofitting buses, vans, and trucks to burn natural gas; limiting CO emissions from vehicles; developing unleaded gasoline and equipping automobiles with catalytic converters, restricting commuter traffic, new and expanded bus routes, extending the "No Driving Today" program which bans private car driving one day per week, a ban on new industries regarded as potentially polluting, emissions control and/or relocation of the 216 foundries and steel mills in the city, and to ensure systematic monitoring and installation of anti-pollution equipment (see Presidencia, 1992). During high pollution episodes, activities of high polluting industries are curtailed and vehicle circulation is restricted.

More recently a joint effort by the Federal District and State of Mexico emphasized incorporation of new air pollution control technology in industry, services, and automobiles, use of alternative energy sources, additional and more efficient public transportation, economic incentives to reduce pollutants, inspection and vigilance in enforcing industrial and vehicular standards, increasing education and spread of information, and more social participation (DDF, 1996). There also has been more recognition of the need for policy integration and coordination among air pollution abatement procedures and governmental units involved in them.

All control strategies require (1) setting standards and (2) then enforcing them. Both of these general approaches have to be adhered to if pollution is to be reduced.

In spite of control strategies, air pollution problems have accelerated in the region. Solutions that have been offered but not put effectively into place are (1) to change the economic foundation of the city from polluting industries to non-polluting industries, (2) to develop more efficient air pollution control technologies, (3) more effective mandating of emission controls, (4) to use better fuels, which presumably would involve the use of unleaded gasoline, and (5) reforestation, e.g., plant more flora and fauna; some of these solutions were suggested by the U.N. (Environment, 1994). Newly considered control strategies involve setting standards to lower dangerous components of LPG and control of LPG transport and storage behaviors. Other suggestions have included more community participation in the fight against pollution, improvement of areas without sewerage, and creation of ecological reserves.

Conclusions

This chapter addressed several different kinds of environmental problems in Mexico Megacity. Clearly many other problems that have been identified and worthy of examination were not discussed. Given the magnitude of housing and air pollution problems shown here, it would be easy to become resigned to the fact that these problems will continue to exist in the future and most likely will become even more serious than they are currently. On the other hand, the first step to overcoming these and other problems of the city are to recognize them and to begin to concentrate resources in overcoming them. Not an easy thing to do, especially given current economic conditions in Mexico and the many other competing uses of scarce resources.

These problems impact in different combinations all parts of the city and external regions as well. In the future, there will be concern with all of the environmental deficits pointed to in this chapter. It is problematic given the current economic situation in Mexico if any of these environmental problems will be overcome in the near future. Even further environmental difficulties will ensue if the population continues to increase in Mexico Megacity -- as it is projected to do! For instances, housing deficits described here are substantial and are likely to increase with an increasing rural to urban migration.

Similarly, air pollution problems examined here are likely to increase unless motor vehicles are more controlled in the city, polluting industries adhere to mandated emission rules and regulations and/or are moved from the city, the newly recognized LPG problem is addressed and more adequate waste disposal technology is employed.

All control strategies made for alleviating various environmental problems in Mexico Megacity are useless unless implemented. Very few environmental problems facing the Megacity can be successfully attacked at the individual and household level or even at the neighborhood or smaller community region. To alleviate most of them requires action at the Megacity level and many of them will have to be dealt with at the national level before any relief will be available. If these problems are not alleviated, it will not be because of "environmental purists" (Feldstein and Felstein, 1991) or because of Free Trade (Reilly, 1991) but rather because of a lack of energy and imagination to utilize available resources.

We have shown that housing and related problems are scattered throughout the city but the most severe conditions are concentrated in certain regions. Similarly, air pollution, while existing throughout city, also is concentrated in certain regions. In general, there is a certain amount of overlap between housing deficits and air pollution; however, the relationship clearly is not isomorphic. Our conclusion is that much needs to be accomplished if environmental problems are to be reduced to safe levels in Mexico Megacity.

8

Socioeconomic Characteristics

Photo courtesy of Tomas Mojarr○

Introduction

Socioeconomic dimensions are essential elements in understanding Mexico City and its citizens. They include literacy and education, social status, indigenous language speaking, religion, consumption, crime, and homeownership. This chapter continues the approach of description combined with statistical and cluster analyses. The chapter builds on the last chapter, which defined among other things the housing dimensions of the city.

First we compare literacy in the nation with literacy in Mexico Megacity and with the state of Chiapas, the state with the lowest literacy rate in Mexico, and then illustrate variation in literacy among various areas of Mexico Megacity. The second part of this chapter examines educational enrollment and attainment by several different age categories.

The next part of this chapter examines socioeconomic variation in 1990 among various delegations and municipios of Mexico Megacity. Specific information is presented on delegations and municipios with a marginality concentration -- that is, areas with a concentration of low or no incomes in 1990, areas with a concentration of high incomes (5 times the minimum wage), and unemployment and underemployment. Because of the importance of the indigenous language speaking population in Mexico the presence of this population and of various individual indigenous populations in Mexico Megacity are examined. The following section of the chapter utilizes 1990 Mexican census data to illustrate the Non-Catholic and other religious segments in the metropolitan complex.

Another section examines home ownership. The next part of the chapter briefly analyzes criminal charge patterns -- misdemeanors, robbery, homicides, and criminal sentences for the Federal District in 1993. Correlations among many of the dimensions included in this chapter are shown on Table 8.1. Finally, the concluding section of the chapter utilizes a number of characteristics examined in this chapter to carry out a cluster analysis to determine if there are underlying, or latent, types of social rank areas in Mexico Megacity.

Literacy

Literacy is defined by the Mexican Census for persons 15 years and older who declare that they know how to read and write a message. Literacy for the nation, Federal District, Mexico Megacity, and Chiapas (for comparison purposes) is shown on Figure 8.1. Chiapas is included in this figure because over the years it consistently has had the lowest literacy rate in Mexico. However, literacy has continued to increase in all sections of Mexico including Chiapas. While the relative proportion of illiteracy has declined, there remains a disparity for all other jurisdictions when compared to the Federal District. As seen in Figure 8.2, male literacy exceeds female literacy only slightly in the Federal District although the gap is very large in Chiapas.

Table 8.2 reports literacy by delegations and municipios of Mexico Megacity. Map 8.1 presents the percent of population literate for 1990 and shows that higher literacy levels are concentrated in the "old core" and nearby peripheral areas north. Mexico Megacity areas with the lowest literacy rates are Atlautla, Axapusco, Cocotitlan, Isidro Fabela, Jilotzingo, Juchitepec, and Otumba. Chalco often regarded as a "slum", has literacy higher than the nation and State of Mexico and Nezahualcoyotl has almost a 95 percent literacy rate.

Figure 8.1
Literacy, 1900 - 1990

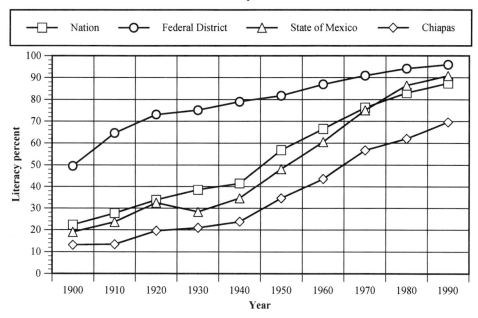

Source: INEGI: *Estadisticas Historicas de Mexico,* 1994

Figure 8.2 Literacy by Gender,
Nation, Federal District, Mexico, Chiapas, 1990

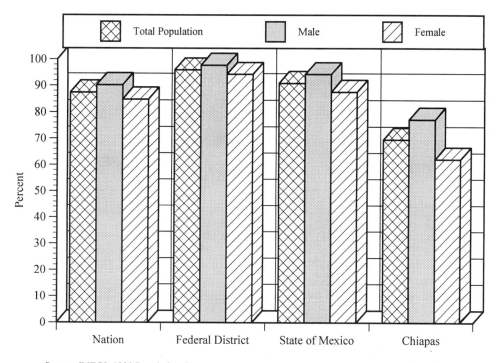

Source: INEGI, 1990 Population Census.

Table 8.1 Correlation Matrix of Socioeconomic Variables

	Literate	Primary Education	Higher Education	Underemployment	Unemployed	No Income	High Income	Indigenous Language	Delta Indigenous 70-90
Primary Education	.780***								
Higher Education	.626***	.918***							
Underemployment	-.374**	-.363**	-.271*						
Unemployed	-.326**	-.389***	-.333**	.681***					
No Income	-.478***	-.397***	-.241*	.244*	.134				
High Income	.563***	.751***	.864***	-.206	-.253*	-.341**			
Indigenous Language	.274*	.293*	.334**	-.216	-.279*	-.440***	.253*		
Delta Indigenous 70-90	.010	-.017	-.024	.003	-.010	.097	.084	-.297*	
Mixteco Language	.145	.034	.088	-.106	-.132	-.285	.116	.672***	.284*
Nahautl Language	.084	.140	.124	-.166	-.276*	-.299	-.029	.779***	-.655***
Otomi Language	.272*	.269*	.329**	-.120	-.083	-.360**	.408***	.521***	-.131
Zapoteco Language	.493***	.555***	.570***	-.284*	-.291*	-.327**	.491***	.562***	.231
Non-Catholic	.183	.200	.277*	-.084	-.072	.113	.292*	.286*	.082
Misdemeanor 1994	.458***	.648***	.661***	-.237	-.238	-.115	.479***	.335**	.129
Felony 1993	.424***	.605***	.607***	-.225	-.227	-.091	.390***	.341**	.144
Home Ownership	-.486***	-.676***	-.665***	.247	.219	.237	-.479***	-.219	-.099
Professional, Technical	.638***	.913***	.978***	-.266*	-.311**	-.236	.890***	.232	.087
Population 1990	.455***	.532***	.499***	-.256*	-.230	-.117	.330*	.316**	.157

Note: Significant Levels

*	.05
**	.01
***	.001

Table 8.1 Correlation Matrix of Socioeconomic Variables (Continued)

	Mixteco Language	Nahuatl Language	Otomi Language	Zapoteco Language	Non-Catholic	Misdemeanor 1994	Felony 1993	Home Ownership	Professional, Technical
Primary Education									
Higher Education									
Underemployment									
Unemployed									
No Income									
High Income									
Indigenous Language									
Delta Indigenous 70-90									
Mixteco Language									
Nahuatl Language	.221								
Otomi Language	.311**	.139							
Zapoteco Language	.573***	.144	.383***						
Non-Catholic	.489***	.005	.176	.420***					
Misdemeanor 1994	.227	.059	.220	.640***	.283*				
Felony 1993	.269*	.055	.214	.605***	.270*	.964***			
Home Ownership	-.122	-.011	-.182	-.597***	-.232	-.709***	-.674***		
Professional, Technical	.076	-.027	.330**	.562***	.273	.647***	.587***	-.655***	
Population 1990	.279	.044	.218	.594***	.249*	.880***	.868***	-.479***	.496***

Note: Significant Levels   *   .05
                         **   .01
                         ***   .001

Table 8.2 Literacy, 1990

No.	Area	Population	Percent Literate
1	Acolman	29,481	0.8999
2	Alvaro Obregon	484,231	0.9512
3	Amecameca	25,349	0.9293
4	Atenco	15,225	0.9447
5	Atizapan de Zaragoza	224,320	0.9437
6	Atlautla	11,807	0.8543
7	Axapusco	10,203	0.8772
8	Ayapango	2,939	0.9357
9	Azcapotzalco	369,990	0.9641
10	Benito Juarez	336,908	0.9709
11	Chalco	179,611	0.9073
12	Chiautla	10,431	0.9419
13	Chicoloapan	38,669	0.9278
14	Chiconcuac	10,165	0.9455
15	Chimalhuacan	155,821	0.9195
16	Coacalco	115,035	0.9749
17	Cocotitlan	5,275	0.8611
18	Coyoacan	504,175	0.9655
19	Coyotepec	15,752	0.8949
20	Cuajimalpa	89,061	0.9769
21	Cuauhtemoc	470,869	0.9607
22	Cuautitlan	34,954	0.9530
23	Cuautitlan Izcalli	235,831	0.9617
24	Ecatepec	886,450	0.9742
25	Ecatzingo	3,464	0.8522
26	Gustavo A. Madero	972,577	0.9620
27	Huehuetoca	16,570	0.9179
28	Huixquilucan	93,611	0.9323
29	Isidro Fabela	3,405	0.8673
30	Ixtapaluca	91,652	0.9228
31	Iztacalco	346,267	0.9642
32	Iztapalapa	1,089,682	0.9515
33	Jaltenco	16,148	0.9554
34	Jilotzingo	5,792	0.8764
35	Juchitepec	9,265	0.8746
36	Magdalena Contreras	145,880	0.9522
37	Melchor Ocampo	18,316	0.9443
38	Miguel Hidalgo	325,244	0.9581
39	Milpa Alta	44,765	0.9242
40	Naucalpan	577,966	0.9461
41	Nextlalpan	7,302	0.9426
42	Nezahualcoyotl	916,055	0.9474
43	Nicolas Romero	125,299	0.9217
44	Nopaltepec	3,467	0.8784
45	Otumba	14,047	0.8825
46	Ozumba	12,239	0.9211
47	Papalotla	1,721	0.9415
48	Paz, La	93,415	0.9343
49	San Martin de las Piramides	9,580	0.9307
50	Tecamac	86,715	0.9421
51	Temamatla	3,673	0.9408
52	Temascalapa	12,625	0.9022
53	Tenango Del Aire	4,367	0.9264
54	Teoloyucan	28,302	0.9221

Table 8.2 Literacy, 1990 (Continued)

No.	Area	Population	Percent Literate
55	Teotihuacan	21,306	0.9362
56	Tepetlaoxtoc	10,638	0.9011
57	Tepetlixpa	8,557	0.9080
58	Tepotzotlan	26,704	0.9210
59	Texcoco	101,316	0.9414
60	Tezoyuca	9,008	0.9543
61	Tlahuac	148,424	0.9488
62	Tlalmanalco	24,468	0.9535
63	Tlalnepantla	524,167	0.9517
64	Tlalpan	362,846	0.9521
65	Tultepec	31,943	0.9344
66	Tultitlan	172,768	0.9538
67	Venustiano Carranza	384,844	0.9210
68	Xochimilco	198,974	0.9504
69	Zumpango	47,380	0.9070
Total		11,415,306	0.8334
Mean		165,439	0.9305
Median		34,954	0.9408
S.D.		251,920	0.0306
C.V.		152.2736	3.2890
Minimum		1,721	0.8522
Maximum		1,089,682	0.9769

Source: INEGI, 1990 Population Census.

Map 8.1
Literacy, 1990

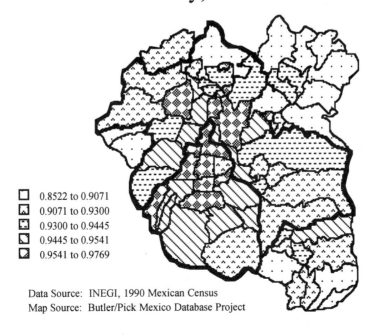

0.8522 to 0.9071
0.9071 to 0.9300
0.9300 to 0.9445
0.9445 to 0.9541
0.9541 to 0.9769

Data Source: INEGI, 1990 Mexican Census
Map Source: Butler/Pick Mexico Database Project

Primary and Higher Education

In 1990, about one third of the population age six and older completed primary education, i.e. the first six school grades (see Table 8.3). The spatial distribution of primary education, seen in Map 8.2, shows much higher primary education in most of the Federal District, except for Milpa Alta, often exceeding 60 percent. The highest level of primary education, 71 percent, is for Benito Juarez, the old city center that contains the Zocolo as well as being an historical center. By contrast the semi-urban periphery in the northeast and southeast has primary education averaging about 25 percent.

All literacy and educational variables are highly inter-correlated. For this reason, only a limited number of them are discussed and only two are displayed. For instance, primary education has high correlations with literacy (r = 0.78) and higher education (r = 0.92). It is also highly related to other educational indicators, such as average grade attained (r = 0.99), school attendance for 15-19 year olds (r = 0.93), and post-primary education (r = 0.80). Although not mapped, higher education averaged 17 percent in the Federal District in 1990, which compares to a national average of 9 percent (Pick and Butler, 1994). As seen in Figure 8.3, higher education in most areas was under 10 percent and in many under 5 percent. These areas are located peripherally in a spatial pattern very close to that for primary education (Map 8.2). At the other extreme are several delegations with higher education at or above 25 percent, i.e. about three times the national average. These are Benito Juarez at 35 percent and Coyoacan at 25 percent. The rest of the old central city and Tlalpan are over 20 percent. This reflects sharp college-level variation in the Megacity. College graduation in Mexico implies entree to management levels of business and government, as well as into some professions.

Map 8.3 shows the distribution of adults enrolled in school in 1990. The rates average about 3 percent, considerably above the nation. By far the highest percentages are in the Federal District.

221

Table 8.3 Education, 1990

No.	Area	Average Grade Attended	Population with Primary Education	Percent of Population with Primary Education	Population with Higher Education	Percent of Population with Higher Education
1	Acolman	7.1	15,535	0.4190	1,497	0.0575
2	Alvaro Obregon	8.5	289,832	0.5170	69,611	0.1636
3	Amecameca	6.8	11,141	0.3592	1,327	0.0617
4	Atenco	6.1	7,358	0.4014	640	0.0502
5	Atizapan De Zaragoza	8.5	127,637	0.4768	30,866	0.1626
6	Atlautla	5.4	4,096	0.2566	272	0.0255
7	Axapusco	5.4	3,339	0.2498	179	0.0201
8	Ayapango	6.2	1,147	0.3241	90	0.0365
9	Azcapotzalco	8.8	233,764	0.5578	49,873	0.1533
10	Benito Juarez	11.1	260,994	0.7117	107,324	0.3513
11	Chalco	5.8	64,607	0.2780	4,225	0.0280
12	Chiautla	6.9	4,920	0.3906	475	0.0537
13	Chicoloapan	6.5	16,835	0.3492	1,254	0.0393
14	Chiconcuac	7.3	5,221	0.4325	572	0.0667
15	Chimalhuacan	5.9	56,533	0.2837	2,827	0.0221
16	Coacalco	9.2	75,791	0.5744	14,891	0.1562
17	Cocotitlan	7.2	2,928	0.4259	312	0.0639
18	Coyoacan	9.8	348,252	0.6134	108,579	0.2472
19	Coyotepec	6.3	7,125	0.3498	490	0.0361
20	Cuajimalpa	7.8	46,455	0.4552	8,630	0.1154
21	Cuauhtemoc	9.5	316,108	0.6017	87,090	0.2066
22	Cuautitlan	7.8	19,446	0.4676	2,497	0.0841
23	Cuautitlan Izcalli	8.7	142,695	0.5124	27,223	0.1401
24	Ecatepec	7.6	452,676	0.4374	57,501	0.0792
25	Ecatzingo	4.5	901	0.1884	26	0.0088
26	Gustavo A. Madero	8.6	595,424	0.5352	122,764	0.1440
27	Huehuetoca	6.3	6,702	0.3181	551	0.0392
28	Huixquilucan	8.1	50,013	0.4449	13,485	0.1654
29	Isidro Fabela	5.5	1,152	0.2600	83	0.0273
30	Ixtapaluca	6.5	39,291	0.3425	3,490	0.0451
31	Iztacalco	8.6	214,824	0.5453	44,512	0.1463
32	Iztapalapa	7.9	607,253	0.4746	100,646	0.1078
33	Jaltenco	7.4	8,044	0.4146	638	0.0496
34	Jilotzingo	5.7	2,000	0.2650	147	0.0275
35	Juchitepec	5.7	3,570	0.2951	293	0.0358
36	Magdalena Contreras	8.4	84,216	0.4956	19,649	0.1549
37	Melchor Ocampo	7.0	8,738	0.3947	784	0.0512
38	Miguel Hidalgo	9.6	217,332	0.6002	67,158	0.2292
39	Milpa Alta	7.4	23,204	0.4257	3,315	0.0850
40	Naucalpan	8.3	326,506	0.4817	78,800	0.1557
41	Nextlalpan	6.6	3,154	0.3504	239	0.0398
42	Nezahualcoyotl	7.6	490,496	0.4560	63,873	0.0813
43	Nicolas Romero	6.6	53,755	0.3463	4,377	0.0412
44	Nopaltepec	5.8	1,338	0.2979	60	0.0196
45	Otumba	5.8	5,246	0.2858	336	0.0273
46	Ozumba	6.5	5,140	0.3386	477	0.0459
47	Papalotla	7.5	839	0.4085	132	0.0916
48	Paz, La	6.8	43,314	0.3808	4,163	0.0531
49	San Martin De Las P.	6.5	4,163	0.3584	374	0.0461
50	Tecamac	7.3	43,273	0.4119	5,526	0.0766

Table 8.3 Education, 1990 (Continued)

No.	Area	Average Grade Attended	Population with Primary Education	Percent of Population with Primary Education	Population with Higher Education	Percent of Population with Higher Education
51	Temamatla	6.7	1,692	0.3771	123	0.0396
52	Temascalapa	5.6	4,200	0.2598	248	0.0229
53	Tenango Del Aire	6.3	1,728	0.3251	166	0.0443
54	Teoloyucan	6.4	12,581	0.3557	872	0.0369
55	Teotihuacan	7.0	10,113	0.3891	1,068	0.0598
56	Tepetlaoxtoc	6.3	4,298	0.3169	329	0.0357
57	Tepetlixpa	5.9	3,179	0.2944	178	0.0238
58	Tepotzotlan	6.8	12,307	0.3704	1,261	0.0552
59	Texcoco	7.9	55,043	0.4541	10,442	0.1212
60	Tezoyuca	7.3	4,570	0.4291	412	0.0555
61	Tlahuac	7.6	79,498	0.4501	9,558	0.0763
62	Tlalmanalco	7.7	13,275	0.4659	1,577	0.0763
63	Tlalnepantla	8.4	307,660	0.5040	63,057	0.1388
64	Tlalpan	9.1	228,725	0.5438	63,841	0.2035
65	Tultepec	7.0	15,489	0.3918	1,553	0.0583
66	Tultitlan	7.9	94,896	0.4564	12,537	0.0876
67	Venustiano Carranza	8.8	253,817	0.5540	54,688	0.1534
68	Xochimilco	8.5	119,457	0.5102	25,956	0.1508
69	Zumpango	6.3	19,862	0.3304	1,973	0.0486
Total			6,596,713		1,363,982	
Mean		7.2	95,605	0.4107	19,768	0.0856
Median		7.1	16,835	0.4085	1,577	0.0583
S.D.		1.3	147,685	0.1041	32,387	0.0657
C.V.		17.41	154.47	25.34	163.84	76.77
Minimum		4.5	839	0.1884	26	0.0088
Maximum		11.1	607,253	0.7117	122,764	0.3513

Source: INEGI, 1992 Population Census.

Figure 8.3 Higher Education by Spatial Unit, 1990

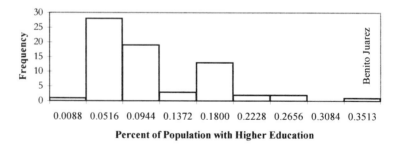

Source: INEGI, 1990 Mexican Census

Map 8.2
Primary Education, 1990

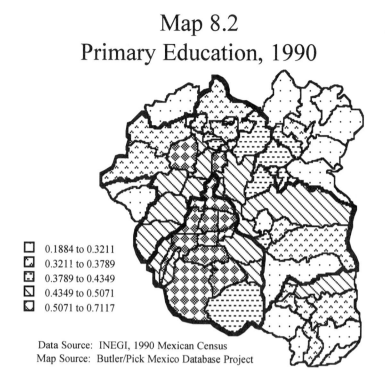

0.1884 to 0.3211
0.3211 to 0.3789
0.3789 to 0.4349
0.4349 to 0.5071
0.5071 to 0.7117

Data Source: INEGI, 1990 Mexican Census
Map Source: Butler/Pick Mexico Database Project

Map 8.3

Adults Enrolled in School, 1990

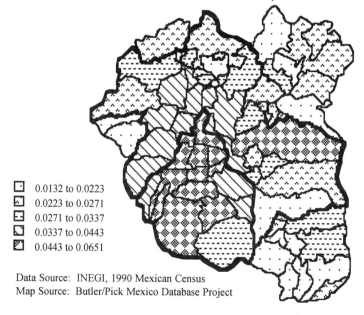

0.0132 to 0.0223
0.0223 to 0.0271
0.0271 to 0.0337
0.0337 to 0.0443
0.0443 to 0.0651

Data Source: INEGI, 1990 Mexican Census
Map Source: Butler/Pick Mexico Database Project

Socioeconomic Level

Marginality

The hourly minimum wage in old pesos (and Log 10) for the Federal District for 1950-51 - 1990-91 is shown on Figure 8.4. These data, of course, have to be balanced with the cost of living for each time period.

On average about one fifth of the metropolitan population has no or low income (see Table 8.4). Low income is defined as income at less than the minimum wage rate. The no/low income is moderately variable (CV = 42 percent), with about two thirds of the range is between 12 and 28 percent no/low income. The geographic distribution in Map 8.4 clearly indicates that poverty as represented by no/low income is heavily concentrated in the northeast and southeast semi-urban zones, with pockets also in the semi-urban zone to the west and Tlahuac in the southeastern Federal District. The heaviest poverty areas are the southeast municipios of Ecatzingo (57 percent), Atlautla (41 percent), and Tepetlixpa (34 percent) as well as in Axapusco (35 percent) in the northeast. By contrast, the percent no/low income for Chalco, often considered the city's prototypical urban slum, is fourteen percent, only about a third below the average. The eleven percent of no/low income in Nezahualcoyotl reflects low poverty, which substantiates the tremendous economic progress of Nezahualcoyotl over the past three decades (Lourdes Vega, 1991).

Certain aspects of marginality shown in Chapter 6 were associated with several different mortality measures. Among them were previous census measures (1970 and 1980) of households without eggs and meat. The analysis demonstrated that there has been substantial continuity in marginal areas located in the metropolitan complex. The lack of households having available meat and eggs is particularly strong in peripheral areas of Mexico Megacity (see Maps 6.2 and 6.3). Not too surprisingly these are the very same areas shown in the last chapter to have housing and neighborhood deficits.

High Level Income

In contrast to marginality, Map 8.5 shows the location of the population that "earned 5 times the minimum wage" (High Income) in 1990 (see Table 8.4). As expected, it is opposite to low/no income (r = -.034). Seven percent of the Mexico City population on average has income that is five times or more the minimum wage. This compares closely to the national average in 1990 of 7.6 percent. There is considerable variability in high income (CV=58 percent), as reflected in a range from Milpa Alta at 0.5 percent in the southeast of the Federal District to Benito Juarez in the central Federal District at 24.1 percent. Several other central Federal district delegations have high income including Coyoacan at 16.3 percent and Miguel Hidalgo at 15.8 percent. In the four delegations in the center of the Federal District about one sixth of the population is in this high income category. This contrasts with many central cities in the United States, in which the central city has lower income than the periphery (Frey, 1995). Most peripheral areas in the northeast and southeast have the lowest percent of population with higher level incomes.

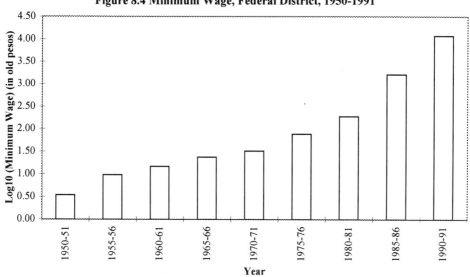

Figure 8.4 Minimum Wage, Federal District, 1950-1991

Supporting Data

Year	Minimum Wage	Log10 Minimum Wage
1950-51	3.39	0.5302
1955-56	9.50	0.9777
1960-61	14.50	1.1614
1965-66	23.25	1.3664
1970-71	32.00	1.5052
1975-76	75.52	1.8781
1980-81	186.50	2.2695
1985-86	1,610.00	3.2068
1990-91	11,802.50	4.0720

Source: *Estadisticas Historicas de Mexico,* Vol 1, 1994
Note: 1000 old pesos = 1 new peso

Table 8.4 Socioeconomic Level, 1990

No.	Area	Employed Population	Population with No or Low Income	Percent of Population with No or Low Income	Unemployed Population	Percent of Population Unemployed	Underemployed Population	Percent of Population Underemployed	Population that Earns 5 Times Minimum Wage	Percent of Population that Earns 5 Times Minimum Wage
1	Acolman	11,404	1,699	0.1490	287	0.0252	602	0.0528	720	0.0631
2	Alvaro Obregon	227,381	47,692	0.2097	3,529	0.0155	8,256	0.0363	25,357	0.1115
3	Amecameca	9,796	2,290	0.2338	262	0.0267	581	0.0593	533	0.0544
4	Atenco	5,452	953	0.1748	106	0.0194	257	0.0471	246	0.0451
5	Atizapan de Zaragoza	98,783	19,405	0.1964	1,661	0.0168	3,902	0.0395	14,424	0.1460
6	Atlautla	4,551	1,856	0.4078	90	0.0198	227	0.0499	164	0.0360
7	Axapusco	3,969	1,383	0.3485	101	0.0254	121	0.0305	119	0.0300
8	Ayapango	1,125	281	0.2498	12	0.0107	46	0.0409	44	0.0391
9	Azcapotzalco	165,830	30,815	0.1858	3,000	0.0181	4,904	0.0296	13,042	0.0786
10	Benito Juarez	168,898	26,324	0.1559	2,464	0.0146	6,781	0.0401	40,681	0.2409
11	Chalco	76,356	10,762	0.1409	1,795	0.0235	4,161	0.0545	3,206	0.0420
12	Chiautla	4,090	894	0.2186	86	0.0210	255	0.0623	217	0.0531
13	Chicoloapan	15,596	1,992	0.1277	309	0.0198	797	0.0511	964	0.0618
14	Chiconcuac	3,786	862	0.2277	74	0.0195	302	0.0798	260	0.0687
15	Chimalhuacan	64,719	8,588	0.1327	1,309	0.0202	3,593	0.0555	2,877	0.0445
16	Coacalco	47,477	7,725	0.1627	855	0.0180	1,794	0.0378	5,215	0.1098
17	Cocotitlan	2,132	352	0.1651	35	0.0164	119	0.0558	88	0.0413
18	Coyoacan	230,840	39,245	0.1700	3,547	0.0154	7,832	0.0339	37,741	0.1635
19	Coyotepec	6,190	1,058	0.1709	127	0.0205	279	0.0451	274	0.0443
20	Cuajimalpa	39,138	8,152	0.2083	713	0.0182	1,150	0.0294	3,385	0.0865
21	Cuauhtemoc	233,676	44,860	0.1920	3,933	0.0168	9,505	0.0407	25,881	0.1108
22	Cuautitlan	14,782	3,133	0.2119	222	0.0150	518	0.0350	1,066	0.0721
23	Cuautitlan Izcalli	97,764	6,965	0.0712	1,770	0.0181	3,032	0.0310	16,568	0.1695
24	Ecatepec	367,801	80,975	0.2202	6,526	0.0177	12,330	0.0335	20,359	0.0554
25	Ecatzingo	1,113	640	0.5750	21	0.0189	68	0.0611	17	0.0153
26	Gustavo A. Madero	428,174	85,142	0.1988	7,583	0.0177	14,381	0.0336	31,731	0.0741
27	Huehuetoca	7,055	1,169	0.1657	114	0.0162	263	0.0373	378	0.0536
28	Huixquilucan	43,505	4,499	0.1034	562	0.0129	2,048	0.0471	7,668	0.1763

Table 8.4 Socioeconomic Level, 1990 (Continued)

No.	Area	Employed Population	Population with No or Low Income	Percent of Population with No or Low Income	Unemployed Population	Percent of Population Unemployed	Underemployed Population	Percent of Population Underemployed	Population that Earns 5 Times Minimum Wage	Percent of Population that Earns 5 Times Minimum Wage
29	Isidro Fabela	1,421	427	0.3005	34	0.0239	122	0.0859	40	0.0281
30	Ixtapaluca	38,648	4,676	0.1210	777	0.0201	1,502	0.0389	2,422	0.0627
31	Iztacalco	158,420	30,674	0.1936	2,716	0.0171	5,233	0.0330	11,312	0.0714
32	Iztapalapa	485,558	108,477	0.2234	8,293	0.0171	17,258	0.0355	26,531	0.0546
33	Jaltenco	6,167	636	0.1031	137	0.0222	194	0.0315	539	0.0874
34	Jilotzingo	2,697	597	0.2214	205	0.0760	563	0.2088	115	0.0426
35	Juchitepec	3,846	879	0.2285	107	0.0278	127	0.0330	127	0.0330
36	Magdalena Contreras	66,789	14,674	0.2197	1,237	0.0185	2,292	0.0343	6,947	0.1040
37	Melchor Ocampo	7,188	821	0.1142	104	0.0145	204	0.0284	445	0.0619
38	Miguel Hidalgo	159,633	28,000	0.1754	2,477	0.0155	5,814	0.0364	25,166	0.1576
39	Milpa Alta	119,106	6,545	0.0550	394	0.0033	1,145	0.0096	584	0.0049
40	Naucalpan	268,488	54,550	0.2032	4,415	0.0164	10,261	0.0382	34,644	0.1290
41	Nextlalpan	2,847	420	0.1475	112	0.0393	119	0.0418	178	0.0625
42	Nezahualcoyotl	399,797	42,175	0.1055	7,214	0.0180	15,921	0.0398	29,167	0.0730
43	Nicolas Romero	52,314	6,657	0.1273	1,149	0.0220	2,391	0.0457	2,930	0.0560
44	Nopaltepec	1,496	507	0.3389	39	0.0261	55	0.0368	53	0.0354
45	Otumba	5,486	1,099	0.2003	118	0.0215	292	0.0532	261	0.0476
46	Ozumba	4,510	1,740	0.3858	91	0.0202	449	0.0996	278	0.0616
47	Papalotla	661	107	0.1619	14	0.0212	69	0.1044	35	0.0530
48	Paz, La	39,529	4,938	0.1249	660	0.0167	1,689	0.0427	2,353	0.0595
49	San Martin de las P.	3,967	1,081	0.2725	79	0.0199	217	0.0547	178	0.0449
50	Tecamac	34,870	3,894	0.1117	619	0.0178	1,501	0.0430	3,383	0.0970
51	Temamatla	1,496	249	0.1664	32	0.0214	65	0.0434	78	0.0521
52	Temascalapa	4,967	1,431	0.2881	113	0.0228	317	0.0638	149	0.0300
53	Tenango del Aire	1,729	361	0.2088	84	0.0486	59	0.0341	64	0.0370
54	Teoloyucan	11,447	1,433	0.1252	223	0.0195	490	0.0428	738	0.0645
55	Teotihuacan	8,430	1,725	0.2046	190	0.0225	438	0.0520	547	0.0649
56	Tepetlaoxtoc	4,320	992	0.2296	95	0.0220	288	0.0667	177	0.0410

Table 8.4 Socioeconomic Level, 1990 (Continued)

No.	Area	Employed Population	Population with No or Low Income	Percent of Population with No or Low Income	Unemployed Population	Percent of Population Unemployed	Underemployed Population	Percent of Population Underemployed	Population that Earns 5 Times Minimum Wage	Percent of Population that Earns 5 Times Minimum Wage
57	Tepetlixpa	3,074	1,060	0.3448	65	0.0211	163	0.0530	123	0.0400
58	Tepotzotlan	11,628	1,693	0.1456	194	0.0167	472	0.0406	836	0.0719
59	Texcoco	39,668	6,784	0.1710	798	0.0201	2,031	0.0512	3,522	0.0888
60	Tezoyuca	3,267	521	0.1595	69	0.0211	168	0.0514	160	0.0490
61	Tlahuac	61,253	15,323	0.2502	1,205	0.0197	2,002	0.0327	1,899	0.0310
62	Tlalmanalco	9,100	1,324	0.1455	176	0.0193	324	0.0356	546	0.0600
63	Tlalnepantla	230,915	44,849	0.1942	3,755	0.0163	7,893	0.0342	23,734	0.1028
64	Tlalpan	165,686	33,083	0.1997	2,778	0.0168	6,091	0.0368	22,421	0.1353
65	Tultepec	12,945	1,474	0.1139	298	0.0230	490	0.0379	1,067	0.0824
66	Tultitlan	72,214	15,082	0.2089	1,355	0.0188	2,652	0.0367	5,095	0.0706
67	Venustiano Carranza	185,595	36,698	0.1977	3,081	0.0166	6,860	0.0370	13,398	0.0722
68	Xochimilco	88,830	20,161	0.2270	1,625	0.0183	3,814	0.0429	6,190	0.0697
69	Zumpango	18,669	3,048	0.1633	353	0.0189	735	0.0394	1,168	0.0626
	Total	5,180,054	940,576		88,573		190,874		482,825	
	Mean	75,073	13,632	0.1979	1,284	0.0205	2,766	0.0472	6,997	0.0716
	Median	14,782	2,290	0.1936	298	0.0193	602	0.0406	964	0.0619
	S.D.	112,459.90	22,115.98	0.0828	1,922.68	0.0088	4,026.24	0.0252	10,936.99	0.0419
	C.V.	149.80	162.24	41.84	149.78	43.09	145.55	53.36	156.30	58.45
	Minimum	661	107	0.0550	12	0.0033	46	0.0096	17	0.0049
	Maximum	485,558	108,477	0.5750	8,293	0.0760	17,258	0.2088	40,681	0.2409

Source: INEGI, 1990 Population Census.

Map 8.4
Low or No Income, 1990

- ☐ 0.0550 to 0.1368
- ▨ 0.1368 to 0.1705
- ▨ 0.1705 to 0.2039
- ◪ 0.2039 to 0.2291
- ▨ 0.2291 to 0.5750

Data Source: INEGI, 1990 Mexican Census
Map Source: Butler/Pick Mexico Database Project

Map 8.5
High Income, 1990

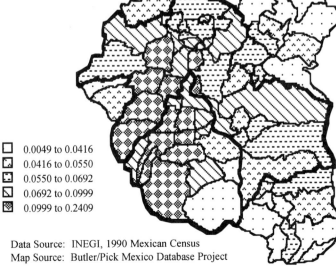

- ☐ 0.0049 to 0.0416
- ▨ 0.0416 to 0.0550
- ▨ 0.0550 to 0.0692
- ◪ 0.0692 to 0.0999
- ▨ 0.0999 to 0.2409

Data Source: INEGI, 1990 Mexican Census
Map Source: Butler/Pick Mexico Database Project

230

Map 8.6
Indigenous Language, 1990

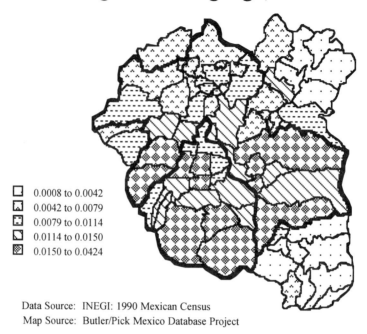

☐ 0.0008 to 0.0042
◩ 0.0042 to 0.0079
⊡ 0.0079 to 0.0114
◪ 0.0114 to 0.0150
▨ 0.0150 to 0.0424

Data Source: INEGI: 1990 Mexican Census
Map Source: Butler/Pick Mexico Database Project

Map 8.7
Change in Indigenous Language, 1970-1990

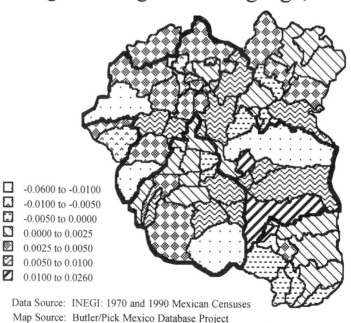

☐ -0.0600 to -0.0100
◩ -0.0100 to -0.0050
⊡ -0.0050 to 0.0000
◪ 0.0000 to 0.0025
▨ 0.0025 to 0.0050
▧ 0.0050 to 0.0100
◪ 0.0100 to 0.0260

Data Source: INEGI: 1970 and 1990 Mexican Censuses
Map Source: Butler/Pick Mexico Database Project

Indigenous Language

The Mexican census contains indigenous language speaking but does not include English language capability. Table 8.5 presents data on indigenous language speaking in Mexico Megacity for 1970 and 1990 and percent change between 1970 - 1990. Map 8.6 illustrates indigenous language in 1990 and Map 8.7 shows the change from 1970 - 1990. The spatial pattern for 1970 indigenous population resembles that for 1990 (r = 0.71).

The major concentration of indigenous language speakers in 1990 was in the Federal District, Chalco, and areas both central to the east and west. The greatest concentration was in Milpa Alta (4.2%) with Chalco, Chimalhuacan, Huixquilucan, Nextlalpan, and Texcoco all having over two percent indigenous speakers. Table 8.4 shows considerable reduction in the C.V. of native language speakers between 1970 and 1990. This reduction may indicate reduction in the segregation of indigenous population or it may imply greater assimilation of native speaking population, so the peak areas are reduced in level.

The major increases of around two percent were in Chalco, Chimalhuacan, and Huixquilucan -- State of Mexico municipios. The largest decrease (almost 6%) of native language speakers was in the Federal District delegation of Milpa Alta.

The change in native language speaking population from 1970 to 1990 reveals that Milpa Alta and several municipios in the periphery lost the largest percentage of indigenous population, while Chalco and the nearby municipios of Chimalhuacan and Temamatla gained in native speaking population (see Map 8.7 and Figure 8.5). It is important to note that the big losers and big gainers are generally areas that still retain high indigenous proportions in 1990. Thus the greatest impact was to re-distribute indigenous population within and among existing high indigenous areas, rather than movement to new areas.

The major indigenous language subgroups in Mexico Megacity are the Mixteco, Nahautl, Otomi, and Zapoteco language speaking. The spatial patterns for these groups, shown in Maps 8.8 - 8.11 tend to be associated. They are significantly correlated with each other and with indigenous language, except for Nahautl, which is not associated with the other language groups. Its association with indigenous language stems from its being the largest language speaking group. One reason for Nahautl's lack of association is its unusual distribution, seen in its histogram (Figure 8.6). There is one major location (Milpa Alta at 3.1 percent) and several other prominent ones (Texcoco and Coyotepec). Nearly all the rest of the localities are highly concentrated in a range under 0.005. This would imply that Nahautl population has greater segregation than the other major language speaking groups. The 50,000+ Nahautl speakers are concentrated in several areas, with greater tendency to be located in the southern Federal District and west central municipios.

Table 8.4 also presented data on Mixteco language ability. In 1990, over 29,000 persons in the metropolitan complex spoke Mixteco with the major concentration being in the far south of the Federal District and central east and west adjacent municipios in the State of Mexico (see Map 8.9). Chimalhuacan has by far the largest proportion of Mixteco speaking population at 0.009 percent.

Over 32,000 persons spoke the Otomi language in 1990. These speakers were distributed throughout the metropolitan complex with little apparent pattern except for a concentration in the central west, adjacent to the Federal District (Map 8.10). As shown on Map 8.11, and reported in Table 8.4, Zapoteco native speakers were concentrated in somewhat similar areas as Otomi speakers but also were scattered throughout the metropolitan complex. By far the largest Otomi speaking locality is Huixquilucan, which is a prosperous western area.

Table 8.5 Indigenous Language, 1970, 1990

Area	Indigenous 1970	Percent Indigenous 1970	Indigenous 1990	Percent Indigenous 1990	Percent Change in Indigenous 1970, 1990	Otomi	Percent Otomi	Zapoteco	Percent Zapoteco	Mixteco	Percent Mixteco	Nahautl	Percent Nahautl
Acolman	75	0.0043	240	0.0055	0.0012	57	0.0013	11	0.0003	6	0.0001	45	0.0010
Alvaro Obregon	3,481	0.0091	8,341	0.0130	0.0039	1,397	0.0022	865	0.0013	1,081	0.0017	1,849	0.0029
Amecameca	43	0.0023	139	0.0038	0.0015	13	0.0004	8	0.0002	8	0.0002	26	0.0007
Atenco	61	0.0069	115	0.0054	-0.0015	2	0.0001	2	0.0001	17	0.0008	45	0.0021
Atizapan De Zar.	267	0.0074	3,912	0.0124	0.0050	719	0.0023	350	0.0011	365	0.0012	890	0.0028
Atlautla	9	0.0009	59	0.0031	0.0022	9	0.0005	0	0.0000	4	0.0002	12	0.0006
Axapusco	8	0.0010	55	0.0035	0.0024	10	0.0006	4	0.0003	1	0.0001	7	0.0004
Ayapango	1	0.0005	13	0.0031	0.0025	1	0.0002	1	0.0002	0	0.0000	3	0.0007
Azcapotzalco	3,782	0.0085	4,443	0.0094	0.0009	940	0.0020	635	0.0013	295	0.0006	862	0.0018
Benito Juarez	6,237	0.0142	6,521	0.0160	0.0018	979	0.0024	853	0.0021	674	0.0017	1,548	0.0038
Chalco	94	0.0028	7,618	0.0269	0.0242	686	0.0024	2	0.0000	2,422	0.0086	1,501	0.0053
Chiautla	34	0.0056	76	0.0051	-0.0005	6	0.0004	3	0.0002	1	0.0001	31	0.0021
Chicoloapan	36	0.0050	753	0.0131	0.0081	142	0.0025	72	0.0013	178	0.0031	132	0.0023
Chiconcuac	140	0.0200	176	0.0124	-0.0076	5	0.0004	2	0.0001	2	0.0001	132	0.0093
Chimalhuacan	44	0.0027	6,891	0.0284	0.0257	446	0.0018	876	0.0036	2,150	0.0089	1,436	0.0059
Coacalco	27	0.0025	1,006	0.0066	0.0041	108	0.0007	189	0.0012	125	0.0008	170	0.0011
Cocotitlan	3	0.0007	17	0.0021	0.0014	4	0.0005	2	0.0002	0	0.0000	17	0.0021
Coyoacan	3,981	0.0139	9,341	0.0146	0.0007	1,245	0.0019	1,113	0.0017	1,205	0.0019	2,405	0.0038
Coyotepec	390	0.0534	474	0.0194	-0.0340	46	0.0019	4	0.0002	15	0.0006	343	0.0140
Cuajimalpa	232	0.0079	1,045	0.0087	0.0008	208	0.0017	76	0.0006	123	0.0010	166	0.0014
Cuauhtemoc	10,843	0.0143	9,677	0.0162	0.0019	1,282	0.0022	1,415	0.0024	825	0.0014	1,836	0.0031
Cuautitlan	114	0.0034	379	0.0078	0.0043	93	0.0019	31	0.0006	16	0.0003	67	0.0014
Cuautitlan Izcalli	114	0.0034	2,093	0.0064	0.0030	269	0.0008	290	0.0009	190	0.0006	492	0.0015
Ecatepec	1,238	0.0072	16,112	0.0132	0.0060	3,114	0.0026	2,247	0.0018	2,028	0.0017	3,622	0.0030
Ecatzingo	10	0.0033	15	0.0026	-0.0007	1	0.0002	1	0.0002	1	0.0002	3	0.0005
Gustavo A. Madero	9,562	0.0097	13,743	0.0108	0.0011	2,626	0.0021	2,150	0.0017	1,196	0.0009	3,047	0.0024
Huehuetoca	7	0.0011	124	0.0049	0.0038	22	0.0009	16	0.0006	5	0.0002	32	0.0013
Huixquilucan	1,322	0.0485	3,329	0.0252	-0.0233	1,226	0.0093	247	0.0019	446	0.0034	465	0.0035
Isidro Fabela	2	0.0009	28	0.0054	0.0045	5	0.0010	0	0.0000	0	0.0000	1	0.0002
Ixtapaluca	133	0.0044	1,865	0.0136	0.0092	173	0.0013	281	0.0020	438	0.0032	386	0.0028

233

Table 8.5 Indigenous Language, 1970, 1990 (Continued)

Area	Indigenous 1970	Percent Indigenous 1970	Indigenous 1990	Percent Indigenous 1990	Percent Change in Indigenous 1970, 1990	Otomi	Percent Otomi	Zapoteco	Percent Zapoteco	Mixteco	Percent Mixteco	Nahautl	Percent Nahautl
Iztacalco	4,530	0.0115	4,834	0.0108	-0.0008	575	0.0013	797	0.0018	694	0.0015	956	0.0021
Iztapalapa	4,032	0.0094	22,242	0.0149	0.0055	2,564	0.0017	2,565	0.0017	4,539	0.0030	4,451	0.0030
Jaltenco	24	0.0062	273	0.0120	0.0058	15	0.0007	10	0.0004	4	0.0002	41	0.0018
Jilotzingo	65	0.0179	77	0.0085	-0.0094	22	0.0024	2	0.0002	3	0.0003	9	0.0010
Juchitepec	21	0.0031	42	0.0029	-0.0001	4	0.0003	0	0.0000	2	0.0001	3	0.0002
Magdalena Contreras	444	0.0073	2,553	0.0131	0.0058	398	0.0020	317	0.0016	292	0.0015	599	0.0031
Melchor Ocampo	41	0.0046	286	0.0109	0.0063	151	0.0058	6	0.0002	19	0.0007	48	0.0018
Miguel Hidalgo	7,824	0.0138	6,111	0.0150	0.0012	1,041	0.0026	883	0.0022	620	0.0015	1,220	0.0030
Milpa Alta	2,875	0.1012	2,696	0.0424	-0.0588	145	0.0023	47	0.0007	127	0.0020	1,988	0.0312
Naucalpan	6,479	0.0208	18,890	0.0240	0.0032	3,358	0.0043	1,724	0.0022	2,143	0.0027	5,225	0.0066
Nextlalpan	29	0.0081	103	0.0095	0.0014	48	0.0044	5	0.0005	4	0.0004	18	0.0017
Nezahualcoyotl	5,531	0.0120	17,582	0.0140	0.0020	1,782	0.0014	2,599	0.0021	2,918	0.0023	3,429	0.0027
Nicolas Romero	824	0.0213	1,994	0.0108	-0.0105	653	0.0035	113	0.0006	155	0.0008	319	0.0017
Nopaltepec	5	0.0022	19	0.0036	0.0014	1	0.0002	0	0.0000	0	0.0000	1	0.0002
Otumba	12	0.0012	85	0.0039	0.0027	10	0.0005	2	0.0001	0	0.0000	3	0.0001
Ozumba	40	0.0044	68	0.0038	-0.0006	3	0.0002	2	0.0001	3	0.0002	21	0.0012
Papalotla	1	0.0011	2	0.0008	-0.0003	0	0.0000	0	0.0000	0	0.0000	1	0.0004
Paz, La	210	0.0081	2,212	0.0164	0.0083	174	0.0013	299	0.0022	435	0.0032	595	0.0044
San Martin De Las P.	5	0.0008	51	0.0038	0.0029	21	0.0015	1	0.0001	2	0.0001	3	0.0002
Tecamac	73	0.0043	1,339	0.0109	0.0066	272	0.0022	134	0.0011	147	0.0012	430	0.0035
Temamatla	1	0.0005	59	0.0110	0.0105	2	0.0004	8	0.0015	12	0.0022	23	0.0043
Temascalapa	1	0.0001	86	0.0045	0.0044	11	0.0006	3	0.0002	0	0.0000	10	0.0005
Tenango Del Aire	65	0.0220	23	0.0037	-0.0183	3	0.0005	1	0.0002	3	0.0005	4	0.0006
Teoloyucan	148	0.0116	273	0.0065	-0.0051	54	0.0013	13	0.0003	35	0.0008	35	0.0008
Teotihuacan	216	0.0161	357	0.0117	-0.0044	52	0.0017	32	0.0010	130	0.0043	41	0.0013
Tepetlaoxtoc	18	0.0031	143	0.0089	0.0058	11	0.0007	11	0.0007	4	0.0002	54	0.0033
Tepetlixpa	65	0.0095	59	0.0047	-0.0049	1	0.0001	1	0.0001	18	0.0014	20	0.0016
Tepotzotlan	62	0.0036	254	0.0064	0.0028	61	0.0015	24	0.0006	22	0.0006	46	0.0012
Texcoco	2,088	0.0383	3,090	0.0220	-0.0163	91	0.0006	93	0.0007	97	0.0007	2,294	0.0163
Tezoyuca	20	0.0050	91	0.0073	0.0023	30	0.0024	8	0.0006	2	0.0002	29	0.0023

Table 8.5 Indigenous Language, 1970, 1990 (Continued)

Area	Indigenous 1970	Percent Indigenous 1970	Indigenous 1990	Percent Indigenous 1990	Percent Change in Indigenous 1970, 1990	Otomi	Percent Otomi	Zapoteco	Percent Zapoteco	Mixteco	Percent Mixteco	Nahautl	Percent Nahautl
Tlahuac	326	0.0063	2,440	0.0118	0.0055	447	0.0022	390	0.0019	359	0.0017	454	0.0022
Tlalmanalco	24	0.0014	89	0.0027	0.0013	9	0.0003	3	0.0001	3	0.0001	6	0.0002
Tlalnepantla	1,846	0.0062	8,533	0.0121	0.0059	1,626	0.0023	823	0.0012	826	0.0012	2,090	0.0030
Tlalpan	1,168	0.0107	7,567	0.0156	0.0049	839	0.0017	758	0.0016	1,016	0.0021	1,862	0.0038
Tultepec	39	0.0041	377	0.0080	0.0038	92	0.0019	47	0.0010	18	0.0004	98	0.0021
Tultitlan	160	0.0038	2,005	0.0081	0.0043	347	0.0014	4	0.0000	198	0.0008	370	0.0015
Venustiano Carranza	8,281	0.0109	5,551	0.0107	-0.0002	712	0.0014	874	0.0017	543	0.0010	1,112	0.0021
Xochimilco	1,055	0.0109	4,447	0.0164	0.0055	1,097	0.0040	378	0.0014	341	0.0013	1,201	0.0044
Zumpango	59	0.0020	363	0.0051	0.0031	67	0.0009	34	0.0005	18	0.0003	67	0.0009
Total	90,997		215,866			32,623		24,757		29,569		50,747	
Mean	1,319	0.0100	3,128	0.0106	0.0005	473	0.0016	359	0.0009	429	0.0012	735	0.0030
Median	75	0.0062	379	0.0095	0.0023	92	0.0014	31	0.0006	35	0.0008	132	0.0021
S.D.	2,522	0.0149	4,964	0.0073	0.0110	763	0.0015	634	0.0008	814	0.0016	1,145	0.0044
C.V.	191.26	148.95	158.67	69.11	2,074.26	161.46	90.31	176.72	91.18	189.96	133.12	155.64	147.40
Minimum	1	0.0001	2	0.0008	-0.0588	0	0.0000	0	0.0000	0	0.0000	1	0.0001
Maximum	10,843	0.1012	22,242	0.0424	0.0257	3,358	0.0093	2,599	0.0036	4,539	0.0089	5,225	0.0312

Source: INEGI, 1990 Population Census.

Map 8.8
Nahautl Language, 1990

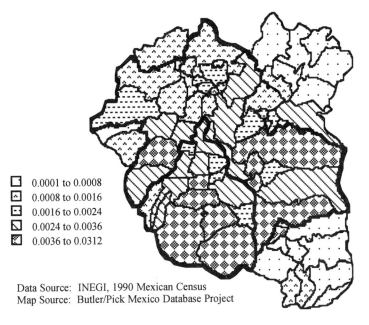

☐ 0.0001 to 0.0008
⊡ 0.0008 to 0.0016
⊟ 0.0016 to 0.0024
◨ 0.0024 to 0.0036
▨ 0.0036 to 0.0312

Data Source: INEGI, 1990 Mexican Census
Map Source: Butler/Pick Mexico Database Project

Map 8.9
Mixteco Languages, 1990

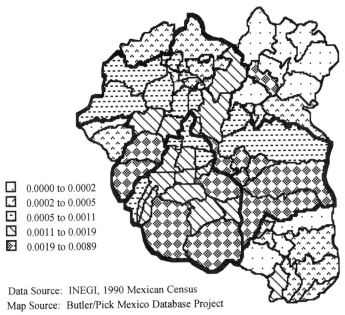

☐ 0.0000 to 0.0002
⊡ 0.0002 to 0.0005
⊡ 0.0005 to 0.0011
◨ 0.0011 to 0.0019
▨ 0.0019 to 0.0089

Data Source: INEGI, 1990 Mexican Census
Map Source: Butler/Pick Mexico Database Project

Map 8.10

Otomi Language, 1990

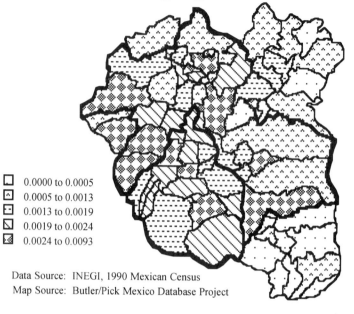

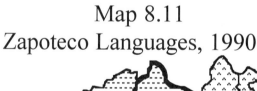

- ☐ 0.0000 to 0.0005
- ▨ 0.0005 to 0.0013
- ⊟ 0.0013 to 0.0019
- ◨ 0.0019 to 0.0024
- ▨ 0.0024 to 0.0093

Data Source: INEGI, 1990 Mexican Census
Map Source: Butler/Pick Mexico Database Project

Map 8.11

Zapoteco Languages, 1990

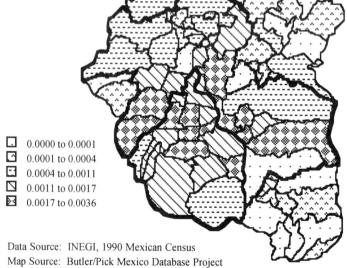

- ☐ 0.0000 to 0.0001
- ▨ 0.0001 to 0.0004
- ⊟ 0.0004 to 0.0011
- ◨ 0.0011 to 0.0017
- ▨ 0.0017 to 0.0036

Data Source: INEGI, 1990 Mexican Census
Map Source: Butler/Pick Mexico Database Project

**Figure 8.5 Change in Indigeous Language
Population in Mexico City 1970-1990**

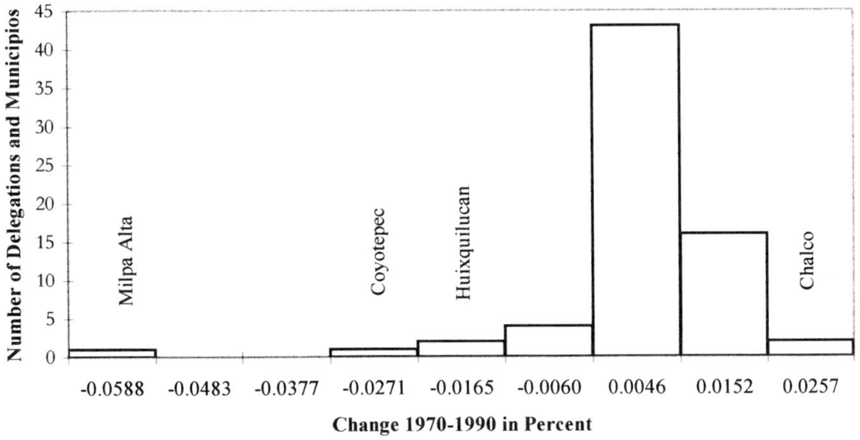

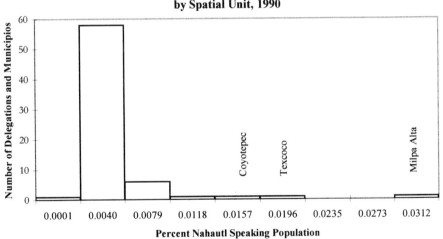

Source: INEGI, 1990 Mexican Census

**Figure 8.6 Percent Nahautl Speaking Population
by Spatial Unit, 1990**

Source: INEGI, 1990 Mexican Census

Religion

Data on self-reported religion for the population aged 5 years and over is shown on Table 8.6. Map 8.12 illustrates the distribution of percent of Non-Catholic population for 1990; this is almost the exact distribution of Non-Catholics in 1970 (r = 0.54). In 1990 in the nation of Mexico, 89.7 percent of the population reported that they were Catholic while 92.4 percent in the Federal District reported themselves as being Catholic. Nationally 4.89 percent were Protestant and/or evangelical but only 3.07 percent were in the Federal District. Nationally, 1.44 percent reported themselves as being "other religion" while in the Federal District the percentage was 1.7 (see Figure 8.7). For the nation, only 0.008 percent were Jewish while in the Federal District 0.27 were Jewish. The religion proportions for the State of Mexico are comparable to the Federal District (see Figure 8.7).

Map 8.12
Non Catholic, 1970

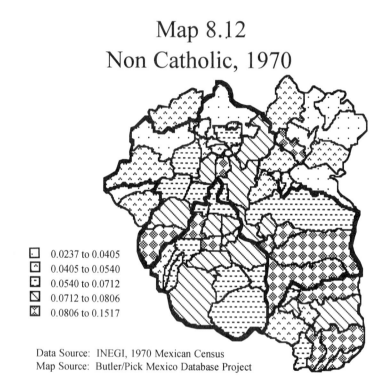

☐ 0.0237 to 0.0405
☑ 0.0405 to 0.0540
☐ 0.0540 to 0.0712
☒ 0.0712 to 0.0806
☒ 0.0806 to 0.1517

Data Source: INEGI, 1970 Mexican Census
Map Source: Butler/Pick Mexico Database Project

Table 8.6 Religion

No.	Area	Non-Catholic, 1990	Non-Catholic, 1970	No.	Area	Non-Catholic, 1990	Non-Catholic, 1970
1	Acolman	0.0406	0.0117	53	Tenango del Aire	0.0726	0.0211
2	Alvaro Obregon	0.0559	0.0324	54	Teoloyucan	0.0348	0.0096
3	Amecameca	0.0713	0.0471	55	Teotihuacan	0.1517	0.0162
4	Atenco	0.0424	0.0187	56	Tepetlaoxtoc	0.0303	0.0231
5	Atizapan de Zaragoza	0.0650	0.0312	57	Tepetlixpa	0.0661	0.0371
6	Atlautla	0.1077	0.0639	58	Tepotzotlan	0.0389	0.0137
7	Axapusco	0.0251	0.0091	59	Texcoco	0.0633	0.0198
8	Ayapango	0.0459	0.0256	60	Tezoyuca	0.0403	0.0126
9	Azcapotzalco	0.0601	0.0316	61	Tlahuac	0.0703	0.0213
10	Benito Juarez	0.0823	0.0509	62	Tlalmanalco	0.0814	0.1245
11	Chalco	0.0907	0.0360	63	Tlalnepantla	0.0645	0.0242
12	Chiautla	0.0267	0.0029	64	Tlalpan	0.0787	0.0408
13	Chicoloapan	0.0914	0.0169	65	Tultepec	0.0448	0.0030
14	Chiconcuac	0.0303	0.0118	66	Tultitlan	0.0719	0.0230
15	Chimalhuacan	0.0805	0.0093	67	Venustiano Carranza	0.0730	0.0382
16	Coacalco	0.0831	0.0198	68	Xochimilco	0.0645	0.0230
17	Cocotitlan	0.0325	0.0556	69	Zumpango	0.0277	0.0095
18	Coyoacan	0.0762	0.0401		Mean	0.0625	0.0268
19	Coyotepec	0.0457	0.0170		Median	0.0645	0.0225
20	Cuajimalpa	0.0529	0.0143		S.D.	0.0243	0.0217
21	Cuauhtemoc	0.0784	0.0514		C.V.	38.81	81.09
22	Cuautitlan	0.0526	0.0114		Minimum	0.0237	0.0026
23	Cuautitlan Izcalli	0.0712	0.0114		Maximum	0.1517	0.1245
24	Ecatepec	0.0728	0.0271				
25	Ecatzingo	0.1043	0.0762				
26	Gustavo A. Madero	0.0687	0.0319				
27	Huehuetoca	0.0510	0.0057				
28	Huixquilucan	0.0950	0.0216				
29	Isidro Fabela	0.0282	0.0027				
30	Ixtapaluca	0.0807	0.0379				
31	Iztacalco	0.0717	0.0348				
32	Iztapalapa	0.0748	0.0339				
33	Jaltenco	0.0535	0.0036				
34	Jilotzingo	0.0533	0.0311				
35	Juchitepec	0.0478	0.0284				
36	Magdalena Contreras	0.0627	0.0225				
37	Melchor Ocampo	0.0332	0.0061				
38	Miguel Hidalgo	0.0970	0.0540				
39	Milpa Alta	0.0544	0.0295				
40	Naucalpan	0.0719	0.0358				
41	Nextlalpan	0.0685	0.0236				
42	Nezahualcoyotl	0.0739	0.0283				
43	Nicolas Romero	0.0433	0.0126				
44	Nopaltepec	0.0385	0.0026				
45	Otumba	0.0458	0.0158				
46	Ozumba	0.1137	0.1034				
47	Papalotla	0.0237	0.0064				
48	Paz, La	0.0845	0.0366				
49	San Martin de las P.	0.0302	0.0152				
50	Tecamac	0.0803	0.0158				
51	Temamatla	0.0606	0.0169				
52	Temascalapa	0.0472	0.0082				

Source: INEGI, 1990 Mexican Census

240

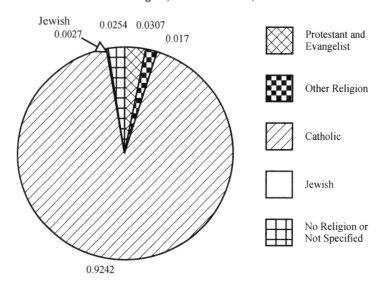

Figure 8.7

Religion, Federal District, 1990

Jewish 0.0027 — 0.0254 — 0.0307 — 0.017

0.9242

Protestant and Evangelist

Other Religion

Catholic

Jewish

No Religion or Not Specified

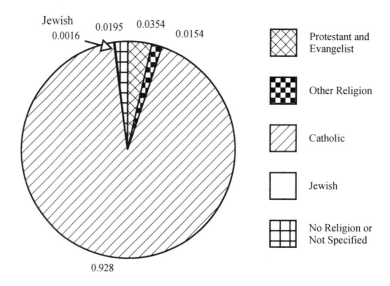

Religion, State of Mexico*, 1990

Jewish 0.0016 — 0.0195 — 0.0354 — 0.0154

0.928

Protestant and Evangelist

Other Religion

Catholic

Jewish

No Religion or Not Specified

Source: INEGI, 1990 Mexican Census of Population
* Counurbation municipios only

Automobiles

Data on automobiles are available only for the Federal District Map 8.13 shows the number per capita distribution of automobiles for 1992 was concentrated in the "old core" of the Federal District; this is virtually the same distribution for per capita automobiles as in 1986. Map 8.14, however, demonstrates that the rate of increase in automobiles was greatest for several delegations in the far southeast and one in the far northwest. The automobile consumption patterns for the Federal District resembles that of absolute population growth 1970-90 (see Map 3.5).

Map 8.13
Automobiles Per Capita, 1992

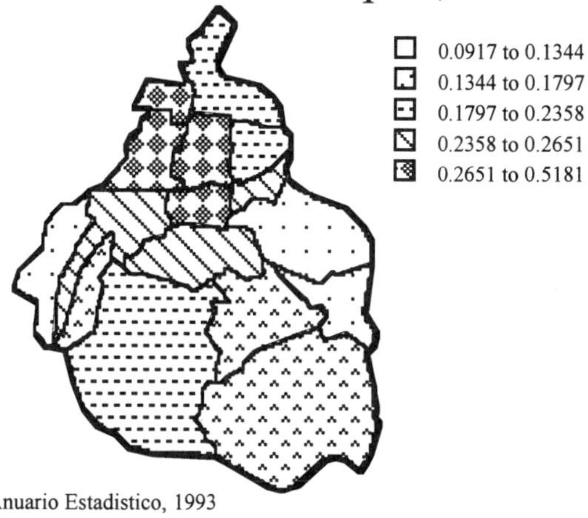

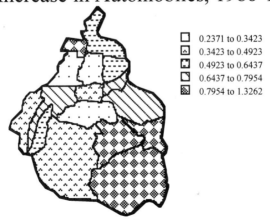

☐	0.0917 to 0.1344
▨	0.1344 to 0.1797
▤	0.1797 to 0.2358
▨	0.2358 to 0.2651
▨	0.2651 to 0.5181

Data Source: INEGI, Anuario Estadistico, 1993
Map Source: Butler/Pick Mexico Database Project

Map 8.14
Rate of Increase in Automobiles, 1986-1992

☐	0.2371 to 0.3423
▨	0.3423 to 0.4923
▨	0.4923 to 0.6437
▨	0.6437 to 0.7954
▨	0.7954 to 1.3262

Map Source: Butler/Pick Mexico Database Project
Data Source: INEGI, Anuarios Estadisticos, Various Years

Crime

Current crime data on the Federal District show a great increase in the past several years. In 1995, there was an average of 550 crimes reported daily in the Federal District, a 25 percent increase over 1994. Over 40 percent of these crimes involved violence. However, the homicide rate for 1995 was about 13/100,000 residents, about half that of New York City. Over 35,000 vehicles were stolen in the Federal District in 1995, an increase of 35 percent over the number stolen in 1994. In addition, Sarmiento (1996) argues that many crimes are not reported to the police and that former police officers and even those now serving are directly responsible for many committed crimes.

Subsequent crime and related data and maps presented in this section utilize primarily 1993 and 1994 data from the *Anuarios Estadisticos*.

All data in this section reflect areas in which the crimes took place. Misdemeanor criminal charges for Mexico Megacity in 1994 are shown on Table 8.7. By far, the highest misdemeanor crime charges per 1,000 persons are in part of the old core -- Benito Juarez, Cuauhtemoc, Gustavo A. Madero, and Iztapalapa. In addition, Ecatepec, Naucalpan, and Nezahualcoyotl in the State of Mexico had high rates in 1994 (see Map 8.15). On the other hand, the lowest rates in 1994 were in State of Mexico municipios of Acolman, Atenco, Atlautla, Ecatzingo, Ozumba, Tepetlaoxtoc, Tepetlixpa, Tezoyuca, and Tlalmanalco. Felony charges followed substantially the same distribution as misdemeanors.

Table 8.7 also shows the rate and number of felony sentences in 1993 for Mexico Megacity (see Maps 8.16) these distributions are substantially similar to those for misdemeanor charges and thus for felony charges. Rates for misdemeanor charges and felony sentences are highly correlated at r = 0.96. Robbery and murder sentences for 1993 are shown on Maps 8.17 and 8.18. The similarity of all crime rates and sentences are remarkable by their congruity. Further consistency is shown by the fact that these also are the same areas that had the highest robberies during the 1983 - 1985 years (see Butler and Pick 1994: Chapter 7). Overall, crime areas coincide with high population and also with economic prosperity. This may be the result of several factors. Crime reporting, charging, and sentencing may be higher in the more advantaged areas. Another factor is that targets of crime, i.e. wealthier individuals and businesses, are concentrated in these areas. In the semi-urban peripheral areas, crime rates are low. This may relate to the lack of targets of crime, as well as stable and traditional social structures that serve as deterrents. Crime is highly related to population (r values of 0.87 and 0.88) and to all indicators of socioeconomic status. Crimes are also related to Non-Catholic population (r = values of 0.27 and 0.28) and to indigenous language population (r = 0.34), although not to all the language categories. This represents a different pattern from U.S. cities, since crime, and minority population, and economic poverty tend to be located together.

Table 8.7 Crime Data

No.	Area	Misdemeanors 1994	Felonies 1993	Robbery 1993	Assaults 1993	Homicides 1993
1	Acolman	0.0264	0.0000	0.0000	0.0000	0.0000
2	Alvaro Obregon	11.4819	0.9195	0.3454	0.2100	0.0467
3	Amecameca	1.8374	0.0933	0.0202	0.0296	0.0047
4	Atenco	0.0825	0.0000	0.0000	0.0000	0.0000
5	Atizapan de Zaragoza	6.4519	0.2552	0.0669	0.0451	0.0249
6	Atlautla	0.0078	0.0249	0.0109	0.0078	0.0000
7	Axapusco	0.0000	0.0233	0.0000	0.0093	0.0000
8	Ayapango	0.0000	0.0000	0.0000	0.0000	0.0000
9	Azcapotzalco	13.7673	0.7017	0.2629	0.1182	0.0264
10	Benito Juarez	22.6432	1.2898	0.6208	0.1447	0.0638
11	Chalco	6.2652	0.8790	0.2505	0.2458	0.0420
12	Chiautla	0.0653	0.0000	0.0000	0.0000	0.0000
13	Chicoloapan	0.5741	0.0000	0.0000	0.0000	0.0000
14	Chiconcuac	0.1042	0.0171	0.0062	0.0047	0.0000
15	Chimalhuacan	4.3687	0.3516	0.1182	0.0793	0.0342
16	Coacalco	3.2921	0.0996	0.0296	0.0140	0.0078
17	Cocotitlan	0.1898	0.0000	0.0000	0.0000	0.0000
18	Coyoacan	18.2558	1.0906	0.4916	0.1883	0.0716
19	Coyotepec	0.2863	0.0000	0.0000	0.0000	0.0000
20	Cuajimalpa	2.1797	0.1074	0.0389	0.0218	0.0093
21	Cuauhtemoc	41.2211	3.0867	1.4671	0.4107	0.1151
22	Cuautitlan	1.9183	0.5523	0.1416	0.1167	0.0498
23	Cuautitlan Izcalli	7.5394	0.2567	0.0840	0.0669	0.0264
24	Ecatepec	23.6825	1.2695	0.4947	0.2287	0.0825
25	Ecatzingo	0.0016	0.0000	0.0000	0.0000	0.0000
26	Gustavo A. Madero	29.5339	2.5095	1.0299	0.4667	0.1665
27	Huehuetoca	0.3516	0.0000	0.0000	0.0000	0.0000
28	Huixquilucan	1.5122	0.1743	0.0669	0.0358	0.0124
29	Isidro Fabela	0.0000	0.0000	0.0000	0.0000	0.0000
30	Ixtapaluca	2.2964	0.1634	0.0498	0.0296	0.0124
31	Iztacalco	9.7300	0.8137	0.3843	0.1276	0.0700
32	Iztapalapa	27.0617	2.2077	0.8230	0.4403	0.2100
33	Jaltenco	0.0000	0.0000	0.0000	0.0000	0.0000
34	Jilotzingo	0.0000	0.0000	0.0000	0.0000	0.0000
35	Juchitepec	0.0000	0.0218	0.0047	0.0093	0.0000
36	Magdalena Contreras	2.0941	0.2738	0.1167	0.0607	0.0156
37	Melchor Ocampo	0.3143	0.0264	0.0000	0.0000	0.0000
38	Miguel Hidalgo	21.7269	1.0813	0.5663	0.1260	0.0607
39	Milpa Alta	0.5834	0.0809	0.0187	0.0327	0.0140
40	Naucalpan	28.8416	1.3800	0.5523	0.2412	0.0700
41	Nextlalpan	0.0000	0.0000	0.0000	0.0000	0.0000
42	Nezahualcoyotl	27.3698	1.5994	0.4310	0.4232	0.1229
43	Nicolas Romero	2.7429	0.2567	0.0669	0.0529	0.0218
44	Nopaltepec	0.0000	0.0000	0.0000	0.0000	0.0000
45	Otumba	0.2069	0.0513	0.0124	0.0093	0.0000
46	Ozumba	0.0093	0.0280	0.0000	0.0000	0.0000
47	Papalotla	0.0233	0.0000	0.0000	0.0000	0.0000
48	Paz, La	3.1474	0.1820	0.0358	0.0342	0.0218
49	San Martin de las P.	0.0000	0.0264	0.0000	0.0000	0.0000
50	Tecamac	1.6865	0.1167	0.0311	0.0109	0.0093
51	Temamatla	0.0000	0.0000	0.0000	0.0000	0.0000
52	Temascalapa	0.0000	0.0000	0.0000	0.0000	0.0000
53	Tenango del Aire	0.0000	0.0000	0.0000	0.0000	0.0000

244

Table 8.7 Crime Data (Continued)

No.	Area	Misdemeanors 1994	Felonies 1993	Robbery 1993	Assaults 1993	Homicides 1993
54	Teoloyucan	0.6317	0.0156	0.0000	0.0062	0.0000
55	Teotihuacan	1.1342	0.0405	0.0000	0.0124	0.0000
56	Tepetlaoxtoc	0.0467	0.0000	0.0000	0.0000	0.0000
57	Tepetlixpa	0.0078	0.0156	0.0000	0.0000	0.0000
58	Tepotzotlan	0.6488	0.0296	0.0140	0.0000	0.0000
59	Texcoco	5.9105	0.3267	0.0669	0.0762	0.0249
60	Tezoyuca	0.0529	0.0000	0.0000	0.0000	0.0000
61	Tlahuac	2.6184	0.2443	0.0980	0.0296	0.0249
62	Tlalmanalco	0.0264	0.0296	0.0000	0.0062	0.0000
63	Tlalnepantla	19.3138	1.0766	0.3501	0.2100	0.0778
64	Tlalpan	10.9078	0.9350	0.3734	0.1789	0.0762
65	Tultepec	0.7670	0.0249	0.0093	0.0000	0.0000
66	Tultitlan	4.3438	0.1307	0.0451	0.0342	0.0093
67	Venustiano Carranza	19.4538	1.3224	0.5865	0.2318	0.0591
68	Xochimilco	4.1322	0.4512	0.1587	0.0933	0.0389
69	Zumpango	1.8001	0.0700	0.0218	0.0140	0.0000
	Mean	5.7575	0.3873	0.1502	0.0715	0.0250
	Median	1.1342	0.0700	0.0187	0.0124	0.0000
	S.D.	9.4396	0.6445	0.2750	0.1157	0.0414
	C.V.	163.95	166.40	183.07	161.76	165.58
	Minimum	0.0000	0.0000	0.0000	0.0000	0.0000
	Maximum	41.2211	3.0867	1.4671	0.4667	0.2100

Source: INEGI, 1990 Mexican Census

Map 8.15
Misdemeanor Charges, 1994
Per 1,000

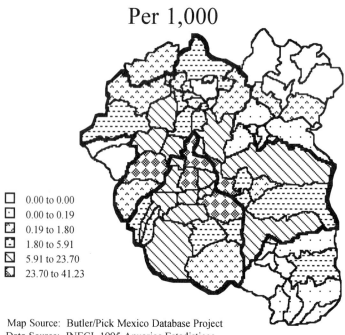

0.00 to 0.00
0.00 to 0.19
0.19 to 1.80
1.80 to 5.91
5.91 to 23.70
23.70 to 41.23

Map Source: Butler/Pick Mexico Database Project
Data Source: INEGI, 1995 Anuarios Estadisticos

Map 8.16
Number of Felony Sentences, 1993

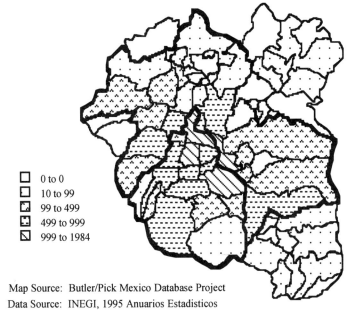

- ☐ 0 to 0
- ☐ 10 to 99
- ▨ 99 to 499
- ⊡ 499 to 999
- ◩ 999 to 1984

Map Source: Butler/Pick Mexico Database Project
Data Source: INEGI, 1995 Anuarios Estadisticos

Map 8.17
Robbery Sentences, 1993, Per 1,000

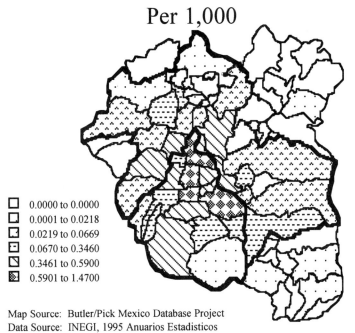

- ☐ 0.0000 to 0.0000
- ☐ 0.0001 to 0.0218
- ☐ 0.0219 to 0.0669
- ⊡ 0.0670 to 0.3460
- ◩ 0.3461 to 0.5900
- ▨ 0.5901 to 1.4700

Map Source: Butler/Pick Mexico Database Project
Data Source: INEGI, 1995 Anuarios Estadisticos

246

Map 8.18
Murder Sentences, 1993,
Per 1,000

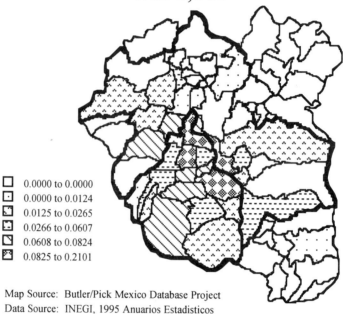

☐	0.0000 to 0.0000
⊡	0.0000 to 0.0124
◩	0.0125 to 0.0265
⊟	0.0266 to 0.0607
◪	0.0608 to 0.0824
▨	0.0825 to 0.2101

Map Source: Butler/Pick Mexico Database Project
Data Source: INEGI, 1995 Anuarios Estadisticos

Map 8.19
Home Ownership, 1990

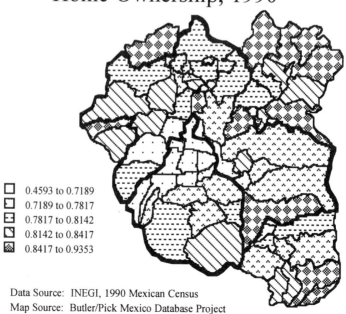

☐	0.4593 to 0.7189
⊟	0.7189 to 0.7817
⊞	0.7817 to 0.8142
◪	0.8142 to 0.8417
▨	0.8417 to 0.9353

Data Source: INEGI, 1990 Mexican Census
Map Source: Butler/Pick Mexico Database Project

Home Ownership

A variety of housing characteristics were examined in Chapter 7. Here the proportion of home ownership in 1990 is shown since this dimension is used in the social rank cluster analysis that concludes this chapter.

One of the major interesting facets of home ownership in Mexico Megacity is that it is almost directly opposite that found in the United States. Map 8.19 shows that the, lowest rates are found in more affluent areas while higher rates are recorded in poorer areas of the city. Home ownership is highest in peripheral, poorer areas of the northeast, Chalco, and southeast, with a scattering of other high rates in peripheral poor areas (see Table 8.8). The opposite effect is seen in home ownership being inversely correlated with primary education (r = -0.676) high income (r = -0.479), and professional/technical/managerial (r = -.655).

Table 8.8 Home Ownership, 1990

No.	Area	Home Ownership	No.	Area	Home Ownership
1	Acolman	0.8068	39	Milpa Alta	0.8334
2	Alvaro Obregon	0.6860	40	Naucalpan	0.6781
3	Amecameca	0.7362	41	Nextlalpan	0.7964
4	Atenco	0.8853	42	Nezahualcoyotl	0.6765
5	Atizapan de Zaragoza	0.8300	43	Nicolas Romero	0.8355
6	Atlautla	0.8667	44	Nopaltepec	0.8775
7	Axapusco	0.8449	45	Otumba	0.8384
8	Ayapango	0.7278	46	Ozumba	0.8222
9	Azcapotzalco	0.5923	47	Papalotla	0.7570
10	Benito Juarez	0.5135	48	Paz, La	0.7033
11	Chalco	0.8581	49	San Martin de las P.	0.8254
12	Chiautla	0.8318	50	Tecamac	0.7929
13	Chicoloapan	0.7685	51	Temamatla	0.6143
14	Chiconcuac	0.9143	52	Temascalapa	0.8532
15	Chimalhuacan	0.8210	53	Tenango del Aire	0.8027
16	Coacalco	0.8434	54	Teoloyucan	0.8048
17	Cocotitlan	0.7925	55	Teotihuacan	0.7903
18	Coyoacan	0.7686	56	Tepetlaoxtoc	0.8428
19	Coyotepec	0.8170	57	Tepetlixpa	0.8382
20	Cuajimalpa	0.7111	58	Tepotzotlan	0.8104
21	Cuauhtemoc	0.4620	59	Texcoco	0.7462
22	Cuautitlan	0.7266	60	Tezoyuca	0.8447
23	Cuautitlan Izcalli	0.8350	61	Tlahuac	0.7969
24	Ecatepec	0.7721	62	Tlalmanalco	0.8001
25	Ecatzingo	0.9353	63	Tlalnepantla	0.7068
26	Gustavo A. Madero	0.6539	64	Tlalpan	0.7840
27	Huehuetoca	0.8620	65	Tultepec	0.8168
28	Huixquilucan	0.8043	66	Tultitlan	0.8116
29	Isidro Fabela	0.8656	67	Venustiano Carranza	0.5875
30	Ixtapaluca	0.7727	68	Xochimilco	0.7614
31	Iztacalco	0.6392	69	Zumpango	0.7917
32	Iztapalapa	0.7357		Mean	0.7720
33	Jaltenco	0.8361		Median	0.7969
34	Jilotzingo	0.8406		S.D.	0.0992
35	Juchitepec	0.7733		C.V.	12.85
36	Magdalena Contreras	0.7579		Minimum	0.4593
37	Melchor Ocampo	0.7795		Maximum	0.9353
38	Miguel Hidalgo	0.4593		Source: INEGI, 1990 Mexican Census	

Social Rank Cluster Analysis

Variables included in the *social rank* cluster analysis are (1) proportion professional / technical managers, (2) percentage with primary education, (3) percent earning five times minimum wage, and (4) tenure status -- home ownership. Results of the cluster analysis are shown on Map 8.20. Table 8.9 presents cluster means and links the delegations and municipios in each cluster..

Clusters 1-5 are characterized by relatively large populations, with clusters 6, 7, and 8 having, on the, much smaller populations per unit.

Cluster 1 consists of the old city core. It has a very high professional / technical / managerial workforce at 15 percent, high grade school graduation, and about a sixth of population in the high income range. On the other hand, it has the lowest proportion of home ownership. Again, this is reverse of the U.S., with home ownership characterizing more disadvantaged households.

The second cluster group is populous at 2.7 million and is the rest of the northern Federal District. It resembles cluster 1 except it has lower social status reflected in a halved high income proportion and greater home ownership. Cluster 3 contains about a third of the Megacity population and consists of a ring surrounding clusters 1 and 2. It follows the trend of lower socioeconomic status, i.e. lower proportion professional/technical/managerial, lower primary education, and higher home ownership.

The first three clusters follow closely the Latin American city framework of Griffin and Ford, with a high status central core surrounded by one or more rings of lower status.

Clusters 4 and 5 together form a wider ring around the cluster 3 ring. They have a combined population of 4.2 million. Cluster 4 has higher social rank than cluster 5, even though they are interwoven spatially. Cluster 4 approximates the SES level of the cluster 3 ring. The remaining clusters 6, 7, and 8 are located in the semi-urban periphery areas, especially in the northeast and southeast. They are the lowest SES, falling below the Megacity average on nearly all parameters. The contrast is shown most sharply in Cluster 8, which has 3 percent professional/technical/managerial, 27 percent grade school graduates, and only 4 percent with high income.

The cluster analysis divides the Megacity into a core, two rings, and periphery with marked socioeconomic differences. It accentuates the idea of sharp contrasts in social status arranged radially in the city. It confirms, for social status, the theories of the Chicago school sociologists as well as Latin American theorists such as Griffin and Ford.

249

Map 8.20
Social Rank Clusters

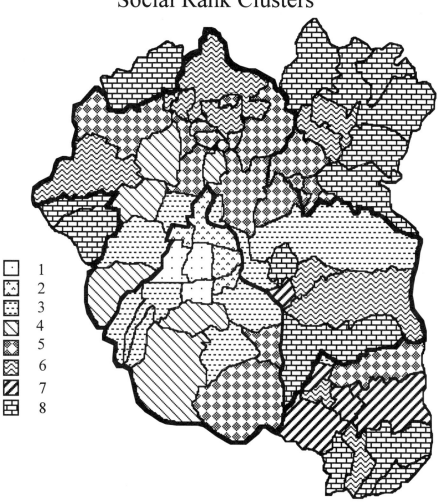

Data Source: INEGI, Population Censuses, 1990
Map Source: Butler/Pick Mexico Database Project

Table 8.9 Social Rank Cluster Means

Variable \ Cluster No.	1	2	3	4	5	6	7	8	Mexico City
Total Population 1990	1,410,693	2,710,706	5,613,022	2,050,882	2,214,667	565,287	194,978	680,565	15,440,746
Professional/Technical/Managerial	0.1499	0.1359	0.1178	0.1128	0.0671	0.0298	0.0960	0.0296	0.0826
Primary Education	0.6378	0.5481	0.4774	0.5306	0.4198	0.3446	0.3472	0.2734	0.4107
Income of Five Times or More Minimum Wage	0.1698	0.0741	0.0861	0.1462	0.0605	0.0558	0.0476	0.0374	0.0716
Home Ownership	0.4728	0.6183	0.7252	0.8061	0.8115	0.8037	0.7110	0.8572	0.8029

Cluster 1	Cluster 2	Cluster 3	Cluster 4	Cluster 5	Cluster 6	Cluster 7	Cluster 8
Benito Juarez	Azcapotzalco	Alvaro Obregon	Atizapan de Zaragoza	Acolman	Chicoloapan	Amecameca	Atlautla
Cuauhtemoc	Gustavo A. Madero	Cocotitlan	Coacalco	Atenco	Coyotepec	Ayapango	Axapusco
Miguel Hidalgo	Iztacalco	Cuajimalpa	Coyoacan	Chiautla	Ixtapaluca	Juchitepec	Chalco
	Venustiano Carranza	Iztapalapa	Cuautitlan Izcalli	Chiconcuac	Nextlalpan	Paz, La	Chimalhuacan
		Magdalena Contreras	Huixquilucan	Cuautitlan	Nicolas Romero	Temamatla	Ecatzingo
		Naucalpan	Tlalpan	Ecatepec	Ozumba		Huehuetoca
		Nezahualcoyotl		Jaltenco	San Martin de las Piramides		Isidro Fabela
		Texcoco		Melchor Ocampo	Tenango del Aire		Jilotzingo
		Tlalnepantla		Milpa Alta	Teoloyucan		Nopaltepec
		Xochimilco		Papalotla	Teotihuacan		Otumba
				Tecamac	Zumpango		Temascalapa
				Tepotzotlan			Tepetlaoxtoc
				Tezoyuca			Tepetlixpa
				Tlahuac			
				Tlalmanalco			
				Tultepec			
				Tultitlan			

9

The Economy

Introduction

Mexico City constitutes an economic engine that is at the heart of the Mexican national economy. This chapter discusses the growth and development of the economy of Mexico City. It traces its expansion from 1930 to 1993, with a focus on industry, commerce, and services. Mexico City's economy grew faster than the national economy from 1930 to 1960, leading to a transformation in the city's industrial base. Economic growth stemmed partly from the city's rapid population growth during this period as well as from productivity increases and broadening of the city's economy to encompass a spectrum of manufacturing and consumption sectors (Garza, 1987). Another reason for growth was the federal government's economic policy of encouraging import substitution, i.e. increased Mexican manufacturing in an import-protected trading environment. In the 80s and early 90s, the city's industrial growth slowed, but other sectors such as services and communications emerged with more rapid growth.

The chapter briefly looks at the Megacity's state and municipio government revenues. These revenues are concentrated in the Federal District and closely surrounding areas in the State of Mexico and amount to about one fifth of the nation's state/municipio revenues. Although in Mexico the federal government is predominant, nevertheless the Department of the Federal District particularly wields impressive economic and political power and has influenced considerably the city's urban growth and development.

The most important basic features of the Mexico City economy in 1993 were metal products and machinery; chemical/petrochemical industry; food, drink, and tobacco; wholesale and retail commerce; professional and technical services; and hotel / restaurant / leisure services sectors. For these sectors the Megacity dominates the national economy.

The spatial distribution of major economic sectors is varied. The industrial sector is concentrated adjoining the northern border of the Federal District in huge industrial zones, especially Azcapotzalco, Miguel Hidalgo, Tlalnepantla, Naucalpan, and Ecatepec. This industrial complex is the largest in Mexico, and is only rivaled by Monterrey. It is remarkable that this huge complex is in close proximity to the city center, i.e. the center of national government, leading corporations, and commercial activity.

Although overall the city's industrial production is centered along the northern Federal District border, there is some variation in locations for major industry categories, such as heavy metals, chemicals, food and drink, etc. Industry located on the semi-urban periphery tends to be textiles/clothing and food/drink/tobacco. However, in raw terms, all categories are heavily centered in the industrial complex.

The commerce sector is primarily centrally located and has remained concentrated in the old city center delegations of Cuauhtemoc, Miguel Hidalgo, Benito Juarez, as well as Iztapalapa. The service sector is likewise centered in the traditional city center. Although in raw terms, all service subsectors are centrally concentrated, some spatial differences exist.

Particular attention is given to high level professional and financial services. Sassen (1991), among others, pointed out the role of advanced megacities as hubs of executive decision-making and high level professional and financial services to support such decision-making. Manufacturing and low level services are becoming more "commodities" that can be transferred to the national and even international "hinterland," i.e. to smaller cities that are tied into the Megacity through modern communications and transportation. As Mexico City develops into a more advanced megacity, we postulate that city qualities pointed to by Sassen will emerge to a greater extent. Location and change in the amount and geographical pattern of high level professional and financial services in the early 90s shows strong centralization as well as recent growth.

This chapter discusses the relationship among economic variables and among the dimensions outlined above and presents an economic cluster analysis. It is clear that raw levels of all economic variables are strongly tied together. These variables are also associated with the more centrally concentrated cluster variables. The economic cluster analysis points to distinct economic zones that are meaningful in terms of this chapter and the next chapter.

Twentieth Century Economic Development

Mexico City became one of the two major economic centers of Mexico in the nineteenth century. It competed back and forth with Puebla during that century for dominance in textile manufacturing, one of the major national industries at the time (Garza, 1987). As seen in the following table, major production industries of Mexico City in 1879 were food, clothing, and textiles.

Major Industries in Mexico City, 1879

Industry Group	Number of Establishments	Number of Workers	Production, in Thousands of 1879 Pesos
Food	128	1,657	5,519
Clothing	214	3,413	3,225
Textiles	6	1,456	1,643
Chemicals	117	452	1,302
Tobacco	20	2,710	1,008
Total (all industries)	728	12,550	15,504

Source: Garza, 1987; cited from Busto, 1880.

At the turn of the century, the dictatorship of Porforio Diaz, known as the Porforiate, was clearly pro-business. In particular the Diaz government emphasized building an infrastructure for industrialization. Government policies led to development of the Mexican national railroad system and the start of a national electrical system (Garza, 1987). Both of these systems were centered on the Federal District. This central location was due to the large population and growing industrial base in the national capital. At the same time, the central location encouraged industrialization in the capital.

Another Diaz policy, encouraging the rising prominence of the capital, was the reduction and elimination of taxation for interstate commerce (Garza, 1987). This also favored Mexico City since its businesses could more profitably sell its goods throughout the nation and also purchase goods more reasonably. The Porforiate also encouraged normalization of international relations with major trading nations including the U.S., Britain, and France. Those nations provided large amounts of capital especially concentrated in Mexico City. This in turn encouraged more rapid industrialization and business growth.

During the first half of the twentieth century, Mexico City was transformed from its early industrializing state to a fully industrialized economy with a variety of economic sectors that enlarged greatly the limited economy of the Pre-Diaz era. Total city production increased vastly from 1930-70. As seen in Table 9.1, the total business sector of the Megacity grew by 10 to 40 times from 1930 to 1970. This greatly exceeded the growth in population, which increased by about sevenfold.

As seen in Table 9.2, the distribution of Megacity industries changed greatly over the forty years. Historically dominant industries of food, drink, textiles, and clothing decreased substantially from a total of two thirds of value added in 1930 to one third in 1970. Industries replacing these declining ones were basic metals, other machinery, petroleum, non-metallic minerals, metal products, and durable goods including automobiles. These industries embodied the industrialization process and are still important in the 1990s.

The rapid growth in industrial goods of the years 1930-70 moderated in the late part of the century, as seen in Table 9.3 In the table, the definition of Megacity broadened from 30 delegations/municipios in 1980 to the 69 delegations/municipios as defined in this book. In spite of the enlarged definition of urban area, the size of the city's industrial sector declined from 1980 to 1993. In particular, the number of workers decreased by about one quarter to 809,000 to approximate the city's workforce estimated at 703,000 in 1975 (Garza, 1987). The number of establishments increased by 12 percent during this period. The slack is made up by productivity that gained an estimated 25 percent over this period.

The Federal District's economy in 1993 reveals a mix of traditional and contemporary features. As reflected in data from the economic census of 1993 in Table 9.4, there are very large economic sectors in metal products/machinery and chemicals/petrochemicals, reflecting their continuing growth from mid-century. The traditional sector of food, drink, and tobacco remains very large, but the traditional area of textiles has diminished. There is a very large commercial sector, as might be expected for the buying and selling center of the nation. This sector accounted for half of the Federal District economy, as reflected in the economic census. Services at 21 percent nearly equals the industrial sector (see Table 9.5).

Within services, professional/technical services and restaurants/hotels/leisure are prominent. These sectors reflect the status of the Federal District as the center of business and government for the nation and for tourism. According to Sassen (1991), megacities in advanced nations are keyed to the support and servicing of an immense scale of business, management, and decision making. The presence of a large professional/technical service sector supports this emerging aspect of Mexico City. The prominence of the hotel/leisure sector reflects the Federal District's status as a center for business and tourist travel (see Pick and Butler, 1994).

In subsequent sections of this chapter, public finance and economic sectors of manufacturing, commerce, communications, services, and the third sector will be examined.[1] Then correlations of economic variables and an economic cluster analysis will be presented.

Table 9.1 Industry in Mexico City, 1930-1970

| Year | Population | Industrial Sector Indicators | | | |
		Number of Establishments	Number of Workers	Total Production*	Value Added*
1930	1,029,068	3,180	54,105	844	475
1940	1,802,679	4,920	89,358	2,182	1,049
1950	3,137,599	12,704	156,697	7,323	3,905
1960	5,251,755	24,624	406,905	13,535	6,513
1970	8,799,937	33,185	658,275	32,437	18,287
Growth '30-'70 (in percent)	855	1,044	1,217	3,843	3,850

* in millions of 1950 pesos

Source: INEGI: *Estadisticas Historicas de Mexico,* 1994; Industrial Census, various years: adjusted by Garza, 1987

---

[1] For more extensive analysis, see Hettrick (1996).

Table 9.2 Change in Megacity Industrial Composition 1930-1970

Industry Sector	1930	1970	Change in Percent 1930-70
Production Goods	16.4	32.9	16.4
Wood and Cork	4.3	1.3	-3.1
Paper and Celuose	2.2	3.3	1.1
Petroleum/Carbon Produc	2.4	5.9	3.5
Non Metallic Minerals	2.3	5.7	3.4
Basic Metals	4.2	8.6	4.4
Metal Products	1.0	5.6	4.6
Non Electrical Machinery	0.0	2.5	2.5
Consumption Goods	83.6	67.1	-16.4
Non-Durable	82.2	54.4	-27.8
Food	19.9	14.7	-5.2
Drink	10.6	6.8	-3.8
Tobacco	5.4	1.8	-3.6
Textiles	30.3	6.8	-23.5
Clothing and Footwear	5.5	3.7	-1.8
Publishing	4.1	2.6	-1.5
Chemicals	4.6	15.4	10.8
Other	1.7	2.5	0.8
Durable	1.4	12.8	11.4
Electrical Goods	0.0	5.2	5.2
Automobiles	0.2	5.4	5.3
Other	1.2	2.2	0.9
Percent Total	100.0	100.0	
Total Industrial Production (in millions of 1950 pesos)	1,749	37,624	

Source: Garza, 1987; data from Industrial Census, 1930-70.

Table 9.3 Change in Industrial Production Indicators, Mexico Megacity, 1980-1993

Year	Establishments	Workers	Salaries*	Capital Investment*	Production*	Ave. Salary*	Productivity	Peso Value
1980	38,492	1,059,182	26,661,400	69,534,986	151,769,894	25,172	143,290	23
1993	43,143	809,256	22,138,104	58,704,061	144,949,102	27,356	179,114	4,360
Percent Change 80-93	12.1	-23.6	-17.0	-15.6	-4.5	8.7	25.0	188.6

Source: Garza, 1987 and INEGI, Industrial Census, 1993.
NOTE: in thousands of 1992 new pesos.

Table 9.4 Features of Economic Sectors, Federal District, 1993

Sector	Establishments	Workers	Salaries	Capital Investment	Production
Industrial Sector - Total	28,059	500,742	13,236.6	36,054.7	84,227.9
Basic Metals	41	4,807	152.9	423.2	2,003.9
Metal Production, Mach.	5,634	117,754	3,196.0	7,402.6	18,713.7
Chemical / Petrochemical	1,801	97,214	3,870.9	9,656.1	22,485.0
Textiles, Clothing	4,501	81,281	1,407.3	3,151.9	8,381.6
Food, Drink, Tobacco	8,009	88,711	2,054.2	9,429.0	18,783.0
Paper, Printing, Pub.	4,605	69,420	1,830.3	4,162.4	9,489.4
Commercial Sector - Total	168,001	567,855	8,694.4	30,768.3	167,599.2
Wholesale	14,111	176,516	4,876.4	17,643.1	98,463.6
Retail	153,890	391,339	3,818.0	13,125.2	69,135.6
Automotive	4,856	28,626	749.0	1,518.2	11,573.8
Communications Sector - Total	187	38,285	3,200.8	6,572.2	9,387.0
Services Sector - Total	108,598	686,456	15,650.3	36,043.6	71,464.9
Real Estate	2,122	15,276	28.1	2,388.6	4,463.9
Restaurants, Hotels, Leisure	33,885	191,740	2,959	8,499	17,817
Finance / Insurance	513	3,983	218.4	357.5	997.9
Professional / Technical	11,324	213,405	7,569.1	15,444.5	28,921.1
Third Sector	16,892	123,861	2,598.5	4,204.6	7,454.3
Federal District - Total	304,845	1,793,338	40,782	109,439	332,679

NOTE: Monetary values are in millions of new pesos.

Source: INEGI: *Censos Economicos,* 1993

Table 9.5 Industrial Variables for Mexico City, 1993

No.	Area	Industry Revenues	Industry Workers	Food, Drink and Tobacco Revenues	Textiles and Clothing Revenues	Paper, Printing and Publishing Revenues	Chemical and Petrochemical Revenues	Basic Metal Revenues	Metal Production and Mach. Revenues
1	Alvaro Obregon	2,619,005.1	19,097.0	306,855.7	225,276.6	80,290.4	876,187.2	0.0	651,217.2
2	Acolman	759,982.2	1,599.0	97,336.4	371.8	222.2	647,322.8	0.0	5,357.7
3	Amecameca	85,011.7	678.0	36,693.0	44,827.5	2,126.2	318.9	0.0	623.4
4	Atenco	40,440.0	431.0	1,900.0	41.6	0.0	0.0	0.0	25,169.7
5	Atizapan De Zaragoza	1,247,359.2	10,643.0	52,219.4	278,363.3	85,999.0	406,359.2	0.0	249,261.0
6	Atlautla	13,546.6	78.0	724.8	12.0	0.0	0.0	0.0	2,756.9
7	Axapusco	3,177.5	150.0	1,584.0	731.5	0.0	234.2	0.0	49.5
8	Ayapango	357.1	11.0	126.1	0.0	0.0	207.0	0.0	0.0
9	Azcapotzalco	20,223,673.4	80,348.0	8,414,082.1	897,179.6	1,659,319.9	3,462,861.1	1,522,868.4	3,581,268.4
10	Benito Juarez	5,249,875.9	36,397.0	606,627.9	579,010.7	1,270,016.6	2,342,871.0	0.0	325,519.6
11	Chalco	556,348.5	4,144.0	232,358.4	7,388.3	34,513.2	14,172.2	5,847.4	229,653.7
12	Chiautla	13,408.8	153.0	11,962.5	1,034.5	0.0	0.0	0.0	226.2
13	Chicoloapan	60,842.6	1,074.0	17,610.1	19,632.1	105.3	2,551.5	0.0	13,407.8
14	Chiconcuac	7,847.6	170.0	1,395.5	6,063.8	46.2	0.0	0.0	203.3
15	Chimalhuacan	85,820.6	1,776.0	38,139.3	6,498.8	375.0	9,320.8	0.0	10,206.4
16	Coacalco	216,181.8	216.0	54,447.6	9,485.7	3,236.2	39,239.3	5,944.6	96,099.5
17	Cocotitlan	701.8	34.0	580.3	0.0	0.0	0.0	0.0	116.3
18	Coyoacan	5,811,921.3	3,612.0	402,826.9	144,348.3	197,682.5	31,947.9	0.0	371,259.2
19	Coyotepec	1,585.4	53.0	1,456.5	0.0	25.1	0.0	0.0	59.7
20	Cuajimalpa	260,900.6	1,817.0	67,983.9	831.2	7,657.6	80,711.1	0.0	26,945.1
21	Cuauhtemoc	8,666,252.8	62,773.0	2,126,569.2	579,010.7	2,888,614.6	2,342,871.0	0.0	325,519.6
22	Cuautitlan	1,364,097.6	7,589.0	185,329.8	213,494.9	1,502.1	674,851.3	0.0	286,448.3
23	Cuautitlan Izcalli	11,074,311.1	32,994.0	2,653,908.1	413,943.8	253,016.5	1,173,442.8	83,013.7	5,853,028.4
24	Ecatepec	10,701,474.4	49,797.0	2,828,834.1	710,778.5	1,310,507.0	3,061,106.9	444,847.4	1,633,817.7
25	Ecatzingo	281.6	20.0	215.3	31.2	0.0	0.0	0.0	22.2
26	Gustavo A. Madero	6,297,249.4	53,981.0	1,064,975.7	540,903.1	410,328.0	1,475,027.7	359,664.2	1,936,766.5
27	Huehuetoca	805,640.7	2,350.0	409,283.5	5,301.2	24,124.2	151,510.8	9,878.3	205,519.1
28	Huixquilucan	100,484.7	624.0	24,675.4	3,321.5	196.0	26,377.6	0.0	3,142.5
29	Isidro Fabela	379.9	9.0	315.7	0.0	0.0	0.0	0.0	38.2
30	Ixtapaluca	1,081,423.6	6,359.0	300,835.0	163,131.9	56,350.3	11,916.8	756.4	442,703.7

Table 9.5 Industrial Variables for Mexico City, 1993 (Continued)

No.	Area	Industry Revenues	Industry Workers	Food, Drink and Tobacco Revenues	Textiles and Clothing Revenues	Paper, Printing and Publishing Revenues	Chemical and Petrochemical Revenues	Basic Metal Revenues	Metal Production and Mach. Revenues
31	Iztacalco	4,762,810.4	45,425.0	797,332.7	1,327,680.8	491,336.7	740,594.0	12,549.8	925,615.2
32	Iztapalapa	7,716,798.5	68,821.0	815,828.3	621,200.0	1,235,808.1	1,895,690.1	42,179.6	2,315,707.7
33	Jaltenco	2,648.6	63.0	1,962.8	131.6	31.7	0.0	0.0	169.1
34	Jilotzingo	1,143.7	38.0	128.6	0.0	0.0	0.0	493.4	0.0
35	Juchitepec	1,584.4	51.0	1,058.9	0.0	0.0	44.4	0.0	142.4
36	Magdalena Contreras	41,349.0	796.0	26,196.4	1,026.1	3,384.1	2,840.7	0.0	2,915.8
37	Melchor Ocampo	20,681.2	207.0	4,404.5	11,570.1	126.0	264.0	0.0	1,040.6
38	Miguel Hidalgo	15,523,161.9	50,511.0	2,969,114.8	868,123.7	786,785.2	3,539,863.9	27,471.8	6,765,840.4
39	Milpa Alta	32,241.1	729.0	25,619.3	529.2	74.3	2,803.5	0.0	2,265.2
40	Naucalpan	12,784,375.8	73,103.0	772,326.2	4,168,834.2	874,273.6	3,476,080.2	0.0	2,927,588.7
41	Nextlalpan	1,994.2	76.0	911.4	409.3	442.0	0.0	0.0	127.5
42	Nezahualcoyotl	798,325.3	13,044.0	428,773.9	59,886.1	27,452.2	64,779.3	75.0	121,142.4
43	Nicolas Romero	101,514.0	1,716.0	24,898.5	28,019.3	22,075.4	2,333.0	0.0	14,389.7
44	Nopaltepec	3,349.0	104.0	449.2	311.2	0.0	310.8	0.0	761.5
45	Otumba	4,403.5	134.0	2,660.3	328.3	89.1	132.2	0.0	339.3
46	Ozumba	9,853.1	366.0	2,108.7	64.7	27.9	373.5	0.0	6,312.7
47	Papalotla	6,391.7	103.0	435.1	60.0	0.0	0.0	0.0	5,731.8
48	Paz, La	1,847,480.5	12,883.0	763,543.6	26,589.6	195,336.1	301,484.1	22,012.8	389,623.5
49	San Martin De Las P.	24,629.2	340.0	2,134.9	9,638.4	0.0	1,002.9		10,068.4
50	Tecamac	681,225.2	3,513.0	236,170.7	109,196.7	2,763.0	10,556.0	15,465.1	274,108.4
51	Temamatla	10,736.3	62.0	10,511.7	0.0	120.0	0.0	0.0	4.5
52	Temascalapa	2,284.2	57.0	814.7	1,265.1	0.0	0.0	0.0	87.1
53	Tenango Del Aire	4,478.4	46.0	4,478.4	0.0	0.0	0.0	0.0	0.0
54	Teoloyucan	52,524.9	601.0	6,383.9	26.0	977.6	11,355.5	0.0	32,980.9
55	Teotihuacan	283,964.7	1,102.0	223,223.5	365.0	16,509.9	0.0	1,333.2	1,311.9
56	Tepetlaoxtoc	15,647.5	244.0	574.9	9,448.2	2,489.9	0.0	0.0	0.6
57	Tepetlixpa	646.2	29.0	557.6	0.0	0.0	0.0	0.0	0.0
58	Tepotzotlan	1,152,732.2	6,264.0	756,277.7	214,552.0	17,741.7	20,588.9	0.0	119,201.4
59	Texcoco	528,722.3	4,607.0	207,085.1	106,385.5	19,585.5	63,388.2	0.0	64,568.6
60	Tezoyuca	13,646.4	116.0	751.0	0.0	6,238.0	5,287.0	0.0	901.0
61	Tlahuac	688,597.7	7,622.0	69,148.9	54,868.4	31,234.4	44,187.1	1,287.0	401,132.2

Table 9.5 Industrial Variables for Mexico City, 1993 (Continued)

No.	Area	Industry Revenues	Industry Workers	Food, Drink and Tobacco Revenues	Textiles and Clothing Revenues	Paper, Printing and Publishing Revenues	Chemical and Petrochemical Revenues	Basic Metal Revenues	Metal Production and Mach. Revenues
62	Tlalmanalco	232,745.9	1,278.0	2,727.7	47,686.4	178,109.4	3,624.0	0.0	217.2
63	Tlalnepantla	16,448,447.3	79,421.0	2,052,877.4	613,383.4	1,211,315.6	3,085,184.1	752,151.4	5,929,813.0
64	Tlalpan	1,808,458.3	14,939.0	303,685.2	32,953.9	120,280.4	788,753.4	0.0	203,194.8
65	Tultepec	375,769.9	2,375.0	4,139.4	17.4	65.5	267.7	0.0	370,226.1
66	Tultitlan	2,153,146.1	13,304.0	119,517.0	24,142.2	162,138.9	781,669.1	183,388.7	755,947.8
67	Venustiano Carranza	2,357,018.1	24,586.0	722,136.2	549,055.5	220,829.8	218,704.5	36,902.3	490,573.6
68	Xochimilco	2,168,554.0	8,022.0	64,053.7	39,216.2	85,787.4	1,906,595.8	0.0	61,085.2
69	Zumpango	77,580.8	1,148.0	23,226.0	13,253.5	370.4	33,204.7	0.0	3,505.1
	Mean	2,175,235.4	11,838.0	454,928.7	199,872.9	202,899.3	490,338.7	51,132.3	557,609.4
	Median	101,514.0	1,148.0	26,196.4	9,448.2	2,489.9	9,320.8	0.0	13,407.8
	S.D.	4,357,474.6	21,594.7	1,183,636.2	555,116.4	495,076.6	973,444.5	212,726.6	1,384,874.4
	C.V.	200.3	182.4	260.2	277.7	244.0	198.5	416.0	248.4
	Minimum	281.6	9.0	126.1	0.0	0.0	0.0	0.0	0.0
	Maximum	20,223,673.4	80,348.0	8,414,082.1	4,168,834.2	2,888,614.6	3,539,863.9	1,522,868.4	6,765,840.4
	Total	150,091,245.0	816,823.0	31,390,081.0	13,791,232.1	14,000,053.9	33,833,371.7	3,528,130.5	38,475,048.1

Note: Values are in thousands of new pesos.

Source: INEGI: 1993 *Censos Economicos*.

Public Finance

Government revenues at the state and municipio levels are important in Mexico, even though the nation's political/governmental system is dominated by the federal versus the state and local levels (Cornelius and Craig, 1991). For the Megacity, state and local government revenues include State of Mexico, municipios in the State of Mexico, and Federal District. Federal District revenues are consolidated, i.e. delegations are not broken out as separate financial entities. Rather, the Department of the Federal District is equivalent to a state government that also provides public financial management, governance, and services at the local level.

In estimating total government revenues for Mexico City, we apportioned the State of Mexico revenues on the basis of the 69.4 percent of population that resides in Mexico City. This is equivalent to Mexico City total state/local revenues of 21.2 billion new pesos in 1993, compared to 97.7 billion for the nation, i.e. 21.6 percent (see Figure 9.1). This closely matches the population proportions, i.e. the Mexico City population constituted 18.5 percent of the national population. It is clear that Mexico City does not stand out economically at the state/local level, but rather the prominence of the Mexico City stems from its being the seat of the federal government.

It is clear in Figure 9.1, that municipio, estimated at only 6.9 percent, versus state revenues are quite small in the Megacity. Municipio revenues in the State of Mexico are located principally in just four municipios -- Naucalpan, Tlalnepantla, Ecatepec, and Huixquilucan. The first three are very populous and Naucalpan and Tlalnepantla have large industrial bases. As seen in Map 9.1, on a per capita basis, government revenues are highest in the northwest, which is heavily industrial. On the other hand, per capita revenues are lowest in Chalco. In fact, Chalco's per capita municipio revenues are only one sixteenth those of prosperous Huixquilucan. The high variation is confirmed by a CV of 123 for gross municipio revenues and 86 for per capita municipio revenues. This great variety in the extent of municipio revenues implies large differences in municipio services which affect quality of life.

Map 9.1
State of Mexico Municipio
Gross Revenues in Thousands of Pesos
Per Capita, 1993

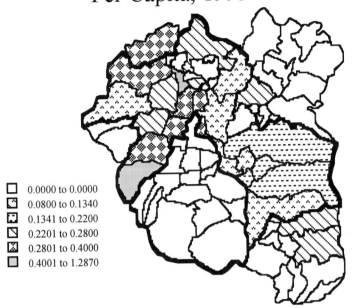

- 0.0000 to 0.0000
- 0.0800 to 0.1340
- 0.1341 to 0.2200
- 0.2201 to 0.2800
- 0.2801 to 0.4000
- 0.4001 to 1.2870

Data Source: INEGI, Finanzas Publicas Estatales y Municipales de Mexico, 1995
Map Source: Butler/Pick Mexico Database Project

**Figure 9.1 Gross Revenues of Megacity
States and Municipios, 1993**

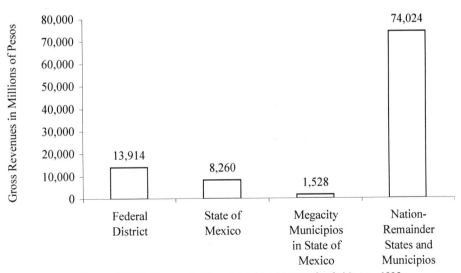

Source: INEGI: *Finanzas Publicas Estatales y Municipales de Mexico,* 1995

Industry

Industry is strongly concentrated in the very populous municipios of Tlalnepantla and Naucalpan in the State of Mexico, as well as the Federal District delegations of Azcapotzalco, Iztapalapa, Cuauhtemoc, and Miguel Hidalgo. These municipios account for 51 percent of industrial workers and 56 percent of industrial production in the metropolis (see Figure 9.2). It is remarkable that several of these zones are also among the wealthiest in the metropolis (compare with Map 10.8). This differs from patterns in advanced nation megacities, in which industrial production is increasingly dispersed to megacity hinterland areas or to outlying and separate smaller cities that may be far removed from the megacity (Sassen, 1991). On the other hand, this corresponds to the theory of Latin American cities, in which the business center coincides with the highest social status (Griffin and Ford, 1983).

The map of industrial workers (Map 9.2) illustrates this concentration. It is important that the semi-urban fringe has very slight industrial workforce production, amounting to about one percent. There is thus a very skewed distribution, as seen in Figure 9.2 that reveals a large number of zones with less than 15,000 workers, i.e. the urban fringe. Also, the CV is very high at 182. There are similar skewed patterns for all indicators of industrial production (see Table 9.5).

Spatial patterns for major industry sectors are similar to those for industrial workers and other overall attributes, with a strong central/north-central concentration. Distributions are very skewed as seen in the table showing the coefficients of variation as well as top municipios for the major industrial sectors.

Beyond the city center's dominance in terms of raw industrial production, it is instructive to examine economic variables that control for total industrial sector size. This is done by estimating for each zone the proportion of revenues in the specific sector to revenues for the overall industry sector (see Table 9.6). For instance, Map 9.3 shows the ratio of basic metal manufacturing revenues to overall industry sector revenues. Municipios with the highest proportionate composition of basic metal manufacturing are located in a corridor that runs from the upper Federal District about five miles north to the top of Tecamac, as well as including Huehuetoca in the far northwest.

On the other hand, proportion of metal production and machinery revenues to total industrial sector are more evenly spread around the metropolis (see Map 9.4). Even a few municipios in the semi-urban fringe, namely San Martin de las Piramides, and Ozumba have high metal production/machinery components exceeding one third. For the traditional manufacturing subsector of textiles, clothing, and leather (see Map 9.5), there are certain municipios spread about the Megacity that have high proportions, i.e. exceeding twenty percent. The wide spatial dispersion of textile industry, measured as sector proportion, stems partly from its historically dominant role in the city.

For chemical and petrochemical manufacturing, revenues are concentrated in the traditional core of the Federal District (Benito Juarez, Miguel Hidalgo), populous northern adjoining municipios of Naucalpan, Tlalnepantla, and Ecatepec, as well as Azcapotzalco, Iztapalapa, and Xochimilco in the Federal District. Miguel Hidalgo, Naucalpan, and Azcapotzalco have the highest total chemical/petrochemical (each has one tenth of the Megacity). On the basis of proportion of total industrial revenues, chemical/petrochemical revenues are high in a north-south axis running from Tlalpan, in the southern Federal District through the northern adjoining industrial municipios and up to the municipios Huehuetoca and Zumpango in the far north. Although not illustrated here, this spatial pattern for chemicals/petrochemical proportion closely resembles (r = 0.49) that for finance / insurance services.

Consistent with other industry factors, textile, clothing, and leather raw revenues are heavily concentrated in the city center. Textile/clothing/leather revenues are half concentrated in the municipios of Naucalpan (thirty percent), Azcapotzalco, and Iztacalco. On a compositional basis, textiles are spread out in the Megacity, with high as well as low concentrations in all major areas (see Map 9.5). Thus textiles/clothing/leather is an industry that can dominate in populous as well as in non-populous areas, in economically advantaged as well as a depressed parts of the city. Since textile/clothing/leather production does not depend on high tech, professional services, access to government power, or financial institutions, there is less need to locate in the city center. The industry is an old one that was a strong element of Mexico City industry until mid twentieth century (Chapter 9 and Garza, 1987). Some areas in the city have a historical tradition of textile/clothing/leather manufacture that persists. An analogy to this is the presence of traditional garment districts in New York City and Los Angeles that have remained in spite of urban change.

In raw revenues, food/drink/tobacco is highly centralized. Thus, four zones have fifty four percent of revenues -- Azcapotzalco, Miguel Hidalgo, Cuautitlan Izcalli, and Ecatepec. This industry sector is no longer under the dominance of the old city center, but has moved slightly northwards. One reason may be environmental pollution constraints for manufacturing in these industries. Also, the city center is so urbanized that locations are limited for firms. The appeal away from the city center is reflected in the spatial pattern on a basis of industry composition (Map 9.6). There are high compositional values in parts of the semi-urban fringes in the southeast, northeast, and west, as well as in Milpa Alta. This may be due to more favorable conditions in certain peripheral areas for locating these industries.

Nationally, paper, printing, and publishing industries are centered on Mexico City. Within the Megacity, these industries are concentrated in the northern Federal District and adjoining State of Mexico municipios. Cuauhtemoc leads with one fifth of the revenues. It is at or near the centers of the federal government, finance, and professional/technical services. The paper/printing/publishing industry is linked to these other city center features. Azcapotzalco, Ecatepec, Benito Juarez, Iztapalapa, and Tlalnepantla account for another half. The semi-urban periphery in the northeast, southeast, and west has practically no revenues in these industries. As seen in Map 9.7, on a compositional basis, paper/printing/publishing remains concentrated in the old core of the Federal District and State of Mexico adjoining municipios to the north/northeast. There are several exceptions of high industry composition in Tezoyuca and Tlalmanalco, which are due to local factors.

264

Map 9.2
Industrial Workers, 1993

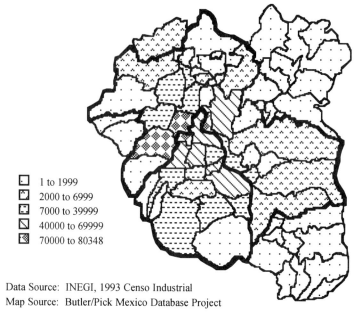

☐	1 to 1999
▨	2000 to 6999
▨	7000 to 39999
◩	40000 to 69999
▧	70000 to 80348

Data Source: INEGI, 1993 Censo Industrial
Map Source: Butler/Pick Mexico Database Project

Figure 9.2 Number of Industrial Workers by Spatial Unit, Mexico City, 1993

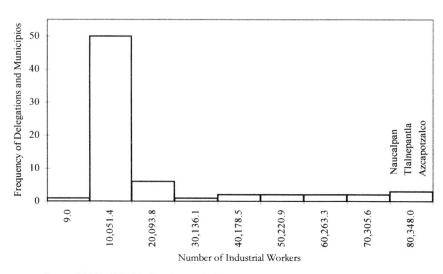

Source: INEGI: 1993 Mexican Economic Census

Map 9.3
Proportion of Revenues
Basic Metal Manufacturing, 1993

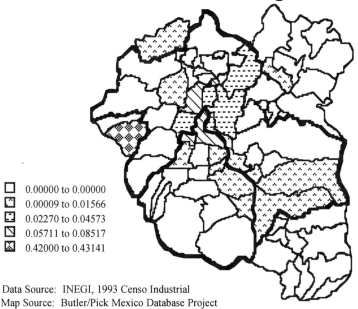

☐ 0.00000 to 0.00000
▣ 0.00009 to 0.01566
▣ 0.02270 to 0.04573
◩ 0.05711 to 0.08517
▧ 0.42000 to 0.43141

Data Source: INEGI, 1993 Censo Industrial
Map Source: Butler/Pick Mexico Database Project

Map 9.4
Proportion of Revenues
Metal Production, Machinery Equipment, 1993

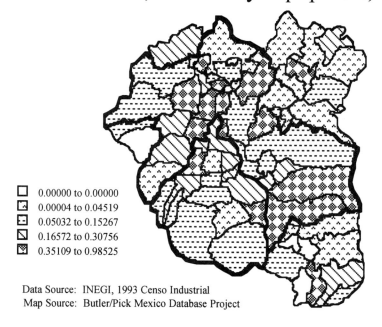

☐ 0.00000 to 0.00000
▣ 0.00004 to 0.04519
▣ 0.05032 to 0.15267
◩ 0.16572 to 0.30756
▧ 0.35109 to 0.98525

Data Source: INEGI, 1993 Censo Industrial
Map Source: Butler/Pick Mexico Database Project

Table 9.6 Commerce and Service Variables for Mexico City, 1993

No.	Area	Commerce Revenues	Wholesale Revenues	Automotive Revenues	Service Revenues	Real Estate Revenues	Education Revenues	Private Scientific Research Revenues	Restaurant, Hotel and Leisure Revenues	Professional and Technical Revenues	Finance and Insurance Revenues
1	Alvaro Obregon	7,634,287.7	4,177,147.1	697,138.7	4,660,962.3	602,366.9	845,476.9	13,940.2	1,192,880.0	1,344,266.9	215,194.6
2	Acolman	63,957.4	10,689.3	1,684.9	95,709.0	17.0	1,182.3	0.0	1,974.5	133.6	0.0
3	Amecameca	122,364.0	30,771.6	20,148.0	16,739.4	0.0	1,873.8	0.0	4,450.2	6,045.2	0.0
4	Atenco	19,104.8	549.5	318.0	3,582.8	0.0	388.2	0.0	1,169.9	23.4	0.0
5	Atizapan De Zaragoza	1,310,656.3	360,663.1	132,452.7	395,365.4	1,895.1	243,543.6	0.0	85,689.9	8,362.0	32.0
6	Atlautla	4,663.7	165.1	0	1,719.2	237.5	30.3	0.0	1,234.9	12.0	0.0
7	Axapusco	5,108.5	20.0	93.6	475.0	0.0	138.0	0.0	108.0	53.6	0.0
8	Ayapango	797.0	20.0	0	102.3	0.0	0.0	0.0	86.3	8.0	0.0
9	Azcapotzalco	11,571,635.4	8,448,960.8	792,623.1	1,534,900.0	70,081.6	146,570.7	1,935.7	209,666.9	596,595.5	309.0
10	Benito Juarez	20,447,735.5	11,699,036.5	1,623,673.7	7,893,996.3	533,475.5	908,580.7	19,886.9	1,777,184.5	3,347,362.5	56,502.3
11	Chalco	525,475.1	157,343.6	101414.2	98,865.5	5,256.4	9,121.7	0.0	29,169.2	4,155.1	195.6
12	Chiautla	13,947.7	1,628.5	0	1,025.8	0.0	567.6	0.0	140.4	0.0	0.0
13	Chicoloapan	167,860.0	82,628.4	5342.6	18,726.3	1,185.0	3,163.1	0.0	5,308.4	293.3	0.0
14	Chiconcuac	131,046.1	655.7	0	8,259.3	0.0	1,451.1	0.0	4,929.9	107.0	0.0
15	Chimalhuacan	286,064.8	43,521.1	2065.7	29,067.6	519.8	5,429.6	0.0	11,133.2	567.0	0.0
16	Coacalco	636,656.3	160,800.4	56886.9	118,606.0	649.0	5,703.6	40.0	40,129.1	5,134.8	0.0
17	Cocotitlan	6,911.3	2,336.8	202	365.7	69.8	22.0	0.0	94.3	13.5	0.0
18	Coyoacan	8,515,802.4	3,105,987.1	829,101.9	3,129,584.5	51,138.8	370,132.2	5,445.9	1,383,094.8	956,930.5	18,546.6
19	Coyotepec	14,550.9	32.1	142.4	2,366.2	0.0	104.1	0.0	1,576.7	47.8	0.0
20	Cuajimalpa	1,059,437.5	133,376.0	395,507.1	658,870.8	19,010.7	243,153.8	0.0	49,749.9	193,778.5	280.0
21	Cuauhtemoc	37,860,107.5	19,761,276.4	2,289,455.5	20,199,249.8	974,453.4	2,053,126.7	10,448.1	7,472,198.6	6,036,682.0	287,504.8
22	Cuautitlan	463,600.5	189,111.4	19305	78,989.9	6,191.7	14,330.9	0.0	14,836.4	22,584.4	0.0
23	Cuautitlan Izcalli	3,056,182.0	1,624,049.1	460,442.0	414,843.8	8,503.7	95,497.6	0.0	98,078.8	51,078.5	1,332.0
24	Ecatepec	7,730,158.3	3,833,790.2	442,986.5	640,465.0	56,089.4	77,738.7	0.0	175,641.4	91,529.7	51.0
25	Ecatzingo	1,071.1	0.0	0.0	122.7	0.0	9.6	0.0	0.0	0.0	0.0
26	Gustavo A. Madero	13,453,260.3	7,689,948.2	1,111,111.8	1,849,471.7	101,795.6	401,064.5	2,472.7	533,894.8	203,486.8	665.8
27	Huehuetoca	22,035.8	3,960.2	764.1	36,226.6	89.9	694.1	0.0	942.4	32,575.3	0.0
28	Huixquilucan	708,676.4	26,070.4	192,435.7	330,826.5	9,143.1	154,406.1	0.0	71,838.5	23,992.7	0.0
29	Isidro Fabela	2,292.7	0.0	0.0	116.3	0.0	9.9	0.0	53.0	0.0	0.0

Table 9.6 Commerce and Service Variables for Mexico City, 1993 (Continued)

	Commerce Revenues	Wholesale Revenues	Automotive Revenues	Service Revenues	Real Estate Revenues	Education Revenues	Private Scientific Research Revenues	Restaurant, Hotel and Leisure Revenues	Professional and Technical Revenues	Finance and Insurance Revenues
30 Ixtapaluca	408,129.8	144,190.7	9,867.5	60,118.1	747.4	5,202.5	0.0	181.0	1,156.3	0.0
31 Iztacalco	5,073,611.6	3,380,996.5	248,605.9	1,042,531.7	119,445.9	68,643.5	18,528.8	419,913.4	222,227.6	2,472.2
32 Iztapalapa	20,397,779.2	14,003,180.0	1,169,983.9	1,232,099.7	50619.6	145,096.1	0.0	327,074.6	263,559.6	310.1
33 Jaltenco	13,641.0	54.6	96.4	4,297.3	0.0	259.4	0.0	927.2	52.0	0.0
34 Jilotzingo	3,407.6	2,222.5	0.0	126.3	0.0	13.2	0.0	43.6	0.0	0.0
35 Juchitepec	13,844.0	156.8	173.4	1,763.3	0.0	42.5	0.0	679.8	15.0	0.0
36 Magdalena Contreras	577,385.0	227781.4	4648.7	676,971.5	6175.5	315,218.6	0.0	260,008.5	67,507.5	0.0
37 Melchor Ocampo	43,225.5	3,135.3	820.3	5,641.3	0.0	1,017.8	0.0	1,301.3	99.6	0.0
38 Miguel Hidalgo	27,469,320.0	19,803,776.0	1,254,403.4	22,621,910.8	2,124,151.0	1,169,897.1	11,633.3	2,565,648.6	14,463,984.0	313,989.0
39 Milpa Alta	114,213.8	9,028.2	1,986.6	20,683.0	0	2,546.4	0.0	12,570.7	394.4	0.0
40 Naucalpan	12,706,341.5	7,420,996.2	837,702.4	2,567,361.3	127,680.6	524,111.0	83.5	667,123.0	759,509.4	17,144.3
41 Nextlalpan	9,845.1	195.1	234.2	2,626.8	0.0	54.6	0.0	190.6	13.0	0.0
42 Nezahualcoyotl	3,681,806.1	1,015,701.9	0.0	531,114.6	8,226.2	99,130.3	0.0	212,876.1	34,426.7	15.0
43 Nicolas Romero	275,905.5	41,623.3	7,509.8	55,276.6	13,656.6	10,956.0	0.0	16,060.6	2,368.8	0.0
44 Nopaltepec	1,971.1	118.8	0.0	135.8	0.0	15.0	0.0	25.7	0.0	0.0
45 Otumba	35,570.0	3,151.5	1,975.7	4,774.8	0.0	705.8	0.0	1,687.5	406.3	0.0
46 Ozumba	43,877.4	12,379.9	819.2	4,838.6	0.0	1,004.9	0.0	2,238.5	263.7	0.0
47 Papalotla	1,603.9	91.8	0.0	486.2	0.0	48.0	0	172.9	0.0	0.0
48 Paz, La	1,005,420.3	566,883.6	41,857.3	85,196.5	375.2	7,847.6	0.0	36,398.4	3,146.2	0.0
49 San Martin De Las P.	41,970.8	712.5	514.5	2,163.1	0.0	315.0	0.0	802.2	87.8	0.0
50 Tecamac	322,586.7	71,378.6	20,543.3	105,573.6	66.8	7,298.1	0.0	9,228.9	2,781.5	0.0
51 Temamatla	3,474.6	82.2	34.1	251.9	0.0	24.0	0.0	139.0	0.0	0.0
52 Temascalapa	12,042.8	552.2	0.0	492.1	0.0	25.8	0.0	168.9	93.4	0.0
53 Tenango Del Aire	3,842.0	433.4	0.0	265.1	0.0	23.2	0.0	158.0	0.0	0.0
54 Teoloyucan	75,025.1	1,972.7	5,007.3	4,783.5	0.0	981.1	0.0	1,238.2	41.2	0.0
55 Teotihuacan	49,350.9	8,121.1	717.2	24,681.9	0.0	3,531.3	2.4	12,202.5	1,605.3	0.0
56 Tepetlaoxtoc	6,866.7	406.0	0.0	806.2	0.0	350.4	0.0	162.8	22.8	0.0
57 Tepetlixpa	6,881.3	556.1	438.2	922.0	0.0	64.9	0.0	527.0	3.6	0.0
58 Tepotzotlan	500,752.5	300,703.5	394.2	307,723.7	1,028.1	4,713.5	0.0	11,229.4	4,867.5	0.0

Table 9.6 Commerce and Service Variables for Mexico City, 1993 (Continued)

	Commerce Revenues	Wholesale Revenues	Automotive Revenues	Service Revenues	Real Estate Revenues	Education Revenues	Private Scientific Research Revenues	Restaurant, Hotel and Leisure Revenues	Professional and Technical Revenues	Finance and Insurance Revenues
59 Texcoco	917,976.8	313,606.8	141,889.5	110,623.1	3,067.5	25,518.8	0.0	34,833.6	17,019.3	927.3
60 Tezoyuca	40,289.7	7,317.1	32,972.6	2,025.1	0.0	87.8	0.0	443.3	26.3	0.0
61 Tlahuac	1,146,203.3	639,250.1	85,857.7	107,654.1	1,048.5	18,026.3	0.0	25,474.8	7,208.7	0.0
62 Tlalmanalco	39,064.5	8,992.9	440.2	17,506.0	13,500.0	864.1	0.0	1,282.6	89.0	0.0
63 Tlalnepantla	11,655,003.2	7,011,704.5	994,637.5	1,429,978.6	50,461.5	159,353.0	0.0	310,452.6	506,450.3	867.1
64 Tlalpan	4,841,125.3	2,085,622.8	266,545.0	2,676,393.0	46,126.1	597,444.3	8,641.5	777,979.6	563,603.4	708.8
65 Tultepec	57,453.8	3,996.3	3,330.0	9,293.5	16.8	2,038.9	0.0	3,354.2	362.6	0.0
66 Tultitlan	506,649.6	209,846.4	66,324.3	189,442.1	145.8	8,568.8	0.0	14,524.5	15,027.7	0.0
67 Venustiano Carranza	5,935,219.6	1,916,997.8	426,454.3	2,843,737.3	24,968.7	105,616.1	7,263.3	714,024.4	622,600.0	10,574.0
68 Xochimilco	1,502,035.6	452,997.7	416,736.0	315,927.1	4,507.6	63,710.0	6,120.2	95,332.1	31,036.0	73,009.8
69 Zumpango	235,252.8	35,703.2	42,501.1	17,691.1	78.3	4,301.5	0.0	6,015.1	1,478.6	18.0
Total	215,611,413.0	121,251,156.6	15,261,317.8	79,305,490.0	5,038,263.6	8,938,178.6	106,442.5	19,711,950.6	30,519,354.7	1,000,649.3
Mean	3,124,803.1	1,757,263.1	221,178.5	1,149,354.9	73,018.3	129,538.8	1,542.6	285,680.4	442,309.5	14,502.2
Median	167,860.0	30,771.6	4,648.7	29,067.6	145.8	3,531.3	0.0	6,015.1	1,478.6	0.0
S.D.	6934054.8	4207402.5	442773.3	3751583.5	292094.2	326573.4	4232.0	983187.3	1910458.6	57179.9
C.V.	221.9	239.4	200.2	326.4	400.0	252.1	274.3	344.2	431.9	394.3
Minimum	797.0	0.0	0.0	102.3	0.0	0.0	0.0	0.0	0.0	0.0
Maximum	37,860,107.5	19,803,776.0	2,289,455.5	22,621,910.8	2,124,151.0	2,053,126.7	19,886.9	7,472,198.6	14,463,984.0	313,989.0

Note: Values are in thousands of new pesos.

Source: INEGI: 1993 *Censos Economicos*.

Map 9.5
Proportion of Revenues Textiles, Clothing, and Leather Industries, 1993

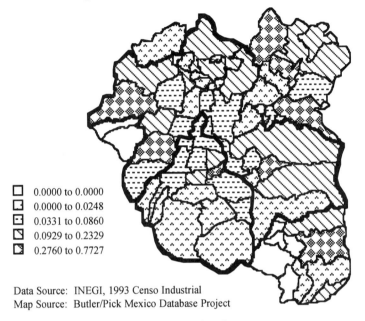

- ☐ 0.0000 to 0.0000
- ☐ 0.0000 to 0.0248
- ⊡ 0.0331 to 0.0860
- ◼ 0.0929 to 0.2329
- ◼ 0.2760 to 0.7727

Data Source: INEGI, 1993 Censo Industrial
Map Source: Butler/Pick Mexico Database Project

Map 9.6
Proportion of Revenues Food, Drink, and Tobacco Industries, 1993

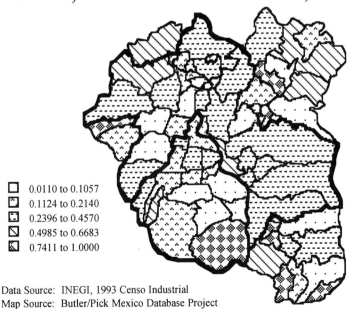

- ☐ 0.0110 to 0.1057
- ⊡ 0.1124 to 0.2140
- ⊡ 0.2396 to 0.4570
- ◼ 0.4985 to 0.6683
- ◼ 0.7411 to 1.0000

Data Source: INEGI, 1993 Censo Industrial
Map Source: Butler/Pick Mexico Database Project

Map 9.7
Proportion of Revenues Paper, Printing, and Publishing Industries, 1993

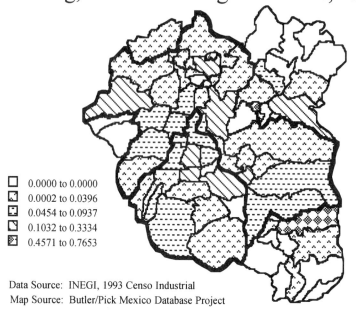

□ 0.0000 to 0.0000
▨ 0.0002 to 0.0396
▣ 0.0454 to 0.0937
◩ 0.1032 to 0.3334
▩ 0.4571 to 0.7653

Data Source: INEGI, 1993 Censo Industrial
Map Source: Butler/Pick Mexico Database Project

Commerce

Commerce accounted for about half of the total revenues measured by the 1993 economic census for the Federal District (INEGI, 1995). As seen in Map 9.8 and Table 9.6, Megacity commerce revenues are concentrated in only a few central delegations. In particular, one sixth of commerce revenues are in the single delegation of Cuauhtemoc, and 13 percent are in Miguel Hidalgo. The next two most important commercial areas, together accounting for another 19 percent, are the central delegations of Benito Juarez and Iztapalapa (see Figure 9.3). Together, these delegations overlap with the modern central business district, and are expected from the theory of Latin American cities (Griffin and Ford, 1983). The hyper-concentration of commerce in the geographically small CBD is consistent with this theory and reinforces the idea that commerce is an older activity that has remained more firmly rooted historically in the center, rather than moving northwards. In particular, the northern municipios of Azcapotzalco and Tlalnepantla that were major ones for industry are much less so for commerce. This may stem from the lack of marketing appeal and conveniences in these areas. The semi-urban periphery is notably low in raw commerce revenues.

For commerce revenues, four central delegations have a disproportionate importance not only for the Megacity but for the nation. As evident in Table 9.7, Cuauhtemoc, Miguel Hidalgo, Benito Juarez and Iztapalapa account for about a fifth of revenues for the nation. This exceeds the average level for dominant delegations/municipios for the industry dimensions, except for paper/printing/publishing, which had about half in four populous delegations and municipios.

Map 9.9 shows the proportion of commerce revenues that are wholesale. The corresponding map for composition retail commerce is not shown, since the proportions are exactly the inverse of wholesale. Considerable variation in wholesale/retail proportions is evident in a CV of 239. Wholesale commerce is more prevalent in the Federal District, and northwestern and eastern parts of the State of Mexico. In the Federal District, Milpa Alta is an exception with a proportion wholesale of only eight percent. Milpa Alta has often in this volume revealed characteristics transitional between the city center and the semi-urban southwest, and this is another instance. The northeastern and southeastern semi-urban fringes have lower wholesale proportions, as well as a far northern zone encompassing Jaltenco, Nextlalpan, Teoloyucan, and Melchor Ocampo. It is not surprising that wholesale activity is very low in these non-populous outlying areas. They do not have proximity to the city's central locus of business activity. They are too outlying to conveniently serve and supply the whole metropolis.

In summary, the commerce sector is huge and overall highly concentrated in the traditional central business district. Within commerce, there are large distributional differences between wholesale and retail, with wholesale more in the center, the northwest and east, and retail more concentrated elsewhere. The patterns are consistent with theoretical and historical trends in Mexico City.

Map 9.8
Commerce Sector Revenues, 1993

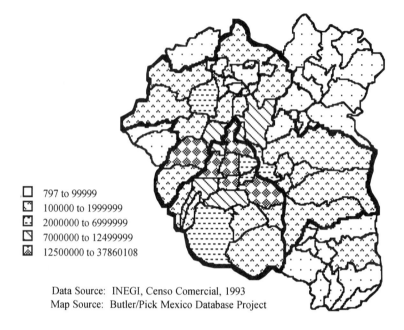

797 to 99999
100000 to 1999999
2000000 to 6999999
7000000 to 12499999
12500000 to 37860108

Data Source: INEGI, Censo Comercial, 1993
Map Source: Butler/Pick Mexico Database Project

Figure 9.3 Mexico City Commerce Sector Revenues. 1993
(in millions of new pesos)

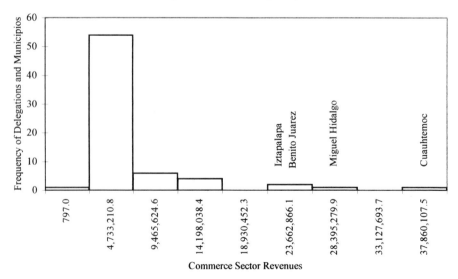

Source: INEGI: 1993 Mexican Economic Census

Map 9.9
Proportion Wholesale of Commerce Revenues, 1993

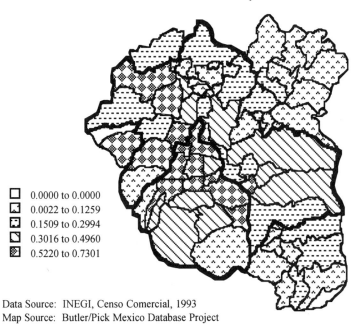

☐ 0.0000 to 0.0000
◪ 0.0022 to 0.1259
▣ 0.1509 to 0.2994
◨ 0.3016 to 0.4960
▨ 0.5220 to 0.7301

Data Source: INEGI, Censo Comercial, 1993
Map Source: Butler/Pick Mexico Database Project

Table 9.7 Comparison of Federal District with Rest of Nation on Industry and Commerce Indicators, 1993

	Federal District	Rest of Nation	Nation	National Percent in Federal District	Dominating Zones in Megacity	National Percent in Dominant Zones
Industry - Total	84,228	438,302	522,530	16	Tlalnepantla, Azcapotzalco, Miguel Hidalgo, Naucalpan	12
Basic Metals	2,004	29,414	31,418	6	Azcapotzalco	7
Metal Production, Mach.	18,714	117,338	136,052	14	Miguel Hidalgo, Tlalnepantla	9
Chemical / Petrochemical	22,485	102,325	124,810	18	Miguel Hidalgo, Naucalpan, Azcapotzalco, Tlalnepantla, Ecatepec	13
Textiles, Clothing	8,382	30,707	39,089	21	Naucalpan, Iztacalco	14
Food, Drink, Tobacco	18,783	107,190	125,973	15	Azcapotzalco	7
Paper, Printing, Pub.	1,533	7,810	9,343	16	Ecatepec, Cuauhtemoc, Iztapalapa, Tlalnepantla	54
Commerce - Total	167,599	330,682	498,281	34	Cuauhtemoc, Miguel Hidalgo, Benito Juarez, Iztapalapa	21
Wholesale	98,464	138,748	237,212	42	Cuauhtemoc, Miguel Hidalgo, Benito Juarez, Iztapalapa	28
Retail	69,136	191,932	261,068	26	Cuauhtemoc, Miguel Hidalgo, Benito Juarez, Iztapalapa	15
Average				21		18

Note: all figures are in millions of new pesos

Source: INEGI: *1994 Censos Economicos*

Communications and Services

Communications revenues are extremely centralized. In fact, 69 percent of communications revenues are in Cuauhtemoc; another 24 percent in Miguel Hidalgo; and five percent in Benito Juarez. The other zones of the city account for only 2 percent of communications revenues. The amount of communications revenues, in new pesos, are: Cuauhtemoc - 7,427.7 million; Miguel Hidalgo - 2,558.9 million; and Benito Juarez - 522.3 million. Thus, a large proportion of national communications revenues is located in the three central delegations. The Federal District accounts for 32.6 percent of national communications revenues and the three aforementioned delegations account for 31.9 percent on a national basis. Communications are extremely concentrated in the center. The core of the Federal District is the national communications revenue center, which is consistent with the core as the national locus of the federal government, large corporations, and high end services and professions.

It is clear that the CBD is dominant in communications. The high concentration corresponds to Sassen's theory of megacities in advanced nations, in which high level services, financial power, and executive decision-making resides in the city center. Communications supports, and is linked to each of these key theoretical characteristics.

The service sector also is highly centralized in an already familiar pattern. As seen in Map 9.10, total services are highly localized in the traditional city center. Two delegations, Cuauhtemoc and Miguel Hidalgo, account for 54 percent of the city's service sector revenues. Table 9.8 reveals that, these two delegations account for one quarter of national service revenues, which emphasizes the importance of the Federal District and its four central delegations for services nationwide. About half of the nation's service revenues are in the Federal District. For individual service subsectors, one to four dominant delegations account for a sixth to over half of service revenues. Dominant delegations tend to be those of the historical city center. The theory of the Latin American city (Griffin and Ford, 1983) which identifies a wealthy and dominant central business district, seems well supported by the service sector. At the same time, elsewhere in this book depopulation of the city center is reported and the industrial sector is seen to have moved somewhat northwards. These shifts outward have not affected the service sector.

The central and northern Federal District and adjoining northern municipios are high in total service revenues, whereas the outlying semi-urban flanks are low (see Map 9.10). The northeast and western semi-urban flanks are very low; the southeast flank is low but substantially higher than the other flanks. The pattern is a familiar one seen earlier for commerce, indeed there is a high correlation between commerce and services (r = 0.71).

Within services, there are three major business components, real estate, restaurants/hotels/leisure and professional/technical services. As seen in Table 9.8, all three subsectors are centrally concentrated in terms of total revenues. Leisure is more concentrated than restaurants and hotels. On a national basis, about two fifths of the nation's professional and technical services are located in the two central and traditional delegations of Miguel Hidalgo and Cuauhtemoc. This further affirms Sassen's hypothesis that megacities have strong concentrations of financial and professional services. These services support both the major national and multinational corporations and the federal government both headquartered in or near these delegations.

Although raw service revenues are greatly concentrated in the city center, the composition of services is more spread out in the surrounding and peripheral sections reflecting differences in the economy and business throughout the city. Service composition is measured, for a particular zone, by the ratio of zonal revenues for a service sector to the total service revenues in the zone. However, in proportion to the total service sector, they differ considerably. As seen in Map 9.11, real estate revenues are higher in the Federal District and northern surrounding municipios as well as in the more dispersed municipios of Nicolas Romero and Tlalmanalco. Those outlying municipios have enlarged business interests and activities in real estate.

Revenue generation by restaurants, hotels, and leisure services is spread out across the Megacity (see Map 9.12). This implies that certain zones, regardless of population or economic size, have touristic/leisure aspects. An example is San Martin de los Piramides, with 37 percent hotels/restaurants/leisure revenue composition, i.e. about 20 percent above the mean. Its high value is tied to attractions of its famous Aztec pyramids. A contrast is Azcapotzalco, which is known as an industrial area, with moderate crime and lack of tourist/leisure sites and concessions. Its 14 percent proportion is about 16 percent below the mean. Chalco compositionally is equivalent to the mean at 30 percent. However its annual revenues for this subsector is only 29.2 million pesos. For this "slum" area, few services are provided in general. In revenues, the Federal District has a low to moderate proportion in this subsector, whereas the southeastern Federal District is high. The city center is still highest in total restaurant/hotel/leisure revenues. Likewise other specific delegations or municipios have qualities that either encourage of discourage tourism or leisure.

Mexico City is the financial, corporate, and governmental center of Mexico. It is expected to have major concentrations of high end services to support intensive corporate/governmental activities. This corresponds to Sassen's contention that megacities in advanced nations increasingly relegate to outlying areas manufacturing and even low level services but retain high level services. One indicator here is finance, securities and insurance service revenues.

For nearly all financial indicators, Mexico City dominates the nation. Several are shown in Table 9.9. It is clear that the Federal District generally accounts for over fifty percent of national financial assets and transactions. By contrast, the Federal District constitutes only about twelve percent of the national population. Financial indicators that predominate in the Federal District are currency exchanges and development bank loans. On other hand, the insurance industry is less centralized, although it is still about forty percent in the Federal District.

Sassen (1991) has pointed to the distinguishing role of advanced megacities as world financial centers. Although Mexico City is not classified as a world financial center, it dominates the nation and is also one of the major financial centers in Latin America. It seems to approach Sassen's criteria by its great hemispheric importance, while even falling short of being a world center. Attainment of that status would depend on very large future growth in the Mexican economy.

Given the Federal District's financial dominance, it is not surprising that financial services predominate there. As seen in Map 9.13, the services are even more concentrated within the Federal District. Eighty two percent of the Megacity's services are in Miguel Hidalgo, Cuauhtemoc, and Alvaro Obregon. In fact as seen in Table 9.9, 58 percent of the nation's financial services are in these three delegations, i.e. in a physical area about seven miles in either direction. Sassen (1991) also pointed to this type of financial hyper-concentration for advanced megacities, although she did not analyze the data spatially.

In service composition, professional, technical, and specialized services appear more evenly across the city (see Map 9.14). Although the Federal District and northern surrounding municipios have the highest proportions of professional/technical services, they are also high in selected peripheral municipios. This implies that professional/technical services are located both in peripheral parts of the Megacity and in the economic engine – the city center. Although generally the southwest fringe area is low in these services, Amecameca is an exception with a very high proportion of professional/technical services. Poorer areas closer to the central city including Chalco, Milpa Alta, and Ixtapaluca have moderate to low proportions of professional/technical services, which is corresponds to their lower educational levels and lack of sophisticated businesses.

Map 9.10
Service Sector Revenues, 1993
(in Thousands of Pesos)

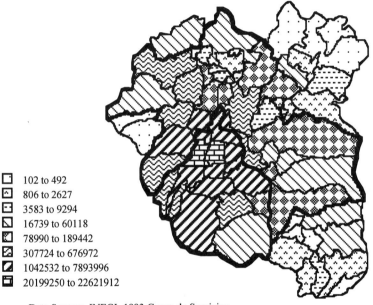

- 102 to 492
- 806 to 2627
- 3583 to 9294
- 16739 to 60118
- 78990 to 189442
- 307724 to 676972
- 1042532 to 7893996
- 20199250 to 22621912

Data Source: INEGI, 1993 Censo de Servicios
Map Source: Butler/Pick Mexico Database Project

Table 9.8 Comparison of Federal District with Rest of Nation on Service Indicators, 1993

	Federal District	Rest of Nation	Nation	National Percent in Federal District	Dominating Zones in Megacity	National Percent in Dominant Zones
Services - Total	71,465	93,412	164,877	43	Cuauhtemoc, Miguel Hidalgo	26
Real Estate	4,729	5,941	10,670	44	Miguel Hidalgo	20
Restaurants, Hotels	9,013	24,410	33,423	27	Cuauhtemoc, Miguel Hidalgo, Benito Juarez	17
Leisure	8,804	5,623	14,427	61	Cuauhtemoc	31
Finance / Insurance	998	405	1,403	71	Cuauhtemoc, Miguel Hidalgo, Alvaro Obregon	58
Professional / Technical	28,921	19,654	48,575	60	Cuauhtemoc, Miguel Hidalgo	42
Third Sector	7,454	13,524	20,978	36	Cuauhtemoc, Miguel Hidalgo, Benito Juarez, Alvaro Obregon	24
Scientific Research in Private Sector	88	108	196	45	Benito Juarez, Iztacalco, Alvaro Obregon, Miguel Hidalgo	33
Average				48		31

Note: all figures are in millions of new pesos
Source: INEGI: 1994 *Censos Economicos*

Table 9.9 Comparison of Federal District with Rest of Nation on Financial Indicators, 1993

Financial Indicators	Federal District	Rest of Nation	Nation	Percent in Federal District
Development Bank Income	434	2,075	2,509	17
Development Bank Loans	113,261	24,968	138,229	82
Financial Funds and Trusts Income	604	700	1,304	46
Financial Funds and Trusts Loans	39,595	16,860	56,455	70
Multiple Bank Income	12,971	7,327	20,298	64
Multiple Bank Loans	201,309	190,714	392,023	51
Currency Exchange Houses Income	14,410	1,779	16,189	89
Securities Institution Personnel	1,437	890	2,327	62
Securities Institution Income	393	408	801	49
Insurance Personnel	8,352	13,076	21,428	39
Insurance Income	7,773	9,833	17,606	44
Average				56

Note: all figures are in millions of new pesos
Source: INEGI: 1994 Censos Economicos

Map 9.11
Proportion of Real Estate
Revenues, 1993

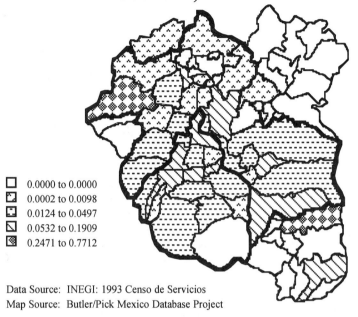

☐ 0.0000 to 0.0000
▨ 0.0002 to 0.0098
▨ 0.0124 to 0.0497
▧ 0.0532 to 0.1909
▦ 0.2471 to 0.7712

Data Source: INEGI: 1993 Censo de Servicios
Map Source: Butler/Pick Mexico Database Project

Map 9.12
Proportion of Restaurants, Hotels,
and Leisure Services Revenues, 1993

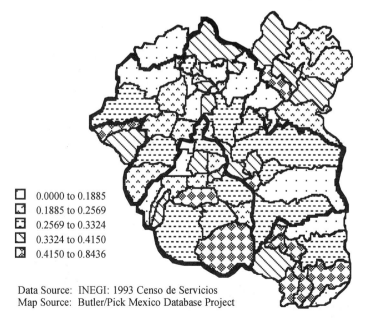

☐ 0.0000 to 0.1885
▨ 0.1885 to 0.2569
▨ 0.2569 to 0.3324
▧ 0.3324 to 0.4150
▦ 0.4150 to 0.8436

Data Source: INEGI: 1993 Censo de Servicios
Map Source: Butler/Pick Mexico Database Project

280

Map 9.13

Finance, Securities, and Insurance Revenues Relative to Entire Service Sector, 1993

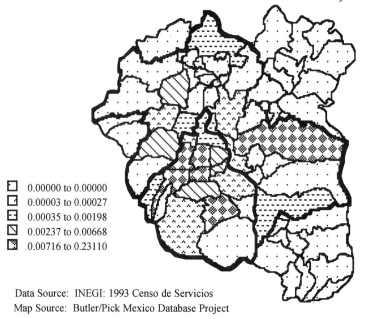

0.00000 to 0.00000
0.00003 to 0.00027
0.00035 to 0.00198
0.00237 to 0.00668
0.00716 to 0.23110

Data Source: INEGI: 1993 Censo de Servicios
Map Source: Butler/Pick Mexico Database Project

Map 9.14

Professional, Technical and Specialized Services Relative to Entire Service Sector, 1993

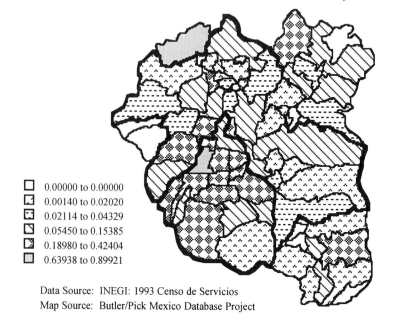

0.00000 to 0.00000
0.00140 to 0.02020
0.02114 to 0.04329
0.05450 to 0.15385
0.18980 to 0.42404
0.63938 to 0.89921

Data Source: INEGI: 1993 Censo de Servicios
Map Source: Butler/Pick Mexico Database Project

Private Education, Medical Services, and the Third Sector

The private educational/medical services and the third, i.e. non-profit, sector are of small size in Mexico City. They constituted about two percent of combined economic revenues in the 1993 economic census. These revenues are lower than the United States, for which these sectors are about four percent of national income (Wiesbrod, 1989). As in the United States, there are more workers involved than revenues would indicate, approximately five to eight percent (Weisbrod, 1989). In Mexico City, workers in these sectors comprise seven percent of the workforce. There is also a higher percent of establishments, in particular 5.5 percent. The sector is characterized by more lower paid workers and with many establishments of smaller revenue size.

Private education/private medical services/third sector continues the pattern of central concentration, with 56 percent of this sector's revenues located in Miguel Hidalgo, Cuauhtemoc, Benito Juarez, and Alvaro Obregon. About a quarter are located in a single delegation, Cuauhtemoc. On a national basis, there is very high concentration of this sector in a few delegations of the Federal District, although the concentration is lower than for financial services and professional/technical services. Nonetheless, one quarter of third sector revenues are in the four delegations.

In service composition, these sectors vary greatly in location throughout Mexico City. This includes the location of educational institutions, private health facilities, research organizations, and numerous other kinds of nonprofit organizations.

An important component of this sector is scientific research services provided to the private sector. Private scientific research is an indicator of a more advanced economy, i.e. scientific R&D is associated with high technology companies and products. Although this sector is overall quite small (see Table 9.8), scientific research services indicate the modernity of the Mexican economy including on a worldwide competitive basis. Private scientific research can be monitored in the future in Mexico City to indicate technology advancement and change.

The spatial pattern for scientific research revenues reflects a high concentration in the historical city center (see Map 9.15), higher than for the service sector as a whole. Iztacalco is surprisingly high accounting for one sixth of the Megacity's scientific research services. This may be due to the location of technological universities in or near this zone. Benito Juarez is also very high, which may be due to the location of many federal government agencies and offices .

Map 9.15
Scientific Research Revenues
In the Private Sector, 1993
(in Thousands of Pesos)

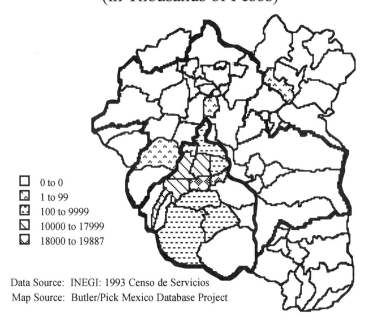

□ 0 to 0
▨ 1 to 99
▣ 100 to 9999
▨ 10000 to 17999
▨ 18000 to 19887

Data Source: INEGI: 1993 Censo de Servicios
Map Source: Butler/Pick Mexico Database Project

Economic Variable Correlations

Prior chapter sections underscored consistency in centralization of the Megacity economy and its subsectors. This consistency is confirmed in strong positive correlations among gross revenue variables examined in this chapter. As seen in summary Table 9.10, all economic revenue variables are strongly correlated with each other, with the exception of basic metals manufacturing. It tends to be correlated with other manufacturing and commerce dimensions, rather than service. The reason is that basic metal manufacturing is not centered in the traditional city center but rather at the northern tip of the Federal District and further north into the State of Mexico. It has low or zero levels in the CBD. Because services are centered in the traditional business district, there is reduced association. Since basic metal production tends to be environmentally polluting, fortunately it is located outside of the populous central business district.

Compared to gross revenues, revenue composition variables have substantially reduced correlations. Of 50 pairs of variables, seventeen were significantly correlated and are summarized in Table 9.11. Significant associations were for the food sector, in particular between food and metal production/machinery ($r = -0.41$), chemicals/petrochemicals ($r = -0.40$) and paper/printing /publishing ($r = -0.28$). Other significant associations were for the wholesale sector and chemical/petrochemical sectors. Several strong retail correlations exist, in particular, retail composition is inversely associated with the composition of chemical/petrochemical, basic metals, and automotive services. Thus retail services are located away from sources of pollution, noise, and visual pollution associated with the latter three sectors. Wholesale composition's strong correlation with professional technical composition may be due to differences in the areal patterns on the city periphery, for which municipios with high wholesale also have high professional/technical. Chemical/petrochemical revenue composition is associated with financial services, professional/technical services, scientific research services, and wholesale commerce. The latter three service sectors support the chemical/petrochemical industry. The positive effect with finance may be an artifact. There is an opposite effect with the food industry. This may stem from differences in location of the chemical/petrochemical and food industries especially in the periphery.

The correlation matrix of economic revenue variables and overall cluster variables reveals strong correlations for most cluster variables. Since economic revenue variables have a spatial continuum from high in the center to low in the periphery, associations are expected for overall cluster variables that have similar center-to-periphery patterns. Correlations are strongly negative for housing variables. This is because housing quality, ranges center-to-periphery from high to low. Overall cluster dimensions not having much correlation with economic revenue variables are relative population growth, inmigration, unemployment, owners/employers/salaried, free union, and indigenous language speaking. These dimensions were shown earlier to lack a center-to-periphery continuum.

Table 9.10 Correlations of Economic Gross Revenue Variables

Economic Revenue Variable	Number of Statistically Significant (p = 0.05) Correlations with Economic Revenue Variables	Non-Significant Correlations for Economic Revenue Variables
TOTAL INDUSTRIAL SECTOR	16	
Chemical / Petrochemical	16	
Food / Drink / Tobacco	16	
Paper / Printing / Publishing	16	
TOTAL COMMERCIAL SECTOR	16	
Wholesale	16	
Metal Production / Machinery / Equipment	15	
TOTAL SERVICE SECTOR	15	Basic Metals
Real Estate	15	Basic Metals
Restaurants / Hotels /Leisure	15	Basic Metals
Professional / Technical	15	Basic Metals
Private Education / Medical Services / Third Sector	15	Basic Metals
Finance / Insurance	14	Basic Metals, Textiles / Clothing / Leather
Textiles / Clothing / Leather	13	Basic Metals, Finance / Insurance, Private Scientific Research
Private Scientific Research	13	Food / Drink / Tobacco, Basic Metals, Metal Production / Machinery / Equipment
Basic Metals	9	Textiles / Clothing / Leather, Real Estate, Restaurants / Hotels / Leisure, Private Scientific Research, Private Education / Medical Services / Third Sector, Finance / Insurance, Professional/Technical

Table 9.11 Correlations of Economic Revenue Composition Variables

	Metal Production	Machinery	Chemical and Petrochemical	Textile, Clothing and Leather	Food, Drink, and Tobacco	Paper, Printing and Publishing	Wholesale	Real Estate	Restaurant, Hotels and Leisure	Finance and Insurance	Professional and Technical	Private Education
Machinery	-.055											
Chemical and Petrochemical	-.048	-.128										
Textile, Clothing and Leather	-.129	-.213	-.213									
Food, Drink, and Tobacco	-.138	-.414***	-.398***	-.213								
Paper, Printing and Publishing	-.048	-.167	.070	.071	-.280*							
Wholesale	.323**	.135	.252*	-.099	-.320**	.163						
Real Estate	-.049	-.091	-.045	.054	-.199	.734***	.146					
Restaurant, Hotels and Leisure	-.038	-.123	-.150	-.092	.256*	-.249*	-.267*	-.149				
Finance and Insurance	-.040	-.088	.490***	-.078	-.171	-.016	.092	.000	-.011			
Professional and Technical	-.022	.018	.255*	-.001	-.176	.033	.457***	.023	-.264*	.063		
Private Education	-.088	-.042	-.058	.159	-.103	-.098	-.048	-.110	-.113	.049	-.089	
Private Scientific Research	-.035	-.081	.393***	.008	-.195	.037	.240*	.053	.036	.725***	.122	-.028

Note: Significance Levels
* .05
** .01
*** .001

Note: all variables represent the proportion of the economic variable to the economic sector, i.e. industry, commerce, or service sector.

Economic Cluster Analysis

An economic cluster analysis portrays the larger spatial patterns in the metropolis. The economic cluster analysis is based on the following economic variables from the overall cluster analysis: metal production and machinery composition, wholesale commerce composition, professional/technical/specialized service composition, economic activity, unemployment, and owners/employers/salaried. The first three dimensions were discussed in this chapter and the latter three were discussed in Chapters 5, 8, and 10. Economic clusters are shown in Map 9.16. The clusters means are summarized in Table 9.12.

A central economic core is apparent consisting of 14 delegations and municipios in clusters 1 and 2. This central core contains over half of the metropolitan population. As seen earlier in the chapter, it contains the preponderance of economic production for the Megacity, whether in industry, commerce, or services. Cluster 1 comprises the oldest parts of the city including the traditional city center of Benito Juarez and Cuauhtemoc. It extends south into Coyoacan and Tlalpan which are less important in economic production due in part to their substantially residential nature. In the next chapter, it will be seen that Coyoacan and Tlalpan group with the city center in high economic activity and low unemployment (see Maps 10.1 and 10.5). Cluster 1 also contains the populous municipio of Ecatepec. Cluster 2 contains seven delegations and municipios surrounding Cluster 1 that include newer industrial areas such as Naucalpan and Tlalnepantla. Clusters 1 and 2 have high economic activity, low unemployment, high proportion of owners/employers/salaried, and high professional/technical composition. They differ among themselves in reduced level of wholesale, i.e. greater retail, presence in the inner core of Cluster 1 and the high level of metal products/machinery in the outer core. This distinction has already been made in this chapter, i.e. that the traditional inner core has higher retail and services, while the outer core to the north mostly is an industrial center.

Surrounding the economic core in a semi-circular ring extending from the northwest to the east are three clusters, Clusters 3, 4, and 5. They contain a little over a third of the metropolitan population. They include a mixture of socioeconomic environments, ranging from areas with rapid population growth and the beginnings of industry growth such as Tepotzotlan to areas of high crime and poor housing such as Chalco. These three clusters are close to the Megacity average on economic activity, unemployment, and owners/employers/salaried, but differ on the economic revenue variables.

Cluster 3 has high wholesale composition, moderate metal products/machinery composition, and low professional/technical. Cluster 4 is located in areas with strong commerce including significant wholesale. Wholesale is closer to average for Clusters 5. Cluster 4 has high metal products/machinery. Cluster 5 is average to low in composition for all three economic sectors. Cluster 5 may be characterized as a zone that is non-industrial with a moderate levels of professional/technical. It is located away from the current economic centers.

Cluster 6 is average in economic activity, unemployment, and owners / employers / salaried. Its commercial composition is strongly retail, while it has very low professional/technical. Its municipios vary in their level of prosperity. Perhaps the most distinguishing feature of cluster 6 is its very high composition of metal products and machinery revenues. Although the cluster includes the highest composition for metal products/machinery, it is dwarfed in gross metal products/machinery revenues by the central zones. Cluster 7 consists of the northern unique municipio of Huehuetoca. It has an extremely high composition of professional/technical revenues. This is unique in the periphery and calls for research exploration.

Cluster 9 is nearly entirely located predominantly in the semi-urban flanks in the northeast, southeast and west. It also includes Milpa Alta and two tiny municipios of Chiautla and Chiconcuac This cluster reflects economic disadvantaged status including low economic activity, high unemployment, very low owners/employers/salaried, and low professional/technical composition. Cluster 8 is partly located as a gradated transition between the semi-urban fringe and more central sections, as well as a less developed area in the far north in the State of Mexico. This cluster resembles Cluster 9 in its economic deprivation but it has about 27 percent higher owners/employers/salaried than Cluster 9 and compositional differences in wholesale and metal products/machinery.

Broadly speaking, the economic cluster analysis points to the presence of an urban core with a surrounding ring and rural extremes. The much more prosperous center emphasizes commerce and services. There is a substantial industrial presence in the ring, and disadvantaged peripheral areas. Huehuetoca is an exceptional municipio for the periphery with very high professional/technical. It may represent an ex-urbanite professional locality that presages outward movement of highly skilled sectors in the future. Note that economic clusters are based on ratios rather than raw economic production. Clustering based on raw economic production indicators would have shown even greater differences between the core and periphery.

Map 9.16
Economic Clusters

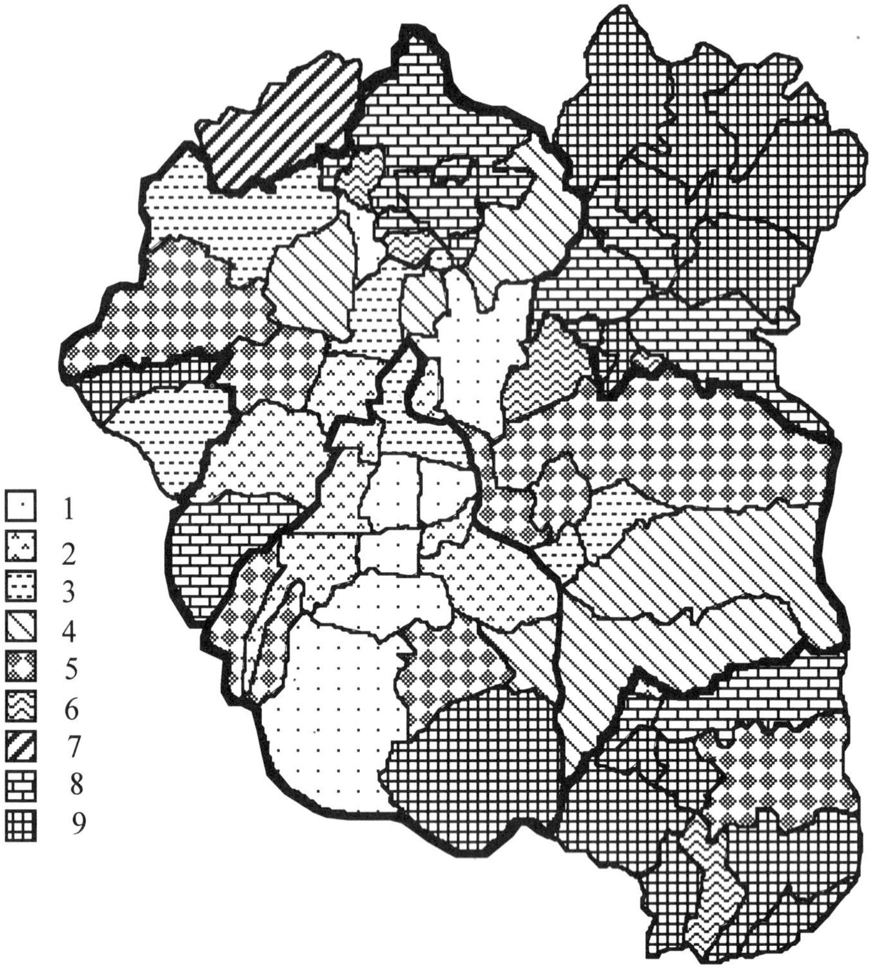

Data Source: INEGI, Population and Economic Censuses, 1990 and 1993
Map Source: Butler/Pick Mexico Database Project

Table 9.12 Economic Cluster Means

Variable	1	2	3	4	5	6	7	8	9	Mexico City
Population 1990	3,915,324	4,952,488	1,755,278	1,229,047	2,768,376	130,945	25,529	428,235	235,524	15,440,746
Economic Activity 12+	0.4792	0.4760	0.3805	0.4166	0.4359	0.3992	0.4360	0.4161	0.3919	0.4222
Unemployment	0.0161	0.0166	0.0276	0.0195	0.0195	0.0207	0.0162	0.0217	0.0220	0.0205
Owners / Employers / Salaried	0.7801	0.7941	0.7108	0.7418	0.7152	0.6117	0.6974	0.6837	0.4143	0.6531
Wholesale Revenue Composition	0.4452	0.6481	0.5491	0.3693	0.2607	0.0928	0.1797	0.0928	0.0455	0.2639
Metal Production and Machinery Composition	0.1209	0.2779	0.1989	0.4633	0.1109	0.7546	0.2551	0.0309	0.0902	0.1975
Prof./Tech./Spec. Service Composition	0.2696	0.3419	0.0430	0.0535	0.1192	0.0217	0.8992	0.0270	0.0372	0.1151

Cluster 1	Cluster 2	Cluster 3	Cluster 4	Cluster 5	Cluster 6	Cluster 7	Cluster 8	Cluster 9
Benito Juarez	Alvaro Obregon	Chicoloapan	Chalco	Amecameca	Atenco	Huehuetoca	Acolman	Atlautla
Coyoacan	Azcapotzalco	Gustavo A. Madero	Coacalco	Atizapan de Zaragoza	Ozumba		Coyotepec	Axapusco
Cuauhtemoc	Iztacalco	Jilotzingo	Cuautitlan Izcalli	Chimalhuacan	Papalotla		Huixquilucan	Ayapango
Cuautitlan	Iztapalapa	Paz, La	Ixtapaluca	Cocotitlan	Teoloyucan		Jaltenco	Chiautla
Ecatepec	Miguel Hidalgo	Tepotzotlan	Tecamac	Cuajimalpa	Tultepec		Melchor Ocampo	Chiconcuac
Tlalpan	Naucalpan	Tultitlan	Tlahuac	Magdalena Contreras			Nextlalpan	Ecatzingo
Venustiano Carranza	Tlalnepantla			Nezahualcoyotl			Temamatla	Isidro Fabela
				Nicolas Romero			Teotihuacan	Juchitepec
				Texcoco			Tepetlaoxtoc	Milpa Alta
				Xochimilco			Tezoyuca	Nopaltepec
							Tlalmanalco	Otumba
							Zumpango	San Martin de las P.
								Temascalapa
								Tenango del Aire
								Tepetlixpa

Conclusions

Relative to the nation, the economy of Mexico City is highly prosperous and has remarkable spatial differences. The economy grew and developed greatly in the twentieth century, enlarged from a nineteenth century economy based on foods and textiles. Today, the modern and varied economy has leading sectors in chemicals/petrochemicals, metal products and machinery, commerce, and the service areas of professional technical and restaurants/hotels/leisure.

Mexico City leads the nation in most economic sectors. Its economic dominance exceeds its large population dominance proportion. In many sectors, Mexico City accounts for over half of the nation's economic revenues. The dominance is particularly evident in finance, financial services, professional/technical sector, and commerce.

Within the city, there is very high concentration in terms of raw revenues in three or four delegations in the old city center and several new municipios just to the north of the district. Industrial centers have moved northwards into these municipios, while the commercial and service center has remained firmly implanted in the traditional city center. Largely, the theory of Latin American cities of Griffin and Ford, which points to a dominant and highly prosperous central business district, is confirmed for Mexico City.

Extreme concentrations, both nationally and for the Megacity, of high-end financial and professional services in a few central delegations, is consistent with Sassen's theory of advanced megacities. What has not taken place yet in Sassen's terms is the dispersion of manufacturing and lower level services farther into the city's hinterland and beyond. Rather, industry has remained firmly rooted only ten or so miles from the central business district, with its corporate and governmental decision-making and attendant high level services. This economic hyper-concentration implies the need for the Mexican government to encourage de-concentration of the center's economic engine in the future. The next chapter will examine the labor force serving the city and, among other things, raise further questions about the need to de-concentrate the economy.

10

Labor Force and Labor Market

Photo courtesy of Tomas Mojarro

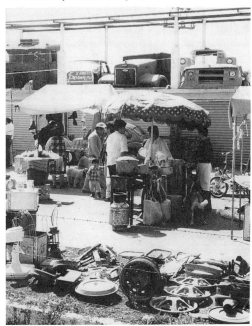

Introduction

This chapter considers the structure of the labor force and labor market in Mexico Megacity. It examines such elements as occupation, economic activity, worker concerns and settlements, and age structure and workforce projections.

The labor force is important to the metropolis because it supports the running of the national capital's economic engine. Differences in the Megacity's labor force from the rest of the nation need to be examined to understand the city's productivity. Likewise geographical patterns of labor force within the city support the spatial concentration of different industries and economic activities.

Since the previous chapter showed that the city's economy is spatially variegated and complex, we can expect that the labor force will not follow simple patterns. In considering metropolitan patterns of the labor force, it is important to recognize that the Mexican population census determines labor force and occupational characteristics by place of residence, whereas the economic censuses account for labor force/occupation by place of work. In the Megacity, work and home are often separated in space, as evidenced by the large volume of commuting that takes place each work day (Fernández-Bremauntz and Merritt, 1992). Hence spatial patterns must be carefully compared not only on characteristics but also evaluated based on the type of census.

Economic activity, occupation, employment, labor concerns and settlement, labor force age structure, and projections of future labor force are examined in this chapter. These dimensions of the labor force reveal many patterns of concentration of labor force in the central and north central parts of the Megacity, gender weighting towards certain parts of the city, higher levels of occupational attainment than for the rest of Mexico, much higher economic activity rates for females in the city center, age structural differences in the labor force, and projections of rapid increase in eligible labor force in the Megacity over the next decade.   These and many more labor force features and trends are analyzed in this chapter.

Labor Force Characteristics Correlations

Labor force variables shown in Table 10.1 are in general highly intercorrelated. As seen in Table 10.2, there are several exceptions in the two strike variables and partial exceptions for unemployment and underemployment. Legal summons to strike is uncorrelated with other labor force dimensions.   It stands out as a rather unique variable in geographic pattern with high concentrations centered in the northeast of the Megacity and low concentrations in the southeast. Strike summons settlements is strongly associated with economic activity, unemployment, and professional, technical, managerial occupation. It reflects greater settlement of labor disputes in areas that are more advanced economically with a higher quality labor force. On the other hand, it is uncorrelated with underemployment, salaried workers, and income variables. Unemployment and underemployment are generally highly correlated with other labor force variables, although less so with certain income and salaried worker attributes. This may reflect the somewhat erratic nature of employment attributes. i.e. stemming from temporary and local conditions.

Labor force variables are mostly correlated with overall cluster variables shown in Table 10.2. Several labor force dimensions with weaker associations with the set of overall cluster variables are unemployment, underemployment, legal summons to strike, and strike summons settlements.   These weaker associations shown in Table 10.2 may again stem from the temporary and local nature of employment variables and from extraneous influences such as legal, judiciary, and union conditions.

Coming at it the other way, overall cluster attributes having the weakest associations with labor force attributes are marital separation and two of the   indigenous language variables, Mixtec language and Nahautlan language. Marital separation in Mexico has not been reported in the literature as linked to employment or labor force. Likewise, Mixtec and Nahautlan language speaking attributes appear unassociated, at least in 1990, with economic activity and other economic dimensions.

Overall, labor force and related dimensions in this chapter are highly correlated with each other and somewhat less highly associated with the overall set of cluster variables. These strong correlations will sometimes be referred to in order to avoid repetitive explanations.

Table 10.1 Labor Force Variables

	Ratio of Econ. Active	Ratio of Econ. Active Males	Ratio of Econ. Active Females	Un-employ-ment	Under-employ-ment	Salaried Employees	No or Low Income	High Income*	Professional, Technical, Managerial	Legal Notice to Strike**	Strike Settlement Ratio***
Acolman	0.387	0.780	0.220	0.025	0.053	0.721	0.149	0.063	0.083	0.000	0.200
Alvaro Obregon	0.484	0.654	0.346	0.016	0.036	0.785	0.210	0.112	0.156	0.000	0.903
Amecameca	0.400	0.793	0.207	0.027	0.059	0.548	0.234	0.054	0.063	0.000	0.400
Atenco	0.376	0.803	0.197	0.019	0.047	0.623	0.175	0.045	0.056	0.000	0.000
Atizapan de Zaragoza	0.459	0.724	0.276	0.017	0.040	0.776	0.196	0.146	0.152	0.000	0.772
Atlautla	0.367	0.857	0.143	0.020	0.050	0.243	0.408	0.036	0.025	0.000	1.000
Axapusco	0.378	0.849	0.151	0.025	0.030	0.468	0.348	0.030	0.026	0.000	0.200
Ayapango	0.405	0.832	0.168	0.011	0.041	0.404	0.250	0.039	0.038	0.000	
Azcapotzalco	0.468	0.661	0.339	0.018	0.030	0.822	0.186	0.079	0.139	0.001	0.984
Benito Juarez	0.520	0.556	0.444	0.015	0.040	0.774	0.156	0.241	0.299	0.001	0.936
Chalco	0.434	0.805	0.195	0.024	0.054	0.679	0.141	0.042	0.032	0.000	0.409
Chiautla	0.406	0.774	0.226	0.021	0.062	0.563	0.219	0.053	0.054	0.000	
Chicoloapan	0.419	0.778	0.222	0.020	0.051	0.076	0.128	0.062	0.046	0.000	0.385
Chiconcuac	0.384	0.791	0.209	0.020	0.080	0.364	0.228	0.069	0.055	0.000	0.250
Chimalhuacan	0.430	0.797	0.203	0.020	0.056	0.717	0.133	0.044	0.027	0.000	0.316
Coacalco	0.334	0.954	0.046	0.018	0.038	0.805	0.163	0.110	0.153	0.000	0.456
Cocotitlan	0.380	0.781	0.219	0.016	0.056	0.656	0.165	0.041	0.078	0.000	
Coyoacan	0.478	0.632	0.368	0.015	0.034	0.795	0.170	0.163	0.215	0.000	0.922
Coyotepec	0.395	0.809	0.191	0.021	0.045	0.648	0.171	0.044	0.035	0.000	2.000
Cuajimalpa	0.468	0.703	0.297	0.018	0.029	0.778	0.208	0.086	0.120	0.000	1.130
Cuauhtemoc	0.514	0.612	0.388	0.017	0.041	0.763	0.192	0.111	0.177	0.002	0.949
Cuautitlan	0.443	0.744	0.256	0.015	0.035	0.752	0.212	0.072	0.089	0.008	0.331
Cuautitlan Izcalli	0.444	0.736	0.264	0.018	0.031	0.812	0.071	0.169	0.138	0.000	0.571
Ecatepec	0.448	0.749	0.251	0.018	0.034	0.771	0.220	0.055	0.083	0.000	0.339
Ecatzingo	0.313	0.930	0.070	0.019	0.061	0.149	0.575	0.015	0.017	0.000	
Gustavo A. Madero	0.459	0.683	0.317	0.018	0.034	0.778	0.199	0.074	0.132	0.000	0.969
Huehuetoca	0.436	0.794	0.206	0.016	0.037	0.710	0.166	0.054	0.041	0.001	0.357
Huixquilucan	0.470	0.670	0.330	0.013	0.047	0.731	0.103	0.176	0.171	0.000	0.585
Isidro Fabela	0.402	0.857	0.143	0.024	0.086	0.388	0.300	0.028	0.025	0.000	

Table 10.1 Labor Force Variables (Continued)

	Ratio of Econ. Active	Ratio of Econ. Active Males	Ratio of Econ. Active Females	Un-employ-ment	Under-employ-ment	Salaried Employees	No or Low Income	High Income*	Professional, Technical, Managerial	Legal Notice to Strike**	Strike Settlement Ratio***
Ixtapaluca	0.434	0.780	0.220	0.020	0.039	0.724	0.121	0.063	0.055	0.000	0.381
Iztacalco	0.476	0.665	0.335	0.017	0.033	0.773	0.194	0.071	0.134	0.001	0.936
Iztapalapa	0.463	0.707	0.293	0.017	0.036	0.762	0.223	0.055	0.101	0.000	0.913
Jaltenco	0.412	0.789	0.211	0.022	0.031	0.757	0.103	0.087	0.071	0.000	0.000
Jilotzingo	0.079	0.823	0.177	0.076	0.209	0.575	0.221	0.043	0.027	0.000	0.000
Juchitepec	0.405	0.843	0.157	0.028	0.033	0.343	0.229	0.033	0.032	0.000	0.000
Magdalena Contreras	0.474	0.665	0.335	0.019	0.034	0.790	0.220	0.104	0.142	0.000	0.524
Melchor Ocampo	0.411	0.794	0.206	0.014	0.028	0.700	0.114	0.062	0.056	0.000	0.400
Miguel Hidalgo	0.506	0.582	0.418	0.016	0.036	0.775	0.175	0.158	0.207	0.001	0.880
Milpa Alta	0.434	0.754	0.246	0.003	0.010	0.084	0.055	0.005	0.009	0.000	0.750
Naucalpan	0.477	0.708	0.292	0.016	0.038	0.781	0.203	0.129	0.143	0.001	0.411
Nextlalpan	0.407	0.785	0.215	0.039	0.042	0.713	0.148	0.063	0.037	0.000	0.000
Nezahualcoyotl	0.454	0.725	0.275	0.018	0.040	0.744	0.105	0.073	0.083	0.000	0.440
Nicolas Romero	0.429	0.772	0.228	0.022	0.046	0.754	0.127	0.056	0.046	0.000	0.432
Nopaltepec	0.419	0.824	0.176	0.026	0.037	0.508	0.339	0.035	0.031	0.001	0.250
Otumba	0.382	0.841	0.159	0.022	0.053	0.432	0.200	0.048	0.036	0.000	0.250
Ozumba	0.378	0.800	0.200	0.020	0.100	0.415	0.386	0.062	0.045	0.000	0.400
Papalotla	0.399	0.770	0.230	0.021	0.104	0.641	0.162	0.053	0.089	0.000	
Paz, La	0.439	0.762	0.238	0.017	0.043	0.739	0.125	0.060	0.052	0.000	0.556
San Martin de las Piramide	0.423	0.811	0.189	0.020	0.055	0.518	0.272	0.045	0.046	0.000	1.000
Tecamac	0.423	0.772	0.228	0.018	0.043	0.725	0.112	0.097	0.059	0.000	0.464
Temamatla	0.421	0.806	0.194	0.021	0.043	0.643	0.166	0.052	0.054	0.000	
Temascalapa	0.395	0.820	0.180	0.023	0.064	0.554	0.288	0.030	0.031	0.000	
Tenango del Aire	0.402	0.837	0.163	0.049	0.034	0.478	0.209	0.037	0.045	0.002	0.333
Teoloyucan	0.418	0.793	0.207	0.019	0.043	0.670	0.125	0.064	0.041	0.000	0.071
Teotihuacan	0.411	0.779	0.221	0.023	0.052	0.639	0.205	0.065	0.059	0.001	0.400
Tepetlaoxtoc	0.496	0.791	0.209	0.022	0.067	0.607	0.230	0.041	0.037	0.000	
Tepetlixpa	0.362	0.875	0.125	0.021	0.053	0.298	0.345	0.040	0.030	0.001	0.286
Tepotzotlan	0.444	0.761	0.239	0.017	0.041	0.707	0.146	0.072	0.055	0.001	0.204
Texcoco	0.405	0.752	0.248	0.020	0.051	0.676	0.171	0.089	0.099	0.000	0.429

Table 10.1 Labor Force Variables (Continued)

	Ratio of Econ. Active	Ratio of Econ. Active Males	Ratio of Econ. Active Females	Un-employ-ment	Under-employ-ment	Salaried Employees	No or Low Income	High Income*	Professional, Technical, Managerial	Legal Notice to Strike**	Strike Settlement Ratio***
Tezoyuca	0.385	0.785	0.215	0.021	0.051	0.713	0.159	0.049	0.072	0.000	0.000
Tlahuac	0.432	0.745	0.255	0.020	0.033	0.753	0.250	0.031	0.075	0.000	0.945
Tlalmanalco	0.397	0.773	0.227	0.019	0.036	0.732	0.145	0.058	0.091	0.000	0.500
Tlalnepantla	0.457	0.706	0.294	0.016	0.034	0.799	0.194	0.103	0.129	0.001	0.395
Tlalpan	0.473	0.660	0.340	0.017	0.037	0.766	0.200	0.135	0.185	0.000	0.776
Tultepec	0.425	0.783	0.217	0.023	0.038	0.739	0.114	0.082	0.061	0.000	0.133
Tultitlan	0.443	0.760	0.240	0.019	0.037	0.792	0.209	0.071	0.092	0.001	0.283
Venustiano Carranza	0.478	0.656	0.344	0.017	0.037	0.759	0.198	0.072	0.139	0.000	0.923
Xochimilco	0.461	0.691	0.309	0.018	0.043	0.726	0.227	0.070	0.128	0.000	0.806
Zumpango	0.400	0.805	0.195	0.019	0.039	0.644	0.163	0.063	0.051	0.000	0.261
Mean	0.422	0.763	0.237	0.021	0.047	0.638	0.198	0.072	0.083	0.000	0.518
Standard Deviation	0.059	0.074	0.074	0.009	0.025	0.180	0.083	0.042	0.057	0.001	0.373
CV	13.9	9.7	31.4	43.1	53.4	28.2	41.8	58.5	68.8	206.0	71.9
Minimum	0.079	0.556	0.046	0.003	0.010	0.076	0.055	0.005	0.009	0.000	0.000
Maximum	0.520	0.954	0.444	0.076	0.209	0.822	0.575	0.241	0.299	0.008	2.000

* Percent of population age 12+ earning equal to or more than 5 times minimum wage.

** Ratio of legal notices to strike in 1994 to total population in 1990.

*** Ratio of strike settlements to legal notices to strike in 1994.

Source: INEGI: 1990 Mexican Census; 1995 *Anuarios Estadisticos*

Table 10.2 Correlations Matrix of Labor Force Variables

	Ratio of Econ. Active	Ratio of Econ. Active Males	Ratio of Econ. Active Females	Unemployment	Underemployment	Salaried Employees	No Income	High Income*	Professional, Technical, Managerial	Legal Notice to Strike**
Ratio of Econ. Active Males	-.689***									
Ratio of Econ. Active Females	.689***	-1.000***								
Unemployment	-.694***	.320**	-.320**							
Underemployment	-.727***	.276*	-.276*	.681***						
Salaried Employees	.417***	-.564***	.564***	-.104	-.231					
No Income	-.288*	.360**	-.360**	.134	.244*	-.485***				
High Income*	.474***	-.693***	.693***	-.253*	-.206	.542***	-.341**			
Professional, Technical, Managerial	.550***	-.813***	.813***	-.311**	-.266*	.599***	-.236	.890***		
Legal Notice to Strike**	.154	-.177	.177	-.030	-.124	.163	.003	.148	.173	
Strike Settlement Ratio***	.422***	-.479***	.479***	-.361**	-.246*	.169	.097	.251*	.432***	-.051

Note: Significance Levels

* .05
** .01
*** .001

297

Economic Activity

Economic activity is the ratio of economically active population to the population age 12 years and older. Economic activity has grown significantly in Mexico over the past twenty five years. Figure 10.1 shows the growth in economic activity for the nation, the Federal District, and the State of Mexico between 1970 and 1990. The 1970 data are directly from the 1970 population census. However, the 1990 data are census-adjusted. The adjustment was necessary because the 1990 census data for the economically active population is regarded as too low (Garcia, 1994). Values were adjusted by referring to accurate surveys, in particular the Encuesta Nacional de Empleo (ENE) of 1989 (INEGI, 1990) and the Encuesta Nacional de Ingresos y Gastos de los Hogares (ENIGH) of 1991 (INEGI, 1993). In this section, the average of economic activity rates of ENE (1989) and ENIGH (1991) are substituted for 1990 census rates.

The national economic activity is seen to have increased from 44 percent in 1970 to 51 percent in 1990. However, the increase is due mostly to changes in female economic activity. In particular, the female economic activity rate nearly doubled from 16 percent in 1970 to 29 percent in 1990. In the same period, the male economic activity rate increased only modestly from 72 to 75 percent. Even with the gains for women, women's economic activity rate was about two fifths that for men. As seen in Figure 10.1, there are comparable changes for the Federal District and State of Mexico.

The trend of rising labor force participation of women has been evident in recent decades in many nations, developing and advanced. In the United States, for instance, female labor force participation grew by 8.7 percent for whites and 5.6 percent for blacks from 1979 to 1989 (Wetzel, 1995). By contrast, over that ten year period, U.S. male labor force participation decreased by 1.5 percent for whites and 2.9 percent for blacks (Wetzel, 1995). The average rate of U.S. female labor force participation for working ages persons in 1990 (by definition somewhat higher than "economic activity" in Mexico) was 70 percent, compared to 88 percent for men (Wetzel, 1995). Thus, in the U.S. the male-female gap in workforce participation is much smaller than in Mexico.

Economic activity rates vary more for women than men. As seen in Figure 10.1, male rates are highly comparable for the two states and the nation. On the other hand, the Federal District female rates are much higher than either the nation or the State of Mexico. This points to the crucial geographical finding that women have very high economic activity in the center of the Megacity, but less so on the periphery. Comparing overall economic activity, the rates are about 5-6 percent higher for the Federal District compared to the State of Mexico and the nation. In other words, the center of the Megacity has enhanced workforce largely due to an enlarged female participation.

The contribution of the Mexico City female workforce has been present for fifty years. As seen in Figure 10.2, the Federal District's percentage of the national female workforce was about two fifths in 1940. Although the absolute female workforce size in 1940 appears small, the Federal District led the nation in the trend toward working women. This percentage steadily dropped to a level of 17 percent in 1990, while the State of Mexico's percentage increased from 3 percent in 1970 to 12 percent in 1990. Together the two states account for about thirty percent of working women in Mexico, substantially higher than the two states' population proportion. In summary, Mexico City has higher economic activity rates than the rest of Mexico and that is particularly true for women and especially within the Federal District.

For small area analysis of economic activity, 1990 population census figures were utilized, even though they have significant undercount as pointed out above (Garcia, 1994). They are utilized rather than the improved ENE Survey and EHIGH Survey data because the latter surveys are not available for small areas. Small area maps of economic activity are nevertheless useful, if the economically active undercount can be assumed to be evenly distributed by zone. We assume this to be the case in the discussion to follow, although an evaluation of 1990 census small area undercount of economic activity in the Megacity zones has not yet been undertaken.

The average 1990 census economic activity in Mexico Megacity in 1990 was 42 percent (see Table 10.1 and Map 10.1). This is close to the national average of 43 percent. However there is considerable range of economic activity, ranging from the unique and problematical outlier of 7.9 percent for Jilotzingo to a high value of 52 percent for Benito Juarez. The value for Jilotzingo may have undercount or compilation problems. The next lowest value is 33 percent for Coacalco. If Coacalco is substituted as the low value, then this implies a range of 19 percent, or about a fifth economic activity differential. This difference is due more to variation in male than female economic activity.(see Table 12.1).

The ratio of economically active represents the proportion of one gender in the economically active population. Males constitute about three quarters of this population, compared to one quarter for females. However, there is considerable variation in ratios. For instance, as seen in Figure 10.3, the ratio of female economic activity varies from five to forty four percent. At the high end, Benito Juarez at 44 percent and Miguel Hidalgo at 42 percent approach gender parity in economic activity, while Coacalco at 5 percent and Ecatzingo at 7 percent reflect a labor force with higher gender ratio than any of the states (Pick and Butler, 1994).

The geographic patterns of economic activity reflect a geographic pattern already familiar from earlier chapters. Economic activity and female economic activity patterns closely resemble those for population, population density, social rank, and economic prosperity. On the other hand, the map of male economic activity is opposite, reflecting a pattern of reduced male economic activity in the central and southwest and high male economic activity in the broad northeast, southeast, and far west semi-urban fringes (see Maps 10.2 and 10.3).

300

Figure 10.1

Economic Activity, 1970 and 1990

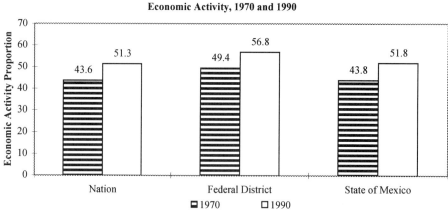

Male Economic Activity, 1970 and 1990

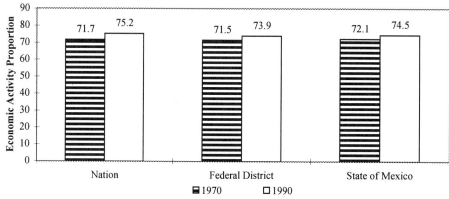

Female Economic Activity, 1970 and 1990

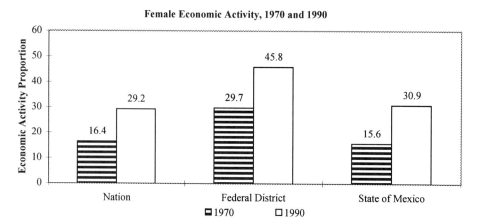

Sources: INEGI: Censuses of Population, 1970 and 1990;
Estadisticas Historicas de Mexico, 1994.
Note: The 1990 economic activity rates were adjusted from the 1990
Census based on the EHIGH Survey and the 1991 ENE Survey.

Map 10.1
Proportion of Economically
Active Total, 1990

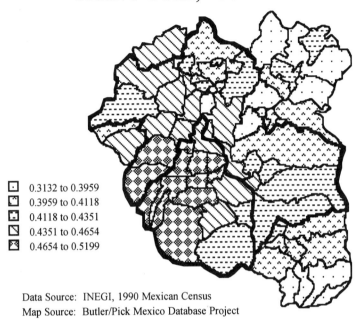

0.3132 to 0.3959
0.3959 to 0.4118
0.4118 to 0.4351
0.4351 to 0.4654
0.4654 to 0.5199

Data Source: INEGI, 1990 Mexican Census
Map Source: Butler/Pick Mexico Database Project

Map 10.2
Ratio of Economically Active Men, 1990

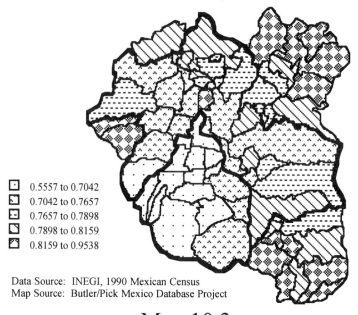

- 0.5557 to 0.7042
- 0.7042 to 0.7657
- 0.7657 to 0.7898
- 0.7898 to 0.8159
- 0.8159 to 0.9538

Data Source: INEGI, 1990 Mexican Census
Map Source: Butler/Pick Mexico Database Project

Map 10.3
Ratio of Economically Active Women, 1990

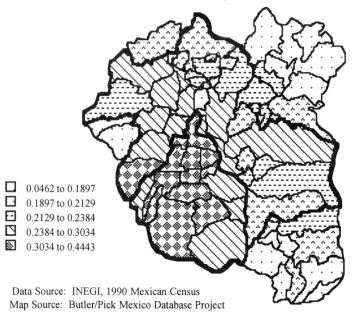

- 0.0462 to 0.1897
- 0.1897 to 0.2129
- 0.2129 to 0.2384
- 0.2384 to 0.3034
- 0.3034 to 0.4443

Data Source: INEGI, 1990 Mexican Census
Map Source: Butler/Pick Mexico Database Project

Figure 10.2 Percentage of National Female Workforce in Federal District and State of Mexico, 1940-1990

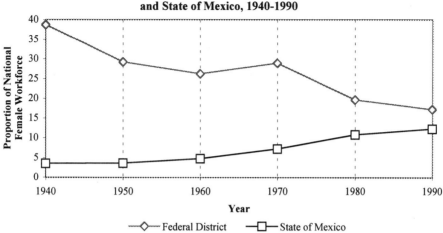

Sources: INEGI: *Estadisticas Historicas de Mexico,* 1994.
Note: The 1990 economic activity rates were adjusted from the 1990 Census based on the 1989 EHIGH Survey and the 1991 ENE Survey.

Figure 10.3 Female Economic Activity by Spatial Unit, 1990

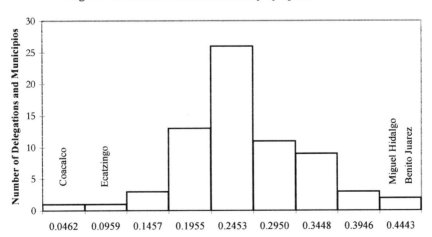

Source: INEGI: 1990 Mexican Census

Occupational Sector Structure of the Labor Force

The occupational distribution of the Mexico Megacity labor force influences the labor force vitality and productivity. Occupational sectors can be examined by selecting broad categories and comparing them for the Federal District, State of Mexico, and remainder of the nation, i.e. the other thirty states combined.   The State of Mexico is used for this comparison, since 69 percent of the State of Mexico population is located within Mexico Megacity. The comparison may be viewed as the Megacity "core," i.e. Federal District, the Megacity "periphery" and surrounding rural area, i.e. State of Mexico, and baseline of the remainder of the nation, i.e. the other 30 states.

Occupational data from the population census were aggregated into the following six categories: (1) professional/technical, (2) educational, (3) managerial/supervisory, (4) service and support, (5) agricultural, and (6) other. The specific aggregations are as follows:

Broad Occupational Category	Specific Occupational Category
Professional/Technical	Professional
	Technical
Educational	Educational workers
Managerial/Supervisory	Managers and Directors
	Supervisors/Inspectors
Service and Support	Assistants
	Office workers
	Commercial workers
	Public Service workers
	Protection/Security workers
Agricultural	Agricultural workers
Other	Art workers
	Artisans and Laborers
	Machine operators
	Transport operators
	Ambulant workers
	Domestic workers

Source: INEGI, 1992.

The occupational distribution (Table 10.3 and Figures 10.4 and 10.5) shows large differences in the agricultural sector from one percent for the Federal District to nine percent for the State of Mexico to twenty eight percent for the nation-remainder. This difference reflects the extreme urbanization of the primate city compared to the rest of the nation (Unikel, 1972; Garza, 1990). For the three higher level occupational categories, education remains steady for the three regions, while the professional/technical and managerial/supervisory categories approximately double in proportion for the Federal District versus the nation-remainder. This reflects constancy in the educational workforce, although the percentages ignore differences in educational quality. The doubling in professional/technical and managerial/supervisory is not surprising given that the core of Mexico City is the center for Mexico's professions as well as the locus of most of the nation's large corporations and federal government structure.

When the occupational structure is examined by gender (Figure 10.5 and 10.6), there are striking differences by gender and by region. Regarding female occupation, it is clear that agricultural occupations for women are virtually non existent in the Federal District and slight in the State of Mexico. In fact, in 1990 there were only 762 female agricultural workers in the Federal District and 7,101 in the State of Mexico. The dominant female occupational category is in service and support, which is about 50 percent in the Federal District and State of Mexico. The greater proportion of women in service occupations corresponds to results for the United States (Bianchi, 1995). It is remarkable that the total proportion of women in the three upper level occupations remains at about one quarter for the three regions. This reflects that those women tend to be in higher level occupations, regardless whether they are in Mexico City or not. A modest shift that occurs is that the female educational proportion increases by about three percent from "core" to nation-Remainder, while the professional/technical proportion decreases by that amount.

The pattern for men is very different. The male proportion in agricultural has a huge shift from one percent in the Federal District to 35 percent in the nation-Remainder. Compared to females, males have relatively lower proportions in service/support and higher proportions in the other category. Since the "other" category contains many blue collar jobs, this difference is not surprising and resembles the gender differences in the U.S. (Bianchi, 1995). For males, the total proportion in the three higher level occupations is double in the Federal District versus the nation-Remainder. This implies that in Mexico City the male workforce is much more skilled and educated than in the rest of the country. A further contrast with females is that males have a much lower relative proportion in educational occupations. As in the U.S., more teachers are women than men (Wetzel, 1995).

In summary, the occupational sector analysis reveals huge differences in occupational structure between Mexico City and the nation-remainder as well as between the genders. The Mexico City occupational structure is much less agricultural. Women workers, although less numerous in the workforce, have a higher proportion of higher level occupations than male workers.

Table 10.3 Occupational Distributions, 1990

	Nation			Federal District			Mexico			Nation-Remainder		
	Total	Male	Female	Total	Male	Female	Total	Male	Female	Total	Male	Female
Professional and Technical	1,398,618	892,900	505,718	313,564	197,776	115,788	179,431	117,678	61,753	905,623	577,446	328,177
Educational	874,411	346,896	527,515	118,408	40,191	78,217	91,010	33,633	57,377	664,993	273,072	391,921
Manager and Supervisor	958,109	787,010	171,099	195,505	158,068	37,437	136,768	115,406	21,362	625,836	513,536	112,300
Service and Support	7,059,078	4,632,071	2,427,007	1,248,536	748,677	499,859	1,035,395	716,202	319,193	4,775,147	3,167,192	1,607,955
Agricultural	5,173,725	4,989,771	183,954	17,187	16,425	762	242,096	234,995	7,101	4,914,442	4,738,351	176,091
Other	7,434,972	5,884,962	1,550,010	954,454	708,873	245,581	1,117,520	897,993	219,527	5,362,998	4,278,096	1,084,902
Total	23,403,413	17,882,142	5,521,271	2,884,807	1,894,371	990,436	2,860,976	2,156,855	704,121	17,657,630	13,830,916	3,826,714
Sex Ratio of Labor Force	3.2388			1.9127			3.0632			3.6143		

Source: INEGI: 1990 Mexican Census

Figure 10.4 Occupational Composition, 1990

Occupations, Federal District

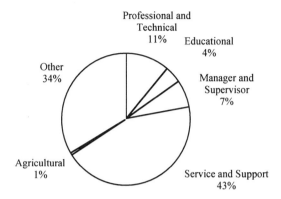

Occupations, State of Mexico

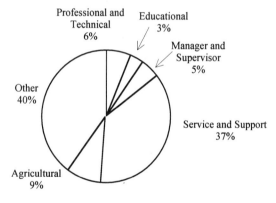

Occupations, Nation-Remainder

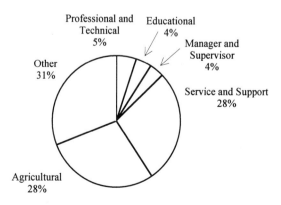

308

Figure 10.5 Male Occupational Distribution, 1990

Male Occupations, Federal District

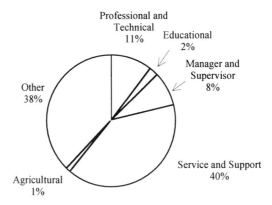

Male Occupations, State of Mexico

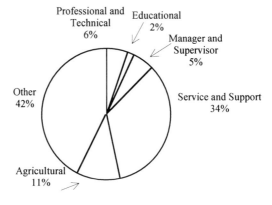

Male Occupations, Nation-Remainder

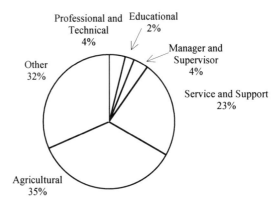

Figure 10.6 Female Occupational Distribution, 1990

Female Occupations, Federal District

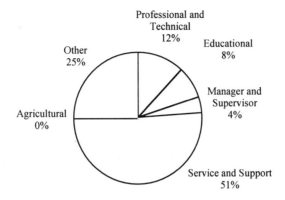

Female Occupations, State of Mexico

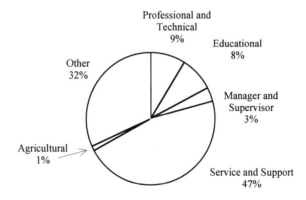

Female Occupations, Nation-Remainder

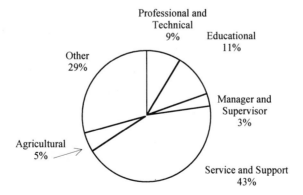

Professional, Technical, Managerial Occupations

The high level occupations of professional, technical, and managerial are given attention for several reasons. First, these occupations encompass the high end professional and financial services that Sassen (1991) are postulated as a characteristic of megacities. Second, these occupations are one of the cluster variable components of social rank discussed in Chapter 8. The attribute of professional/technical/managerial occupations encompasses the census categories professional, technical, and managers/directors. Comparing to definitions in the last sections, it includes the professional/technical category and half of the managerial/supervisory category, i.e. it excludes supervisors and inspectors.

The mean value is 8.3 percent. There is wide variation as seen in a coefficient of variation of 69. Values range from 0.9 percent for Milpa Alta in the southeastern Federal District to values of one fifth or higher for central Federal District delegations, namely Benito Juarez (29.9 percent), Coyoacan (21.5 percent), and Miguel Hidalgo (20.7 percent). The geographical distribution pattern seen in Map 10.4 reflects high percentages in the western Federal District and western neighboring municipios and very low levels generally under 3 percent in the northeast and southeast semi-urban arms and northwestern semi-urban area. There is also a very low level in Chimalhuacan of 2.7 percent (see Map 10.4).   The geographical pattern is highly correlated with and strongly resembles those of high income (r = 0.89) shown in Chapter 8 and female economic activity (r = 0.81). Economically prosperous zones tend to have high values on all three of these characteristics.

The very high levels for professional/technical/managerial workers in the central Federal District are consistent with Chapter 9's findings on high-end professional and financial services and with corporate headquarters locations in the next chapter. It further reinforces the disproportion of economic power and prosperity of the central business district.

Map 10.4
Population Professional,
Technical, Managerial, 1990

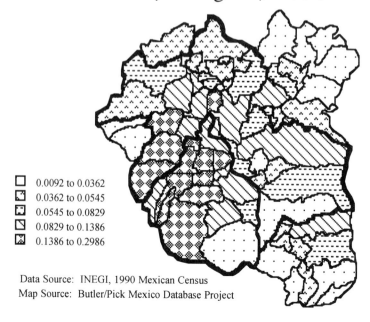

☐	0.0092 to 0.0362
▨	0.0362 to 0.0545
▨	0.0545 to 0.0829
▨	0.0829 to 0.1386
▨	0.1386 to 0.2986

Data Source: INEGI, 1990 Mexican Census
Map Source: Butler/Pick Mexico Database Project

Employment

Unemployment averages 2.1 percent in Mexico Megacity, comparable to the national average rate of 2.0 percent. As seen in Table 10.3, there is moderate variation as reflected in a CV of 43. The geographical pattern of unemployment shown in Map 10.5 reflects low unemployment in the Federal District and mixed unemployment in Counties adjoining to the north and high unemployment in the northeastern areas as well as several areas to the southwest north. The extremes of high unemployment are Jilotzingo in the far east at 7.6 percent, Tenango del Aire in the south at 4.9 percent and Nextlalpan in the far north at 3.9 percent. These areas are all semi-urban and have low population size. Their extreme values must be ascribed to local labor market conditions in 1990, since they do not otherwise have very distinctive characteristics in the cluster analyses. It is important to note in general that the seemingly low value for unemployment may reflect INEGI's particular census definition of unemployment; other alternative definitions imply a higher unemployment level.

Underemployment averaged 4.7 percent for the metropolis, which closely resembles the 1990 state mean of 4.8 percent. However, the pattern within the Megacity has considerable variation as shown in a coefficient of variation of 53. Since, the geographical pattern shown in Map 10.6 is highly similar to that for unemployment as reflected in a highly significant correlation (r = 0.68), the reader is referred to the general explanation for unemployment. The highest underemployment is again for Jilotzingo at 21 percent. In fact, Jilotzingo has 28 percent of its labor force unemployed or underemployed, i.e. more than a quarter of eligible workers.

The proportion of owners/employers/salaried employees is about 2/3 of the workforce. It is highly correlated with high income (r = 0.54) and inversely related to low income (r = -0.48). It has a broad range from 8 percent in Chicoloapan in the west to a high of 82 percent in Azcapotzalco, a small delegation in the northwest Federal District.

Map 10.5
Unemployed, 1990

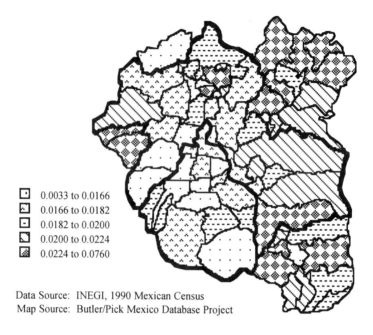

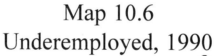

0.0033 to 0.0166
0.0166 to 0.0182
0.0182 to 0.0200
0.0200 to 0.0224
0.0224 to 0.0760

Data Source: INEGI, 1990 Mexican Census
Map Source: Butler/Pick Mexico Database Project

Map 10.6
Underemployed, 1990

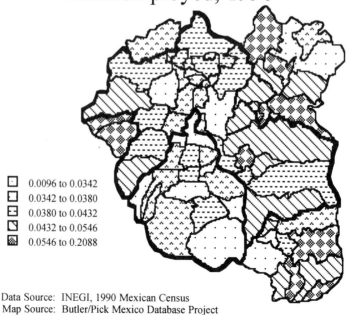

0.0096 to 0.0342
0.0342 to 0.0380
0.0380 to 0.0432
0.0432 to 0.0546
0.0546 to 0.2088

Data Source: INEGI, 1990 Mexican Census
Map Source: Butler/Pick Mexico Database Project

Labor Concerns and Settlement

Mexico has had a strong labor movement and labor laws since early in the twentieth century. Mexico's major labor union, the Federation of Mexican Workers (CTM) is a powerful federation of 11,000 unions. It has been aligned with the federal government since 1941 and under the same leader, Fidel Velazquez. The aging leader is now in his late 90s. Although there were some signs of change in the 1990s, generally the CTM/government coalition still dominates (Sheridan, 1996).

The establishment and increases in the minimum wage has been one labor milestone in Mexico. The minimum wage in the Federal District, seen in Figure 8.4, has had both crude and peso-adjusted increase since 1950. When discounted by the rise in value of the peso, it is clear that the minimum wage increased in peso value by about three times over the three decades from 1960 to 1990. However, this seeming increase is reduced to little gain, if the purchasing power of the peso is considered. A recent survey study by leading Mexican newspapers reveals the following decline in purchasing power equivalency from 1976 to 1996:

Consumption Item	1976	1983	1996
Milk (quarts)	21.2	19.8	6.4
Beans (pounds)	4.8	5.9	2.2
Tortillas (pounds)	12.4	14.7	6.1
Beef (pounds)	0.9	0.6	0.3
Sugar (pounds)	15.8	13.4	2.5
Gasoline (gallons)	11.0	4.4	2.3

Source: *Reforma*, Mexico and *El Norte*, Monterrey, Cited by Sheridan, 1996.

In Mexico City in 1990, one fifth of the workforce had no or low income (see Map 8.4). This impoverished segment of the city's workforce totaled nearly one million workers. The lack of increase over thirty years in the purchasing power of the minimum wage has limited the living standards and potential for economic and social advancement of this population.

Another element of labor concerns is labor conflicts and strikes and the potential for settling them. This discussion focuses on legal summons to strikes, strikes, and strike settlements. These reflect collective rather than individual labor concerns and protests. They are generally of greater magnitude to the businesses and organizations than individual worker concerns and grievances.

In Mexico Megacity in 1994, there were 8,295 legal notices of intent to strike (INEGI, 1995). In the same year in the city, there were 5,528 solutions to strike (INEGI, 1995). Since the solutions applied to strikes in 1994 or earlier, the two attributes refer to somewhat different strike events, but are comparable, since they each represent one year of activity. The 1994 ratio of solutions of strike notices to strikes is 2/3. The ratio of legal notices to strike in 1994 to total population in 1990 indicates city areas that are more prone to strike on a per capita basis. The geographical pattern seen in Map 10.7 shows high intensities shifted to the northwest including the northwest Federal District and bordering State of Mexico areas to the northwest. The areas of lowest strike notice proclivity are in the south and southeast, as well as most of the central-east. By far the highest rate of legal notice is for Cuautitlan to the north at 0.0077, while the next five highest in the range of 0.0019 to 0.0012 are Tenango Del Aire, Cuauhtemoc, Tlalnepantla, Tepotzotlan, and Miguel Hidalgo (see Figure 10.7). These include the traditional city core, which has large concentrations of economic and corporate decision-making might, as well as industrial areas to the northwest.

314

Map 10.7
Legal Notices to Strike, 1994;
Ratio to Total Population, 1990

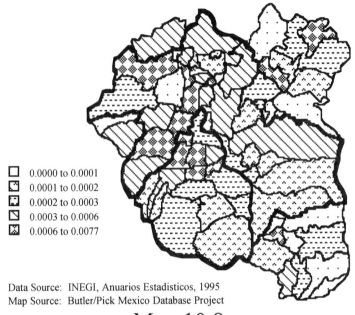

☐	0.0000 to 0.0001
▣	0.0001 to 0.0002
▣	0.0002 to 0.0003
▨	0.0003 to 0.0006
▦	0.0006 to 0.0077

Data Source: INEGI, Anuarios Estadisticos, 1995
Map Source: Butler/Pick Mexico Database Project

Map 10.8
Settlements of Notices to Strike, 1994;
Ratio of Settlements to Summons

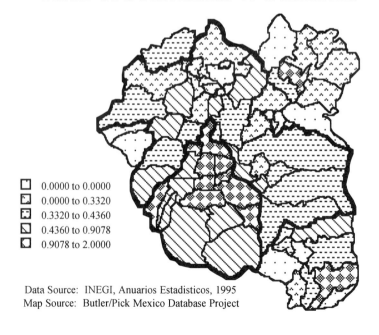

☐	0.0000 to 0.0000
▣	0.0000 to 0.3320
▣	0.3320 to 0.4360
▨	0.4360 to 0.9078
▨	0.9078 to 2.0000

Data Source: INEGI, Anuarios Estadisticos, 1995
Map Source: Butler/Pick Mexico Database Project

As seen in Figure 10.7, the distribution is skewed to resemble a Poisson distribution with a tail having a few high values. The geographical pattern is so different that it shows nearly no correlations with other labor force or overall cluster attributes. The only associations in this set are inverse ones with crowding (r = -0.31) and home ownership (r = -0.25). The lack of any economic associations is remarkable. It may point to historical legal or union reasons that certain city areas are more prone to legal notice of strike.

The ratio of strike settlements to strike notices reflects higher settlement ratios in the city center and lower ratios around the periphery (see Map 10.8). It may be that mechanisms for settlements, i.e. courts, attorneys, union officials, and negotiators/mediators are more available for strike summons in the more populous and prosperous city center and less so on the outskirts. The standard center and ring pattern leads to more associations with other attributes. Ratio of strike settlements to notices is related to economic activity (r = 0.42), unemployment (r = -0.48), professional/technical/managerial occupation (r = 0.43), population density (r = 0.44), sex ratio (r = -0.63), primary education (r = 0.45), and home ownership (r = -0.44). In other words, strike settlements, are correlated with higher economic prosperity and social rank in patterns resembling those of earlier chapters.

In 1994, 161 strikes broke out in Mexico City. This is a mere two percent of legal notices to strike, which points to the vast preponderance of potential disputes being settled or otherwise resolved short of an actual strike. As seen in Figure 10.8, strikes were about three quarters located in only eight areas in the old central city (Cuauhtemoc, Benito, Juarez, Gustavo Madero) and an adjoining areas to the north and northwest of the center (Iztapalapa, Tlalnepantla, Azcapotzalco, Ecatepec). These zones represent the economic, and industrial heart of the city. It is not surprising that actual strikes would be largely located there, since the organizations and industrial facilities being targeted by the strikes are also located there. Many strikes occurring in Mexico City are important ones having nationwide significance   because of   the importance of the Megacity for national economic and business decision-making.

Figure 10.7 Legal Notices to Strike by Spatial Unit, 1994

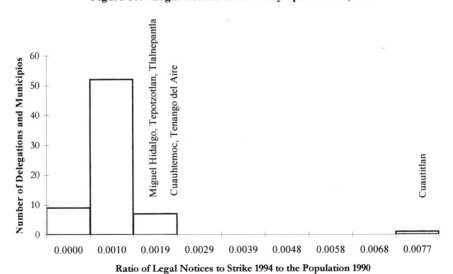

Ratio of Legal Notices to Strike 1994 to the Population 1990

Source: INEGI: *Anuarios Estadisticos* ; 1990 Mexican Census

316

Figure 10.8 Location of Strikes in Mexico City in 1994

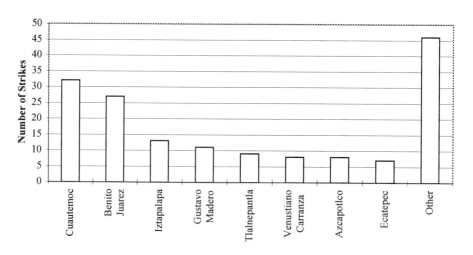

N = 161

Source: INEGI, 1995 *Anuarios Estadisticos*

Figure 10.9 Economically Active Population Total by Gender, 1970 and 1990, Combined Federal District and State of Mexico

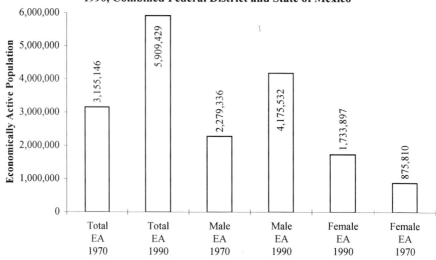

Source: INEGI, 1970 and 1990 Mexican Censuses

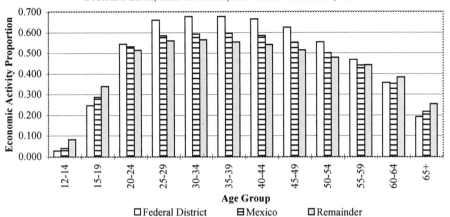

Figure 10.10 Economic Activity by Age Group
Federal District, State of Mexico, and Nation-Remainder, 1990

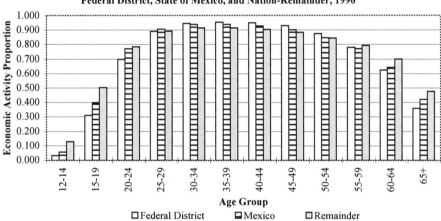

Figure 10.11 Male Economic Activity by Age Group
Federal District, State of Mexico, and Nation-Remainder, 1990

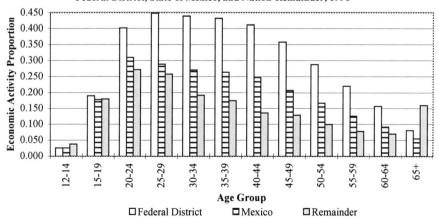

Figure 10.12 Female Economic Activity by Age Group
Federal District, State of Mexico, and Nation-Remainder, 1990

Source: INEGI, 1990 Mexican Census

Labor Force Age Structure and Labor Force Projections

The labor force has increased significantly over the last two decades and has shifted in gender and age composition. The data utilized in this chapter section are from the Mexican population census which underestimates the number of female workers, as pointed out earlier in the chapter. As seen in Figure 10.9, the total labor force approximately doubled from 1970 to 1990, with the female labor force growing more rapidly than the male labor force.

Economic activity by age and gender for the Federal District, State of Mexico, and nation-remainder is shown in Figure 10.10 and Table 10.4. Economic activity rates are highest for the Federal District for the prime working ages of 20-59, but lowest for the Federal District for ages under 19 or over 65. This reversal is also apparent when the age structure of the labor force is examined by gender in Figures 10.11 and 10.12. The reason for this reversal may be greater prevalence of educational opportunities at ages under 20 and improved retirement options for the older population.

Differences in economic activity among the Federal District, State of Mexico, and nation-remainder are particularly pronounced for women (see Figure 10.12). Differences are greatest for the ages 20-64, i.e. women born from 1925 to 1970. Those women were part of age cohorts that included large streams of migration into Mexico City. It may be that economic pressures of migration combined with more acceptance of women in the labor force led to the large differences for those age groups. For the young age group of women age 20-24 in 1990, there still is substantial difference, but it is not as pronounced as for older age groups. However, there also may be anticipated large increments of female entrance into the labor force in the Megacity, especially the urban core, as the 20-24 year age group ages, increasing the differences.

The future labor force of the Megacity may be projected based on national projections (Pick, Butler, and Gonzalez, 1992). The year 2005 projected figures for the nation were adjusted for Mexico City population by using the United Nations forecast of a percentage of population in Mexico City in year 2005 of 79.8 percent (United Nations, 1995). Doing this gives the following projection of future Mexico City labor force:

Year	Total Labor Force	Male Labor Force	Female Labor Force
1990	6,125	3,867	2,258
2005 (Series I)	7,533	5,005	2,528
2005 (Series II)	8,331	5,102	3,229

Series I assumes moderate international migration and moderate increase in female labor force participation, while Series II assumes moderate international migration and a large increase in female labor force participation (see Pick, Butler, and Gonzalez, 1992).

The Series II projection implies that eligible labor force will increase between 1990 and 2005 by 36 percent. There is greater increase for females (43 percent) than for males (32 percent). Based on this projection, there will be need for substantial economic growth and a large number of new jobs created over the next decade to accommodate this large growth in eligible labor force. Given the economic woes that have characterized the early years of the Zedillo administration, there is some doubt that the necessary economic growth and job creation will be present. This may imply increasing unemployment or underemployment or alternatively growing migration out of the Megacity.

Table 10.4 Economic Activity, 1990

Total Econ. Activity by Age, 1990

	Federal District			Mexico			Nation			Nation - Remainder		
	Pop. Econ. Active	Pop. 12+	Ratio of Econ. Active	Pop. Econ. Active	Pop. 12+	Ratio of Econ. Active	Pop. Econ. Active	Pop. 12+	Ratio of Econ. Active	Pop. Econ. Active	Pop. 12+	Ratio of Econ. Active
12-14	14,758	519,604	0.028	30,515	759,010	0.040	459,445	6,302,971	0.073	414,172	5,024,357	0.082
15-19	241,077	976,029	0.247	343,308	1,198,496	0.286	3,119,778	9,664,403	0.323	2,535,393	7,489,878	0.339
20-24	487,510	898,114	0.543	537,593	1,010,653	0.532	4,072,548	7,829,163	0.520	3,047,445	5,920,396	0.515
25-29	513,601	778,695	0.660	487,219	834,509	0.584	3,678,222	6,404,512	0.574	2,677,402	4,791,308	0.559
30-34	446,519	659,098	0.677	419,504	709,181	0.592	3,130,191	5,387,619	0.581	2,264,168	4,019,340	0.563
35-39	368,830	544,706	0.677	347,903	584,990	0.595	2,626,213	4,579,116	0.574	1,909,480	3,449,420	0.554
40-44	277,234	417,720	0.664	250,838	429,384	0.584	1,958,831	3,497,770	0.560	1,430,759	2,650,666	0.540
45-49	211,312	338,444	0.624	192,408	348,862	0.552	1,577,718	2,971,860	0.531	1,173,998	2,284,554	0.514
50-54	151,921	274,523	0.553	132,042	264,020	0.500	1,171,126	2,393,791	0.489	887,163	1,855,248	0.478
55-59	104,571	223,519	0.468	87,995	200,166	0.440	840,762	1,894,484	0.444	648,196	1,470,799	0.441
60-64	68,344	192,053	0.356	54,743	156,005	0.351	606,294	1,611,317	0.376	483,207	1,263,259	0.383
65+	75,593	394,930	0.191	64,091	294,916	0.217	822,155	3,376,841	0.243	682,471	2,686,995	0.254
Total	2,961,270	6,217,435	0.476	2,948,159	6,790,192	0.434	24,063,283	55,913,847	0.430	18,153,854	42,906,220	0.423

Male Econ. Activity by Age, 1990

	Federal District			Mexico			Nation			Nation - Remainder		
	Pop. Econ. Active	Pop. 12+	Ratio of Econ. Active	Pop. Econ. Active	Pop. 12+	Ratio of Econ. Active	Pop. Econ. Active	Pop. 12+	Ratio of Econ. Active	Pop. Econ. Active	Pop. 12+	Ratio of Econ. Active
12-14	8,132	257,687	0.032	21,123	378,700	0.056	351,651	3,159,216	0.111	322,396	2,522,829	0.128
15-19	145,911	472,392	0.309	235,954	592,244	0.398	2,239,342	4,759,892	0.470	1,857,477	3,695,256	0.503
20-24	299,951	430,901	0.696	376,195	488,297	0.770	2,882,025	3,738,128	0.771	2,205,879	2,818,930	0.783
25-29	331,438	372,514	0.890	361,842	399,918	0.905	2,724,910	3,050,595	0.893	2,031,630	2,278,163	0.892
30-34	293,320	310,444	0.945	320,051	341,203	0.938	2,375,366	2,578,736	0.921	1,761,995	1,927,089	0.914
35-39	243,891	255,606	0.954	269,347	287,047	0.938	2,037,646	2,210,565	0.922	1,524,408	1,667,912	0.914
40-44	186,285	196,228	0.949	197,647	213,167	0.927	1,554,465	1,705,013	0.912	1,170,533	1,295,618	0.903
45-49	146,780	158,036	0.929	156,184	173,369	0.901	1,293,409	1,452,573	0.890	990,445	1,121,168	0.883
50-54	108,808	124,635	0.873	109,811	129,860	0.846	983,837	1,161,875	0.847	765,218	907,380	0.843
55-59	77,268	99,161	0.779	75,150	97,577	0.770	723,624	918,864	0.788	571,206	722,126	0.791
60-64	51,214	82,016	0.624	47,236	73,584	0.642	527,802	769,917	0.686	429,352	614,317	0.699
65+	56,699	158,604	0.357	55,295	131,270	0.421	724,618	1,578,808	0.459	612,624	1,288,934	0.475
Total	1,949,697	2,918,224	0.668	2,225,835	3,306,236	0.673	18,418,695	27,084,182	0.680	14,243,163	20,859,722	0.683

Table 10.4 Economic Activity, 1990 (Continued)

Female Econ. Activity by Age, 1990

	Federal District			Mexico			Nation			Nation - Remainder		
	Pop. Econ. Active	Pop. 12+	Ratio of Econ. Active	Pop. Econ. Active	Pop. 12+	Ratio of Econ. Active	Pop. Econ. Active	Pop. 12+	Ratio of Econ. Active	Pop. Econ. Active	Pop. 12+	Ratio of Econ. Active
12-14	6,626	261,917	0.025	9,392	380,310	0.025	107,794	3,143,755	0.034	91,776	2,501,528	0.037
15-19	95,166	503,637	0.189	107,354	606,252	0.177	880,436	4,904,511	0.180	677,916	3,794,622	0.179
20-24	187,559	467,213	0.401	161,398	522,356	0.309	1,190,523	4,091,035	0.291	841,566	3,101,466	0.271
25-29	182,163	406,181	0.448	125,377	434,591	0.288	953,312	3,353,917	0.284	645,772	2,513,145	0.257
30-34	153,199	348,654	0.439	99,453	367,978	0.270	754,825	2,808,883	0.269	502,173	2,637,285	0.190
35-39	124,939	289,100	0.432	78,556	297,943	0.264	588,567	2,368,551	0.248	385,072	2,221,840	0.173
40-44	90,949	221,492	0.411	53,191	216,217	0.246	404,366	1,792,757	0.226	260,226	1,930,842	0.135
45-49	64,532	180,408	0.358	36,224	175,493	0.206	284,309	1,519,287	0.187	183,553	1,436,856	0.128
50-54	43,113	149,888	0.288	22,231	134,160	0.166	187,289	1,231,916	0.152	121,945	1,235,239	0.099
55-59	27,303	124,358	0.220	12,845	102,589	0.125	117,138	975,620	0.120	76,990	1,004,969	0.077
60-64	17,130	110,037	0.156	7,507	82,421	0.091	78,492	841,400	0.093	53,855	783,162	0.069
65+	18,894	236,326	0.080	8,796	163,646	0.054	97,537	1,798,033	0.054	69,847	441,428	0.158
Total	1,011,573	3,299,211	0.307	722,324	3,483,956	0.207	5,644,588	28,829,665	0.196	3,910,691	23,602,382	0.166

Note: Census data are utilized to examine age structure since the census has more complete information on age structure than the 1989 ENE or 1991 ENIGH surveys, both of which are more accurate regarding female workforce.

Source: INEGI, 1990 Mexican Census.

Conclusions

The metropolitan labor force had about six million workers in 1990. Although the workforce had among the lowest gender ratio of any state or city in the nation, it reflected over two male workers for every female worker. The workforce sex ratio follows the population sex ratio in being substantially lower in the city center and higher in the periphery in the State of Mexico. This may reflect the more modern and advanced economy in the city center. The center's occupations and jobs are especially attractive to skilled women workers. In particular, there is a greater proportion of service occupations in the city center and more blue collar occupations around the periphery. Since women work differentially more in service and less in blue collar, the spatial patterning of women workers may be affected.

Economic activity is a critical variable measuring the number of people who are able and willing to work, although they may be out of work temporarily. Historically the trend in proportion of economically active population has risen consistently since the early 70s. In recent years the increase may partially reflect the very large cohort of "Mexican baby boomers," which entered the workforce in substantial numbers. Spatial patterns for economic activity attributes reinforce the gender difference of greater intensity of economic activity for women in the center versus for men in the periphery.

Analysis of the city's occupational distribution reveals sharp gender differences in occupational weightings as well as a strong distinction between the Megacity's occupational mix and that of the rest of the nation. In the most educationally-qualified occupations, analysis reveals a large and comparable proportion of professional/technical workforce for both genders, but substantially reduced proportion of males for educational jobs and higher male proportion for management/supervisory jobs. In comparing service/support occupations versus the "other" category, which is mostly blue collar, there is much higher proportion of women who work in service/support occupations and many more men in blue collar jobs. As is expected for a giant city, there are agricultural jobs in only one percent of the Federal District versus the nearly one third of the workers in agriculture in the rest of the nation.

The metropolitan labor force approximately doubled from 1970 to 1990, which surpassed the city's population growth for the two decades. The higher rate of labor force additions is largely due to increases in female labor force participation over the two decades. Currently the Megacity's female economic activity is about 37 percent which is about half that for males and much lower than comparable U.S. female economic activity rates of 70 percent. This points to the likelihood of a continuing substantial growth in the city's labor force from women's continuing increase in participation. This latent jump of greater labor force should continue for several decades in the future. New women workers, combined with the huge "Mexican baby boom" generation currently in its late twenties, implies a large increase in the Mexican labor force over the next ten years, estimated as approximately one million annually (Pick, Butler, and Gonzalez, 1992). Much of the increase will take place in the Megacity. If jobs are not available there, there may be large volumes of economically motivated outmigration.

In summary, the labor force is relatively more employed and productive in Mexico City than in other parts of the nation. These combine with higher educational level to provide long-term economic productivity to the metropolis. One of the attractions of multi-national corporations for locating in the center of Mexico City is the availability of a productive labor force that is inexpensive relative to the U.S. and other advanced nations. The dilemma for the future is whether that growing labor force will be supplied with enough jobs to continue to sustain it in order to avoid increased unemployment and substantial outmigration.

11

Economic Transformation in Mexico Megacity

Introduction

This chapter focuses upon economic transformation in Mexico, with special attention being devoted to major enterprises in Mexico and their concentration in Mexico Megacity. Also featured is the corporate and legal historical background of changes in the relationship of Mexico and the United States in respect to U.S. investment, import/export, manufacturing, and transnational corporations in Mexico.

Corporate and Legal Historical Background

Corporate Background

The emergence of *global corporations*, or *transnational corporations* (TNCs), has occurred primarily since the 1950s (Taylor and Thrift, 1982).[1] TNCs have a fundamental objective of seeking locations in nations which enable maximal returns of investment. Increasingly, TNCs have sought countries in which there are uneven regulatory frameworks and ones in which monetary transfers can be made with minimum interference from and to the host country. The reasons for this are rather obvious -- a TNC needs to produce a profit and it must be able to transfer funds rapidly from one country to another. The movement of money by TNCs has accelerated in recent years and individual corporations insist upon being able to transfer resources from one country to another, more profitable one, quickly (Wolfe, 1977:618).

Further, given the worldwide character of TNCs, they are able to react swiftly to prevailing political and fiscal conditions. One implication of this rapid reaction time to changing circumstances is that any given investment is continually checked against potentially more profitable locations in another country.[2] This is apparently true despite the fact that a plant in any given location may be productive and profit making. Thus, the questions are whether or not a plant would be more profitable in another country, rather than if profit is currently being produced. This has led several investigators to describe TNCs as being locationally "fickle;" that is, when changing conditions warrant it, they can move without notice to a better location defined as one with greater profit potential (Taylor and Thrift, 1982:141).

Insofar as Mexico is concerned, prior to World War II, Mexico exchanged imported manufactured goods for primary exports. President Cardenas in the 1930s stimulated foreign investment by providing tax incentives for private industry, state investments in the infrastructure, and the maintenance of a disciplined labor force receiving low wages with no social-welfare benefits (Cockcroft, 1981:262-263). Development over the next three decades focused on producing consumer goods rather than on production of industrial equipment for further industrialization. Direct foreign investment almost doubled between 1940 and 1960 and tripled between 1960 and 1970. Most of this investment was from the United States.

TNCs do not limit investments to one country but have increasingly diversified their investments to many countries, including the so-called developed nations. For example, the largest amount of direct investment by Japan is to the United States and continental European investment has been heavy to the United Kingdom (Taylor and Thrift, 1982:5ff).

---

[1] "TNCs are corporations which have their base in one country but draw much of their income, raw materials, and operating capitals from several other countries, through their ownership of foreign subsidiaries, joint ventures with foreign governments or investors, and a host of other means" (Belshaw, 1977: 620).

[2] This ability is similar in some respects to "program trading" on Wall Street.

Implications of these trends for Mexico is that most jobs developed under the terms of foreign investment are likely to be labor-intensive with labor that is cheap and untrained, such as in the tourist and maquiladora industries.

A more recent contrary trend evolving in Mexico is that of capital intensive industries such as automobiles with an emphasis on robotics. The rationale for the emergence of more sophisticated industry must be the ability to manipulate costs and taxes involving parts received from throughout the world and the completed product being exported, primarily to the United States.

Legal Background

Fundamental goals stressed by former Mexican president, Carlos Salinas, involved controlling inflation, renegotiating the external debt, rationalizing foreign trade, and attracting foreign investment (Salinas, 1989). Currently, in Mexico, as in many other countries, only advantages of foreign investment are emphasized. Little attention has been paid to the potential negative impact that TNCs may have upon traditional values, spatial locations, and the labor force. For example, the generation of jobs for women will likely weaken the traditional family, while developing tourism along the coasts will engender migration patterns. Developing primarily lower level manual labor positions does not engender a skilled labor force.

Preoccupation of the Mexican government in attracting foreign investment has resulted in legal changes that make investing in Mexico more attractive. For example, until May of 1989, a 1973 Law to Promote Mexican Investment and Regulate Foreign Investment controlled foreign investment in Mexico. The 1973 law divided economic activities in Mexico into those (1) reserved exclusively for the State, (2) reserved for Mexican citizens, (3) those subject to limits on foreign capital, and (4) all others, subject to general regulations. Decisions regarding foreign investment were discretionary and administrative policies unduly complicated. Generally, the law specified that foreign investors could own not more than 49 percent of a company.

New guidelines established in May, 1989, included the following requirements for the *automatic authorization* of up to 100 percent foreign ownership in every sector not specifically restricted by law: (1) A minimum of 100 million dollars invested in fixed assets, (2) direct external funding obtained through subscriptions of capital, external credit, or foreign funds, channeled through Mexican financial institutions, (3) investment made in industrial establishments located outside of the three largest metropolitan areas -- Mexico City, Monterrey, and Guadalajara, (4) the maintenance of an equilibrium in its foreign-exchange transactions over the first three years of operation, (5) the creation of permanent jobs and establishment of training and personal development programs for the workers, and (6) the use of appropriate technologies that satisfy current environmental requirements.

The new regulations also required that the government make a decision in 45 days, to expand the duration of ownership of real estate for tourism, to allow foreign majority ownership in maquiladoras and other export oriented companies by registering with the National Foreign Registry, to increase foreign access to the stock market, and to give temporary outside control over sectors that under usual circumstances were reserved exclusively for Mexicans, e.g., those with high export potential or facing financial difficulties.

The Mexican government emphasized foreign investment in the tourist sector by setting goals of doubling the access of tourists during the next five years (Salinas, 1989) and in the maquiladora sector by the expansion of in-bond plants. Leaders of both opposition political parties also have gone on record as encouraging foreign investment, the PAN via its party platform and the PRD in a speech by Cardenas (1989). The emerging emphasis in Mexico upon privatization also allowed foreign investors to gain access to economic sectors prohibited by foreigners, e.g., the telephone company (Salinas, 1989).

Up until recently, most foreign investment in Mexico was from the United States; however, increased investment is being made by Pacific Rim countries. The average annual inflow of foreign investment in Mexico over the past few years has approximated two and one-half billion dollars. New foreign investment in 1990 surpassed five billion dollars. In subsequent years the government anticipates that 20 to 25 percent of total new investment will be from outside of the country as compared to ten percent currently. Recent examples of outside investment are Nissan (Japan) investing one billion dollars during the first three years of the 1990s (McDonnell, 1989), Ford (United States) increasing its investment by 300 million dollars, Nestle (Switzerland) investing a like amount, and a joint venture group (United States, Germany, and Mexico) investment in a movie studio (*Wall Street Journal*, 1989).

Mexico during the past several years has accepted wholeheartedly a positive view of foreign investment. Thus, Mexico is in concert with most other developing countries and their leaders who have accepted the modernization theoretical perspective. This positive view assumes that TNC capital investment will generate jobs and income (other possible contributions are listed by Kissling, 1978). Another assumption is that TNCs will enhance Mexico's ability to participate in the world's major commodity flows. Thus, more jobs, contributions to national income, increased government revenues and foreign reserves, and enhanced participation in world trade are all viewed as being advantageous to Mexico. In addition, TNCs are assumed to contribute to local populations by offering training otherwise not available. Further, employees trained by TNCs may pass on or use their learned skills in other host country enterprises. There are, however, possible disadvantages to foreign investment that are often neglected.

A more critical perspective from dependency theory implies that negative consequences may result from a country relying upon TNC investment (Moran, 1978; Newfarmer and Topik, 1982; Gereffi, 1980). The potential influence of transnational investment in Mexico is especially important since benefits of direct investment in some instances are viewed as being 'unequally' or 'unfairly' distributed to the detriment of the host country and in favor of the TNC (Enderwick, 1985:67). Johnson (1978) argues that over 80 percent of funds for TNCs are raised locally in the host country while 80 percent of the profits are removed from the country by the TNCs. Also, in some countries, TNCs have created distortions in local economies by squeezing out local businesses, utilizing inappropriate technologies, creating inequalities in distribution of income among the population, and distorting consumer patterns.

Another negative effect has been that foreign investors pervert or subvert host country political processes. This is possible because some TNCs are larger economic entities than the host country. For example, in 1972 Mexico's economy ranked 14th in the world while if measured in the same manner, General Motors would rank 16th (Newfarmer and Mueller, 1975:7). The economic power of TNCs then is great and their ability to obtain credit to build plants and facilities may be greater than a host country such as Mexico. Thus, economic resources available to some TNCs are at least as great as they are to Mexico and larger than many nations with smaller economic resources (Taylor and Thrift, 1982: 142).

A further complication in some instances has been that national and regional policies begin to reflect needs of the TNCs rather than the host country and/or local population (Gedicks, 1978). When a government negotiates with a TNC, Plaza (1978) argues that the government is eroding its most important element -- its sovereignty. Examples of foreign influence upon policy are the impact that the international financial community has had upon the periodic devaluation of the peso imposed upon Mexico and the imposition of terms by the IMF to determine the "'credit-worthiness'' of Mexico (Cockcroft, 1981: 275).

This chapter examines both the potential positive and negative consequences of transnationals on the Mexican economy and its population. Future changes in Mexico may be influenced more by transnational corporations than political parties. That is, as transnational corporations locate throughout Mexico, especially in Mexico Megacity, they are having a profound influence upon contact with the global economy and with foreign cultures, e.g., United States, Germany, England, and now the Orient, especially Japan, Korea, and Taiwan.

The Mexican 500 in 1986

Data Sources

This chapter utilizes data and information from a variety of sources, including the agricultural, commercial, economic, and population and housing censuses of 1989 - 1993. In addition, data on major Mexican enterprises in 1986 and 1993 were obtained from *Expansión, Commercial Exterior*, and other publications from the World Bank, International Monetary Fund, and United Nations. Since many Mexican 500 corporations are TNCs, one important feature of this chapter is to compare Mexican corporations with those that are transnational in character.

Concentration by State

In 1986, 58 percent of corporate enterprises in Mexico were concentrated in the urban centers of the states of Nuevo Leon, Mexico, and Federal District (see Table 11.1). This concentration reflected the dominance of Monterrey, Guadalajara, and Mexico Megacity (the Federal District and surrounding municipios of the State of Mexico) in finance, business, and manufacturing.

As shown on Map 11.1, Mexico's 500 largest enterprises in 1986 were not equally distributed throughout Mexico. Mexico City proper (the Federal District) contained 29.8 percent of them and State of Mexico municipios surrounding the Federal District contained 15.5 percent; thus 45.4 percent of the total were located in Mexico Megacity. The two states of Nuevo Leon and Jalisco, containing the secondary metropoli of Monterrey and Guadalajara, had 12.6 and 7.2 percent of major enterprises, respectively. These several cities, then, contained 65 percent of the total major 500 enterprises in Mexico in 1986. In addition, two states with major enterprises -- Puebla and Queretaro -- are located adjacent to Mexico Megacity. Five states had no major enterprises; four were located in the poor, deep south and the fifth one of Nayarit, one of the poorest states in Mexico, was located on the Pacific-Central coast.

In 1986 there was clear spatial demarcation by state of major economic enterprises in Mexico. In 1986, 68 percent of *total investment* by the 500 was in the Federal District. In addition, 57 percent of *total employees* of the 500 were employed in the Federal District. For the entire State of Mexico, the figures were 2.5 percent investment and 6.0 percent of employees. This concentration, primarily in the Federal District, existed despite of prior and then current federal administration's attempts to decentralize such activities.

This hyperconcentration of Mexican 500 employees in the Federal District is not surprising in lieu of the heavy concentration in the Federal District of service employees, in particular that about half of the nation's service sector workers were located in the Federal District in 1993. These proportions were even higher for professional/technical and financial service workers. Commerce had a concentration in the Federal District of 34 percent, while industry's concentration was 16 percent. Employees in the Mexican 500 are more highly skilled and so should be expected to be proportionately more located in the Federal District.

The 1989 law allowing firms outside of the Mexico Megacity, Guadalajara, and Monterrey regions to be held completely by foreigners apparently had little impact upon the location of major corporations, including those foreign owned.

Within State Concentration

Within states in 1986, there was further concentration with 29.8 percent of the major 500 enterprises being located in the Federal District. Further, virtually all major corporations located in Mexico City were concentrated in two of its sixteen delegations, Miguel Hidalgo and Cuauhtemoc. In the State of Mexico, 42 of 78 enterprises were located in two municipios -- Ecatepec and Tlalnepantla, both adjacent to the Federal District. In Nuevo Leon, 38 of 63 corporations were located in Monterrey and 12 were located in the municipio of San Nicolas de los Garza. In Jalisco, 22 of 36 enterprises were located in Guadalajara. In the states of Puebla and Queretaro, all top 500 enterprises were located in the two major cities -- Puebla and Queretaro.

Thus, the Mexico 500 in 1986 was geographically concentrated within a few states and primarily in the largest cities of those states. Further concentration existed in particular zones of major cities, especially in Mexico Megacity.

TNCs and the Mexican 500 in 1986

In 1986, 96 of the Mexican 500 were United States corporations; of these, 29.2 percent (N = 28) also were prominent in the "Fortune 500" in the United States. Among these corporations were three of the top ten in both countries -- General Motors, Ford, and Chrysler. Two others in the top ten in the United States also were prominent in the Mexico 500 -- IBM and Mobil. Thus, five of the top ten in the United States also were in the Mexico 500. U.S. 500s in Mexico were primarily associated with automobiles, chemicals, computers and related products, food products, and scientific equipment. Other than automobile enterprises, most U.S. corporations sold products in Mexico rather than manufacturing them in Mexico.

Figure 11.1 shows ownership of Mexico's major 500 enterprises in 1986, with 17.2 percent being foreign owned. Figure 11.2 shows the total origin of capital for the Mexican 500 in 1986 from Mexico, United States, Europe, and other countries. In 1986, the main source of foreign capital was primarily the United States and Europe.

Table 11.2 shows the principal activity of the 500 major enterprises in 1986. In 1986, federally owned enterprises had the largest number of employees while TNCs typically had a larger number of employees than did Mexican owned enterprises (see Figure 11.3). Figure 11.4 shows the number of employees by type of enterprise. Figure 11.5 shows occupational distributions by type of principal activity and by three broad categories of administrators, operatives, and technical occupations. In 1988, over 68 percent of investment by the 500 was in the Federal District and over 57 percent of employees of the major 500 corporations worked in the Federal District.

Table 11.1 The Location of Mexico's 500 Major Enterprises, 1986 and 1993

Locaiton	No. 1986	No. 1993
Federal District	149	206
State of Mexico	78	64
Nuevo Leon	63	75
Jalisco	36	38
Chihuahua	15	13
Puebla	17	5
Queretaro	17	5
Coahuila	16	26
Veracruz	14	6
Sinaloa	NA	10
Five States	0	0

Source: *Expansion,* August 17, 1987.

Map 11.1
Mexico's 500 Major Corporations, 1986

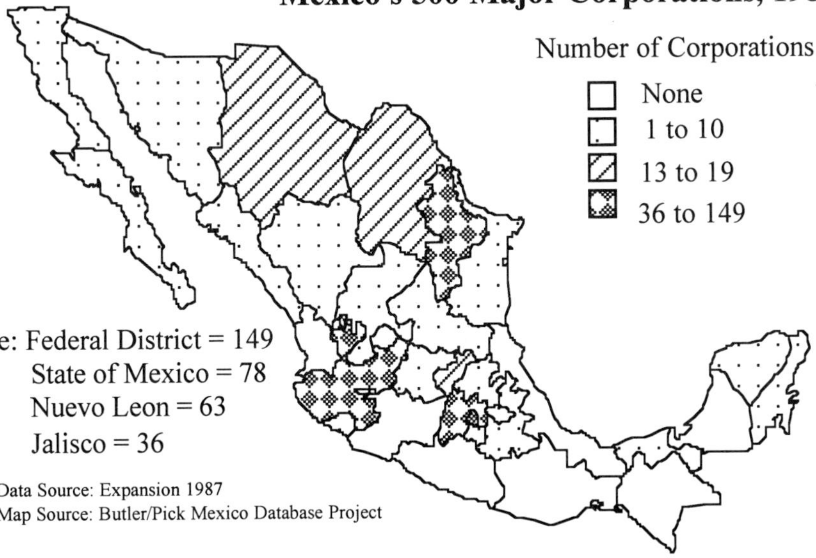

Number of Corporations

☐ None
☐ 1 to 10
▨ 13 to 19
▦ 36 to 149

Note: Federal District = 149
State of Mexico = 78
Nuevo Leon = 63
Jalisco = 36

Data Source: Expansion 1987
Map Source: Butler/Pick Mexico Database Project

330

Figure 11.1 Ownership of Enterprises: Mexico's 500, 1986

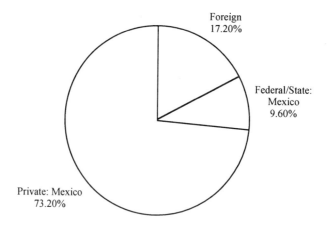

Foreign
17.20%

Federal/State:
Mexico
9.60%

Private: Mexico
73.20%

Source: *Expansion,* August 17, 1987

Figure 11.2 Origin of Capital: Mexico's 500 Major Enterprises, 1986

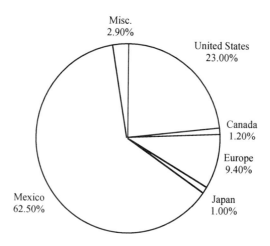

Misc.
2.90%

United States
23.00%

Canada
1.20%

Europe
9.40%

Japan
1.00%

Mexico
62.50%

Source: *Expansion,* August 17, 1987

Table 11.2 Origin and Composition of Capital for the Mexican 500: 1986

Composition of Capital	Amount	Percent
Private - 100%	2,375,457	23.5
Foreign - 100%	2,773,212	27.5
State - 100%	195,176	1.9
Private and State	2,984,252	29.6
Private and TNC	1,656,321	16.4
State and TNC	86,944	0.9
Private/State/TNC	15,890	0.2
Not classified	4,851	NS
Totals	10,092,103	100.0

Note: Amounts are in millions of pesos.
Source: *Expansion,* August 17, 1987.

Figure 11.3 Type of Enterprise and
Mean Number of Employees, 1986

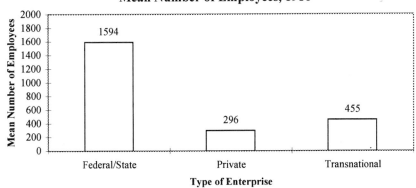

Source: *Expansion,* August 17, 1987.

332

Figure 11.4 Mean Number of Employees by Type of Enterprise, 1986

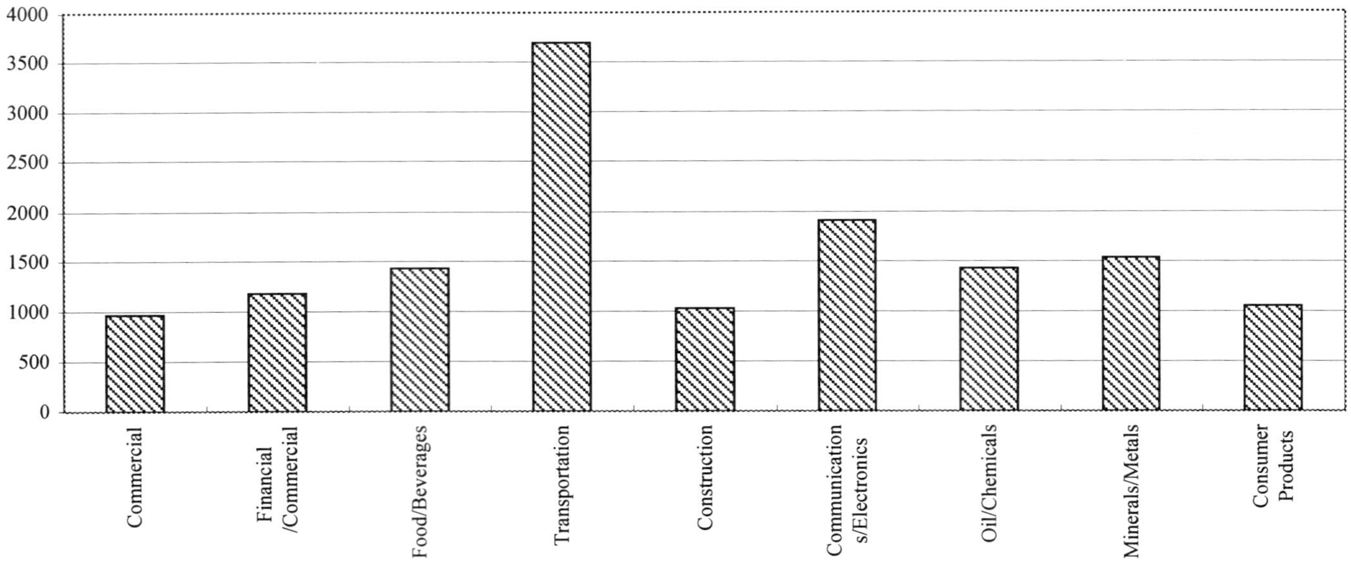

Source: *Expansion,* August 17, 1987.

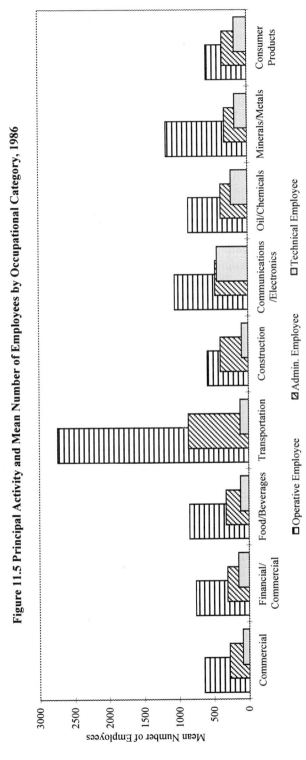

Figure 11.5 Principal Activity and Mean Number of Employees by Occupational Category, 1986

Source: *Expansion*, August 17, 1987

Changes in the Mexican 500: 1986 - 1993

Concentration by State

The basic overall distribution of the 500 in 1993 shown on Map 11.2 remained nearly the same as in 1986 (see Map 11.1 and Table 11.1). However, some changes did take place. Concentration in the Federal District increased from 149 corporations in 1986 to 206 in 1993. The State of Mexico had a decline from 78 to 64. Jalisco remained virtually the same with an increase of two. Nuevo Leon, primarily Monterrey, had an increase from 63 to 75. Queretaro had a decline from 17 to five. Overall, then, the federal government's effort to decentralize corporate activities failed since there was an increased concentration of major enterprises, especially in the Federal District portion of Mexico Megacity between 1986 and 1993.

It should be recalled from Chapter 2 that the Salinas administration promulgated the 100 cities plan, which had a goal of decentralizing the population and economy from the over-concentrated Mexico City to medium sized cities throughout the nation (see Map 2.5). This plan intended also to attract private corporations to the medium sized cities. Obviously, the plan failed.

Concentration in Mexico Megacity

Map 11.3 shows the number of 500 corporations in Mexico Megacity by delegation and municipio in 1993. The concentration that existed in 1986 continued in 1993. Table 11.3 shows the distribution in the Federal District of the 206 of 500 (41%) corporations headquartered there, with the two delegations of Cuauhtemoc and Miguel Hidalgo containing 105 (21%) of the total 500 corporations in Mexico (see Map 11.3). Only Magdalena Contreras, Milpa Alta, and Tlahuac delegations in the Federal District did not have a major 500 corporation. Map 11.4 shows the concentration of workers in these major firms in the Mexico Megacity region. The concentration is in the Federal District and a ring around the Federal District.

Maps 11.5 and 11.6 illustrate that 1993 assets and sales by major corporations also were concentrated in the Cuauhtemoc and Miguel Hidalgo, several other delegations in the Federal District, and Tlalnepantla in the State of Mexico. Net profit margin, however, was greatest in Venustiano Carranza of the Federal District (see Map 11.7).

Mexico's top ten corporations have substantial foreign ownership and are concentrated in the heart of Mexico City. As seen in Table 11.4, top ten corporations account for 49 percent of the revenues and 51 percent of assets for the Mexico 500. This disproportion at the top exceeds that of the other countries of North America. For instance, the ratio of sales of the nation's top 25 corporations to the top 500 is much higher in Mexico (68 percent) than in the United States (42 percent) or Canada (38 percent) (*Expansion*, 1995). This is partly due to the huge size of PEMEX, the national petroleum company. It is also clear that the top 10 corporations are located in two central delegations in the Federal District. These are also the delegations that tend to have a disproportionate concentration of services, especially high end services, and commerce (see Chapter 10). It further supports the conclusion of extreme concentration already seen for the 500 as a whole.

TNCs and the Mexican 500 in 1993

Map 11.8 shows that foreign owned corporations in 1993 were primarily situated in Miguel Hidalgo. There also was a concentration in Cuauhtemoc, Coyoacan, and Iztapalapa in the Federal District, and in Tlalnepantla in the State of Mexico adjacent to the Federal District. Thus, the change in laws in 1989 for foreign owned corporations did not alter the concentration of foreign ownership of corporations in Mexico Megacity. In fact, concentration continued unabated after that date.

For the top 10 corporations, there is strong foreign ownership. The largest firm Petroleos Mexicanos remains nationalized, as it has been for most of the century. In the past decade, it has become in some ways a symbol of national sovereignty to the government to retain state ownership, even under difficult economic conditions. Three of the top 10 are completely foreign owned, while two are 49 percent foreign owned. In addition, a sixth firm, Telefonos de Mexico, originally nationalized, has yielded minority ownership to U.S. firms. Included in the top ten are familiar multinational corporate names of GM, Chrysler, and Nestle. This underscores the transnational impact of certain companies and products on Mexico and its citizens/consumers. It is probable that Ford Motor would also have been included in the top 10, but Ford is excluded because it did not respond to Expansion's 1993 survey (*Expansion*, 1994).

The origin of capital was different for 1986 and 1993. In Figure 11.6, which compares 1986 with 1993, there was a slight decline in private Mexican and a substantial decrease in foreign origin of capital in the 500 major Mexican firms. In contrast, there was a substantial increase in Mexican state origin of capital when 1986 is compared to 1993. In the next section, it is demonstrated that this substantial increase in state origin of capital has been accompanied by a severe reduction in the number of state owned enterprises! This may imply that privatization has resulted in subsidization.

Regarding foreign ownership between 1986 and 1993 there was a decline in U.S. capital investment from 23.0 to 19.8 percent while European capital contribution increased from 9.4 to 10.6 percent. Japan's contribution remained the same while Canada's decreased from 1.2 to 0.6 percent.

Privatization

One of the major changes in the Mexican 500 between 1986 and 1993 was privatization. In 1987, 64 of the 500 were state owned enterprises, ranging from food products (N = 8), commercial enterprises (N = 7), production of metal products (N = 5), auto parts (N = 4), the petroleum industry -- the number 1 enterprise in both 1986 and 1993, petrochemicals, minerals, transportation and related industries.

As seen in Table 11.5, in 1993, only six Mexican 500 were state-owned enterprises; three of these entities were state-owned in 1987 -- the petroleum industry (No. 1); a corporation exporting salt from Baja California Sur (184); and an enterprise transporting salt from Baja California Sur (No. 409). The three new state-owned enterprises listed in the 1993 500 were the Postal Service (No. 80), the production and importing of paper (No. 91), and a group concerned with hotels (No. 211).

Private ownership of the 500 increased from 73.1 percent in 1986 to 77.8 percent in 1993, while foreign ownership increased from 17.2 percent in 1986 to 20.9 percent in 1993. These increases were a result of the decline in state owned enterprises .

Foreign Owned Mexican 500: 1986 and 1993

Table 11.6 shows the foreign owned Mexican 500 in 1986 and 1993. The table includes all foreign owned Mexican 500 listed in 1986, with those enterprises not responding being excluded. The base comparison, then, is with the Mexican 500 in 1986 compared with the 1993 500. The two columns show respective ratings for the two time periods. An asterisk in the 1993 column indicates that the firm was surveyed but did not respond. ND indicates that while the enterprise was listed in 1986 it was not listed in 1993.

Not being listed in 1993 presumably means that these firms were (1) no longer a major enterprise in 1993, (2) may have been absorbed by some other enterprise, or (3) no longer existed. In addition, a number of other firms surveyed in 1993 did not respond. Among non-responders were Nissan, Pizza Hut, Proctor & Gamble, and Industrias Kores de Mexico (*Expansion,* 1994: 346).

Figure 11.5 illustrated origin of capital for the Mexican 500 enterprises in 1986 and 1993. Between 1986 and 1993 there was a slight decline in Mexican private origin of capital. The two major differences in 1986 and 1993 were (1) a decline in the foreign origin of capital and (2) a substantial increase in Mexican state origin of capital. The increase in Mexican state origin of capital took place despite of a decline in state owned enterprises from 64 in 1986 to six in 1993! There were 70 foreign corporations in 1993.

A more refined breakdown of origin of capital illustrates that in fact the state's contribution to the total was greater than 19.9 percent because of its contribution to other Mexican private and foreign majority owned firms. Given its partial contribution to Mexican private and foreign firms, the state's origin of capital approached 25 percent. This figure ignores that the more than 10 percent of capital not allocated may actually have increased the state's contribution. One conclusion reached from these data is that while extensive privatization took place between 1986 and 1993, this may be an illusion rather than reality. That is, loss of state control of many major enterprises has been replaced by extensive state capital subsidies. A major question, of course, is what happens to the accrued to profits (if they exist)? Are they distributed to private investors and to the state, or only to private investors?

Only 29 percent of Mexican private firms were 100 percent funded by Mexican nationals and slightly more than half of the 70 foreign owned firms were 100 percent owned by foreigners (N = 45).

Mexico Megacity as a Global City

Of particular interest to us has been an examination of aspects of Mexico City as a Megacity. Our analysis has focused on services that are considered essential to the formation of a Megacity (Sassen 1991). This perspective argues that certain higher level services are the primary indicators of a global city. Examples are computer and data processing and other information services, research and development, financial related services, and other business related endeavors. Here we examine only a few of these service industries (for more extensive analysis, see Butler and Pick, in progress; Hettrick, 1996).

In examining Mexico Megacity as a global city, we first carried out a cluster analysis of the 69 delegations and municipios that make up Mexico Megacity (see Chapters 1, 12, and 13). The cluster analysis resulted in 10 clusters. The primary cluster shown on Maps 1.5 and 12.1, covers the "old core" region of the Federal District. Mexico Megacity has a concentration of important service sectors in two delegations and it remained consistent across time and by various service categories (see Hettrick, 1996). Our analysis of service sector revenues showed that both in 1989 and 1993, the "old core" -- especially the delegations of Cuauhtemoc and Miguel Hidalgo -- was the primary service area of Mexico Megacity, which, of course, means for all Mexico. In addition, there was a decline in service revenues the further away a delegation or municipio was from this core. Of all service revenues in Mexico Megacity in 1992, 3/4 were in cluster one -- or the very same areas that had a concentration of 500 corporations and of the 500 corporations that were foreign owned (see Figure 11.6).

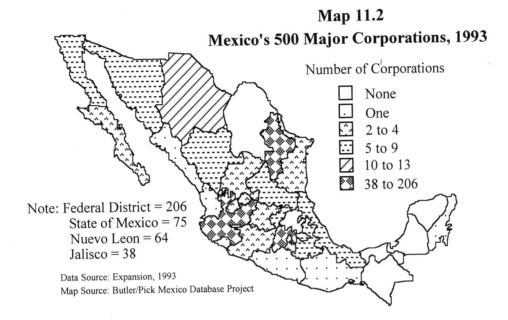

Map 11.2

Mexico's 500 Major Corporations, 1993

Number of Corporations

- None
- One
- 2 to 4
- 5 to 9
- 10 to 13
- 38 to 206

Note: Federal District = 206
State of Mexico = 75
Nuevo Leon = 64
Jalisco = 38

Data Source: Expansion, 1993
Map Source: Butler/Pick Mexico Database Project

Map 11.3
Number of 500 Major
Mexican Corporations, 1993

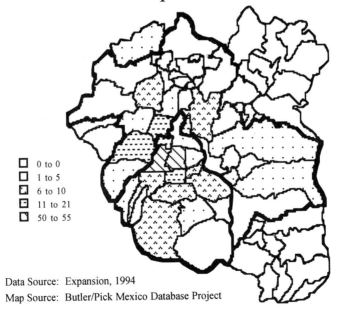

- 0 to 0
- 1 to 5
- 6 to 10
- 11 to 21
- 50 to 55

Data Source: Expansion, 1994
Map Source: Butler/Pick Mexico Database Project

338

Table 11.3 Mexican 500 by Delegation in Federal District, 1993

Area	Count
Alvaro Obregon	10
Azcapotzalco	11
Benito Juarez	16
Coyoacan	7
Cuajimalpa	3
Cuauhtemoc	50
Gustavo Madero	4
Iztacalco	6
Iztapalapa	10
Miguel Hidalgo	55
Tlalpan	10
Venustiano Carranza	3
Xochimilco	3
Total	188

Magdalena Contreras, Milpa Alta, and Tlahuac do not have a '500'.

Source: *Expansion,* 1994

Note: the delegation location was not available for 18 Mexico 500 firms.

Map 11.4
Number of Workers in 500 Major
Mexican Corporations, 1993

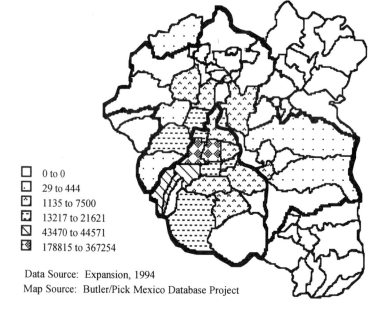

☐	0 to 0
⊡	29 to 444
⊡	1135 to 7500
⊡	13217 to 21621
◩	43470 to 44571
▦	178815 to 367254

Data Source: Expansion, 1994
Map Source: Butler/Pick Mexico Database Project

339

Map 11.5
Assets of 500 Major
Mexican Corporations, 1993

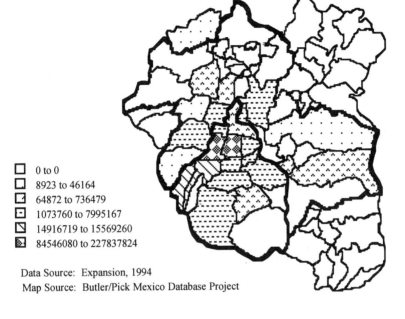

- 0 to 0
- 8923 to 46164
- 64872 to 736479
- 1073760 to 7995167
- 14916719 to 15569260
- 84546080 to 227837824

Data Source: Expansion, 1994
Map Source: Butler/Pick Mexico Database Project

Map 11.6
Sales by 500 Major
Mexican Corporations, 1993

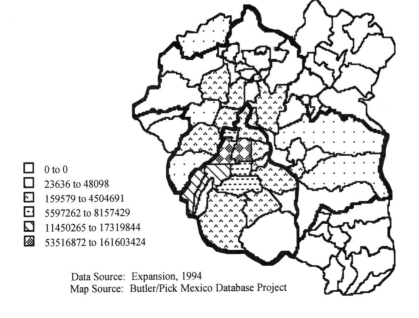

- 0 to 0
- 23636 to 48098
- 159579 to 4504691
- 5597262 to 8157429
- 11450265 to 17319844
- 53516872 to 161603424

Data Source: Expansion, 1994
Map Source: Butler/Pick Mexico Database Project

Map 11.7

Profit Margin of 500 Major
Mexican Corporations, 1993

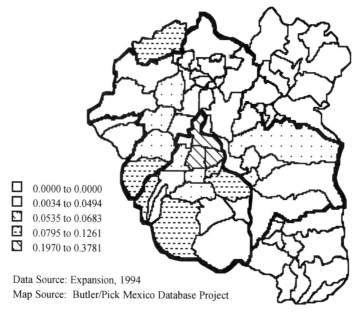

☐	0.0000 to 0.0000
☐	0.0034 to 0.0494
▨	0.0535 to 0.0683
▣	0.0795 to 0.1261
◩	0.1970 to 0.3781

Data Source: Expansion, 1994
Map Source: Butler/Pick Mexico Database Project

Map 11.8

Number of Foreign Owned Corporations,
Mexico Megacity, 1993

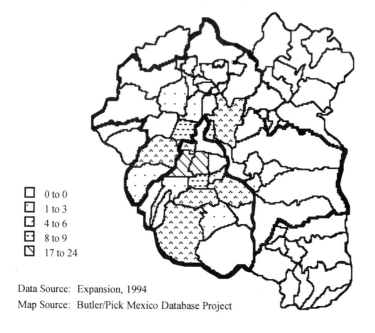

☐	0 to 0
☐	1 to 3
▨	4 to 6
▣	8 to 9
◩	17 to 24

Data Source: Expansion, 1994
Map Source: Butler/Pick Mexico Database Project

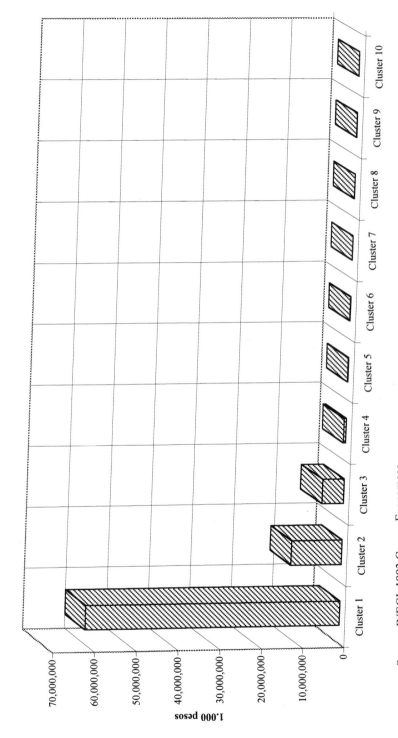

Figure 11.6 Service Revenues by Overall Cluster Area, 1993

Source: INEGI, 1993 Censos Economcos

Table 11.4 Mexico's Top Ten Corporations, 1993

Name	Business	Revenues*	Assets*	Capital Composition**	Origin of Foreign Capital	State/Municipio
Petroleos Mexicanos	Petroleum and Gas	82,790	153,102	State (100)	none	DF/Miguel Hidalgo
Telefonos de Mexico	Communications	24,602	52,902	ND	U.S.	DF/Cuauhtemoc
Cifra y Subsidiarias	Auto Service/Sales	14,231	10,204	Private (100)	none	DF/Cuajimalpa
General Motors de Mexico	Auto	13,409	8,610	Foreign (100)	U.S.	DF/Miguel Hidalgo
Chrysler de Mexico	Auto	11,153	4,544	Foreign (100)	U.S.	DF/Miguel Hidalgo
Gigante	Auto Service/Sales	7,944	5,231	Private (51),Foreign (49)	ND	DF/Miguel Hidalgo
Controlodora Comercial Mexicana	Cement	7,160	4,583	Private (51),Foreign (49)	ND	DF/Cuauhtemoc
Grupo Modelo	Beverage	5,106	8,234	Private (99.98)	ND	DF/Miguel Hidalgo
Grupo Industrial Bimbo	Food	5,097	4,148	Private (100)	none	DF/Alvaro Obergon
Compania Nestle	Food	4,205	2,762	Foreign (100)	Switzerland	DF/Miguel Hidalgo
Total - Top 10		175,697	254,320			
Total - Mexico 500		361,700	501,600			
Top 10 - Percent of Total		49	51			

* in millions of new pesos.

** the number in parentheses is the percent of ownership.

ND = not determined

Source: *Expansion*, 1994

Table 11.5 Mexican State Owned '500' Enterprises in 1986 and 1993*

Firm	1986 Position	Principal Activity	1993 Position
Petroleos Mexicanos	1	Petroleum	1
Telefonos de Mexico	4	Communications	
Altos Hornos de Mexico	6	Iron and Steel	
CIA. Mexicana de Aviacion	9	Transport	
Fertilizantes Mexicanos	15	Fertilizer	
Aseguradora Mexicana	19	Financial Services	
Siderurgica L. Cardenas Las Truchas	21	Iron and Steel	
Compania Mindera de Cananea	32	Mining	
Tereftalatos Mexicanos	37	Petrochemical	
Minera Carbonifera Rio Escondido	38	Mining	
Hules Mexicanos	60	Petrochemical	
Distribuidora Conasupo Metropoli	86	Rubber	
Exportadora de Sal	99	Mining	
Constructsora Nal. de Carros de Ferpo	100	Transportation Equipment	184
Rassini	110	Auto Parts	
Industrias Conasupo Monterrey	111	Food	
Conscorcio Minero B. Juarez P. Color	113	Mining	
Telefonos del Noroeste	114	Communications	
Industrias Conasupo Gomez Palacio	119	Food	
Industrias Conasupo Tultitlan	120	Food	
Tetraetilo de Mexico	128	Petrochemical	
Motores Perkins	141	Auto Parts	
Alimentos Blanceados de Mexico	158	Food	
Algodonera Comercial Mexicana	160	Commerce	
Industrias Conasupo Puebla	167	Food	
Grupo Contelmex	174	Construction	
Industrias Conasupo Co. Obregon	175	Food	
Arrendadora Internacional	183	Financial Services	
Turboeactores	207	Professional Services	
Dina Rockwell Nacional	259	Auto Parts	
Industrias Conasupo Mexicali	264	Food	
Compania Operadora De. Est. de Serv.	268	Commerce	
Envases Passini	273	Metal Production	
Moto Diesel Mexicana	320	Auto Parts	
Procesadora de Aceros Rassini	323	Metal Production	
Tornillos Rassini	324	Metal Production	
Torres Mexicanas	335	Metal Production	
Prograsa	356	Printing/Publishing	
Compania Mexicana de Exploraciones	373	Professional Services	
Industrias Conasupo Nvo. Laredo	381	Food	
Aceros Rassini	411	Iron and Steel	
Transportes Centrales	417	Transport	
Estructuras de Acero	436	Metal Production	
Transportadora de Sal	474	Transport	409
Servicio Postal Mexicano		Postal Service	80
Producto y Importado de Papel		Paper	91
Grupo Hotelero Brisas		Hotels	211
Totals	N = 64		N = 6

* Data are from *Expansion*, 1987 and 1994.

344

Table 11.6 Foreign Owned '500' Enterprises in 1986 and 1993**

	1986 Position		1993 Position
Chrysler de Mexico	2	Automobiles	5
General Motors	3	Automobiles	4
Ford Motor	5	Automobiles	*
Volksvagen	8	Automobiles	*
IBM	14	Electronics	14
Compania Nestle	18	Food	10
American Express	22	Financial Services	28
Teleindustria Ericcson	33	Electronic Equipment	48
Industrias Fogografica	39	Other Manuf.	77
Xerox Mexicana	42	Commerce	59
Anderson Clayton	43	Food	50
Carton y Papel de Mexico	46	Paper and Cellulose	ND
Kodak Mexicana	48	Commerce	69
Barcardi y CIA	56	Beverages	ND
Renault Industrias	58	Auto Parts	ND
Quimica Hoechst de Mexico	63	Chemicals	92
Bayer de Mexico	66	Chemicals	63
Hewlett Packard	71	Electronics	47
BASF Mexicana	81	Chemicals	196
ICI de Mexico	87	Chemicals	*
Unisys de Mexico	90	Commerce	ND
Uniroyal	91	Rubber	ND
General Foods de Mexico	94	Food	ND
Siemens	122	Electronic Equipment	71
Mobil	124	Petrochemical	ND
Mem-Mex	133	Electronics	ND
Black & Decker	143	Electronic Equipment	ND
Componentes Mecanicos de de Matamoros	148	Auto Parts	ND
Square D de Mexico	149	Machinery	157
Singer Mexicana	159	Machinery	111
Olympia de Mexico	162	Machinery	217
Sandoz	163	Pharmaceuticals	167
RIMR	166	Auto Parts	ND
AGA de Mexico	168	Chemicals	*
Grolier	170	Commerce	ND
Nichimen de Mexico	201	Commerce	ND
Fermentaciones Mexicanas	215	Chemicals	ND
SKF Mexicana	219	Commerce	ND
Upjohn	222	Pharmaceuticals	ND
Materias Primas	224	Commerce	ND
Grupo Camilar	241	Commerce	ND
Becton Dickinson	243	Pharmaceuticals	185
Berol	247	Pencils	222
Rio Bravo Electricos	248	Auto Parts	ND
Prove-Quin.	253	Commerce	ND
Industrias Mexicanas Unisys	255	Electronics	ND
Editorical Cumbre	269	Printing/Publishing	ND
American Ref. Products	270	Electronic Equipment	164
Inmont de Mexico	281	Chemicals	ND
Sperry	282	Commerce	ND
Nashua de Mexico	285	Commerce	ND
Sandvix	290	Metal Production	ND
Federal Pacific Electric	296	Electronic Equipment	256
Laboratorios y Agencies Unidas	300	Food	218
NCR Industrial	301	Electronics	174
Deltronicos de Matamoros	309	Auto Parts	ND
Sonoco de Mexico	310	Paper and Cellulose	ND
Byron Jackson	314	Non Electrical Equipment	ND
Eds de Mexico	317	Professional Services	ND

Cajas Corrugadas	318	Paper and Cellulose	ND
SAF de Mexico	326	Food	*
Durr de Mexico	328	Non Electrical Equipment	*
Campbell's	332	Food	ND
Delredo	354	Auto Parts	ND
Quimica Sumex	358	Chemicals	384
Conductores y Componentes	361	Auto Parts	ND
Recold	376	Non Electrical Equipment	ND
Gestetner	379	Commerce	ND
Cableados de Juarez	382	Auto Parts	ND
Productos Darex	401	Chemicals	ND
Sistemas Elec. y Commutadores	429	Auto Parts	290
G.F.T. de Mexico	438	Control Systems	ND
Delnosa	445	Auto Parts	ND
Degussa	446	Chemicals	242
Garlock	452	Minerals	ND
Louis Mulas Sucs	453	Commerce	ND
Burroughs Wellcome	456	Pharmaceuticals	ND
Cajas y Empaques	459	Paper and Cellulose	ND
Sinalopasta	464	Food	ND
A.C. Nielson Co.	477	Professional Services	ND
Quimica Knoll	484	Pharmaceuticals	377
Cutler-Hammer	495	Electronic Equipment	ND
Ediciones Larousse	496	Printing/Publishing	320
Firsche Dodge y Olcott	497	Chemicals	ND

** Data are from *Expansion*, 1987 and 1994.
* Indicates surveyed but did not respond.
ND indicates not listed in 500.

Conclusions

A comparison of ownership and investment in 1986 with 1993 points to apparent substantial policy changes in Mexico. There has been extensive privatization of major enterprises in Mexico. On the other hand, origin of capital by the state has increased substantially. Thus, extensive privatization of the major enterprises in Mexico has been accompanied by a substantial increase in state origin of capital for these private enterprises. There was, then, a decline in state owned enterprises accompanied by more state capital being infused into private enterprises which gives the appearance of the replacement of state-owned enterprises by state-subsidies. In essence this may mean the release of government control of these enterprises but with government funds allowing them to continue. These policy changes lead to a whole host of issues about control and profits foreign versus domestic ownership, and many others.

Sassen (1991) postulated that advanced megacities would retain executive decision-making and related services. On the other hand, manufacturing plants, middle level service offices, and support functions could move away from the Megacity, even to another country.

This chapter shows that the Megacity is attracting in great numbers the major companies of the nation. In addition to the centralized government decision making, corporate executive decision-making also is taking place in a small central area of Mexico City. However, contrary to Sassen's hypothesis for advanced megacities, the industry sector has remained huge in Mexico City, with the center i.e. Federal District accounting for a quarter of national industrial production revenues. Nevertheless, there are some signs that some industrial production may be moving away from the center. There are large industrial parks being built in the mid to far northern municipios of the Megacity, which results in some 500 firms and industries moving away from the center. Production facilities for several enterprises have moved entirely away from Mexico City.

As Mexico City develops in the next few decades, it will be important to monitor for shifts in the location of industrial production versus corporate decision making. The last chapter will return to the topic of industrial and corporate concentration, or perhaps hyperconcentration in the city center and examine more issues involved in this centralization.

12

Spatial Structure of Mexico Megacity

Introduction

Spatial analysis of Mexico City reveals distinctive zones that characterize broadly the social and economic structure of the Megacity. This structure is informative in understanding the overall urban development context of the city and in anticipating future growth. The methodology utilized is cluster analysis applied in a casewise manner, with further descriptive comparisons of the cluster-zones. Cluster variables were selected based on several different theoretical and demographic perspectives. Six variable groups enable more refined analysis along particular dimensions. For the overall cluster analysis and five of the six subsets, there is a common set of key zones. The key zones consist of the (1) traditional urban core, (2) concentric circles, (3) Chalco and other poverty areas, and (4) the semi-urban periphery and neighboring buffer zones.

Key cluster zones are compared with urban growth patterns since 1950 and with other studies of the growth and differentiation of Mexico City. Key zones are discussed in terms of their relevance to the broad metropolitan picture.

Variable groups of social rank and urbanism/familism are closely interlinked. This is confirmed through cluster comparisons and cross-correlations. The broad linkage between social rank and urbanism/familism is supported by social theories, including contemporary social theories of fertility.

The ethnicity cluster analysis reveals spatial patterns highly different from that of the other five dimensions. The magnitude of indigenous ethnic proportions is, however, reduced in the conurbation compared to the nation.

Methodology

Cluster analysis may be applied case-wise to identify cases that are similar to each other based on a measure that averages similarity for many variables (Hartigan, 1975; Chatfield and Collins, 1980). Cases are grouped starting with those two most alike. Once grouped, two or more cases are represented by average values for many variables. The averaged values are subject to further grouping, just as an individual case would be. The clustering process continues until eventually all cases are in one large cluster. The clustering process can be stopped at any point of interest to the investigator or at a specially determined point.

Clustering in this study was based on Euclidean squared distance, as a measure of the closeness between the values of a variable for any two cases and/or clusters. This means that the similarity between two cases and/or clusters is computed as the sum of the differences squared, summing over all variables (Hartigan, 1975; SPSS, 1993).

The clustering process utilized was Ward's hierarchical clustering method (Chatfield and Collins, 1980). In this method within groups sum of squares is calculated for each cluster that has formed. Then the number of clusters and/or cases is reduced by one, in the way that gives the smallest value for sum of within cluster group sum of squares. Euclidean squared distance is very appropriate and commonly utilized as the distance measure for Ward's hierarchical clustering (Chatfield and Collins, 1980).

The research framework calculated overall clusters for variables covering the six key socioeconomic areas of the book. Specific clusters are established for each of six key socioeconomic variable groups. The variable groups and their component variables are shown in Table 12-1.

Variable groups were chosen based on groupings from various urban area analysis theories combined with groups of key demographic, economic, and housing variables. The theory of social area analysis, which also was used in selecting variables, is well developed in the urban literature. Social area analysis customarily includes variables for social rank, urbanism/familism, and race/ethnicity. It has been applied extensively to studies of U.S. and elsewhere. It has been especially relevant to studies of social stratification, segregation, and longitudinal growth and change in cities.

Demographic variables chosen are basic demographic parameters including population, population growth, density, migration, and gender balance. Housing dimensions characterize the size, crowding, plumbing, and utilities of housing units. These variables are keyed to a developing nation, since in the U.S. they would reflect considerable modernization and have much lower values. In the economic variables group, there is a mixture of basic microeconomics and macroeconomics parameters.

Variables for cluster analysis were chosen from a set of variables about 30 percent larger, based on elimination of highly correlated variables. Variables eliminated are highly correlated with variables selected; hence their elimination does not have major effects on the cluster results.

Table 12.1 List of Variables for Cluster Analysis

Variable Group	Description
Population	Log of Population
	Relative Population Growth 1970-1990
	Log of Population Density
	Sex Ratio
	Inmigration in Past 5 Years
Housing	Lack of Running Water
	Housing with One Room
	Household Crowding
	Septic Tank of Open Flow for Housing Unit
	No Toilet in Housing Unit
	Firewood or Coal for Heating
Economic	Economic Activity for Population Age 12+
	Unemployment
	Percent Owners/Employers/Salaried Workers
	Percent of Chemical and Petrochemical Revenues, 1993
	Percent of Metal Production and Equipment Manufacturing Revenues, 1993
	Percent of Professional and Technical Services Revenues, 1993
Social Rank	Professional/Technical/Managerial Occupation
	Primary Education
	High Income (more than 5 times minimum wage)
	Home Ownership
Urbanism/Familism	Cumulative Fertility to Women 20-29
	Free Union
	Separated and Divorced
	Ratio of Women Economically Active
Race/Ethnicity	Mixtec Language
	Nahautl Language
	Otomi Language
	Zapotec Language
	Indigenous Language - Remainder

Note: all variables are for 1990 unless otherwise indicated.
Source: 1990 Mexican Census of Population; 1993 Mexican Economic Censuses.

Map 12.1
Overall Clusters- 30 Variables
(Squared Euclidean Distance)

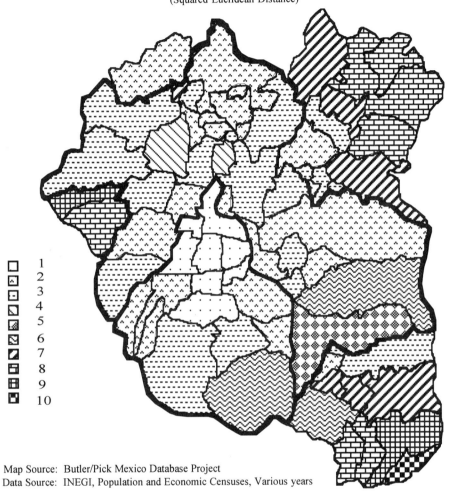

Map Source: Butler/Pick Mexico Database Project
Data Source: INEGI, Population and Economic Censuses, Various years

Broad Spatial Structure: Key Zones

The overall results reflect clustering based on all 30 variables. This discussion builds and expands on results initially presented in Chapter 1. The hierarchical cluster analysis results in the ten clusters shown in Map 12.1. The data results are summarized in Table 1.3. The major zones are the following:

Traditional Urban Core.

This cluster, labeled 1 on Map 12.1 is in the north half of the Federal District and consists of the delegations of Azcapotzalco, Benito Juarez, Coyoacan, Cuauhtemoc, Gustavo Madero, Iztacalco, Miguel Hidalgo, Tlahuac, and Venustiano Carranza. This is the original old core of Mexico City dating back to the 19th century (Garza, 1985, 1987). This urban core roughly corresponds to twelve smaller zones given in the Mexican censuses of 1930-1970 referred to as *cuartels* (INEGI, 1930, 1950, 1970). This area is characterized by:

-- high population (about 4.8 million persons)
-- population decrease from 1970 to 1990 (about 8 percent population loss)
-- low gender ratio (a gender ratio of 0.89 indicates a majority of women)
-- good housing conditions (for instance only 7 percent of housing units lack a toilet)
-- economic prosperity (only 2 percent are unemployed and 79 percent are owners, employers, or salaried workers).
-- low indigenous population (1 percent)

In many respects this urban core resembles that of the urban cores of advanced nations, with high population and density, economic prosperity, good housing, and ongoing population de-concentration.

In terms of one theory of Latin American Cities (Griffin and Ford, 1983), this zone is termed the "central business district." Their CBD is relatively dominant and prosperous because of continuing dependence on public transportation which is centered in and focused toward the CBD and by the influence of affluent residential areas that are within the CBD or nearby. These factors apply to the Mexico City urban core for the following reasons. First, there is continuing great dependence on public transportation, especially the subway system and the very large number of small buses accounting for perhaps a fourth of city passenger transport. Second, the urban core is surrounded closely by the highly affluent Las Lomas and other residential areas. The Las Lomas and other nearby affluent residential areas would correspond to what Griffin and Ford call the "elite residential sector" that surrounds the "spine." The spine is a linear extension of the CBD that contains the fine buildings and amenities. For Mexico City, the "spine" is clearly Paseo de La Reforma, the grand boulevard of the city. It is partly surrounded on both sides by fine residential areas and it terminates in the west in the Las Lomas zone. Third, as shown in Chapter 11, there is an extremely high concentration of the nation's largest corporations in the urban core.

Concentric Ring Surrounding the Urban Core Consisting of Several Zones.

There is a large and populous concentric ring surrounding the traditional urban core that consists of three zones (labeled 2, 3, and 4 on Map 12.1). These zones are interwoven with each other.

In the theory of Latin American cities referred to earlier (Griffin and Ford, 1983), these zones are referred to as the "zone of maturity" and "zone of *in situ* accretion." The zone of maturity is an area of good but older residences, often colonial, while the zone of *in situ* accretion consists of housing that started out modestly but moved through self improvement, i.e. accretion, towards a state of maturity. A prominent example of the "zone of *in situ* accretion" is the delegation of Nezahualcoyotl, which is included in Zone 2 on Map 12.1, i.e. within the concentric ring around the urban core.

The three zones (2, 3, and 4) within the concentric ring may be characterized as follows:

Zone 2
- high population (5.9 million persons in 20 cluster areas)
- very high population growth rates (close to doubling 1970-90)
- somewhat low gender ratio (0.97)
- fair housing quality (16 percent lacking toilet; 17 percent with septic tank or open flow)
- good economic prosperity (2 percent unemployment; 71 percent owners, employers, and salaried workers)
- low indigenous population (1 percent)

Zone 3
- high population (3.6 million persons in 19 areas)
- modest positive population growth 1950-1970 (about 3 percent)
- somewhat low gender ratio (0.97)
- fair housing quality (17 percent of housing units lack a toilet)
- economic prosperity (2 percent unemployment and 70 percent are owners, employers, and salaried workers)
- low indigenous population (1 percent)

Zone 4
- modest population (478,000 in two clusters)
- high relative population growth (10 percent 1970-90)
- somewhat low gender ratio (0.96)
- good housing quality (4 percent lacking a toilet; 4 percent dependent on a septic tank or open flow)
- high economic prosperity (2 percent unemployment, 94 percent are owners, employers, and salaried workers)
- very low indigenous population (0.65 percent)

Chalco - Impoverished and Indigenous Area.
Chalco is often recognized as the most impoverished area in Mexico City (Hiernaux, 1991). On the other hand, in the context of the nation of Mexico, it is not very impoverished (Pick and Butler, 1994). It developed as a result of in-migration after 1950 and is located in an area lacking many public utilities and urban amenities. It is labeled 5 on Map 12.1. It may be characterized as follows:
- moderate population (282,940 persons)
- equal gender ratio (equal at 1.00)
- fair housing quality (17 percent lack toilet; 13 percent depend on septic tank or open flow)
- fair economic prosperity (2.4 percent unemployed; 67 percent of workers are owners, employers, or salaried)
- high indigenous language population (3 percent) for Mexico Megacity. It should be noted that this percent is well below the average for Mexico as a whole (Pick and Butler, 1994).

Semi Urban Periphery and Gradated Transition Zone.

Semi-urban zones are located on the urban fringes in the west, northeast, and southeast of the conurbation. These areas have many rural characteristics, but are classified as being part of the Mexico City conurbation due to economic, labor force, and commuting dependencies. The urban sprawl of Mexico City has been moving in the direction of these fringes, and it is likely in the next 25 years they will be overrun by metropolitan sprawl. They are labeled as 8 and 9 on the Map.

They are characterized as follows:

– very low population (only 107,000 persons)
– high relative population growth 1970-90 (79 percent relative growth)
– gender ratio slightly above average (1.00).
– poor housing quality (48 percent lack toilet; 16 percent depend on septic tank or open flow)
– high use of wood and coal (one sixth lack running water)
        fair to poor economic level (3 percent unemployment; 38 percent owners, employers, and salaried workers)
– very low indigenous population (0.3 percent)

These semi-urban fringe zones are more impoverished and with somewhat worse housing than Chalco, which is often perceived in public image as being the worst poverty zone of Mexico City. There is a relatively small indigenous population in this outlying poverty zone.

Gradated Transition Zones Next to the Semi-Urban Fringe.

There is a transition zone next to the semi-urban fringe. It is shown in Map 12.1 diagonals and labeled 7 on the map (transition zone II).

It is characterized as follows:

– very low population (120,000)
– slightly above average gender ratio (1.04)
– high relative population growth 1970-90 (58 percent)
– fair housing quality (32 percent without toilet)
– fair economic poverty (2 percent unemployed: 8 percent are owners, employers, and salaried workers)

Ecatzingo

Ecatzingo is a very small population zone (5,800 persons) which shows extreme urban poverty, very low housing quality, and very low indigenous population. It is shown on the Map as checkerboard and labeled 10. In the cluster analysis, it represents the poorest and least developed area. It is located on the rough terrain adjacent to a huge volcanic mountain. (see Map 1.4). It fits into the semi-urban periphery, representing an extreme in the far southeast.

Comparison and Relevance of Key Zones

The key zones are consistent with the historical growth and change of Mexico City and with other studies of Mexico City's development. There is a particularly strong association with the growth of the metropolis 1950-1990 and with the history and growth of incorporated areas within the city.

Key Zones and Population Growth 1950-1970

The relative population growth of Mexico Megacity was discussed in Chapter 3. The growth from 1950-70 relates to the 1990 key zones in the following way:

-- *Traditional urban core*. It grew moderately in the center four delegations but rapidly in the remaining four delegations. It may be viewed as a smaller core within the present urban core that grew slowly while rapid growth occurred outwards, i.e. within the present core.

-- *Concentric ring surrounding the urban core*. There is a ring of high growth, but its radius is about 3/4 that of the concentric ring of 1990.

-- *Chalco*. Chalco does not stand out as distinctive in terms of 1950-70 growth. It is in the lower moderate portion of growth. Its relative 1950-70 growth rate was 77 percent.

-- *Semi Urban Periphery and Gradated Transition Zones*. These areas formed a distinctive slow growing zone 1950-1970. Their growth was approximately 0-50 percent, which varies between zero and two percent per year. The areas were rural and outside of the metropolis.

Key Zones and Population Growth 1970-1990

Overall, the key zones reveal a very close correspondence with growth patterns, 1970-90 (see Map 3.7).

-- *Traditional urban core*. There is an area of slow growth that closely approximates the size of the urban core key zone. The growth rates are in the range of -2.4 percent to 2.5 percent annually. Parts of this zone in the center are depopulating.

-- *Concentric ring surrounding the urban core*. There is a large concentric ring of high growth in the range of four to ten percent annually. The size and shape of the high growth ring approximates that of the key zone concentric ring.

Chalco. Chalco does not stand out as a distinctive, but is included with eleven municipios of high growth. From a growth standpoint, Chalco is included in a ring of high growth.

Semi Urban Periphery and Gradated Transition Zone. The northeast and southeast are distinctive as zones of slow growth, i.e. in the range of -2.4 to 3.3 percent annually. The rates of growth are comparable to rates for the urban core 1970-90. However, the semi urban periphery and transition zones to the west have moderate growth rates.

Generally there is some correspondence between population growth 1950-70 to the key cluster zones, but quite high correspondence between population growth 1970-90 and key cluster zones.

This correspondence is reflected in the patterns for 1970-90 population growth being closely tied to 29 socioeconomic characteristics in the set of thirty.

As seen in Table 12.2, seven out of 29 variables are significantly correlated at the $p=0.05$ level with population growth 1970-90. The highest correlations are with inmigration 1985-90, home ownership, and no toilet (inverse relationship). The inmigration is logically correlated as a component of population growth. The history of Mexico City urban growth is tied to shifts in home ownership (Schteingart, 1991), with a tendency to higher home ownership in more rapidly growing zones (compare Map 3.7 with Map 8.19). Areas having housing units with toilets tended to grow more rapidly in population 1970-90. This reflects the availability of better housing in the 70-90 exapnsion ring (see Chapter7), among other things.

The close correspondence between the 1990 overall cluster zones and population growth 1970-90 is further corroborated by examining the strength of correlations between each overall set of cluster variables and population growth 1970-90. Looking at results given in Table 12.2, there is a highly significant positive correlation with inmigration in the past five years. This result is quite plausible, since inmigration is one of the components in population growth, even though the time periods for the two variables differ considerably. The association with home ownership may reflect that Mexican urban patterns of ownership/renting differ from the urban U.S. In Mexico, renting is characteristic of the older and more affluent parts of the urban area the opposite of home ownership in Map 3.7, whereas in the U.S. home ownership is more characteristic of older and better off areas. The explanation is that population growth tends to take place in newer and less affluent zones. There are also positive associations with Mixtec language and indigenous language-remainder reflecting migration of the relevant language-speaking groups into growing areas of the conurbation.

This close correspondence is supported by several inverse associations. The reverse association for population density reflects reduced population growth in the urban core and higher growth in the large inner ring. There are negative associations with two housing indicators of no toilet and firewood/coal for housing. This reflects poor housing in the outer fringes and better housing in the large ring.

Population growth since 1950 corresponds closely to the overall pattern of cluster zones. This is corroborated by examining correlations of growth 1970-90 with the overall cluster set of variables. Results point to population growth as influential in forming the zones of the metropolis. It is likely that rapid growth of the metropolis since 1950 has led decade by decade to the formation of distinctly new growth zones and they have tended to remain distinct. One example of this may be Chalco, which has undergone large population growth since 1970 and is identified as a unique zone. This pattern of metropolitan differentiation may apply more to a rapidly growing metropolis than to a slow growing or stable metropolis.

Overall cluster zones for 1990 can be compared to other empirical and theoretical studies of overall socioeconomic patterning of the Mexico City metropolis (Rubalcava and Schteingart, 1985, 1987; Negrete et al., 1994), as well as to theories of spatial patterning for Latin American cities (Griffin and Ford, 1983). The comparison reveals many similarities and some differences that shed light on overall patterning of the metropolis.

This comparison moves from the more general and theoretical to the more empirical. Griffin and Ford (1983) discuss the transformation of Latin American cities into modern form through a series of stages and they present a model of the spatial structure of a typical Latin American City. They mention several trends that have transformed earlier "colonial" city structures into modern ones: (1) growth in the central business district (CBD), (2) industrialization, (3) expansion of urban-related services, (4) suburbanization, (5) architectural change, and (6) squatter settlements and later accretion in housing.

The CBD has changed from a traditional Spanish colonial Zócolo central plaza by expanding into what were formerly well-to-do residential areas near the core and beyond. In some cases, the CBD has expanded linearly along a major boulevard with building expansion on both sides of the boulevard extending for some distance. Industrialization has occurred in areas near the urban core, since the transportation, communications, and service infrastructure is more built up near the core. The expansion of urban services has occurred in cities as the housing stock in the newer, peripheral areas has been upgraded and developed. This upgrading of urban services is documented in the case of Mexico in Nezahualcóyotl (Lourdes, 1991; also see Relez-Igamez, 1983), Chalco (Hiernaux, 1991), and in many other areas (Castañeda, 1988; Duhau, 1991). Suburbanization is more limited in Latin American metropolises due to a steep income pyramid and limited high speed commuting highways.

Squatter settlements are typically Latin American and were discussed in Chapter 7. They tend to enter cycles of improvement with slow but persistent housing upgrading often done initially by the householders (Ward, 1978; Lourdes, 1991). Housing is further benefited by improving utilities and government services (Castañeda, 1988).

In the Griffin and Ford formulation, Latin American cities have undergone transformation over many decades from a traditional Spanish colonial model into modern metropolises based on these processes. The modern metropolis model shown in Figure 12.1 consists of the following zones: (1) CBD which is largely commercial and industrial, (2) Spine which is a linear extension of the CBD, (3) elite residential sectors on either side of the spine, (4) a zone of maturity which is mostly older and moderate quality residential housing, (5) zone of "in situ" accretion consisting of upgraded housing stock generally from squatter settlements originally, and (6) zone of peripheral squatter settlements (Griffin and Ford, 1980). There are also (6) zones of disamenity, which are disadvantaged areas extending as radial arms from the CBD through the two inner rings. These often tend to occur in physically degraded areas (Griffin and Ford, 1983). In traditional terms they reflect the axial theory of Homer Hoyt (1939), although Hoyt ascribes such wedges to transportation corridors rather than physical degradation.

It is important to note that the Griffin-Ford model is draws strongly on the Burgess model (Burgess, 1924), since it consists of a center and concentric rings. However, the Burgess theory was developed in the United States and includes a core and four surrounding rings, which are zones with improving socioeconomic level from center to periphery (see Figure 1.1). By contrast, in the Griffin-Ford model, the socioeconomic level declines from center to periphery (Butler, 1976). Both models tend to support cities that are expanding in population and physical size (Butler, 1976; Griffin and Ford, 1983). In both instances, the development of rings is the result of historical expansion in city size and area.

The Griffin-Ford theory supports part of the overall cluster pattern for Mexico City (Map 12.1). The traditional urban core may be considered equivalent to a CBD, several spines, and elite residential neighborhoods. The spines are the major traffic corridors especially Paseo de la Reforma and Insurgentes. Elite residential neighborhoods include Las Lomas, Coyoacan, and the Pedregal, among others. The urban core is more complex than the one outlined by Griffin and Ford, but this reflects the huge size of the city. There is one large ring consisting of three interleaved zones, rather than the two inner concentric rings of Griffin/Ford. These zones are not distinguished on the basis on "maturity" versus "accretion." Rather the three zones are distinguished on the basis on density, population growth 1970-90, and several indices of housing quality. Economically, the three zones are quite similar. There is a "wedge" of disamenity that centers on Chalco as a unique cluster and includes the surrounding cluster of Milpa Alta, Juchitepec, and Ixtapaluca. Included in the overall clusters but not in the Griffin/Ford model are the semi-urban periphery and gradated transition zones. This difference may reflect a somewhat different concept of metropolitan area, i.e. Griffin/Ford considered the urban area somewhat more narrowly than our concept of conurbation.

The second comparison is with an empirical study that utilized factor analysis to classify the zones of Mexico City. Rubalcava and Schteingart (1985, 1987) performed a factor analysis based on eight variables from the 1970 and 1980 population censuses.[1] Variables of social and physical-spatial aspects of urban differentiation were population economically active, self employed workers, completed primary education, and population with income more than five times the minimum wage. Socioeconomic variables were home ownership, housing units with potable water, index of persons per room, and urban population proportion. These were selected from a larger group on the basis of importance and reduced inter-correlations. After performing factor analysis, two factors were identified, which were termed "urban consolidation" and "socio-economic conditions" for the years 1970 and 1980.

These factors shown in Maps 12.2 and 12.3 are highly correlated. Since factor results are for 1980, the metropolitan area was smaller, so comparison with the overall clusters must be qualified. The rough comparison indicates that both factors distinguish an urban core, albeit smaller than that from our cluster analysis. There is a socioeconomically disadvantaged zone ("very low level") in Map 12.3 that has some overlap with clusters three and five, although the zone is larger than for clusters three and five than for factor II. An inner ring is apparent for "urban consolidation," although it is smaller than the "concentric ring" for the cluster analysis. This may reflect the smaller metropolitan area a decade earlier.

For both factors, there is generally a lowering in factor value from center to periphery. This may reflect the choice of variables, which individually follow such radial lowering. In comparing results, it is important to note that the eight factor variables would fall into our variable groups of social rank, housing, and economic. The factor analysis excludes demographic, urbanism/familism, and race/ethnicity dimensions. In this sense, the overall cluster results represent a broader geographical classification of zones. Another difference is the smaller concept of metropolitan area in the factor analysis, excluding the urban periphery and gradated transition zones of the conurbation. Finally, the factor analysis differs from cluster analysis in its objective of sorting variance into new combined variables, i.e. factors, whereas cluster analysis seeks to group similar zones hierarchically based evenly on variables. As a result, cluster analysis creates more homogenous and distinctive geographic zones than factor analysis.

In summary, viewed broadly, our cluster results conform well with the theoretical model for Latin American cities and somewhat with a factor analysis of Mexico City 1980 geographical patterns. The overall cluster analysis provides a division of the Megacity into distinctive parts: urban core, large concentric ring, Chalco and surrounding impoverished zone, and semi-urban periphery and gradated transition zone. This broad division retains the high density, rich central business district with an intermediate medium density and moderate socioeconomic ring, a poor "wedge" of Chalco and surroundings, and low-density, poor, semi-urban arms extending prominently in the northeast and southeast and slightly in the far west. The development of this broad pattern is due to historical expansion outwards from the original city in the CBD, housing history including squatter settlements, successions, accretions, and interactions with natural topography especially in Chalco and the southeast.

The overall pattern differs substantially from that of advanced megacities such as New York, Los Angeles, London, and Tokyo. Major differences are the following: (1) the urban

---

[1] Rubalcava and Schteingart's definition of the metropolitan region was smaller than ours.

core represents the highest standards of living in Mexico City, versus moderate standards in advanced megacities, (2) there are two types of poor areas, a disamenity zone nearer the core and urban periphery poor zones, (3) The periphery is poor whereas it is middle class or better in advanced megacities, and (4) Mexico Megacity has expanded much more rapidly in the late 20th century than many other megacities; for Mexico the geographical pattern of expansion has strongly influenced the development of overall zones.

Table 12.2 Correlations of Population Growth 1970-1990 with Other 29 Variables in the Overall Cluster Analysis Set of 30 Variables

Correlations with Population Growth 1970-1990	
0.21	Log of Population 1990
-0.25	Log of Population Density 1990
0.17	Sex Ratio
0.70	Inmigration in Past 5 Years
0.21	Lack of Running Water
0.13	Housing with One Room
0.04	Household Crowding
0.03	Septic Tank or Open Flow for Housing Unit
-0.28	No Toilet in Housing Unit
-0.24	Firewood or Coal for Heating
-0.04	Economic Activity for Population Age 12+
-0.06	Unemployment
0.16	Percent Owners/Employers/Salaried Workers
-0.07	Percent of Chemical and Petrochem. Revenues
0.20	Perc. of Metal Prod. and Equip. Manuf. Revenues
-0.17	Perc. of Prof. and Technical Services Revenues
-0.03	Professional/Technical/Managerial Occupation
-0.03	Primary Education
0.16	High Income (more than 5 times minimum wage)
0.31	Home Ownership
0.22	Cumulative Fertility to Women 20-29
-0.15	Free Union
-0.10	Separated and Divorced
-0.19	Ratio of Women Economically Active
0.26	Mixtec Language
0.01	Nahautl Language
0.10	Otomi Language
0.23	Zapotec Language
0.26	Indigenous Language - Remainder

Bold = statistically significant at 0.05 level

Figure 12.1

Latin American City Structure

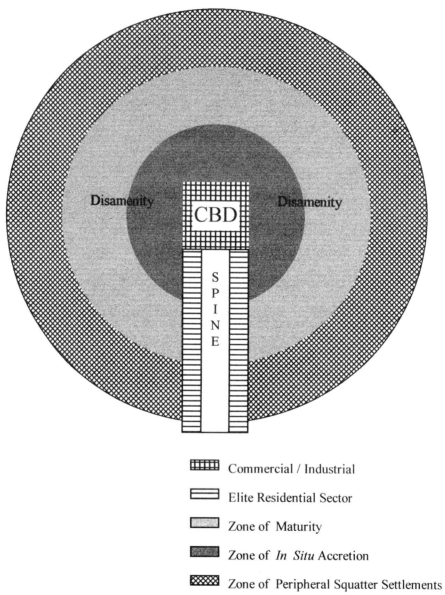

Source: Griffin and Ford in Brunn and Williams (eds.), *Cities of the World: World Regional Urban Development*, 1983

Social Rank and Urbanism/Familism

As pointed out in Chapter 1, the selection of variables for Social Rank, Urbanism/Familism, and Race/Ethnicity were selected in conformance with the theory of social area analysis. The theory of social area analysis is a more elaborate theory than those of Burgess (1925) and Hoyt (1939) to account for urban growth and differentiation. Social area analysis (Shevky and Bell, 1955) includes three dimensions for urban differentiation: (1) social rank, (2) urbanism/familism, and (3) race/ethnicity. Social rank is a socioeconomic factor that generally contains the most important variable in statistically explaining urban differences. It includes indicators of social rank and status (see Table 12-1 for indicators). Urbanism/familism reflects family size and composition. It reflects the adaptation of the family to the urban environment at various points in the family life cycle. Race/ethnicity, sometimes referred to as segregation, has generally been the most independent of the three factors. There are a variety of studies that have been accomplished utilizing social area analysis (Butler, 1976). These include cross-sectional studies, longitudinal studies, and comparative across one or more nations.

In earlier chapters, the cluster results for the three dimensions of social area analysis were discussed in the context of particular variable groups. It is important to go further and point to similarities and differences between the three dimensions. Two dimensions of social rank and urbanism/familism are tightly connected, but the third race/ethnicity dimension is only slightly correlated with the other two. This result reflects the general empirical results in the literature that race/ethnicity is less connected (Butler, 1976).

The close relationship between social rank and urbanism/familism can be observed spatially and confirmed statistically. The close eyeball comparison is evident by examining Maps 12.4 and 12.5. The clusters are remarkable similar, with the exception of the far western quadrant. The cluster groupings have almost no similarity for about ten municipios in the far west, in contrast to almost exact replicas elsewhere. It must be concluded that a very strong association in clusters elsewhere does not hold in the far west, and that in that area the social forces connecting these groupings weaken. We could find no literature on the little-studied far west to shed light on this.

In spite of the lack of association in the west, the overall association between the variable groups is very strong (see Table 12.3). For the sixteen individual correlations between variables in the two groups, eleven are statistically significant at the 0.05 level. It is interesting that the associations lack significance for free union. It may be that free union is present across a spectrum of social ranks and so is uncorrelated.

The overall strong association between social rank and urbanism familism is supported by many studies. In the demographic literature, there are numerous consistent results linking social rank with fertility (Kasarda et al., 1986). Many researchers postulate that social rank is influential on women's employment which in turn influences fertility (Kasarda et al., 1986). This points also to the well known strong relationship between female economic activity and fertility (Gendell et al., 1970; Davidson, 1973; Davidson, 1977; Alan and Casterline, 1984). Marital status variables have also been closely linked to social rank (Quilodrán, 1991). Overall then social theory strongly supports the close relationship between these two variable groups.

362

Map 12.2
Factor I Scores for
Mexico City, 1980

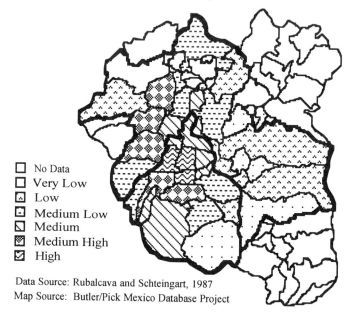

	No Data
	Very Low
	Low
	Medium Low
	Medium
	Medium High
	High

Data Source: Rubalcava and Schteingart, 1987
Map Source: Butler/Pick Mexico Database Project

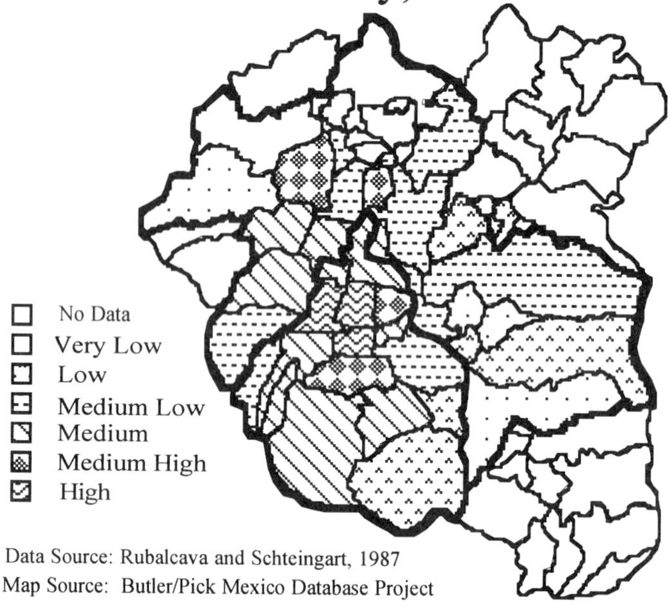

Map 12.3
Factor II Scores for
Mexico City, 1980

	No Data
	Very Low
	Low
	Medium Low
	Medium
	Medium High
	High

Data Source: Rubalcava and Schteingart, 1987
Map Source: Butler/Pick Mexico Database Project

Map 12.4
Social Rank Clusters

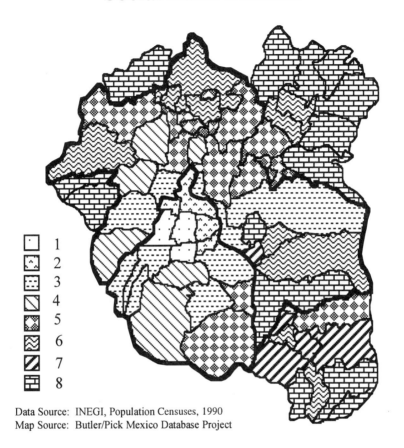

Data Source: INEGI, Population Censuses, 1990
Map Source: Butler/Pick Mexico Database Project

Map 12.5
Urbanism/Familism Clusters

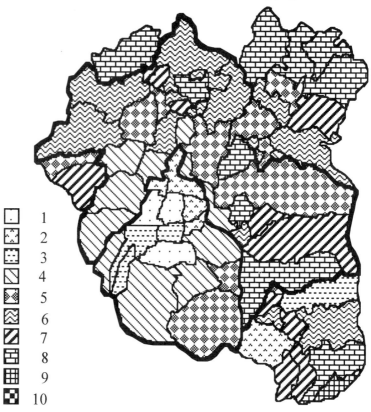

☐	1
☒	2
☐	3
☒	4
☒	5
☒	6
☒	7
☒	8
☷	9
☒	10

Data Source: INEGI, Population Census, 1990
Map Source: Butler/Pick Mexico Database Project

Table 12.3 Correlations Between Social Rank and Urbanism/Familism Variable Groups

	Cum. Fertility to Women 20-29	Free Union	Separated and Divorced	Ratio of Women Econ. Active
Prof./Tech./Mgr. Occupation	**-0.79**	0.05	**0.26**	**0.81**
Primary Education	**-0.82**	0.09	**0.29**	**0.78**
High Income (> 5 x min. wage)	**-0.60**	0.02	0.14	**0.64**
Home Ownership	**-0.63**	-0.20	**-0.29**	**-0.68**

Bold = statistically significant at 0.05 level

Ethnicity as a Contrasting Pattern

Social area analysis points to the likelihood that race/ethnicity will vary from other social area dimensions. This is indeed the case for Mexico City, as seen by comparing the cluster pattern for ethnicity (Map 12.6) with the overall cluster pattern (Map 12.1) and with the other social area analysis clusterings (Maps 12.4 and 12.5), as well as with the population, housing, and economic cluster results (Maps 3.18, 7.8 and 9.16). There is only modest comparability.

One comparison is the near uniqueness of Chalco as an ethnicity cluster, which is similar to the overall cluster results. For ethnicity, Chalco is grouped with Chimalhuacan. Chalco in the 70s and 80s grew rapidly in part from substantial inflow migrants from the south of Mexico, areas of high indigenous population (see Chapter 5 and Hiernaux, 1991). It is not surprising that Chalco has among the highest indigenous proportion in the conurbation and that its ethnic composition is quite different than other parts of the metropolis (see Chapter 8).

Another similarity between ethnicity clusters and overall clusters involves the northeast and southeast. These have unique ethnic composition, which includes among the lowest proportions of minority population in Mexico City. The northeast and southeast are also similar in the overall cluster results, if the gradated transition zones are also included.

Beyond these two similarities, there are large differences. For instance, in the ethnicity clusters, there is an urban core but it is shifted to the lower part of the Federal District. For the overall clusters it is in the upper part of the Federal District. Similarly there is an ethnicity cluster consisting of Iztapalapa, La Paz, and Chicoloapan, and Teotihuacan, (Cluster 3 on Map 12.6) which is quite unique not appearing in any other cluster maps. This cluster is very high in Nahautl Language speaking population. Huixquilucan which forms Cluster 8 is also unique in its very high proportion of Otomi language speaking, combined with elevated Mixtec language speaking and Zapotec language speaking population. The language speaking composition of all the clusters is shown in Table 12.4.

The unique patterning of ethnicity has been discussed with limited explanation in Chapter 8. The ethnic geographic patternings have had very limited study, so explanation is difficult. This study area may become much more important in the future if increased minority inmigration occurs, as is occurring in the most advanced megacities including London and New York and even Tokyo in the late 20th century (Sassen, 1991).

Map 12.6
Race / Ethnicity Clusters

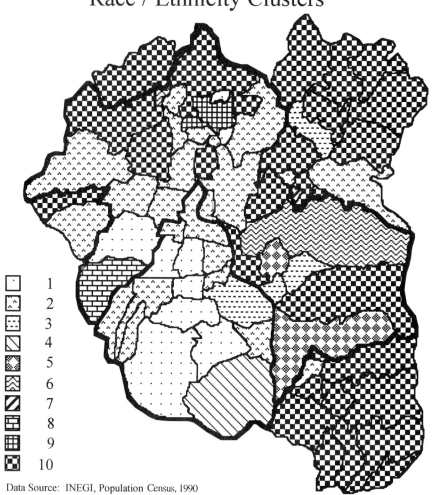

⊡	1
⊡	2
⊡	3
◩	4
◼	5
▨	6
▨	7
⊞	8
⊞	9
▩	10

Data Source: INEGI, Population Census, 1990
Map Source: Butler/Pick Mexico Database Project

Table 12.4 Race/Ethnicity Cluster Means

Variable / Cluster No.	1	2	3	4	5	6	7	8	9	10	Mexico City
Total Population 1990	3,616,076	6,845,877	1,713,073	63,654	525,257	164,819	14,179	131,926	36,994	2,328,891	15,440,746
Indigenous Language	1.6230	1.0183	1.4046	4.2354	2.7681	2.0700	1.2413	2.5234	1.0219	0.4852	1.0552
Mixtec Language	0.1587	0.1022	0.3411	0.0000	0.8716	0.0652	0.0141	0.3381	0.0548	0.0446	0.1235
Nahuatl Language	0.3793	0.2322	0.2762	3.1231	0.6160	1.5185	0.9310	0.3525	0.1748	0.1013	0.2995
Otomi Language	0.2470	0.1913	0.1799	0.2278	0.2133	0.1265	0.0353	0.9293	0.5101	0.0621	0.1635
Zapotec Language	0.1745	0.1086	0.1561	0.0738	0.1811	0.0413	0.0141	0.1872	0.0345	0.0385	0.0888
Other Indigenous Languages	1.1623	0.3840	0.4513	0.6111	0.9406	0.3184	0.2413	0.7163	0.2477	0.2415	0.3809

Cluster 1	Cluster 2	Cluster 3	Cluster 4	Cluster 5	Cluster 6	Cluster 7	Cluster 8	Cluster 9	Cluster 10
Benito Juarez	Alvaro Obregon	Chicoloapan	Milpa Alta	Chalco	Coyotepec	Chiconcuac	Huixquilucan	Melchor Ocampo	Acolman
Coyoacan	Atizapan de Zaragoza	Iztapalapa		Chimalhuacan	Texcoco			Nextlalpan	Amecameca
Cuauhtemoc	Azcapotzalco	Paz, La							Atenco
Jaltenco	Cuajimalpa	Teotihuacan							Atlautla
Miguel Hidalgo	Cuautitlan								Axapusco
Naucalpan	Ecatepec								Ayapango
Tlalpan	Gustavo A. Madero								Chiautla
Xochimilco	Iztacalco								Coacalco
	Jilotzingo								Cocotitlan
	Magdalena Contreras								Cuautitlan Izcalli
	Nicolas Romero								Ecatzingo
	Tecamac								Huehuetoca
	Temamatla								Isidro Fabela
	Teoloyucan								Ixtapaluca
	Tepetlaoxtoc								Juchitepec
	Tezoyuca								Nezahualcoyotl
	Tlahuac								Nopaltepec
	Tlalnepantla								Otumba
	Tultepec								Ozumba
	Tultitlan								Papalotla
	Venustiano Carranza								San Martin de las P.
									Temascalapa
									Tenango del Aire
									Tepetlixpa
									Tepotzotlan
									Tlalmanalco
									Zumpango

Conclusions

This chapter has distinguished the overall defining areas of the Megacity that include the urban core, large ring, Chalco and surrounding poverty zones, and semi-urban periphery and gradated transition zones. The overall zones can be better understood by comparing them to urban theories and empirical classification studies. The overall classification is well supported by a theory of Latin American city development which enhances traditional theories of urban core and concentric rings as well as urban "wedges." The Latin American theory adds new twists including reversal of direction of socioeconomic gradations from center to periphery.

The overall cluster results may be compared to Rubalcava and Schteingart's factor analysis of Mexico City zones based on 1980 data. The comparison is weak due to temporal, variable, and methodological differences.

When clustering patterns for the variables groups are compared, social rank and urbanism/familism are highly similar except for differences in the west. The comparison is supported by correlations as well as by relevant social and demographic theories.

Race/ethnicity cluster patterns are different from all other cluster results. Although a few areas resemble the overall cluster results, most are entirely different. These patterns cannot be explained entirely at present, but will be important for the future Megacity.

13

Mexico Megacity in the Future

Introduction

We have three goals for this final chapter. First, to briefly recap the most important conclusions engendered by our research on Mexico Megacity. This will be accomplished by exploring a number of matters involving important decisions and policy alternatives related to (a) population, (b) environmental management, (c) land use and physical planning, (d) multifunctional and societal planning, and (e) evaluation of policy decisions, feedback, and adjustments. Second, to enumerate a list of future research priorities, albeit from our personal perspective. Third, to paint a sweeping overview of Mexico Megacity that is based upon our research and to discuss briefly projections for the future.

The 1978 national urban economic development plan[1] had as its goals redistributing the population away from Mexico City, Monterrey, and Guadalajara by concentrating industry and services in different priority zones of (1) the coasts, primarily for tourism; (2) areas rich in natural resources; and (3) the Mexican - U.S. border region. As seen on Map 13.1, the plan included tourist development areas such as Cancun, Ixtapa, the coast of Oaxaca, Cabo San Lucas at the tip of Baja California Sur, etc. Emphasis on tourism has so far ignored that there is no consensus that exists on the central question of whether or not tourism actually benefits more than it damages (Goulet, 1983: 147).[2] The planned border zones raise similar questions to that of tourism -- are interactions between Mexico and the U.S. horizontal and mutually advantageous or vertical and exploitative? (Goulet, 1983: 151).

Among relevant aspects of the current proposed National Development Plan 1995-2000[3], there is recognition of the need to overcome inequities between individuals, regions, and economic sectors (President of Mexico, 1995). The plan includes programs to increase the coverage and quality of education, social security, housing, and health care. Housing will be advanced through housing promotion agencies, improving administrative procedures, and strengthening procedures and financing for issuing housing and land title.

The current National Development Plan 1995-2000 continues the earlier objective of balancing national growth of population, regions, micro-regions within states, and cities. Among other realities noted in the plan is that the four major Mexican cities, Mexico Megacity, Guadalajara, Monterrey, and Puebla, contained 45 percent of the national population in 1990. Thus, there is endeavor to promote the development of 100 medium sized cities. This portion of the current plan stems directly from CONAPO's System of Cities, which was developed and proposed in 1991-1992 (see Chapter 2). Development of the 100 cities, many in regions away from major metropolitan areas, will be facilitated by transferring resources from the major cities to these regions and cities.

There is recognition in the 1995-2000 plan that "least favored groups" who include the extremely poor, indigenous peoples, women, and migrant workers, require priority attention to improve their well being. Among other things, attention will be given to shelter, education, training, urban services, sewage disposal, electricity, and food availability.

The current plan favors policies to advance economic growth through improved savings, foreign exchange, monetary policy, employment and productivity, training, technological advances, infrastructure improvement, and promotion of competition. Enhanced economic growth would favor Mexico City since this book has shown that it constitutes up to half of the national economy. The question is whether economic growth

---

[1] *Plan Nacional de Desarrollo Urbano 1978.*

[2] *Plan Nacional de Desarrollo Industrial, 1979-1982.*

[3] *Plan Nacional de Desarrollo, 1995-2000.*

would benefit the Megacity's highly varied zones and sectors equitably. Another concern expressed in the 1995-2000 plan is how to make economic growth compatible with environmental protection. Hindering all of these economic policies and efforts is Mexico's currently high debt, high inflation, and high primary export economy.

Attempts to decentralize the government and economy, for the most part, have been resisted. The most notable successes have been in the maquiladora and tourism sectors. Despite all contrary efforts, Mexico Megacity continues to grow and to disproportionately form the center of the nation's population, services, commerce, and industry. New rural migrants and enterprises continue to enter Mexico City, providing the basis for further economic and population concentration (Lo, 1994).

372

Map 13.1 Planned Development Zones, 1978 National Urban Development Plan

Key
Priority zones of urban growth

1. Tampico
   Port, industry, energy, agriculture.
2. Manzanillo
   Tourism, port.
   Ciudad Juárez
   Commerce.
3. León
   Commerce, industry.
4. Commerce, industry.
5. Coatzacoalcos-Villahermosa-Salina Cruz
   Energy, agriculture.
6. Tijuana-Mexicali
   Commerce, agriculture.
7. Gómez Palacio-Lerdo-Torreón
   Agriculture, industry.
8. Ciudad Obregón
   Industry, agriculture, tourism.
9. Lázaro Cárdenas-Acapulco
   Industry, tourism.

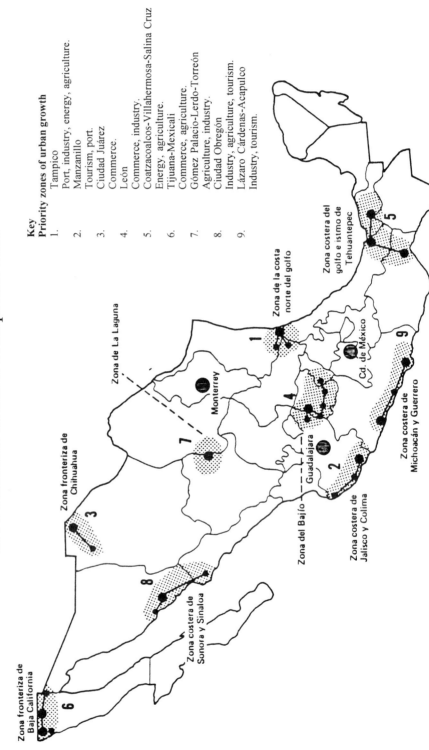

Source: Florescano, 1984:219. Reprinted with permission from Enrique Florescano.

Policy Alternatives

If policy alternatives are to be implemented successfully they must have clearly defined goals, objectives with timelines specified, and activities geared to ensuring that goals and objectives are successfully met (Butler, 1976). Rhetoric will not succeed. Much like the United States, Mexico does not currently have a national plan of urban development although there have been attempts at decentralization and regional development. While some plans for regional development exist and have been implemented, especially in the construction of tourist centers, no effective national plan currently exists. Mexico also has issues of economic inequity, social and political conflict, inadequate utilization of physical resources, some administrative inefficiency, and no plan for development of the Megacity. Clearly, policy will have to address the fact that the Megacity dominates the rest of the country financially, industrially, in communications, and in investment. Much effort is going to have to be expended if the "Political, social, economic, and ecological forces that have conspired to make the capital increasingly unmanageable, overpopulated, unproductive, and insalubrious" are to be overcome (Kandell, 1996: 187).

In addition to a national plan of urbanization development, important policies must be advanced for specific land development in various areas of the Megacity and especially for *ejido* areas that will be enveloped by Megacity expansion. How does the Megacity and other urban expansion in Mexico impact agrarian reform? Associated with a national plan of urbanization might be one related to industrialization. At the national level, is the oil industry, maquilas, and tourism an adequate economic base for the future?

Mexico has attempted to decentralize population and economic activities. However, population and economic activities have increasingly concentrated in Mexico Megacity. Unikel (1976) pointed out that up to that time much of the limited decentralization that had taken place had been in larger nearby locations -- Toluca, Queretaro, Cuernavaca, and Puebla. Part of the pull to the larger metropolitan region, of course, is that Mexico Megacity is the financial, corporate, cultural, political, and decision-making center of the country. Without question these very same areas will continue to be attractive locations because of proximity to the Megacity.

Of course, one possible policy alternative is to make it virtually impossible because of regulations or financial disincentives for people and economic activities to locate in the greater Megacity region. However, this is highly unlikely. Another possible approach is to offer financial incentives for both people and economic activities to locate elsewhere throughout the country. To be successful, such an alternative undoubtedly would have to stress location into other major metropolitan regions. It would also enlarge the already burdened national budget (see Vargas and Garcia, 1996). Unikel (1976) stressed possible development in the Bajio region stretching from Guadalajara over the northeastern section of the country and a zone including Veracruz and Tabasco and the Monterrey-Saltillo area. Another possible focus is on major border cities -- Tijuana, Mexicali, Ciudad Juarez, and others shown in Table 2.6.

There are substantial environmental problems in the Megacity region, including infrastructure deficits. The need to develop additional housing to overcome the housing deficit, develop basic urban facilities, employment, and services may overwhelm the metropolis. There are substantial areas in the Megacity with a lack of running water, electricity, and sewage disposal, among others (see Chapter 7). If the current population and economic concentration continues, current deficits most likely will increase rather than decrease. Clearly, basic policies need to be developed to overcome current environmental deficiencies. Also, it appears that definite policies will have to be developed and implemented in regard to *ejidos*, especially in respect to adequate payment for expropriated land (Negrete et al., 1993). As Unikel (1976) noted, the government may be required to use them as areas for development and possibly to   control prices. However, pressure from speculators and developers requires definitive policy decisions.

Further, the Megacity has the worst air pollution problem in the world (U.N., 1994). Although there appears to be greater awareness and some recent abatement measures, air pollution so far appears not to be moderating . A number of alternatives have been proposed and were reviewed in an earlier chapter. So far what appears to be missing is the will to solve the problem. Other problems that need immediate attention are the water supply, waste water disposal, and waste disposal. Water must come from further and further reaches to satisfy the needs of the Megacity. Waste water disposal has become more costly and may threaten the quality of water in Mexico Megacity.

Population

Population growth and urbanization in Mexico has continued at a rapid pace over the past thirty years. The population doubled in that time with most of the expanding population living in urban areas, especially Mexico Megacity. Over half of the Mexican population now lives in overcrowded cities of over 100,000 population. Further, it is anticipated that population will continue to grow at a rate which will lead to half again as much population in 30 years (Population Reference Bureau, 1996). Substantial numbers of persons will be born in rural areas and many of them will become rural to urban migrants, and with the population being born in urban places, will account for most of the increasing proportion of the population that will be living in the major urban places in Mexico.

Mexico Megacity will be the destination for large numbers of rural to urban migrants and others will be moving to the Megacity from other urban places. Mexico Megacity, now the largest city in the world by some estimates, will continue to be the largest or one of the largest with an increasing population. While the Megacity is growing in population, the old core in the Federal District actually is losing population (see Chapter 3). Thus, most future Megacity population growth will be in peripheral areas; spatial expansion outward will continue. One estimate places 40 percent of the population in the Megacity as living in informal (squatter) settlements, primarily located on newly squatted peripheral land (Mathur, 1994: 355).

Unikel (1977) pointed out that two factors will determine the degree of Mexican urbanization in the future: (1) overall population growth and (2) that proportion of the population living under urban conditions. Overall population growth, of course, is determined by natural increase (excess of births over deaths) and net international migration. It is anticipated that fertility rates in all regions and areas of Mexico will outstrip death rates at more or less the same rate as current. In Mexico, it is anticipated that international inmigration will be insignificant so the major component of population growth will be natural increase. Urban growth is dependent upon natural increase, internal net migration to urban areas from rural areas, outward growth of already existing urban complexes, and reclassification of formerly rural areas as urban.

Natural increase is expected to continue in Mexico into the forseeable future. In addition, rural areas undoubtedly will persist in having higher natural increase than the Mexican urban population; thus, it can be anticipated that there will be sustained rural to urban migration. Most rural to urban migrants will have lower level education and lack skills necessary to survive in an urban labor force. As a result of natural increase in both urban and rural areas, already existing urban complexes will proceed to grow and probably expand outward absorbing smaller localities. In addition, some smaller places will expand enough in population to be defined as an urban place.

Mortality in Mexico has reached a low level. As a result, any future reduction in mortality rates will have little impact upon the total Mexican population. Thus, fertility, especially of the rural population, will be a greater influence upon future population growth in Mexico than mortality. In the past, fertility declines in Mexico have first taken place in urban regions; it remains problematic, however, how much more urban fertility will decline in the future. What is predictable is that if excess fertility continues in rural areas, there will be substantial rural to urban migration in the future. Thus, population growth will continue in Mexico; a central question about it concerns to what degree rural fertility will be further reduced, if at all.

Environmental Management

Migration to the Megacity most likely will continue unabated with primary areas of origin being rural and from urban places in the central region of the country, areas with infrastructure deficits. While there will be outmigration and the core (Federal District) will actually lose population, gains in the periphery will offset core losses and thus there will be a large net gain. Morbidity and mortality rates are expected to remain substantially as current. Environmental problems that currently plague the Megacity may get worse and possibly lead to more diseases. Air pollution, inadequate drainage and sewage disposal, lack of running water, etc. are rampant in many areas of the Megacity, especially in the periphery. The Megacity has a serious water problem that undoubtedly is going to get much worse before it gets better. Water is needed both for urban development and for agricultural purposes or the urban population will not be fed.

Given the anticipated large influx of new migrants and that the overall infrastructure of the Megacity already is in deep trouble because basic urban services, especially in the periphery, have not kept pace with an ever increasing Megacity population, it is not likely that the infrastructure will be able to accommodate and support this expanding population. Thus, only increased problems can be anticipated in the future unless there is a much larger expenditure of resources than currently to correct and expand the infrastructure.

Resources available to be expended on the infrastructure, however, will be minimal. Even now there are not enough resources to overcome current neighborhood and housing deficiencies. With an increasing population in peripheral areas many substantially without an infrastructure, a huge amount of investment will be required to ensure even minimum access to drinking water, electricity, and sanitation. Many newly born Mexico Megacity residents will be poor, undereducated, and probably without a job. They will pay little attention to environmental problems; their focus will be on obtaining adequate food, housing, and clothing. It is highly unlikely that the Mexico City economy will generate hundreds of thousands or more new jobs a year to accommodate the labor force demand of this expanding population (see Chapter 10 and Pick et al., 1993). Mexico Megacity, however, will persist as having a much higher standard of living compared to the rest of Mexico.

Thanks to INEGI, unlike many other countries, Mexico excels in collection of information. INEGI in the mid-1990s has increased its responsibility for and enhanced its collection and distribution of environmental information. However, there are organizational barriers in the utilization of data and in many instances a lack of coordinated efforts in their use by other agencies. Thus, while data are available, there is a need for more adequate utilization of these data by Mexican organizations in addition to INEGI.

Land Use and Physical Planning

Most planning is concerned with land use and physical environment. Generally, such plans focus on physical forms and utilize untested assumptions about individual and group behavior. In Mexico and Mexico Megacity, many aspects of land use and physical planning have been incorporated into a variety of schemes, some successful and some not so successful. In the future, land use and physical planning undoubtedly will have to be concerned with its impact upon how they are influenced by individuals and groups and in turn how they influence individuals and groups. Such planning will of necessity involve multifunctional and overall societal planning. This planning will have to address the transportation difficulties that exist in the Megacity and will require coordination of various agencies and groups to overcome its deficiencies and costs.

Of particular concern in Mexico Megacity has been the utilization of *ejido* land.[4] *Ejidal* land was established after the Mexican Revolution and is agricultural land held by the community but worked individually by named peasants (Gilbert and Ward, 1985: 284). In 1988 almost 45 percent of the land in the Federal District and just over 50 percent in the State of Mexico was *ejidal*. On the other hand, there were only 20,373 *ejidarios* in the Federal District and 219, 301 in the State of Mexico (INEGI, 1991).

As shown on Map 13.2, *ejido* land was spread throughout the greater Mexico City area; however, the northern areas in the State of Mexico were more substantially ejido than other parts of the complex (Varley, 1985: 4; Gilbert and Varley, 1989). In 1970, the State of Mexico took the first legal steps to institute a wide-ranging tenure legalization program. Anticipated results of legalization were better housing conditions, security, and better access to urban services. Of course, not all of these lofty goals were always met.

By 1970, at least 16 percent of the Mexico City population was residing on *ejido* lands. Expropriation of *ejido* and communal land are supposed to be limited to public use or social benefit purposes. However, while about half of the uses of *ejido* land in 1976 was for low-income housing (*colonias populares),* 39 percent was being used for public works, three percent for middle class, and nine percent for luxury housing. It was estimated that three-fifths of the population of Naucalpan (adjacent east-central to the Federal District) lived in poor-quality housing on formerly *ejido* lands (Varley, 1987).

Legalization of urban land ownership took place for 325,000 owners in 1989, 450,000 in 1990, and 450,000 in 1991, for a total of 1,225,000 during the three year period (Presidencia, 1992). Undoubtedly this process will continue but with the diminution of *ejidal* lands.

Multifunctional and Societal Planning

Mexico Megacity will continue to be the cultural, financial, and communications center of the country. It undoubtedly will remain as one of the primary urban centers in Latin America and expand its influence far beyond its borders -- becoming an important "global city." Most major corporations and main foreign corporations will continue to locate in the Megacity and in only certain locations, all near each other in part of the old core. National planning that does take place will be in Mexico Megacity, whether it is for the oil industry, border maquilas, tourism, or other endeavors.

For effective future planning for Mexico Megacity, there is a need for (1) knowledgeable and skilled planners, (2) basic data and information systems, (3) adequate funding, (4) a capable and honest administration, (5) at least some level of common agreement on goals and objectives of the plans, and (6) the political will and power to carry out the plan.

---

[4]   *Ejido* property was originally intended for agricultural purposes by people living in specific communities. But beginning in the 1940s, some of this land was being sold illegally to people in search of a home site.

Evaluation of Policy Decisions, Feedback, and Adjustments

It is probably highly unreasonable to assume accompanying sustained population growth of the Megacity that there will be substantial changes in (1) population composition, (2) environmental management problems, (3) land use and physical planning needs, and (4) necessity for multifunctional and societal planning. What is imperative, however, will be a systematic evaluation of policy decisions regarding these elements, feedback, and the will to make adjustments. Resource expenditures should be directed toward the very real and extensive problems that exist. However, without adequate evaluation and thence feedback for adjustments, such attempts will prove to be futile. Policy decisions that will have to be made and evaluated properly will have to come to grips with two counteracting tendencies. There clearly is a need for a national population and urbanization plan in Mexico. On the other hand, there seems to be a clearly emerging trend for more participatory democracy at the local level. How to accommodate the macro with mini view will require delicate balancing act.

Map 13.2 Ejido Lands of Mexico City

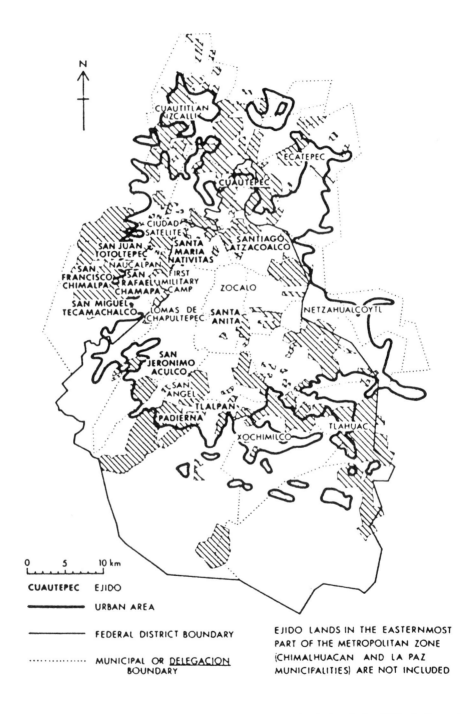

N

CUAUTITLAN IZCALLI

ECATEPEC

CUAUTEPEC

CIUDAD SATELITE

SANTA MARIA NATIVITAS

SANTIAGO ATZACOALCO

SAN JUAN TOTOLTEPEC

NAUCALPAN

SAN FRANCISCO CHIMALPA

SAN RAFAEL CHAMAPA

FIRST MILITARY CAMP

ZOCALO

SAN MIGUEL TECAMACHALCO

LOMAS DE CHAPULTEPEC

SANTA ANITA

NETZAHUALCOYTL

SAN JERONIMO ACULCO

SAN ANGEL

TLALPAN

PADIERNA

XOCHIMILCO

TLAHUAC

0   5   10 km

CUAUTEPEC   EJIDO

——————   URBAN AREA

——————   FEDERAL DISTRICT BOUNDARY

·············   MUNICIPAL OR DELEGACION BOUNDARY

EJIDO LANDS IN THE EASTERNMOST PART OF THE METROPOLITAN ZONE (CHIMALHUACAN AND LA PAZ MUNICIPALITIES) ARE NOT INCLUDED

Reprinted from *Bulletin of Latin American Research*, Volume 4, Number 1, Ann Varley, "Urbanization and Agrarian Law," pp. 1-16, Copyright 1985, with kind permission from Elsevier Science Ltd, The Boulevard, Langford Lane, Kidlington OX5 1GB, UK.

Research Priorities

Research priorities can be approached from varying perspectives. Each policy area requires extensive research to make adequate decisions and determine if viable programs are to be developed. Here we first focus on population growth as it is related to urban development and especially to Mexico Megacity. Second, we present a number of other potential priorities that deal with rural to urban and urban to urban migration. Since rural migration, in part is engendered by high fertility rates in rural areas, this leads to additional research priorities and programmatic implications. The relationship between economic development and an expanding Megacity population certainly deserves an examination. One of the most important considerations for future Megacity is how large and what gender balance the potential the labor force will have and what skills the labor force will have.

If current population projections are anywhere near correct, this means that give-or-take one million persons a year for the next 15 years will be old enough to enter the national labor force in Mexico (Pick et al., 1993). Yet, most modern industrialization is designed to save labor rather than utilize a larger labor force. Current economic resources in Mexico are primarily from the nationalized oil industry, maquiladoras, and tourism. The oil industry may expand its labor force; however, that labor force undoubtedly will have to be relatively highly trained. On the other hand, the maquila and tourism industries, for the most part, engender a labor force that is relatively low-level and weighted toward females. Surplus labor in Mexico is expected to gravitate primarily to Mexico Megacity, other larger Mexican cities, including those in the U.S. - Border region, and to the U.S.

Unless there is substantial change in fertility in the near future, there will be continued population growth and urbanization in Mexico. Undoubtedly, the surplus rural population will continue to be city bound. Mexico Megacity - and other large cities in Mexico will be the destination of rural to urban migrants. Large scale industrialization is not foreseen in the future and agricultural production is not expected to increase substantially unless there are more water projects developed. If these assumptions are correct, there will be little surplus money for substantial economic development.

All of these trends lead to pressing research priorities on how to guide urban development - especially in Mexico Megacity and the development of an effective urban policy. Great attention probably should be devoted to mechanisms that would encourage decentralization. Research on past and current trends needs to be expanded since they may be the best portents of the future.

It is clear in Mexico that subsequent urbanization and growth of Mexico Megacity are not necessarily related to industrialization. How to incorporate the large number of rural to urban and migrants from other urban centers to Mexico Megacity is of substantial concern. Expansion of the Megacity will require utilizing land not now in urban uses. Already in Mexico Megacity there are huge areas with a substantial population that lack the most basic urban services. How to spawn new areas of housing with adequate urban services while not ignoring areas already with substantial housing and neighborhood deficits will require substantial effort and research. An emphasis on fertility notes rural-urban differences and there is ample research evidence showing variation in fertility within the Megacity (see Chapter 4). Little explored, however, is the relationship between extreme environmental conditions in the Megacity and their relationship to morbidity and mortality.

Research could focus on where migrants are coming from, what they expect, and what happens to them after they have arrived in the Megacity. Past research has shown the importance of social networks in migration. Could these networks be used to resettle surplus migrants and population to underpopulated areas (if there are such areas). Another research effort might focus on how migrants to the metropolis and population movement within the Megacity has influenced behavior. "Migrant selectivity" perhaps would determine if there has been a "brain drain" from rural areas to the Megacity and if a similar circumstance exists for other urban migrants to the metropolitan complex. Given the lack of economic development in rural areas, is this a sufficient push for migration to urban centers such as Mexico Megacity? Would extensive rural development inhibit or blunt the urbanward migration? Or is the pull at destination of family and/or "bright lights" stronger than economic push factors in urban migration in Mexico?

There is relatively little research now available on social stratification in Mexican cities and Mexico Megacity. How does stratification of various areas emerge in the city and what are implications for attitudes and behavior of emerging areas filled with different kinds of population. Little research has been accomplished on intergenerational mobility in the Megacity. That is do rural migrants come to the Megacity with relatively few urban skills remain forever after at lower levels or do they move up in the labor force over time. Similarly, do second-generation migrants remain in a "culture of poverty" or do they begin the climb up the educational, occupational, and income ladder?

Many new jobs in the maquila and tourism industries appear to be at the lower level and substantially for females. Given the family structure and values in Mexico what does this mean for the family in the future? Also, related to these expanding jobs are locations at the U.S. - Mexican border and substantially along the sea coasts. This in itself generates migration of younger women away from their home of origin. Within the Megacity, there are clear gender ratio differences (see Chapter 3) What does this mean for the future?

Finally, there is a whole litany of other issues and research priorities that could be listed. For examples, there is a need to enhance research concerned with environmental protection, solid waste collection, the transportation system, cross-governmental cooperation, and property rights, among others (Cheema, 1994: 427).

An Overview of Mexico Megacity

This concluding section provides a broad overview of contemporary Mexico Megacity based upon our analyses presented in this book and then briefly presents a projection of future population growth of Mexico Megacity. The overview paints from specific research results a more abstract view of the City. Undoubtedly, this contemporary overview also describes substantially what the Megacity is likely to be like in the year 2000.

The spatial structure of Mexico Megacity was a primary focus of our endeavor. One important aspect of our work was to carry out cluster analyses seeking to identify common areas of the Megacity based on sets of variables. That is, our effort was guided by including a large number of variables/dimensions to determine if there were identifiable areas in the Megacity that were relatively homogeneous within but different from other areas -- e.g., homogeneous areas within but different from other areas. One cluster analysis involved 30 variables (see Chapters 1 and 12). Then several "subcluster" analyses were carried out on six subsets of the larger number of dimensions. From the major cluster analysis, the "old core" of the city emerged as one cluster. This cluster included an extremely large population, high density, and had the lowest gender ratio among ten clusters -- e.g., more females than males. Several other clusters were located on the periphery and one cluster clearly identified those areas with severe environmental and housing deficits. Cluster analyses of other dimensions were found extremely useful in describing the spatial structure of Mexico Megacity. What is clear from the cluster analyses is that how Mexico Megacity is described depends at least partially upon what one wants to emphasize. While the broad view presented here is based upon several analyses, adding, deleting, or changing the dimensions in the analysis plainly would somewhat alter the view of Megacity presented.

Chapter 12 presented the basic statistical analysis carried out in our research. Variables utilized in the 30-variable cluster and specialized cluster analyses were selected from several theoretical perspectives. It is clear from these analyses that Mexico Megacity dimensions do not fit the traditional view of U.S. cities. However, there are similarities in structural form, albeit with different dimensions making up various zones. As a result of the descriptive and cluster analyses reported in this volume, an idealized model of Mexico Megacity strongly implies that there are major "concentric zones" in the metropolitan complex with some sectorization. Our analyses lead us to the conclusion that there are four relatively homogeneous zones with several areas that are relatively unique. The four clearly demarcated zones are (1) the old urban core, (2) an inner ring, (3) an outer ring or what might be labeled as the transition zone, (4) the periphery, urban fringe, poverty zone. The populous unique area of Chalco is included on Map 13.3 as part of the urban poverty fringe. However, they are labeled for identification. The ethnicity cluster, indigenous population, appears to be completely different than all other clusters and is not included here as part of the idealized model. Thus, Map 13.3 is based upon analytical results presented in previous chapters but presented as a broader idealized model, but excludes race/ethnicity which is so important in U.S. research. Ethnicity should be viewed alongside it as a differing perspective.

Idealized Model of Mexico Megacity

The Core. Without exception, all cluster analyses picked out the old core from the other areas of the Megacity. In addition, other analyses consistently demonstrated that the old core of Mexico City was distinctive from other areas in Mexico City. However, the exact dimensions of the old core cluster varied by the 30-variable analysis and or subcluster analyses. For example, the old core population cluster focused almost entirely on only the various oldest delegations in the Federal District, whereas the economic cluster contained most of these same delegations but also consisted of a sector from the old core to the slightly west-south. These two perspectives of the core were only slightly in variance with an industrial cluster which, in contrast, was slightly north but contained most of the old core of Mexico City. The idealized model shown on Map 13.3 is broader than the old core and demonstrates how the core has expanded.

The core was considered as having expanded because economic, housing, population, and housing cluster analyses included all of the original core areas but also several peripheral areas of longer term settlement. The expanded core includes a sector from the traditional old core to somewhat to the south-central.

The core contains a huge population and is central in many other ways including the home of the majority of major economic institutions and corporations in Mexico, the center of the federal government, more females than males, and relatively good housing conditions, although with substantial environmental degradation in air pollution, and other deficits.

Inner Ring. Partially surrounding a substantial part of the traditional old core is an inner ring concentrated from central west and east and to the south but covering only partially the southern areas which are now included in the "new core."

Outer Ring/Transition Zoen. The outer ring, for the most part beyond the inner ring, includes delegations and municipios covering the entire Megacity. These areas are in transition from either formerly smaller places now being inundated by the Megacity or former *ejido* and/or other rural lands being converted to urban usage in the metropolitan complex.

Urban Fringe. There are substantial urban fringe areas, especially on the far northeast and far southeast. These municipios in the State of Mexico are just now beginning to undergo accretion into the Megacity. There are also a few areas to the central-west that remain urban fringe. Some of these areas still retain their rural character but undoubtedly will soon be "lost" in the larger metropolitan complex.

Distinctive Areas. In addition to the above, there are several municipios in the State of Mexico included in the larger metropolitan complex that do not fit the above characterization. Among them are (1) *Chalco,* (2) *Ecatzingo,* (3) *Atlautla,* and (4) *Isidro Fabela,* either as a single municipio cluster or combined only with a few other units to make up an unusual cluster. Several other municipios on occasion were the only unit in a cluster. However, for this presentation they were included in the broader perspective shown here. All of these relatively unique areas are in the State of Mexico and not the Federal District. Atlautla and Ecatzingo are both located in the far southeast of the metropolitan complex. For some analyses they were in the same cluster while in others they were separate and at times joined with other units in a cluster. Similarly, Isidro Fabela clearly is a rather unique area. Perhaps the most often distinctive unit is Chalco. Since Chalco is much more populous than the other unique areas, it is the only unique area shown on Map 13.3.

Theoretical Implications

Map 13.3, generalized from the data and different cluster analyses reported in this volume, shows quite clearly that there are some spatial consistencies. These consistencies do vary somewhat depending upon variables included in the analysis. However, just as obvious there are theoretical implications of our analyses. Early "traditional" studies of U.S. cities reported concentric zones (Burgess, 1925) and concentric zones with sectors (Hoyt, 1943). While these approaches have been extensively criticized, these "ideal" types of areas *within* cities have been shown to exist in a number of cities in the U.S. One criticism argued that there are not zones but rather gradients (Alihan, 1938). Gradients in fact may exist in Mexico Megacity; however, data by spatial units that we were able to collect and analyze do not allow such an exploration. Further, it should be noted that the heterogeneous/homogeneity of areas are important to consider. Our analyses utilized 69 delegations and municipios, all of which had varying degrees of heterogeneity. While all of these points have implications for Mexico Megacity, perhaps the one of most interest is that of the *generality* of the traditional approach to all types of cities and, of course, cities outside of the U.S.

Studies of Latin American cities, in general, have not called into question the traditional approach. One of the very first studies of Merida, Mexico actually showed some remarkable similarity with the traditional approach with the exception that there was a reversal of population characteristics in concentric zones but with some sectorization (see Hansen, 1934). Subsequent studies have substantially conformed this early study of Merida. That is, there exists a pattern in which higher status persons tend to be located near the core of the city but with some outward movement of the higher classes, generally in specific sectors (Schnore, 1965; Griffin and Ford, 1983). Lower status persons are located on the periphery or in more central zones of diameinity. There is a gradual tendency for cities in Latin America, including Mexico Megacity, to move toward the U.S. pattern.

The traditional approach to intra-city differentiation postulated that topography and transportation patterns influence a city's growth and hence its settlement pattern. A finer-grained analysis would have to be carried out on Mexico Megacity before such a determination can be made. So far, the topography clearly has influenced the growth pattern but has not distorted the concentric zones and sectorization of the city, although the zones and sectorization have different qualities than for U.S. cities. In the greater metropolitan complex, the conversion of *ejidos* would have been expected to rule how the city would grow and expand. However, such does not appear to be the case in Mexico Megacity.

Map 13.3

Idealized Model of Mexico Megacity Structure

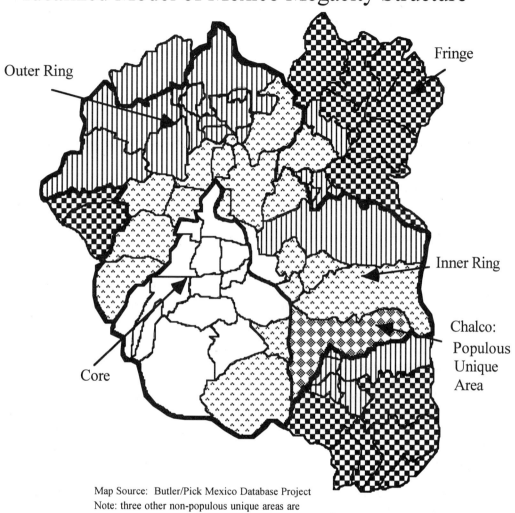

Map Source: Butler/Pick Mexico Database Project
Note: three other non-populous unique areas are
Ecatzingo, Atlautla, and Isidro Fabila

Future Population Growth

In 1950 and 1960, Mexico City was not listed as one of the world's ten largest megacities (Chen and Heligman, 1994; United Nations, 1995). However between 1960 and 1970 the population grew at such a pace that it moved into the top five world cities, with one estimate at fourth (Chen and Heligman, 1994) and another at fifth (United Nations, 1995).

Figure 13.1 shows the United Nations recent estimates of the population size of six selected megacities between 1950 and 2000. If we use the UN classification of megacity as one with a population of 8 million or more (Fuchs, 1994), the number of megacities grew from 2 in 1950 to 15 in 1980, 21 in 1990, and is projected to reach 25 in 2000, and 30 in 2010. Figure 13.1 illustrates the acceleration of Mexico Megacity's growth beginning in the decade of the 60s. The only city in the figure with a comparable increased pace of growth was Sao Paulo, which was in third place worldwide in total population in 1995 according to the United Nations.

In 1994, Tokyo was the largest city in the world, but this is due to the Japanese government re-defining the metropolis to encompass 87 neighboring cities and towns including the large city of Yokohoma (Population Reference Bureau, 1993). Bunched together in 2nd, 3rd, and 4th place worldwide in 1994 were New York, Sao Paulo, and Mexico City, with 16.3, 16.1, and 15.5 million population respectively (United Nations, 1995).

In the future, the UN predicts Tokyo will continue as the largest Megacity with 28.7 million persons in 2010, while Mexico City is predicted to drop to sixth place with 16.4 million. Sao Paulo will move to third place with 17.8 million, while Bombay (not shown on the figure) will move up rapidly to second place at 18.1 million. (United Nations, 1995).

It is likely that Mexico City will be larger in year 2000 than the UN projects, since INEGI reported a Mexico City population of 16.4 million in its 1995 mid-decennial census (INEGI, 1996). Extrapolating INEGI's census figure for 1995 to year 2000, we estimate Mexico City will have about 17.5 million in 2000, which would move it up to 4th place in the UN projection.

The UN projection and an alternative Megacity projection by Chen and Heligman are shown in Figure 13.2. The substantial reduction in growth rate for the UN projection starting in 1980 is due to the lowered Mexico City 1990 census population versus what some had expected (Population Reference Bureau, 1993). Chen and Heligman's higher figure is because they used earlier UN projections that did not include the 1990 Mexican census results. It may be that the 1980 Mexican census overestimated the Mexico City population.

Chen and Heligman's study predicted that Mexico City would be the world's largest city in 2000 at 25.6 million. Another earlier projection listed the potential for the Federal District and State of Mexico in 2000 to be over 29 million (FEMAP, 1987).

In addition to now being the world's fourth most populated city according to the UN in 1995, it also has an extremely high percent of Mexico's urban population living in Mexico Megacity -- the primate city of Mexico. As shown in Figure 13.3 its percentage of total population is higher than for Sao Paulo, New York, Los Angeles, and London, although lower than for Tokyo. The crossover in position between Tokyo and Mexico City between 1980 and 1990 relates to the Tokyo's expanded metropolitan re-definition and Mexico's lower than expected 1990 census count, a point mentioned above.

In the future, natural increase both in rural areas and the Megacity will influence its growth rate. Internal migration to the Megacity and its broader hinterland undoubtedly will continue since Mexico Megacity is the core of the nation in respect to the economy, jobs, and the corporate sector. Megacity extended growth may include more municipios in the State of Mexico and one each from the states of Tlaxcala and Hidalgo (Schteingart, 1988: 289). Thus, it will include parts of four federal entities. It may merge with rapidly growing Toluca and very likely Cuernavaca. It may encompass a larger number of surrounding cities and towns, as was the case in the Japanese census re-definition of Tokyo (Population Reference Bureau, 1993).

While substantial industrial capacity has developed outside of the Megacity, such as in Monterrey, the large border cities, Aguascalientes, and other locations, the largest portion of the nation's industrial capacity it is still located in the Megacity. Government efforts at economic deconcentration have been notable by a lack of success, with a few visible exceptions such as the late 80s relocation of INEGI, an entire Federal department, from the Megacity to Aguascalientes. All of this leads to the conclusion that Mexico Megacity will continue to be the focal point of economic and governmental activities, with the Megacity continuing to be the primate city of Mexico and one of the world's largest.

Figure 13.1. Population Size of Selected Megacities, 1950 - 2010

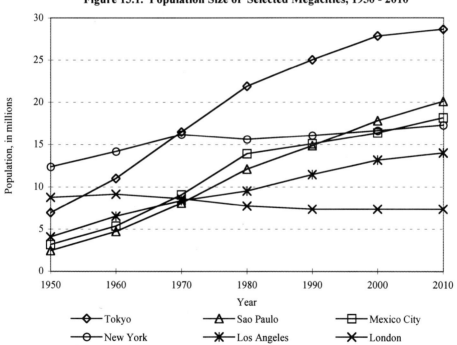

Data Source: United Nations, 1995.

386

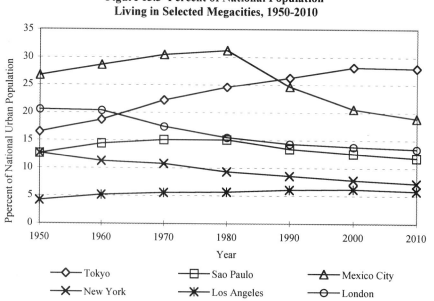

Figure 13.2   Population Projections for Mexico Megacity to Year 2010

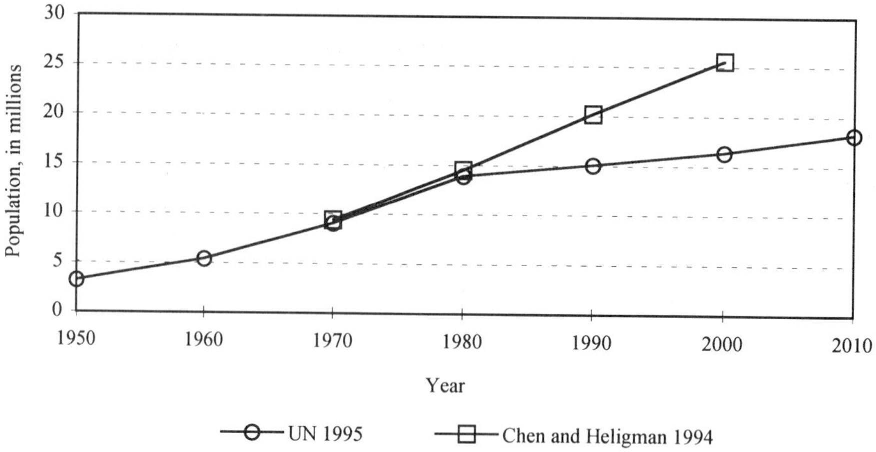

Sources: United Nations, 1995
Chen and Heligman, 1994.

Figure 13.3 Percent of National Population
Living in Selected Megacities, 1950-2010

Data Source: United Nations, 1995.

Appendix: Definitions of Variables

Chapter	Variable Name	Definition
1,3	population	total population
1,3	relative population growth 1970-1990	(population 1990 - population 1970)/population 1970
1,3	population density	population/area in square kilometers
1,3	sex ratio	male population/female population
1,5	inmigration in the past five years	inmigrants into an area in the past five years/total population for an area
1,7	lack of running water	housing units without running water inside the housing unit/total housing units
1,7	housing with one room	housing units with one room/total housing units
1,7	household crowding	number of individual housing units with 3 or fewer rooms and 6 or more occupants/total housing units
1,7	septic tank or open flow	housing units with plumbing connected to a septic tank or open flow to the soil, a river or lake/total housing units
1,7	no toilet in housing unit	housing units without a toilet/total housing units
1,7	firewood or coal for heating and cooking	housing units with firewood or coal for heating or cooking/total housing units
1,10	proportion of economic activity	population economically active age 12 and older/population age 12 and older
1,8,10	unemployment	persons who had a job and were not working in the reference week for a temporary reason/employed population
1,10	owners/employers/salaried workers	employed persons who are owners, employers, or salaried workers/employed population
1,9	chemical and petrochemical revenues, 1993	revenues in chemical and petrochemical industries/total industry sector revenues
1,9	metal production and equipment manuf. revenues,	revenues in basic metal production and equipment manufacturing/total industry sector revenues
1,9	professional and technical services revenues	revenues in professional, technical, and specialized services/total service sector revenues
1,10	professional/technical/managerial occupation	employed population who are professionals, technical workers, managers and administrators/employed population
1,8	primary education	population age 6 and older with some post-primary instruction/population age 6 and older
1,8	high income (more than 5 times minimum wage)	employed population earning more than five times the minimum wage/total employed population
1,8	home ownership	occupied housing units that are owned/all occupied housing
1,4	cumulative fertility to women 20-29	number of live births for women age 20-29/female population age 20-29
1,4	free union	population in a free union 12 years and older/population 12 years and older
1	separated and divorced	divorced and separated population 12 years and older/population 12 years and older
1,10	ratio of economically active women	economically active females age 12 and older/economically active population age 12 and older
1,8	Mixteco language speaking	population 5 years or older who speak Mixteco language/population 5 years or older
1,8	Nahuatl language speaking	population 5 years or older who speak Nahautl language/population 5 years or older
1,8	Otomi language speaking	population 5 years or older who speak Otomi language/population 5 years or older
1,8	Zapotec language speaking	population 5 years or older who speak Zapoteco language/population 5 years or older
1,8	Indigenous language-Remainder	population 5 years or older who speak an indigenous language other than Mixteco, Nahautl, Otomi, or Zapoteco/population five years or older
2	urbanization (also called urban ratio)	population living in places of size 2,500 or more/total population
2	urbanization change, 1970 - 1990	urbanization 1990 - urbanization 1970

3	absolute population growth 1970-1990	total population in year 1990 - total population in year 1970
3	population age 0-17	population age 0-17/total population
3	population 18-64	population age 18-64/total population
3	population 65+	population age 65+/total population
3	dependency ratio	(population age 0-17 + population age 65 and older)/population 18-64
4	percent married	married population 12 years and older/population 12 years and older
4	percent divorced	divorced population 12 years and older/population 12 years and older
4	percent separated	separated population 12 years and older/population 12 years and older
4	crude fertility rate	number of annual births/total population
4	children ever born to women 12 years and older	total number of children ever born to women age 12 and older
4	cumulative fertility to women	average number of live births for women age 45 or
5	population native to state	population born in the state/total population for a small area
5	foreign born population	population born in a foreign country/total population for a small area
5	sex ratio of inmigration	male inmigrants in the past five years/female inmigrants in the past five years
5	region-specific inmigration	population born in a designated region or state/total population for a small area
5	inmigration between Federal District and State of Mexico	inmigrants from the Federal District to the State of Mexico 1985-1990/population of the State of Mexico in 1990
5	inmigration between State of Mexico and Federal District	inmigrants from the State of Mexico to the Federal District 1985-1990/population of the Federal District in 1990
5	major migration stream between state A and state B	number of migrants between State A and State B over a designated five year period
6	life expectancy at birth	average number of years of expected lifetime at the time of
6	crude mortality rate	number of annual deaths/total population
6	infant mortality rate	deaths in one year for infants age less than one year/live births in one year
6	standardized cause-specific mortality rate	indirect age standardization of the cause specific mortality rate, i.e. annual deaths from a specific cause/total population (indirect age standardization is explained under "Causes of Death" in Chapter 6)
6	no meat	population not eating meat/total population
6	no eggs	population not eating eggs/total population
6	medical services provided by government, per capita	number of medical services provided by the ISSSTE + number of medical services provided by the Department of the Federal District per capita
6	government medical centers, per 100,000	number of ISSSTE medical centers + number of Department of the Federal District Medical Centers per 100,000
6	government hospital beds, per 10,000	hospital beds in ISSSTE medical centers + hospital beds in Department of the Federal District medical centers per 10,000 population
6	medical services provided by DDF per capita	number of medical services provided by the DDF per capita
6	DDF hospital beds per 10,000	hospital beds in the service of the Department of the Federal District
6	DDF medical center personnel, per 100,000	medical personnel in the service of the Department of the Federal District per 100,000 population
6	adult deaths with no prior federal government medical benefits, per capita, 1992	adult deaths in 1992 having received no prior medical benefits/population in 1990
6	adult deaths in medical centers from communicable diseases per capita, 1992	adult deaths in 1992 in medical centers from communicable diseases/population in 1990

6	adult deaths with no prior medical attention, 1992	adult deaths in 1992 where no prior medical attention was received/population in 1990
7	total number of housing units	total number of housing units
7	average number of rooms per housing unit	total number of rooms in housing units/total number of housing units
7	no electricity	housing units with no electricity available/total housing units
7	no drain	housing units without drainage/total housing units
7	kitchen in bedroom	housing units with the kitchen in a bedroom/total housing
7	total landfill area, in hectares	total area of landfill, in hectares
7	non-sanitary landfill area, in hectares	area of non-sanitary landfill, in hectares
7	sanitary landfill area, in	area of sanitary landfill, in hectares
8	literacy	population 10 years or older who state they know how to read and write a message/population 10 years or older
8	average grade attended	the average of highest grade level attended for the population
8	higher education	population 16 and older with superior level instruction/population 16 and older
8	adults enrolled in school	population 25 years or older attending school/population 25 years and older
8	no or low income	employed population earning no income or income less than the minimum wage/employed population
8	indigenous language population	population 5 years or older who speaks an indigenous language/population 5 years or older
8	change in indigenous language population, 1970-1990	percent of population speaking an indigenous language in 1990 - percent of population speaking an indigenous language
8	non-Catholic religion	population age 5 and older that is not Catholic and not unspecified in religion/population age 5 and older
8	automobiles, per capita	number of automobiles in a given year, per capita
8	rate of increase in automobiles, 1986-1992	change in the ratio of automobiles per capita between to given years
8	misdemeanor charges, per 1,000	number of misdemeanor charges in 1993 per 1,000 population
8	felonies, per 1,000	number of felony sentences in 1993 per 1,000 population
8	robberies, per 1,000	number of robbery sentences in 1993 per 1,000 population in 1990
8	assaults, per 1,000	number of assault sentences in 1993 per 1,000 population in
8	homicides, per 1,000	number of homicide sentences in 1993 per 1,000 population in 1990
9	industry revenues, 1993	total industry sector revenues in 1993
	industrial workers, 1993	total industrial workers in 1993
9	food, drink, and tobacco revenues, 1993	food, drink, and tobacco industry revenues/total industry sector revenues
9	textile and clothing revenues, 1993	textile and clothing industry revenues/total industry sector revenues
9	paper, printing, and publishing revenues, 1993	paper, printing, and publishing industry revenues/total industry sector revenues
9	basic metals revenues, 1993	basic metals industry revenues/total industry sector revenues
9	state of Mexico municipio gross revenues, in 1000s of pesos per capita, 1993	state of Mexico municipio gross revenues in thousands of pesos per capita, 1993
9	commerce revenues, 1993	total commerce sector revenues in 1993
9	wholesale revenues, 1993	wholesale revenues/total commerce sector revenues
9	automotive revenues, 1993	automotive retail revenues, 1993
9	service revenues, 1993	total service sector revenues in 1993
9	real estate revenues, 1993	real estate revenues/total service sector revenues
9	education/medical service/third sector revenues,	revenues in private education, medical services, and third sector/total service sector revenues
9	private scientific research revenues, 1993	private scientific research revenues, 1993

9	restaurant, hotel, and leisure revenues, 1993	restaurant, hotel, and leisure revenues/total service sector revenues
9	finance and insurance revenues, 1993	finance service, securities service, and insurance service revenues/total service sector revenues
10	ratio of economically active males	economically active male population age 12 and older/economically active population age 12 and older
10	underemployment	employed population who were working less than 1 hour to 16 hours per week/employed population
10	legal notices to strike	ratio of legal notices of intent to strike in 1994 to total population in 1990
10	strike settlement ratio	ratio of settlements of notices of intent to strike in 1994 to notices of intent to strike in 1994
11	number of Mexico 500 corporations	number of Mexico 500 corporations in an area
11	number of workers in Mexico 500 corporations	number of workers in Mexico 500 corporations in an area
11	assets of Mexico 500 corporations	total assets of Mexico 500 corporations in an area
11	sales by Mexico 500 corporations	total sales of Mexico 500 corporations in an area
11	profit margin of Mexico 500 corporations	average profits margin of Mexico 500 corporations in an area. Profit margin is defined as the ratio of profit ("utilidades") to
11	number of foreign owned corporations	number of companies for which the origin of capital is foreign

NOTE: variables appearing in more than one chapter are designated by two or three chapter numbers

References

AbuLughod, Janet I. "Testing the Theory of Social Area Analysis: The Ecology of Cairo, Egypt." *American Sociological Review*. 14: 198-212, 1969.

Aguilar, Adrián Guillermó, Luis Javier Castro Castro, and Eduardo Juárez Aguirre (Coords.). *El Desarrollo Urbano de México a Fines del Siglo XX*. Monterrey, Nuevo Leon, Instituto de Estudios Urbanos de Nuevo León and Sociedad Mexicana de Demografía, 1995.

AIC-ANIAC. "El Agua y la Ciudad de México." México, D.F.: Academia de la Investigacion Cientifica, A.C. y Academia Nacional de Ingenieria, A.C., 1995.

Alam, I. and J.B. Casterline. "Socio-economic Differentials in Recent Fertility." *World Fertility Survey Comparative Studies, Cross-National Summaries*, No. 33. Voorburg, Netherlands, International Statistical Institute, 1984.

Alba, Francisco. *La Poblacion de México: Evolucion y Dilemas* (3d edition). Mexico City: El Colegio de México, 1984.

Alihan, Milla A. *Social Ecology: A Critical Analysis*. New York: Columbia University Press, 1938.

Alvarez, Humberto Bravo et al. *Cinco Conclusiones Sobre el Problema de la Contaminacion en la Ciudad de México*. Mexico City: Comisión Nacional de Ecologia, 1986.

Anderson, Theodore R. and Janice A. Egeland. "Spatial Aspects of Social Area Analysis." *American Sociological Review*. 26:392-398, 1961.

Arreloa, Daniel D. and James R. Curtis. *The Mexican Border Cities*. Tucson: University of Arizona Press, 1993.

Arriaga, Eduardo E. "Measuring the Level and Change of Mortality by Causes of Deaths. The Use of Years of Life Lost." Paper presented at the Annual Meeting of 1994 Population Association of America. Miami: Florida, May 5-7, 1994.

Arriaga, Eduardo E. "Comparación de la Mortalidad en las Américas." *Estudios Demograficos y Urbanos* 7(2-3):407-449, 1992.

Belshaw, Cyril S. "Comments," *Current Anthropology*, 18 (No. 4):620, 1977.

Bennett, Vivienne. "Urban Public Services and Social Conflict: Water in Monterrey," in *Housing and Land in Urban Mexico*. San Diego: Center for U.S.-Mexican Studies, University of California, pp. 79-99, 1989.

Beristain, Javier. 1996. "Mexico City: Toward Its Sustainable Development," in Laura Randall (ed.), *Changing Structure of Mexico: Political, Social, and Economic Prospects*. Armonk, New York: M.E. Sharpe, pp. 391-395.

Berry, Brian J.L. "City Size and Economic Development," *Economic Development and Cultural Change*, 9(No. 4): 573-588, 1961.

Berry, Brian J.L. *Comparative Urbanization*. New York: St. Martin's Press, 1981.

Bianchi, Suzanne. "Changing Economic Roles of Women and Men," in Reynolds Farley (ed.), *State of the Union: America in the 1990s*, Vol. 1, New York: Russell Sage Foundation, pp. 107-154, 1995.

Black, Henry R. "Cardiovascular Risk Factors," in Zaret, Barry L, Marvin Moser, and Lawrence S. Cohen (eds.), *Yale University School of Medicine Heart Book*. New York: Hearst Books, pp. 23-35, 1992.

Bluestone, Barry and Bennett Harrison. *The Deindustrialization of America*. New York: Basic Books, 1982.

Bobadilla, José Luis and Cristina de A. Possas. "Health Policy Issues in Three Latin American Countries: Implications of the Epidemiological Transition," in Gribble, James N. and Samuel H. Preston (eds.), 1993, *The Epidemiological Transition: Policy and Planning Implications for Developing Countries*, Washington, D.C.: National Academy Press, pp. 145-169, 1993.

Bronfman, Mario and José Gómez de León. *La Mortalidad en México: Niveles, Tendencias y Determinantes*. Mexico, D.F.: El Colegio de México, 1988.

Brown, Jane C. *Patterns of Intra-Urban Settlement in Mexico City: An Examination of the Turner Thoery.* Ithaca: Cornell University, 1972.

Brunn, Stanley D. and Jack F. Williams (eds.). *Cities of the World.* New York: Harper and Row, 1983.

Bulatao, Rodolfo A. "Mortality by Cause, 1970 to 2015," in Gribble, James N. and Samuel H. Preston (eds.), *The Epidemiological Transition: Policy and Planning Implications for Developing Countries,* Washington, D.C.: National Academy Press, pp. 42-68, 1993.

Burgess, Ernest W. "The Growth of the City: An Introduction to a Research Project," in Robert E. Park, Ernest W. Burgess, and Roderick D. McKenzie, *The City,* Chicago: University of Chicago Press, pp. 47-62, 1925.

Bush, Virgilio Partida. "Natalidad y Mortalidad en la Ciudad de México, 1950-1980," in Garza, Gustavo (ed.), *Atlas de la Ciudad de México.* Mexico City, D.F.: Departamento del Distrito Federal y El Colegio de Mexico, pp. 129-134, 1987.

Butler, Edgar W. *Urban Sociology: A Systematic Approach.* New York: Harper and Row, 1976.

Butler, Edgar W. *Urban Problems and Prospects.* Pacific Palisades, California: Goodyear Publishing Company, 1977

Butler, Edgar W., James B. Pick and W. James Hettrick. *Globalization of the Mexican Economy.* In progress.

Butler, Edgar W. and James B. Pick. "Poverty in Mexico: 1970-2000." Paper presented at the Association for the Advancement of Policy Research and Development in the Third World, Las Vegas, November 19-22, 1995.

Butler, Edgar W. and William J. Barclay. "A Longitudinal Examination of Two Models of Urban Spatial Differentiation," *Research Previews,* 14:2-25, 1967.

Butler, Edgar W., James B. Pick, and Hiroshi Fukurai. "Twentieth Century Mexico: Continuity Within Change," in Leonard Hochberg, Carville Earle, and David Miller (eds.), *Geographic Information Systems: A Handbook for the Social Sciences,* Oxford: Basil Blackwell, in press.

Butler, Edgar W., James B. Pick, and Hiroshi Fukurai. "A Systematic Approach to a Demographic and Geographic Database System on Mexico." Paper presented to Simposium Binacional Sobre Poblacion y Desarrollo, Cuidad Juarez, Chihuahua, Mexico, September, 1987.

Butler, Edgar W., James B. Pick, Hiroshi Fukurai, and Suhas Pavgi. *"Migration to Baja California 1900-1980."* The Center for Inter-American and Border Studies, The University of Texas at El Paso." *Research Paper Series,* 54 pp., 1987.

Camposortega, Sergio. "Evaluación y Corrección de la Poblacion Mexicana Censada en 1970." *Revista de Estadistica y Geografia* 3(10). Mexico, D.F., Secretaria de Programación y Presupuesto, 1982.

Cantú Gutiérrez, Juan José. "La Migración A Las Grandes Ciudades Del País: Principales Características," in *Memoria de la IV Reunión Nacional de Investigación Demográfica en Méxcio.* Tomo II. 263-272, 1990.

Cárdenas, Cuauhetomoc. Speech given at the University of California, Riverside, November 13, 1989.

Cárdenas, Rosario. "Características de la Mortalidad en México: Tendencias Recientes y Perspecitivas." Paper presented at the V Reunión Nacional de Investigación Demográfica en México. Mexico City, June 5-9, 1995.

Castañeda, Victor. "Mercado Inmobiliario en la Periferia Metropolitana: Los Precios del Suelo. Estudio de Casos. In Terrazas, Oscar and Eduardo Preciat (Coords.), *Estructura Territorial de la Ciudad de México,* Mexico, D.F.: Plaza y Valdés and Departamento del Distrito Federal, 221-247, 1988.

Centro de Estudios Economicos y Demograficos. *Dinamica de la Poblacion de México.* 2nd edition. Mexico City, D.F.: El Colegio de México, 1981.

Chatfield, Christopher and Alexander J. Collins. *Introduction to Multivariate Analysis.* London: Chapman and Hall Ltd., 1980.

Cheema, G. Shabbir. "Priority Urban Management Issues in Developing Countries: The Research Agenda for the 1990s," in *Mega-city Growth and the Future*. New York: United Nations University Press, pp. 412-428, 1994.

Chen, Nancy Yu-ping and Larry Heligman, "Growth of the World's Megalopolises," in Roland Fuchs, Ellen Brennan, Fu-Chn Lo, and Juhn I. Uitto (eds.) *Mega-City Growth and the Future*, Tokyo: United Nations University Press, pp. 17-31, 1995.

Chiswick, Barry R. and Teresa A. Sullivan. "The New Immigrants," in Reynolds Farley (ed.), *State of the Union: American in the 1990s*, Vol. 2 Social Trends, 211-270, 1995.

Cisneros Sosa, Armando. "Organizaciones Sociales en la Reconstrucción Habitacional de la Ciudad de México." *Estudios Demograficos y Urbanos* 3(2):339-352, 1988.

Cockcroft, James D. "Subordinated Technological Development: The Case of Mexico," *Research in Social Movements, Conflict and Change*, 4:253-282, 1981.

COMPLAMAR. *Necesidades Esenciales en México: Vivienda* (Vol. 3). Mexico City: Siglo XXI Editores, 1982.

COMPLAMAR. *Necesidades Esenciales en México*. Five Volumes. Mexico, D.F.: Siglo XXI Editores, 1983.

CONAPO. *Sistema de Ciudades y Distribución Espacial de la Población en México*. Tomo I. Integración de Resultados de los Estudios de los Subsistemas de Ciudades de México. México, D.F.: Consejo Nacional de Población, 1991.

Cone, Marla. "Study Links New Culprit to Smog in Mexico City." *Los Angeles Times*, pp. A1, A28. August, 18, 1995.

Connolly, Priscilla, Rene Coulcomb, and Emilio Duhau. *Cambiar de Casa Pero No de Barrio*. Mexico: Universidad Autonoma Metropolitana-Azcapotzalco, 1991.

Cornelius, Wayne A. "Introduction." *Latin American Review* 6:7-24, 1976.

Cornelius, Wayne A. and Ann L. Craig. *The Mexican Political System in Transition*. La Jolla, California: Center for U.S.-Mexican Studies, University of California San Diego, 1991.

Corona Cuapio, Reina and José Rodolfo Luque González. "Cambios Recientes en Los Patrones Migratorios a la Zona Metropolitana de la Ciudad de México (ZMCM)." *Estudios Demograficos y Urbanos* 7(2-3): 575-586, 1992.

Corona Vazquez, Rodolfo. "Confiabilidad de Los Resultados Preliminares de XI Censo General de Población y Vivienda de 1990." *Estudios Demograficos y Urbanos* 6(1):33-68, 1991.

Davidson, Maria. "A Comparative Study of Fertility in Mexico City and Caracas." *Social Biology* 20(4):460-472, 1973.

Davidson, Maria. "Female Work Status and Fertility in Latin America." In S. Kupinsky, ed., *The Fertility of Working Women: A Synthesis of International Research*, New York: Praeger, pp. 342-354, 1977.

Davis, Diane E. "Crisis Fiscal Urbana y Los Cambios Políticos en la Ciudad de México: Desde Los Orígenes Globales a Los Efectos Locales." *Estudios Demograficos y Urbanos* 8(1):67-103, 1993.

DDF. "Agua 2000: Estrategia Para la Ciudad de México, México, D.F. :Departamento del Distrito Federal, 1991.

DDF. "1992 Compendio DCGOH." Mexico, D.F.: Departmento del Distrito Federal, Direccion General de Construcion y Operacion Hidraulica, Secretaria General e Obras, 1992.

DDF. *Resumen del Programa para Mejorav la Calidad del Aire en el Valle de México 1995-2000*. México: Departamento del Distrito Federal, Gobierno del Estado de México, Secretaria de Medio Ambiente, Recursos Naturales y Pesca, Secretaria de Salud, 1996.

Delgado, Javier. "El Patron de Ocupación Territorial de la Ciudad de México al Año 2000, " in Terrazas, Oscar and Eduardo Preciat (Coords.), *Estructura Territorial de la Ciudad de México*, Mexico, D.F.: Plaza y Valdés and Departamento del Distrito Federal, 103-141, 1988.

Delgado, Javier. "La Estructura Segregada de la Ciudad de México, 1970-1986," in Zenteno, Raúl Benítez and José Benigno Morelos (Coords.), *Grandes Problemas de la Ciudad de México*, México, D.F.: Plaza y Valdés and Departamento del Distrito Federal, 185-211, 1988.

Delgado, Javier. 1990. "De Los Anillos a La Segregación. La Ciudad de México, 1950-1987." *Estudios Demograficos y Urbanos* 5(2):237-274, 1990.

Delgado, Javier. "Centro y Periferia en la Estructura Socioespacial de la Ciudad de México," in Schteingart, Martha A. (coord.)., *Espacio y Vivienda en la Ciudad de México*, Mexico, D.F.: El Colegio de México and I Asamblea de Representantes del Distrito Federal, 85-105, 1991.

Departmento de Distrito Federal. *Resumen del Programma pare Mejorar la Calidad del Aire en el Valle de Mexico 1995-2000*. Mexico: Departmento del Distrito Federal, Gobierno del Estado de Mexico, Secretaria de Medio Ambiente, Recursos Naturales y Pesca, Secretaria de Salud. No date.

DeSoto, Hernando. *The Other Path: The Invisible Revolution in the Third World.* New York: Harper and Row, 1989.

Dogan, Mattei and John D. Kasarda. *The Metropolis Era.* 2 Volumes. Newbury Park, California, Sage Publications, 1988.

Dolan, Robert and H. Grant Goodell. "Sinking Cities." *American Scientist* 74:3(January-February), 8-47 1986.

Doremus, Anne. "Air Pollution Killing Desierto de Los Leones Trees." *Mexcico City News*, November 16, 1988.

Duhau, Emilio. "Planeación Metropolitana y Política Urbana Municipal en la Ciudad de México." *Estudios Demograficos y Urbanos* 3(1):115-142, 1988.

Enderwick, Peter. *Multinational Business & Labor.* New York: St.Martin's Press, 1985.

Environment Magazine. "Air Pollution in the World's Megacities." *Environment* 36:2:5-13,25-37, 1994.

Espino, E., M. Vazquez, and F. Flores. "Pilot Studies of Wastewater Stabilization in Mexico City." In Proceedings of Water Resuse Symposium 4, August, Denver, Colorado: American Water Works Association, pp. 693-703, 1987.

Everitt, B.S. *Cluster Analysis.* London: Chapman and Hall, 1980.

ESRI. *Atlas Pro.* Redlands, California: Enviromental Systems Research Institute, 1996.

Expansión. "Las Empresas Individuales Mas Importantes de México," Mexico, D.F., *Expansión*, August 17, 1987.

Expansión. "Localización Geográfica de las 500." *Expansión*, pp. 154-156, Agosto 17, 1988.

Expansión. "Las Empresas Individuales Mas Importantes de México," Mexico, D.F., *Expansión*, August 17, 1994.

Expansión. "Las 500 de *The Financial Post, Fortune,* and *Expansión*." *Expansión*, p. 285, August 1995.

Ezcurra, Exequiel and Marisa Mazari-Hiriat. "Are Megacities Viable: A Cautionary Tale from Mexico City." *Environment* 38(1):6-34, 1996.

Ezcurra, Exiquiel. "The Basin of Mexico," in Turner, B.L. II (ed.), *The Earth As Transformed By Human Action: Global and Regional Changes in The Biosphere Over the Past 300 Years.* New York, New York: Cambridge University Press, pp. 577-588, 1991.

Farley, Reynolds (ed.). *State of the Union: American in the 1990s*, Volume 1: Economic Trends, New York: Russell Sage Foundation, 1995.

Farley, Reynolds (ed.). *State of the Union: American in the 1990s*, Volume 2: Social Trends, New York: Russell Sage Foundation, 1995.

Feldstein, Martin and Kathleen Feldstein. "Environmental Purists May Be Mexico's Curse." *Los Angeles Times*, April 16, 1991.

FEMAP. *Mexico: 1980-2010*. Ciudad Juarez: Departmento de Estudios Sociodemograficos, 1987.

Fernández-Bremauntz, Adrian A. and Michael R. Ashmore. "Exposure of Commuters to Carbon Monoxide in Mexico City 2. Comparison on In-Vehicle and Fixed Site Concentrations." Paper presented at Symposium on Motor Vehicle Pollution, Joint Conference of the International Society for Exposure Analysis and the International Society for Environmental Epidemiology. Research Triangle Park, North Carolina, September 18-21, 1994.

Fernández-Bremauntz, Adrián A. and Michael R. Ashmore. "Exposure of Commuters to Carbon Monoxide in Mexico City 1. Measurement of In-Vehicle Concentrations." *Atmospheric Environment* 29(4):525-532, 1995.

Fernández-Bremauntz, Adrián and J. Quentin Merritt. "A Survey of Commuter Travel Habits in the Metropolitan Area of Mexico City." *Journal of Exposure Analysis and Environmental Epidemiology* 2(Supp. 2):95-111, 1992.

Fernández-Bremauntz, Adrián, Michael R. Ashmore, and J. Quentin Merritt. 1993. "A Survey of Street Sellers' Exposure to Carbon Monoxide in Mexico City." *Journal of Exposure Analysis and Environmental Epidemiology* 3(Supp. 1):23-35.

Fernández-Bremauntz, Adrián. 1994. "Monitoreo Personal de Contaminantes: Lo Que Efectivamenta Respira La Gente." *Ambiente y Desarrollo*, Septembre, 79- 84, 1994.

Figueroa Campos, Beatríz (ed.). *La Fecundidad en Mexico: Cambios y Perspectivas*. Mexico, D.F., El Colegio de Mexico, 1989.

Florescano, Enrique (coordinator). *Atlas Historico de Mexico*. Mexico: Siglo XXI Editores, 1984.

Frey, William. "The New Geography of Population Shifts: Trends Toward Balkanization," in Reynolds Farley (ed.), *State of the Union*, New York: Russell Sage Foundation, pp. 271-336, 1991.

Frieden. "The Search for a Housing Policy in Mexico City," *Town Planning Review*, 36 (No.2):75-94, 1965.

Friedrich, Otto. "A Proud Capital's Distress: Overcrowded, Polluted, Corrupted, Mexico City Offers the World a Grim Lesson." *Time*, pp. 26-35, August 6, 1984.

Fuchs, Roland J., Ellen Bresman, Joseph Chamie, Fu-Chen Lo, and Juha I. Uitto. *Mega-City Growth and The Future,* Tokyo: United Nations University Press, 1995.

García Guzmán, Brígida. "La Medicion de la Población Economicamente Activa en México al Inicio de la Años Noventa." *Estudios Demograficos y Urbanos*, 1994.

García y Garma, Irma Olaya. "Diferenciales de Fecundidad en México. *Demografia y Economía* 13(1):49-81, 1979,

García y Garma, Irma Olaya. "Fuentes de Datos y Tratamiénto de la Información en el Análisis de la Mortalidad," in Bario Bronfman and José Gómez de Léon (eds.), *La Mortalidad en México: Niveles, Tendencias, y Determinantes*, Mexico, D.F.: El Colegio de México, pp. 71-79, 1988.

Garza, Gustavo. *El Proceso de Industrialización en la Ciudad de México (1821-1970)*. Mexico, D.F., El Colegio de México, 1985.

Garza, Gustavo. "Distribución de la Industria en La Ciudad de México (1960-1980)," in Gustavo Garza (ed.), *Atlas de la Ciudad de México*, Mexico City, D.F.: Departamento del Distrito Federal y El Colegio de Mexico, pp. 102-107, 1987.

Garza, Gustavo. "Hacia La Superconcentración Industrial en La Ciudad de México," in Gustavo Garza (ed.), *Atlas de la Ciudad de México*, Mexico City, D.F.: Departamento del Distrito Federal y El Colegio de Mexico, pp.100-102, 1987.

Garza, Gustavo. (ed.). *Atlas de la Ciudad de México*. Mexico City, D.F.: Departamento del Distrito Federal y El Colegio de Mexico, 1987.

Garza, Gustavo. 1990. "El Carácter Metropolitano de la Urbanización en México, 1900-1988." *Estudios Demograficos y Urbanos* 5(1):37-59, 1990.

Garza, Gustavo and Araceli Damián. "Ciudad de México. Etapas de Crecimiento, Infraestructura y Equipamiento," in Schteingart, Martha A. (coord.), *Espacio y Vivienda en la Ciudad de México*, Mexico, D.F.: El Colegio de México and I Asamblea de Representantes del Distrito Federal, 21-49, 1991.

Garza, Gustavo and Martha Schteingart. "La Accion Habitacional del Estado de Mexico." Mexico City: El Colegio de Mexico, 1978.

Gedicks, Al. Panel Member: "Multinational Enterprise in Latin America: An Historical Perspective," in *Multinational Corporations in Latin America: Private Rights - Public Responsibility*, in Donald P. Irish (ed.). Ohio University: Center for International Studies, Series No. 2, 1978.

Gendell, M., M.N. Maraviela, and P.C. Kreitner. "Fertility and Economic Activity of Women in Guatemala City." *Demography* 7:273-278, 1970.

Gereffi, Gary A. "'Wonder Drugs' and Transnational Corporations in Mexico: An Elaboration and a Limiting-Case Study of Dependency Theory," Unpublished doctoral disssertation, Yale University, 1980.

Gilbert, Alan and Ann Varley. "From Renting to Self-Help Ownership? Residential Tenure in Urban Mexico Since 1940," in *Housing and Land in Urban Mexico*. San Diego: Center for U.S.-Mexican Studies, University of California, Monograph Series, 31, pp. 13-37, 1989.

Gilbert, Alan and Peter M. Ward. *Housing, the State and the Poor: Policy and Practice in Three Latin American Cities*. Cambridge: Cambridge University Press, 1985.

Goddard, Haynes. "Air Pollution and Its Control in Mexico," in Laura Randall (ed.), *Changing Structure of Mexico: Political, Social, and Economic Prospects*. Armonk, New York: M.E. Sharpe, pp. 207-216, 1996.

Goldman, Noreen and Anne R. Pebley. "Legalization of Consensual Unions in Latin America." *Social Biology* 28(1-2): 49-61, 1981.

Goldstein, Sidney and David F. Sly (eds.), *The Measurement of Urbanization and Projection of Urban Population*. Dolhain, Belgium: Ordina Editions, 1975.

Goulet, Denis. *Mexico: Development Strategies for the Future*. Notre Dame: University of Notre Dame Press, 1983.

Griazbord, Boris. "El Comportamiento Electoral en la Magalópolis." *Estudios Demograficos y Urbanos* 8(3):641-654, 1993.

Graizbord, Boris and Héctor Salazar Sánchez. "Expansión Física de la Ciudad de México, Gustavo Garza (ed.), *Atlas de la Ciudad de México*, Mexico City, D.F.: Departamento del Distrito Federal y El Colegio de Mexico, pp. 120-125, 1987.

Graizbord, Boris and Alejandro Mina. "La Geografía de la Descentralización Demográfica del la Ciudad de México," in Aguilar, Adrián Guillermo, Luis Javier Castro Castro, and Eduardo Juárez Aguirre (coords.), *El Desarrollo Urbano de México a Fines Del Siglo XX*, Monterrey: Instituto de Estudios Urbanos de Nuevo Leon, 101-114, 1995.

Greenwood, Michael J. and Jerry R. Ladman. "Economia de al Movilidad Geografica de la Mano de Obra en Mexico," *Demografia y Economia*, 11: 155-166, 1977.

Gribble, James N. and Samuel H. Preston (eds.). *The Epidemiological Transition: Policy and Planning Implications for Developing Countries*. Washington, D.C.: National Academy Press, 1993.

Griffin, Ernst and Larry Ford. "A Model of Latin American City Structure." *Geographical Review* 70:397-422, 1980.

Griffin, Ernst and Larry Ford. "Cities of Latin America." in Stanley D. Brunn and Jack F. Williams (eds.), *Cities of the World: World Regional Urban Development*, New York: Harper and Row, pp. 199-242, 1983.

Guia Roji. "1995 Ciudad de México: Area Metropolitana y Alrededores." México, D.F.: Guia Roji, 1995.

Gutiérrez Sánchez, Sergio and Alejandro Arcila Ponce. *La Distribucion Espacial de La Población en El Estado de México, 1950-1980.* Cuadernos de Trabajo 9. Zinacantepec, State of Mexico, 1988.

Hansen, Asael T. "The Ecology of a Latin American City," Edward B. Reuter (ed.), Race and Culture Contacts. New York: McGraw-Hill, pp. 124-152, 1934.

Hardoy, Jorge E., Diana Mitlin, and David Satterthwaite. *Environmental Problems in Third World Cities.* London: Earthscan, 1993.

Hartigan, John A. *Clustering Algorithms.* New York, John Wiley and Sons, 1975.

Haub, Carl. "Tokyo Now Recognized as World's Largest City." *Population Today* 21(3). Washington, D.C.: Population Reference Bureau, 1993.

Heligman, Larry, Nancy Chen , and Ozer Babakol. 1993. "Shifts in the Structure of Population and Deaths in Less Developed Regions," in Gribble, James N. and Samuel H. Preston (eds.). *The Epidemiological Transition: Policy and Planning Implications for Developing Countries,* Washington, D.C.: National Academy Press, pp. 9-41, 1993.

Henderson, Brian.E., Ronald.K Ross, and Malcom C. Pike. "Toward the Primary Prevention of Cancer." *Science* 254(5035): 1131-1137, 1991.

Herrera-Revilla, I., r. Medina-Banuelos, J. Carrillo-Rivera, and E. Vazquez-Sanchez. Diagnostico del Estado Presente de las Aguas Subterraneas de la Ciudad de Mexico y Determinacion de sus Condiciones Futuras. Contracto No. 3-33-1-6684. Mexico, D.F.: DGCOH, DDF, Instituto de Geofisica, UNAM, 1994.

Hettrick, W. James. "Regional Distribution and Change in Professional/Technical Services in the Mexico City Conurbation, 1989-1993, MBA Project, Redlands: University of Redlands, 1996.

Hiernaux Nicolas, Daniel. "Ocupación del suelo y producción del espacio construido en el valle de Chalco, 1978-1991," in Martha Schteingart (coord.), *Espacio y Vivienda en La Ciudad de México,* Mexico, D.F.: El Colegio de México, pp. 179-202, 1991.

Holian, John. "Fertility Differentials in México: An Individual Level Analysis. *Secolas Annals* 14:47-60, 1983.

Hoover, Edgar M. and Raymond Vernon. *Anatomy of a Metropolis.* New York: Anchor Books, 1962.

Hoyt, Homer. *The Structure and Growth of Residential Neighborhoods in American Cities.* Washington, D.C.: Federal Housing Administration, 1939.

Huxhold, William E. *Introduction to Urban Geographic Information Systems.* New York: Oxford University Press, 1991.

INEGI and STPS. "Encuesta Nacional de Empleo (ENE) de 1991. " Aguascalientes, Aguascalientes, Instituto de Estadística, Geografía e Informática and Mexico, D.F.: Secretaría del Trabajo y Previsión Social, 1993.

INEGI. *Atlas Ejidal Nacional: Estados Unidos Mexicanos.* Aguascalientes: INEGI.

INEGI. "Encuesta Nacional de Ingresos y Gastos de los Hogares (ENIGH) de 1989. Aguascalientes, Aguascalientes: Instituto de Estadistica, Geografía e Informática, 1990.

INEGI. *XI Censo General de Población y Vivienda: Estados Unidos Mexicanos.* Aguascalientes: México, Instituto Nacional de Estadística, Geografía, e Informática: 1992.

INEGI. *Censos Economicos, 1989.* Various Volumes, 1993.

INEGI. *Anuario Estadístico de los Estadoos Unidos Mexicanos.* Aguascalientes, Aguascalientes, Instituto Nacionál de Estadística, Geografía, e Informática, 1984-93.

INEGI. *Estadisticas Historicas de México.* 2 vols. Mexico City, D.F.: Instituto Nacional de Estadística, Geografía, e Informática, 1993.

INEGI. "Defunciones en los Estados Unidos Mexicanos, 1976-1992. Aguascalientes: Instituto Nacional de Estadística Geografía e Informática, 1994.

INEGI. *ENADID: Encuesta Nacional de la Dinamica Demografica, 1992.* Aguascalientes, Aguascalientes, Instituto Nacional de Estadistica Geografica e Informatica: 1994.

INEGI. *Anuario Estadistico del Distrito Federal.* Edición 1995. Aguascalientes: Instituto Nacionál de Estadística, Geografía, e Informática, 1995.

INEGI. *Niveles de Bienstar en México.* Aguascalientes: Aguascalientes, 1993.

INEGI. *Anuario Estadistico del Estado del México .* Edición 1995. Aguascalientes: Instituto Nacionál de Estadística, Geografía, e Informática, 1995.

INEGI. *Censos Económicos 1994. Resultados Oportunos Tabulados Básicos.* Aguascalientes,: Instituto Nacional de Estadística, Geografía e Informática, 1995.

INEGI. Los Datos Preliminares del Censo de Población de 1995. Aguascalintes: México, Instituto, Nacional de Estadistica, Geografia, e Informática, 1996.

Iracheta Cenecorta, Alfonso X. "Metropolización y Política Urbana en la Ciudad de México: en Busco de Un Nuevo Enfoque." *Estudios Demograficos y Urbanos* 3(1):143-162, 1988.

Jefferson, Mark. "The Law of the Primate City," *Geographical Review*, 29:226-232, 1939.

Johnson, Douglas. Panel Member: "The Hemispheric Challenge: Profit or Justice for Whom?" in *Multinational Corporations in Latin America: Private Rights - Public Responsibility*, in Donald P. Irish (ed.). Ohio University: Center for International Studies, Series No. 2, 1978.

Juarez, G., Gl Martinez, and J. Diaz. "Installation of a Water Disinfection System in a Mexico City Hospital." *Bulletin of the Pan American Health Organization* 26(2):121-127, 1992.

Kandall, Jonathan. *La Capital.* New York: Random House, 1988.

Kandall, Jonathan. "Mexico's Megalopolis," in *I Saw A City Invincible*, Gilbert M. Joseph and Mark D. Szuchman (eds.). Wilmington, Delaware: Jauguar Books Latin America, pp. 181-201, 1996.

Kasarda, John D., J.O.B. Billy, and K. West. *Status Enhancement and Fertilty.* Orlando, Florida: Academic Press, 1986.

Kemper, Robert V. and Anya P. Royce. "Mexican Urbanization Since 1821: A Macro-Historical Approach," *Urban Anthropology*, 8 (Winter):267-289, 1977.

Keyfitz, Nathan and Wilhelm Flieger. *Population: Facts and Methods of Demography.* San Francisco: W.H. Freeman, 1971.

Keyfitz, Nathan and Wilhelm Flieger. *World Population Growth and Aging.* Chicago, Illinois: University of Chicago Press, 1990.

Kissling, Walter. "The Operation of Multinational Companies in Latin America: Problems, Advantages, and Contributions to the Host Counries," *Multinational Corporations in Latin America: Private Rights - Public Responsibility*, in Donald P. Irish (ed.). Ohio University: Center for International Studies, Series No. 2, 1978.

Knight, Richard V. and Gary Gappert (eds.). *Cities in a Global Society.* Newbury Park: Sage Publications, 1989.

Lacy, Rodolfo. *La Calidad del Aire en el Valle de México.* México, D.F.: El Colegio de México, 1993.

Lawrence, E.N. "Urban Climate and Day of the Week." *Atmospheric Environment* 5:935-948, 1971.

Lewis, Oscar. *Los Hijos de Sachez.* México: Edicion Limusa, 1961.

Lewis, Oscar. *Cinco Familias.* Mexico: Fondo de Cultura Economica, 1974.

Lo, Fu-chen. "The Impacts of Current Global Adjustment and Shifting Techno-Economic Paradigm on the World City System," in *Mega-city Growth and the Future*. New York: United Nations University Press, pp. 103-129, 1994.

Lourdes Vega, Ana. "Proceso de Poblamiento en la Zona Oriente de la Ciudad de México. El Caso de Ciudad Netzahualcóyotl," in Schteingart, Martha A. (coord.)., *Espacio y Vivienda en la Ciudad de México*, Mexico, D.F.: El Colegio de México and I Asamblea de Representantes del Distrito Federal, 161-178, 1991.

Luna Santos, Silvia. "Mortalidad Adulta en La Ciudad de México: Una Perspectiva Desde El Acceso a Los Servicios de Salud y El Estilo de Vida." Unpublished Masters Thesis. Mexico, D.F.: El Colegio de México, 1995.

Maguire, D.J., M.F. Goodchild, and D.W. Rhind (eds.), *Geographical Information Systems*, Essex, England: Longman Scientific and Technical, 1991.

Mathur, Om Prakesh. "The Duel Challenge of Poverty and Mega-Cities: An Assessment of Issues and Strategies," in *Mega-city Growth and the Future*. New York: United Nations University Press, pp.349 ff., 1994.

Martin, Linda G. and Samuel H. Preston, Eds. *Demography of Aging*. Washington, D.C.: National Academy Press, 1994.

Mazari, M., and M.D. Mackay. "Potential Groundwater Contamination by Organic Compunds in the Mexico City Metropolitan Area." *Environment, Science, and Techology* 27(5):794-802, 1993.

McElrath, Dennis. "The Social Areas of Rome." *American Sociological Review*. 27:376-390, 1962.

McLanahan, Sara and Lynne Casper. "Growing Diversity and Inequality In the American Family." in Reynolds Farley (ed.), *State of the Union: American in the 1990s*, Volume 2: Social Trends, New York: Russell Sage Foundation, pp. 1-45, 1995.

Mehta, Surinden. "Some Demographic and Economic Correlates of Primate Cities: A Case for Reevaluation." *Demography* 1: 136-147, 1964.

Monge, Raúl. "Contingencia Ambiental: La Capital recoge La Sucia Cosecha de 48 Años de Incapacidad, Improvisación y Contradicciones." *Proceso*, pp. 6-13, January 29, 1996.

Moran, T. "Multinational Corporations and Dependency: A Dialogue for Dependistas and Nondependistas," *International Organization*, 32:79-100, 1978.

Morena Mejia, S. "Sistema hidraulico del Distrito Federal," in Gustavo Garza (ed.), *Atlas de la Ciudad de México*, Mexico, D.F.: El Colegio de Mexico and DDF, pp. 183-186, 1987.

Mumme, Stephen. "Clearing the Air: Environmental Reform in Mexico." *Environment* 33(10):6-30, 1991.

Negrete Salas, M.E. "La Migración a la Ciudad de México: Un Proceso Multifacético." *Estudios Demográficos y Urbanos* 5(3):641-654.

Negrete Salas, Mariá Eugenia. "Dinámica Demográfica y Densidad Poblacional en la Zona Metropolitana del Valle de México." *TRACE* (Travaux et Recherches dan Les Amériques du Centre). No. 26 (Decembre). Mexico, D.F.: Mexico, 1994.

Negrete, María Eugenia and Héctor Salazar. "Dinámica de Crecimiento de la Población de la Ciudad de México (1900-1980), in Gustavo Garza (ed.), *Atlas de la Ciudad de México*, Mexico City, D.F.: Departamiento del Distrito Federal y El Colegio de Mexico, 1987, 125-128.

Negrete, María Eugenia, Boris Graizbord, and Crescencio Ruiz. *Población, Espacio, y Medio Ambiente en la Zona Metropolitana de la Ciudad de México*. Mexico, D.F.: El Colegio de México, 1993.

Nelson, Joel I., and Jon Lorence. "Employment in Service Activities and Inequality in Metropolitan Areas." *Urban Affairs Quarterly* 21(11): 106-125, 1985.

Newfarmer, Richard S. and Willard F. Mueller. *Multinational Corporations in Brazil and Mexico: Structural Sources of Economic Power and Noneconomic Power*. Report to the U.S. Senate. Washington, D.C.: U.S. Government Printing Office, 1975.

Newfarmer. Richard S. and S. Topik. "Testing Dependency Theory: A Case Study of Brazil's Electrical Industry," in *The Geography of Multinationals*, Michael Taylor and Nigel Thrift (eds.). New York: St. Martin's Press, 1982.

NRC/AIC/ANI. *Mexico City's Water Supply: Improving the Outlook for Sustainability.* Washington, D.C.: National Academy Press, 1995.

Nunez, Leopoldo F. and Lorenzo Moreno N. *Proyecciones de Poblacion Urbana y Rural: 1980-2010.* Mexico: D.F. Academia Mexicana de Investigacion en Demografia Medica, 1986.

OECD. *Cities for the 21st Century.* Paris: Organisation for Ecnonomic Co-operation and Development, 1994.

Omran, A. "A Century of Epidemiological Transition in the United States. *Preventive Medicine.* 6:30-51, 1977.

Ortega, E., L. Schroeder, and S. Wynne. *Institutional Incentives and Sustainable Development: Infrastructure Policies in Perspective* Boulder, Colorado: Westview Press, 1993.

Palloni, A. "Mortality in Latin America: Emerging Patterns." *Population and Development Review* 7(4):623-649, 1981.

Partida Bush, Virgilio. "Natilidad y Mortalidad en la Ciudad de México, 1950-1980." in Gustavo Garza (ed.), *Atlas de la Ciudad de México*, Mexico City, D.F.: Departamento del Distrito Federal y El Colegio de Mexico, pp. 129-134, 1987.

Pendleton, B.F. and S.O. Yang. "Socioeconomic and Health Effects on Mortality Declines in Developing Countries." *Social Science and Medicine* 20(5):453-460, 1985.

Pezzoli, Keith. *Mexico City: Autonomous Urban Movements and the Production of Residential Space.* Unpublished M.A. Thesis, University of California, Los Angeles, 1985.

Pick, James B., Swapan Nag, Glenda Tellis, and Edgar W. Butler. "Geographical Distribution and Variation in Selected Socioeconomic Variables for Municipios in Six Mexican Border States, 1980." *Journal of Borderlands Studies* 2(1):58-92, 1987.

Pick, James B., Swapan Nag, and Edgar W. Butler. "A Cluster Analysis Approach to Marketing Research in the Borderlands Region of Mexico." In Kuklan, Hooshang, Joan Anderson, and Denise Dimon (eds.), *1988 BALAS Proceedings*, Business Association of Latin American Studies, 19-25, 1988.

Pick, James B., Edgar W. Butler, and Elizabeth Lanzer. *Altas of Mexico.* Boulder, Colorado: Westview Press, 1989.

Pick, James B., Glenda L. Tellis, Edgar W. Butler, and Suhas Pavgi. "Determinantes Socioeconomicas de Migración en México." *Estudios Demograficos y Urbanos* 5(1):61-101, 1990.

Pick, James B., Edgar W. Butler, and Raul Gonzalez Ramirez. "Projection of the Mexican National Labor Force, 1980-2005." *Social Biology* 40(3-4):161-190, 1992.

Pick, James B. and Edgar W. Butler. *The Mexico Handbook: Economic and Demographic Maps and Statistics.* Boulder, Colorado: Westview Press, 1994.

Pick, James B. and Edgar W. Butler. "La Influencia De Los Factores Socioeconómicos En Las Principales Causas De La Mortalidad En México, 1990. Paper presented at the V Reunion Nacional de Investigación Demografica en Mexico, June, 1995. Submitted for publication.

Pick, James B. and Edgar W. Bulter. "Application of Cluster Analysis in the Study of Urban Growth and Differentiation." *Proceedings of the American Statistical Association*, Social Statistics Section 1996, in press.

Plan Nacional de Desarrollo Urbana 1978.

Plan Nacional Desarrollo Industrial, 1979-1982.

Plaza, Alvaro. Panel Member: "The Hemispheric Challenge: Profit or Justice for Whom?" in *Multinational Corporations in Latin America: Private Rights - Public Responsibility*, in Donald P. Irish (ed.). Ohio University: Center for International Studies, Series No. 2, 1978.

Population Reference Bureau. "World Population Data Sheet." Washington, D.C.: Population Reference Bureau, various years.

Portes, Alejandro and Robert Bach. *Latin Journey: Cuban and Mexican Immigrants in the United States*. Berkeley: University of California Press, 1985.

Presidencia. *Mexico: The Path Towards Modernity*. Mexico, D.F.: Presidencia de la Republica, 1992.

Presidencia. *Mexican Agenda: Background Information on Mexico*. Mexico, D.F.: Presidencia de la Republica, 1995.

Presidencia. *Plan Nacional de Desarrollo, 1995-2000* Mexico, D.F.: Presidencia de la Republica, 1995.

Preston, Samuel H. and Paul Taubman. "Socioeconomic Differenences in Adult Mortality and Health Status," in Martin, Linda G. and Samuel H. Preston (eds.), *Demography of Aging*, Washington, D.C.: National Academy Press, pp. 279-318, 1994.

Preston, Samuel H., Nathan Keyfitz, and Robert Schoen. *Causes of Death: Life Tables for National Populations*. Studies in Population Series. New York: Seminar Press, 1972

Quilodrán, Julieta. *Niveles de Fecondidad y Patrones de Nupcilalidad en México*. Mexico, D.F.: El Colegio de México, 1991.

Rabell, Cecilia, Marta Mier, and Teran Rocha. "El Descenso de la Mortalidad en México de 1940 a 1980." *Estudios Demograficos y Urbanos* 1(1):39-92, 1986.

Randall, Laura. *Changing Structure of Mexico: Political, Social, and Economic Prospects*. Armonk, New York: M.E. Sharpe, 1996.

Reilly, William K. "Mexico's Environment Will Improve With Free Trade." *Wall Street Journal*, April 19, 1991.

Roberts, Leslie. *Cancer Today: Origins, Prevention, and Treatment*. Washington, D.C.: Institute of Medicine/National Academy Press, 1984.

Rubalcava, Rosa Mária and Martha Schteingart. "Diferenciación Socioespacial Intraurbana en el Area Metropolitana de la Ciudad de México." *Estudios Sociológicos*, 9, 1985.

Rubalcava, Rosa Mária and Martha Schteingart. "Estructura Urbana y Diferenciación Socioespacial en la Zona Metropolitana de la Ciudad de México (1970-1980), in Gustavo Garza (ed.), *Atlas de la Ciudad de México*, Mexico City, D.F.: Departamiento del Distrito Federal y El Colegio de Mexico, pp. 108-115, 1987.

Rubin-Kurtzman, Jane R. *The Socioeconomic Determinants of Fertility in Mexico: Changing Perspectives*. Monograph Series No. 23. San Diego: Center for U.S.-Mexican Studies, Univerisity of Caliornia San Diego, 1987.

Rubin-Kurtzman, Jane R. "Los Determinantes de la Oferta de Trabajo Femenino en la Ciudad de México, 1970." *Estudios Demograficos y Urbanos* 6(3):545-582, 1991.

Rutstein, S.O. "Levels, Trends, and Differentials in Infant and Child Mortality in the Less Developed Countries, in Hill, K. (ed.), *Child Survival Priorities for the 1990s*, Baltimore, Md.: Johns Hopkins University, Institute for International Programs, 1992.

Salinas de Gotari, Carlos. Speech given at the National Press Club, Newsmaker Luncheon Series. Washington, D.C., October 4, 1989.

Sarmiento, Sergio. "My Encounter With Mexico City's Crime Wave," *Wall Street Journal*, A15, January 12, 1996.

SAS. *SAS Users Guide*. Cary, N.C.: SAS Institute, Inc., 1985.

Sassen, Saskia. *The Global City: New York, London, Tokyo*. Princeton: Princeton University Press, 1991.

Sassen, Saskia. *Cities in a World Economy*. Thousand Oaks, California: Pine Forge Press, 1994.

Sassen-Koob, Saskia. "New York City's Informal Economy," in Alejandro Portes et al. (eds.), *The Informal Economy: Studies in Advanced and Less Developed Countries*, Baltimore: Johns Hopkins University Press, 1989.

Schteingart, Martha. "Expansión Urbana, Conflictos Sociales y Deterioro Ambiental en la Ciudad de México. El Case del Ajusco. *Estudios Demograficos y Urbanos* 2(3):449-477, 1987.

Schteingart, Martha. "Mexico City," in Dogan, Mattei and John D. Kasarda, *The Metropolis Era*, Vol. 2, *Mega-Cities*, pp. 268-293, 1988.

Schteingart, Martha. "Dinámica Poblacional, Estructura Urbana y Producción del Espacio Habitacional en la Zona Metropolitana de la Ciudad de México." *Estudios Demograficos y Urbanos* 4(3):521-548, 1989.

Schteingart, Martha A. (coord.). *Espacio y Vivienda en la Ciudad de México*. Mexico, D.F.: El Colegio de México and I Asamblea de Representantes del Distrito Federal, 1991.

Schteingart, Martha. "Producción Habitacional en la Zona Metropolitana de la Ciudad de México 1960-1987," in Schteingart, Martha A. (coord.). *Espacio y Vivienda en la Ciudad de México*, Mexico, D.F.: El Colegio de México and I Asamblea de Representantes del Distrito Federal, 225-250, 1991.

Sector Salud. *La Contaminacion Atmosferica en la Zona Metropolitana de la Ciudad de Mexico: Riesgos a la Salud y Recommendaciones a la Población*. Mexico, D.F.: IMSS, DIF, 1987.

Shannon, Thomas Richard. *World-System Perspective*. Boulder, Colorado: Westview Press, 1989.

Sheridan, Mary Beth. "State of the Unions: Mexican Labor, Like Its Leader, is Showing Signs of Age." *Los Angeles Times*, pp. D1,D2, March 13, 1996.

Shevky, Eshref, and Wendell Bell. *Social Area Analysis*. Berkeley and Los Angeles: University of California Press, 1955.

Shryock, Henry S., Jacob S. Siegel, and Associates. *The Methods and Materials of Demography*. New York: Academic Press, 1976.

Smith, Carol A. "Modern and Premodern Urban Primacy," *Comparative Urban Research*, IX (No. 1):79-96, 1982.

Smith, Carol A. "Theories and Measures of Urban Primacy: A Critique," in M. Timberlake (ed.), *Urbanization in the World-Economy*, New York: Academic Press, 1985.

Smith, David P. *Formal Demography*. New York: Plenum Press. 1992.

Smith, K.R. "The Risk Transition." *International Environmental Affairs* 2(3):227-251, 1990.

Sokal, R.R. " A Statistical Method for Evaluating Systematic Relationships," *University of Kansas Science Bulletin*, 38:1409-1438, 1958.

Spring, Ursula Oswald. *Estrategias de Supervivencia en la Ciudad de México*." Cuernavaca, Morelos: Centro Regional de Investigaciones Multidisciplinarias, UNAM, 1991.

SPSS Inc. *SPSS 6.1*. Chicago: SPSS Inc., 1994.

State of Mexico. "Plan Maestral de Agua Potable," in *Alcantarillado y Saneamiento del Estado de Mexico 1994-2000*, Tomo 2, Comision Estatal de Agua y Saneamiento, Estado de Mexico, 1993.

Tamayo, Jesus. "Borderlands, Border Policies, and National Policies," paper presented at the Annual Conference of Borderlands Scholars, Reno, Nevada, April, 1986.

Taylor, Michael and Nigel Thrift (eds.). *The Geography of Multinationals*. New York: St.Martin's Press, 1982.

Terrazas, Oscar and Eduardo Preciat (Coords.). *Estructura Territorial de la Ciudad de México*. Mexico, D.F.: Plaza y Valdés and Departamento del Distrito Federal, 1988.

Timberlake, Michael (ed.). *Urbanization in the World-Economy.* Orlando, Florida, Academic Press, 1985.

Tudela, Fernando. "Usos del Suelo, Vivienda, y Medio Ambiente," in Schteingart, Martha A. (coord.)., *Espacio y Vivienda en la Ciudad de México*, Mexico, D.F.: El Colegio de México and I Asamblea de Representantes del Distrito Federal, 203-222, 1991.

U.S. Bureau of the Census. *1990 Census of Population and Housing: Summary Social, Economic, and Housing Characteristics.* 1990 CPH-5-1. Washington, D.C.: U.S. Government Printing Office, 1992a.

U.S. Bureau of the Census. *1990 Census of Population and Housing: Summary Social, Economic, and Housing Characteristics.* 1990 CPH-5-1. Washington, D.C.: U.S. Government Printing Office, 1992b.

Unikel, Luis. "La Dinámica del Crecimiento de la Ciudad de México." Fundación para Estudios de la Población, A.C., 1972.

Unikel, Luis. "Urbanization in Mexico: Process, Implications, Policies, and Prospects," in Goldstein, Sidney and David F. Sly (eds.), *Patterns of Urbanization: Comparative County Studies.* Dolhain, Belguim: Ordina Editions, pp. 465-568, 1977.

Unikel, Luis, et al. El Desarollo Urbano de Mexico: Diagnostico e Implicasiones Futuras. Mexico: El Colegio de Mexico, 1976.

Unikel, Luis et al. *El Desarrollo Urbano de México: Diagnóstico e Implicaciones Futuras.* Mexico, D.F.: El Colegio de México, 1978.

United Nations. *Population Growth and Policies in Mega-Cities: Mexico City.* Population Policy Paper No. 32. New York: United Nations, 1991.

United Nations. *World Population 1994.* Data sheet. New York: United Nations, Department for Economic and Social Information and Policy Analysis, Population Division, 1994.

U.N. *Estimates and Projections of Urban, Rural and City Populations, 1950-2015: The 1982 Assessment.* New York: United Nations, 1985.

UnoMasUno. July 5, 1983.

United Nations. *World Urbanization Prospects: the 1994 Revision.* New York: United Nations, 1995.

Van Arsdol, Maurice, Nadia Youssef, Michel Antochiw, Dennig Berg, and John Brennan Jr. "Migration and Population Redistribution in the State of Mexico, Replublic of Mexico." ICP work Agreement Reports, *Occasional Monography Series*, 5(1), Washington, D.C., Smithsonian Institution, 133-176, 1976.

Vargas, Martín and Mario Garcia II. "El Plan de Cien Ciudades, 'Atorado' por La Crisis." *Uno Más Uno*, pp. 1, 8, May 6, 1996.

Varley, Ann. "The Relationship Between Tenure Legalization and Housing Improvements: Evidence from Mexico City," *Development and Change*, 18:463-481, 1987.

Varley, Ann. "Urbanization and Agrarian Law: The Case of Mexico City," *Bulletin of Latin American Research*, 4 (No. 1):1-16, 1985.

Velez-Ibanez, Carlos. *Rituals Of Marginality.* Berkeley: University of California Press, 1983.

Vining, Daniel. "Population Redistribution Towards Core Areas of Less Developed Countries, 1950-1980." *International Regional Science Review* 10(1):1-45.

Wall Street Journal. "Group Plans to Build Mexican Movie Studio at Cost of $100 Million," *Wall Street Journal*, November 17, 1989.

Ward, J.H. "Hierarchial Grouping to Optimize an Objective Function," *Journal of the American Statistical Association*, 58:236-244, 1963.

Ward, Peter M. "Self-Help Housing in Mexico City." *Town Planning Review* 49:38-50, 1978.

Wetzel, James R. "Labor Force, Unemployment, and Earnings." in Reynolds Farley (ed.), *State of the Union: American in the 1990s*, Volume 1, Economic Trends, New York: Russell Sage Foundation, pp. 59-105. 1995.

Whetten, Nathan and Robert C. Burnight. "Internal Migration in Mexico," *Rural Sociology*. 21 (June):140-151, 1956.

Wiesbrod, Burton A. "Rewarding Performance That Is Hard to Measure: The Private Nonprofit Sector." *Science* 244:541-546, 1989.

Winnie, William W. "Componentes del Crecimiento y Redistribución de la Población Mexicana: Implicaciones de los Resultados Preliminares Del Censo De 1980." *Demografía y Economía* 15(3:359-376, 1981.

Wolfe, Alvin W. "The Supernational Organization of Production: An Evolutionary Perspective," *Current Anthropology* 18 (No. 4):615-620, 1977.

World Health Organization and United Nations Environment Programme. "Air Pollution in the World's Megacities." *Environment* 36(2):5-37, 1992.

World Health Organization and United Nations Environment Programme. *Urban Air Pollution in Megacities of the World.* Oxford, England: Blackwell Publishers, 1992.

Zambrano Lupi, Jorge H. 1979. "Fecundidad y Escolaridad en la Ciudad de México." *Demografía y Economía* 13(4):405-448, 1979.

Zaret, Barry L, Marvin Moser, and Lawrence S. Cohen (eds.). 1992. *Yale University School of Medicine Heart Book.* New York: Hearst Books.

Zenteno, Raúl Benítez and José Benigno Morelos (Coords.). *Grandes Problemas de la Ciudad de México.* México, D.F.: Plaza y Valdés and Departamento del Distrito Federal, 1988.

Index

About the Book and Authors

With a population of 15 million in 1990, Mexico City is one of the world's largest cities. It is a famous center of civilizations and culture and one of the economic capitals of the Americas, but it also has serious social and economic problems, including large impoverished zones, severe environmental degradation, crime, and overpopulation.

This book describes and analyzes growth, change, and spatial patterns in Mexico City, looking at urbanization, population, marriage and fertility, health and mortality, migration, environment and housing, social characteristics, the economy, labor force, and corporate structure. Applying modern techniques of geographic information systems and spatial analysis, the authors reveal many previously unknown or unrecognized trends and patterns. In a capstone chapter, they summarize the spatial patterns in a series of cluster analyses that identify distinctive zones within the metropolis—a prosperous core, surrounding complex ring patterns, an impoverished zone, and semi-rural arms. They also compare the pattern of Mexico City's cluster zones to the classical and developmental literature on cities. In closing, the authors suggest government policies that would foster optimal future development of an even larger metropolis.

This book addresses a topic of growing importance. The United Nations predicts the emergence of many more giant cities worldwide over the next quarter century, most of which will appear in the developing world. Mexico Megacity is a milestone work that increases our knowledge about one developing world megacity while offering analytical tools for studying others.

James B. Pick is professor and chair of the Department of Management and Business at the University of Redlands. **Edgar W. Butler** is professor emeritus of sociology at the University of California at Riverside.